Web Privacy with P3P

Web Privacy with P3P

Lorrie Faith Cranor

O'REILLY®

Beijing · Cambridge · Farnham · Köln · Paris · Sebastopol · Taipei · Tokyo

Web Privacy with P3P
by Lorrie Faith Cranor

Published by O'Reilly & Associates, Inc., 1005 Gravenstein Highway North,
Sebastopol, CA 95472.

O'Reilly & Associates books may be purchased for educational, business, or sales promotional use. Online editions are also available for most titles (*safari.oreilly.com*). For more information contact our corporate/institutional sales department: (800) 998-9938 or *corporate@oreilly.com*.

Editor:	Linda Mui
Production Editors:	Leanne Clarke Soylemez and Rachel Wheeler
Cover Designer:	Ellie Volckhausen
Interior Designer:	David Futato

Printing History:

September 2002:   First Edition.

ISBN: 0-596-00371-4
[M]

For Chuck and Shane

Table of Contents

Foreword . . . . **xi**

Preface . . . . **xv**

Part I. Privacy and P3P

1. Introduction to P3P **3**
    How P3P Works   4
    P3P-Enabling a Web Site   9
    Why Web Sites Adopt P3P   9

2. The Online Privacy Landscape **12**
    Online Privacy Concerns   12
    Fair Information Practice Principles   22
    Privacy Laws   24
    Privacy Seals   27
    Chief Privacy Officers   28
    Privacy-Related Organizations   29

3. Privacy Technology **30**
    Encryption Tools   31
    Anonymity and Pseudonymity Tools   36
    Filters   40
    Identity-Management Tools   41
    Other Tools   41

4. P3P History **43**

The Origin of the Idea   43

The Internet Privacy Working Group   45

W3C Launches the P3P Project   46

The Evolving P3P Specification   47

The Patent Issue   51

Feedback from Europe   52

Finishing the Specification   53

Legal Implications   55

Criticism   56

Part II.   P3P-Enabling Your Web Site

5. Overview and Options **61**

P3P-Enabled Web Site Components   61

P3P Deployment Steps   63

Creating a Privacy Policy   65

Analyzing the Use of Cookies and Third-Party Content   68

One Policy or Many?   73

Generating a P3P Policy and Policy Reference File   74

Helping User Agents Find Your Policy Reference File   75

Combination Files   76

Compact Policies   77

The Safe Zone   78

Testing Your Web Site   79

6. P3P Policy Syntax **81**

XML Syntax   81

General Assertions   82

Data-Specific Assertions   89

The P3P Extension Mechanism   104

The Policy File   107

7. Creating P3P Policies **110**

Gathering Information About Your Site's Data Practices   110

Turning the Information You Gathered into a P3P Policy   121

Writing a Compact Policy   128

Avoiding Common Pitfalls   131

8. Creating and Referencing Policy Reference Files **133**

Creating a Policy Reference File 133

Referencing a Policy Reference File 144

P3P Policies in Policy Reference Files 149

Changing Your P3P Policy or Policy Reference File 150

Avoiding Common Pitfalls 151

9. Data Schemas **153**

Sets, Elements, and Structures 153

Fixed and Variable Categories 154

P3P Base Data Schema 154

Writing a P3P Data Schema 164

10. P3P-Enabled Web Site Examples **170**

Simple Sites 170

Third-Party Agents 179

Third Parties with Their Own Policies 180

Examples From Real Web Sites 180

Part III. P3P Software and Design

11. P3P Vocabulary Design Issues **191**

Rating Systems and Vocabularies 191

P3P Vocabulary Terms 195

What's Not in the P3P Vocabulary 201

12. P3P User Agents and Other Tools **203**

P3P User Agents 203

Other Types of P3P Tools 207

P3P Specification Compliance Requirements 210

13. A P3P Preference Exchange Language (APPEL) **214**

APPEL Goals 214

APPEL Evaluator Engines 216

Writing APPEL Rule Sets 216

Processing APPEL Rules 225

Other Privacy Preference Languages 229

14. **User Interface** 236
    Case Studies   236
    Privacy Preference Settings   254
    User Agent Behavior   259
    Accessibility   262
    Privacy   264

Part IV.   Appendixes

A. **P3P Policy and Policy Reference File Syntax Quick Reference** 269

B. **Configuring Web Servers to Include P3P Headers** 284

C. **P3P in IE6** 289

D. **How to Create a Customized Privacy Import File for IE6** 301

E. **P3P Guiding Principles** 306

Index 311

Foreword

The problem of privacy on the Internet is the most pressing policy concern of ordinary Internet users. Uncertainty about privacy keeps many users away; frustration with spam drives many to lie about who they are or where they come from. The privacy debate has attracted a great deal of regulatory attention, but it has not yet produced any significant, broad-based regulatory reform.

And for good reason—for much of the slowness in regulation is explained by an ambiguity in the "privacy problem" itself. There are certainly some kinds of data that should not be traded—you shouldn't be able to buy my credit card number on Creditcards.com; there shouldn't be a place where the nosey can find out what I told my doctor last time I had a checkup. These invasions, and many others, are properly considered violations. Laws that ban them would be completely appropriate.

But there are other kinds of data that we as a society are more uncertain about. Trades with respect to them don't have a simple legislative solution. You might think it insulting that Amazon.com monitors purchases you make there, so that it can recommend other things to buy; I love the idea, and wish the company Godspeed. I might hate the idea of Amazon sending me emails to tell me about the latest sale in gardening supplies; you might love the signs of life budding from your email inbox. People are different, and where we differ, we need not simple, absolute rules, but simple technologies for finding agreement.

In the early days of the consumer Internet, this agreement was sought through privacy policies posted on web sites. The Federal Trade Commission (FTC) and many privacy advocates pushed web sites to state what they intended to do with the data they collected. The FTC was proud of the number of web sites that displayed privacy-policy statements, and their press statements bragged about the increase in postings that they had effected.

The problem with privacy pages, however, was that no one read them—or could read them, as they were written in a strange mix of English and lawyerspeak. But more fundamentally, the whole idea of a privacy page had no connection with how people used the Internet. No one surfs to a web page and then pulls to the side of the road to read the associated privacy policy. And even if they did, what would they do with that knowledge? Keep charts by their terminals, indicating the different privacy policies of different sites? Amazon promises not to resell email addresses, but Yahoo does not? The whole idea that this was a "solution" to any problem (except the underemployment of a strange variety of lawyer) was absurd.

What this spin through the history of posted privacy policies begins to make clear is that, in the space where individuals need to make choices, more words on the Web won't help. What's needed instead is better code to enable machines to understand privacy policies, rather than words for humans to read. In other words, P3P: a technology to enable web sites to express their privacy policies in machine-readable form and hence to enable users to set their preferences about the sort of sites they're willing to frequent. Computer code thus replaces lawyers' code, with the consequence of more and more effective understanding.

P3P alone won't solve the privacy problems of cyberspace. Understanding is just a first step. Even if P3P were universally implemented, it would not end legitimate questions about whether privacy was properly protected. Choices within a market are not self-justifying; they need the law to back them up. Moreover, as we come to see how people choose, we may learn that we all essentially choose in the same way. If so, elaborate mechanisms to facilitate that choice may no longer be necessary.

However, we are a long way from understanding either what people really want or what choices the market will produce. Thus, while there is uncertainty about whether and how data about individuals is collected, technology to reduce the cost of resolving that uncertainty is progress. P3P is one such technology, one important step in moving society to a place where it understands the problem of data enough to see a solution.

In this book, one of the authors of P3P introduces the technology. Her clear and lively presentation has something for everyone who has any interest in this question of privacy on the Internet. For privacy advocates, the book demonstrates both the promise of the technology and its limits. For technologists, the book offers a clear and complete picture of how the technology might be implemented. And finally, for policymakers, the book demonstrates one particular example of how policy gets implemented through technology.

It is this last lesson that will ultimately prove to be the most important, not just for the values of privacy, but also for values generally. In the world that cyberspace will build, the technology that builds cyberspace will also set its policies. Code is law. If policymakers are not to be displaced by technologists, they must begin to examine the details of this interaction between code and law. The law embeds values that many centuries of social life have taught are important. Privacy is one such value. Whether those values in general, or privacy in particular, will continue to be a part of life in cyberspace depends fundamentally on how cyberspace is built. There are choices to be made. They should be made by people who understand what those choices are.

Lawrence Lessig
May, 2002

Preface

The Platform for Privacy Preferences (P3P) is a standard for communicating the privacy policies of web sites to the clients that connect to them. With P3P, a web client can retrieve a machine-readable privacy policy from a web server and respond appropriately. This book covers how P3P evolved, how to P3P-enable a web site, and how to design P3P applications.

I was first introduced to the idea of machine-readable privacy labels for web sites in October 1996, about two weeks after completing my dissertation and beginning work at AT&T Labs-Research. Little did I know at the time that I had begun a journey that would take over five and a half years to complete.

My work on the project that eventually came to be known as P3P was largely motivated by a personal desire to help improve the state of individual privacy. Obviously, there are many important online and offline privacy concerns on which P3P is unlikely to have any impact. However, I am optimistic that P3P, in conjunction with other efforts, will result in eventual improvements in the protection of data privacy online. The extent to which this goal is achieved remains to be seen, as we are still in the early days of P3P adoption and use. While the technical work behind the P3P 1.0 specification is now finished, much work remains to be done to bring about widespread P3P adoption by web sites, development and deployment of useful P3P tools for users, and consumer education about data privacy. Hopefully, this book will serve as a useful guide for all of these endeavors.

I have included a lot of history in this book, and in an attempt to provide an accurate account, I have spent much time digging through the P3P mailing list archives and my personal notes and talking with others who were involved in the early days of P3P. Some readers may ask whether the details of who was responsible for what or when a meeting took place really matter. They may seem inconsequential, but I include them here because I believe that an understanding of how technology and technical standards are created provides useful and important insights.

Who Should Read This Book?

This book was written for a broad audience. I have tried to address a wide range of questions about P3P that I have been asked by web site operators, software developers, policymakers, and individuals concerned about protecting their privacy online. Whether you are interested in deploying P3P on a web site or in a software product, or are just curious about what P3P is and how it works, this book is for you.

Readers of this book are expected to have some experience using a web browser. While some parts of this book will be understood most readily by readers who have some programming experience, most of it should be accessible to those with only a basic knowledge of computers.

How This Book Is Organized

This book is organized into four sections.

Part I, *Privacy and P3P*, reviews online privacy concerns and various technical, regulatory, and self-regulatory initiatives that address them. This section includes an introduction to P3P that describes the history of the P3P specification and the motivations behind it. It contains four chapters:

Chapter 1, *Introduction to P3P*
Chapter 2, *The Online Privacy Landscape*
Chapter 3, *Privacy Technology*
Chapter 4, *P3P History*

Part II, *P3P-Enabling Your Web Site*, provides webmasters with all of the information they need to use P3P on their sites. It includes an overview of the steps involved in P3P-enabling a web site, instructions for creating P3P files, and examples of P3P-enabled web sites. This part of the book also includes detailed explanations of all of the elements of the P3P vocabulary and P3P Base Data Schema. It contains the following chapters:

Chapter 5, *Overview and Options*
Chapter 6, *P3P Policy Syntax*
Chapter 7, *Creating P3P Policies*
Chapter 8, *Creating and Referencing Policy Reference Files*
Chapter 9, *Data Schemas*
Chapter 10, *P3P-Enabled Web Site Examples*

Part III, *P3P Software and Design*, discusses design issues related to both the P3P vocabulary and P3P software. These chapters provide some of the design rationale behind the P3P vocabulary, as well as information on how the vocabulary can be translated into P3P user agent interfaces. They describe different kinds of P3P implementations, introduce the APPEL language, and offer advice on user interface issues.

This part of the book is intended primarily for software developers interested in building P3P into their products and individuals who want to develop P3P preference settings. However, these chapters also serve to tie together the concepts introduce in the previous sections of the book and demonstrate how everything comes together in P3P software implementations. Part III contains the following chapters:

Chapter 11, *P3P Vocabulary Design Issues*
Chapter 12, *P3P User Agents and Other Tools*
Chapter 13, *A P3P Preference Exchange Language (APPEL)*
Chapter 14, *User Interface*

Part IV, *Appendixes*, provides technical details and materials from other sources. There are five appendixes:

Appendix A, *P3P Policy and Policy Reference File Syntax Quick Reference*
Appendix B, *Configuring Web Servers to Include P3P Headers*
Appendix C, *P3P in IE6*
Appendix D, *How to Create a Customized Privacy Import File for IE6*
Appendix E, *P3P Guiding Principles*

While not all readers are likely to be interested in the entire book, it does contain something for everyone, and I hope that most readers will at least take a cursory look at all of the sections of the book. For example, while software developers may be most interested in Parts II and III, I think they will find the background information on privacy issues provided in Part I to be valuable, and important to consider as they develop user interfaces and default settings for their tools.

If you are interested in deploying P3P on a web site, you will probably want to take a quick look at Part I, then focus on Part II. A brief examination of Part III will help you understand the range of P3P user agents that might be used to view the P3P policies on your web site.

If you are interested in developing software for a P3P user agent, policy generator, or other P3P tool, you should review the entire book, but focus your attention on Chapters 6, 8, 9, 12, 13, and 14.

If you are a policymaker interested in understanding how P3P works and what it can do, or an individual who is simply curious about P3P, you will probably find Part I and Chapters 12 and 14 most interesting. Chapters 5 and 6 will give you a deeper understanding of P3P policies, and Chapter 11 will provide more insight into the design of the P3P vocabulary. If you want to try your hand at creating P3P preference files using the APPEL language, also read Chapter 13.

P3P Specification Compliance

The Platform for Privacy Preferences 1.0 (P3P1.0) Specification (*http://www.w3.org/ TR/P3P/*) is the authoritative source for information on the P3P protocol and vocabulary. I have done my best to make sure that this book is accurate and consistent with the P3P specification. However, in the unlikely event that there is a discrepancy between the P3P specification and this book, the P3P specification is "right." (And should you find such a discrepancy, please let us know!)

The P3P specification uses the term "MUST" to indicate requirements. A P3P implementation or a P3P-enabled web site that violates such a requirement is not considered P3P compliant. In this book, whenever I say that a site or P3P user agent "must" do something, it is because the specification requires it.

The P3P specification also uses the term "SHOULD" to indicate conditional requirements—requirements that can be violated if there is a good reason. A site or implementation that violates one or more of these conditional requirements (but satisfies all of the MUST requirements) is said to be "conditionally compliant." In this book, I use the term "should" when I describe conditional requirements. However, I sometimes also use the term "should" when I describe practices that I recommend, but that are not necessarily addressed in the P3P specification.

Conventions in This Book

The following typographical conventions are used in this book:

Italic
> Used for file and directory names, for URLs, and to emphasize new terms and concepts as they are introduced

`Constant width`
> Used for code examples

`Constant width italic`
> Used in code examples for text that should be replaced with something more specific.

 This icon indicates a tip, suggestion, or general note.

Online Resources

We have created a web site for this book at *http://p3pbook.com*. At this site, you will find electronic versions of most of the examples used in this book, as well as lists of the online resources referenced in this book. By using the web site, you can avoid having to type in lengthy examples or URLs. We will also update the URLs on the web site as we discover new references and as resources move to new locations.

How to Contact Us

Please address comments and questions concerning this book to the publisher:

O'Reilly & Associates, Inc.
1005 Gravenstein Highway North
Sebastopol, CA 95472
(800) 998-9938 (in the United States or Canada)
(707) 829-0515 (international/local)
(707) 829-0104 (fax)

There is a web page for this book, which lists errata, examples, or any additional information. You can access this page at:

http://www.oreilly.com/catalog/webprivp3p/

To comment or ask technical questions about this book, send email to:

bookquestions@oreilly.com

For more information about books, conferences, Resource Centers, and the O'Reilly Network, see the O'Reilly web site at:

http://www.oreilly.com

Acknowledgments

I would like to begin by thanking all of the P3P working group members, without whom there would be no P3P specification and no reason for this book. Developing the P3P specification proved to be a much longer and more time-consuming project than I could ever have imagined. At times the process of developing this specification proved extremely frustrating, but it has been rewarding to watch the implementation and adoption of P3P and to see the P3P vocabulary used as a basis for other privacy-related endeavors. I am also grateful for all the friends I have met along the way. In the process of developing the P3P specification, I have made friends all over North America and in Europe, Asia, and Australia. This unexpected outcome of chairing a W3C working group is certainly one of the factors that helped motivate me to stick with the project and see it through to completion.

I would also like to thank all of my colleagues and friends who reviewed chapters of this book and provided constructive criticism: Manjula Arjula, Chuck Cranor, Brooks Dobbs, Aaron Goldfeder, Eszter Hargittai, Giles Hogben, Patrick McDaniel, Deirdre Mulligan, Martin Presler-Marshall, Joseph Reagle, Joel Reidenberg, Paul Resnick, Avi Rubin, Ari Schwartz, and Sander van Zoest. I am especially grateful to Martin Presler-Marshall, who reviewed multiple drafts of this book, was a major contributor to the development of P3P, and served as acting chair of the P3P Specification Working Group during my absence.

I would like to thank Simson Garfinkel, for encouraging me to submit the proposal for this book to O'Reilly, and Linda Mui, my editor at O'Reilly, for helping me through the process of completing this book.

I would like to thank Bill Aiello and all of my other current and former managers at AT&T Labs-Research for supporting my work on P3P and allowing me to spend time working on this book.

Finally, I would like to thank my family for all their support and encouragement. I would especially like to thank my husband, Chuck, for entertaining Shane during the many evenings and weekends I spent working on this book, and I would like to thank *Law and Order* for entertaining Chuck while I worked on this book.

PART I

Privacy and P3P

This part of the book introduces P3P and reviews online privacy concerns and various technical, regulatory, and self-regulatory initiatives that address them.

- Chapter 1, *Introduction to P3P*, provides an overview of what P3P is, how it works, and why web sites are adopting it. This chapter is a good "executive summary" on P3P.
- Chapter 2, *The Online Privacy Landscape*, looks at online privacy concerns and discusses fair information practice principles and privacy laws.
- Chapter 3, *Privacy Technology*, reviews tools for anonymity, encryption, filtering, identity management, and other privacy-related services.
- Chapter 4, *P3P History*, details the P3P development process and discusses some of the issues faced as the specification was being created.

CHAPTER 1

Introduction to P3P

Internet users are becoming increasingly concerned about what personal information they may reveal when they go online and where that information might end up. It's common to hear about companies that derive revenue from personal information collected on their web sites. Information you provide to register for a site might later be used for telemarketing or sold to another company. Seemingly anonymous information about your web-surfing habits might be merged with your personal information. Web sites use cookies to gather information about users, but disabling cookies prevents you from doing online banking or shopping at some web sites.

Web sites might email you to say that their privacy policies are changing, but most of us find it difficult and time-consuming to read and understand privacy policies or to figure out how to request that the use of our personal information be restricted. Privacy concerns are making consumers nervous about going online, but current privacy policies for web sites tend to be so long and difficult to understand that consumers rarely read them.*

The Platform for Privacy Preferences (P3P) project addresses this problem by providing both a standard, computer-readable format for privacy policies and a protocol that enables web browsers to read and process privacy policies automatically. The World Wide Web Consortium (W3C) developed P3P as a standard way for web sites to communicate about their privacy policies. P3P enables machine-readable privacy policies that can be retrieved automatically by web browsers and by other user agent tools that can display symbols, prompt users, or take other appropriate actions. Some of these tools can also compare each policy against the user's privacy preferences and assist the user in deciding when to exchange data with web sites.

Unlike anonymity tools, which seek to prevent any transfer of personally identifying information, the P3P project seeks to enable the development of tools for making informed decisions about when and if personal information should be revealed.

---

* Privacy Leadership Initiative, "Privacy Notices Research Final Results" (conducted by Harris Interactive, December 2001), *http://www.ftc.gov/bcp/workshops/glb/supporting/harris%20results.pdf*.

These tools may work hand-in-hand with anonymity software or filters that actually prevent the transmission of personal information in situations when users do not want their information revealed.

P3P tools are currently available that allow users to configure their web browsers with their personal privacy preferences. P3P-enabled web browsers check for P3P privacy policies at web sites and display symbols to alert users at sites that do not match their preferences. They can also provide summaries of web site privacy policies and use P3P policies to make decisions about cookies.[*]

How P3P Works

The Platform for Privacy Preferences 1.0 (P3P1.0) Specification is the authoritative source for information on the P3P protocol and vocabulary. Throughout this book, I generally refer to it simply as the "P3P specification." You can retrieve the specification from *http://www.w3.org/TR/P3P/*.

P3P was developed through a consensus process involving several dozen W3C working group members. Participants came from around the world and included representatives from industry, government, nonprofit organizations, and academia. In addition, public comments on the many P3P working drafts helped shape the final P3P specification. This section gives a brief summary of how P3P works.

Privacy policies are intended to describe a company's *data practices*—what they do with the information they collect from individuals (usually customers and potential customers, but sometimes also employees and others). The P3P specification includes a standard *vocabulary* for describing these data practices and a *base data schema* for describing the kinds of information collected. A P3P *policy* is a collection of vocabulary and data elements that describes the data practices of a particular web site (or section of a web site).

A P3P policy is essentially composed of the answers to a number of multiple-choice questions and thus does not always contain as much detailed information as a human-readable privacy policy (i.e., a policy written in English or another spoken language that is intended for people, rather than computers, to read). The standard format of a P3P policy allows it to be processed automatically.

The P3P specification also includes a protocol for requesting and transmitting P3P policies. The P3P protocol is built on the same HTTP protocol[†] that web browsers

---

[*] Cookies are bits of text that web sites can send in their HTTP headers and ask web browsers to send back to them on subsequent visits to the same web site. They help enable features such as electronic shopping carts and logging into a web site without a password. Cookies are discussed in more detail in Chapter 2.

[†] HTTP is short for HyperText Transfer Protocol (*http://www.ietf.org/rfc/rfc2616.txt*). For in-depth information on how HTTP and related protocols work, see Balachander Krishnamurthy and Jenifer Rexford, *Web Protocols and Practice: HTTP/1.1, Networking Protocols, Caching, and Traffic Measurement* (Boston: Addison Wesley, 2001).

use to communicate with web servers. As shown in Figure 1-1, P3P user agents use standard HTTP requests to fetch a P3P *policy reference file* from a well-known location on the web site to which a user is making a request. The policy reference file indicates the location of the P3P policy file that applies to each part of the web site. There might be one policy for the entire site, or several policies that each cover a different part of the site. The user agent can then fetch the appropriate policy, parse it, and take action according to the user's preferences.

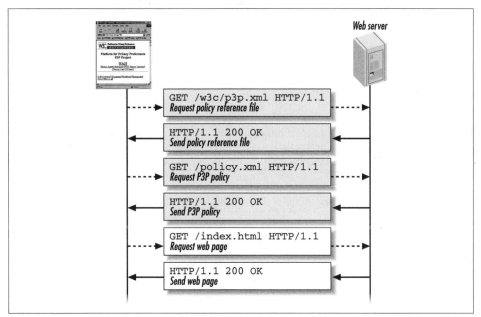

Figure 1-1. The basic protocol for fetching a P3P policy

P3P also allows sites to place policy reference files in locations other than the well-known location. In these cases, the site must declare the location of the policy reference file by using a special HTTP header or by embedding a LINK tag in the HTML files to which the P3P policies apply. Special HTTP headers are also used to transmit an optional P3P *compact policy* whenever cookies are set. Compact policies are very short summaries of full P3P policies that describe only the data practices related to cookies. They do not have the full expressive capabilities of P3P policies.

Here's a plain English example of the kind of disclosure a web site might make in a P3P policy:

> We do not currently collect any information from visitors to this site except the information contained in standard web server logs (your IP address, referer, information about your web browser, information about your HTTP requests, etc.). The information in these logs will be used only by us and the server administrators for web site and system administration, and for improving this site. It will not be disclosed unless required by law. We may retain these log files indefinitely. Please direct questions about this privacy policy to *privacy@p3pbook.com*.

And here's what this policy would look like using the P3P syntax and encoding:

```
<POLICIES xmlns="http://www.w3.org/2002/01/P3Pv1">
<POLICY discuri="http://p3pbook.com/privacy.html"
        name="policy">
  <ENTITY>
  <DATA-GROUP>
    <DATA
      ref="#business.contact-info.online.email">privacy@p3pbook.com
    </DATA>
    <DATA
      ref="#business.contact-info.online.uri">http://p3pbook.com/
    </DATA>
    <DATA ref="#business.name">Web Privacy With P3P</DATA>
  </DATA-GROUP>
  </ENTITY>
  <ACCESS><nonident/></ACCESS>
  <STATEMENT>
    <CONSEQUENCE>We keep standard web server logs.</CONSEQUENCE>
    <PURPOSE><admin/><current/><develop/></PURPOSE>
    <RECIPIENT><ours/></RECIPIENT>
    <RETENTION><indefinitely/></RETENTION>
    <DATA-GROUP>
      <DATA ref="#dynamic.clickstream"/>
      <DATA ref="#dynamic.http"/>
    </DATA-GROUP>
  </STATEMENT>
</POLICY>
</POLICIES>
```

If you are familiar with the eXtensible Markup Language (XML), this encoding may look familiar to you. But if not, don't worry! I'll get to the details of writing policies in later chapters and introduce you to some tools you can use to create policies without having to write any XML yourself. It is also important to note that P3P policies are designed to be read by computers, not people. User agents will interpret these policies on a user's behalf. In addition, every policy should contain the URL of the web site's human-readable privacy policy, so that users have someplace to turn for more detailed information.

The example policy above is fairly brief, because this web site does not collect much information from visitors. Commercial web sites typically have lengthier policies that describe their more complicated data practices.

P3P user agents typically allow users to specify their privacy preferences so that they can automatically compare a web site's policies to these preferences. P3P user agents can also provide tools that make it easier for users to quickly assess a site's privacy practices for themselves. Some user agents display symbols that summarize a site's privacy policy or indicate that it has a privacy seal (a certification that the site follows its stated privacy policy and/or complies with some set of privacy standards) or is bound by certain privacy laws. Some user agents also include buttons that load a site's human-readable privacy policy without the users having to search for it on the site.

User Agents

The P3P specification rarely uses the terms *browser* or *client*; instead the term *user agent* is used. Although end-user P3P implementations might naturally be built into web browsers, P3P implementations can also be built into electronic wallets, standalone applications, ISP software, or other tools. Thus, the more general term "user agent" is used in the specification and in many places throughout this book.

The P3P specification places few requirements on user agents, so what P3P user agents do varies considerably. This book contains descriptions of several P3P user agents and a variety of possible user agent functions.

Figure 1-2 shows an example of the kind of information displayed by one P3P user agent, the AT&T Privacy Bird beta 1.1 (*http://privacybird.com*). The AT&T Privacy Bird displays a green, "happy" bird icon at sites with P3P policies that match a user's privacy preferences and a red, "angry" bird icon at sites with P3P policies that do not match a user's preferences. Users can click on the bird icon to view a summary of the site's privacy policy that is generated automatically from the site's P3P policy. At sites that do not match a user's preferences, the policy summary also explains where the policy differs from the user's preferences.

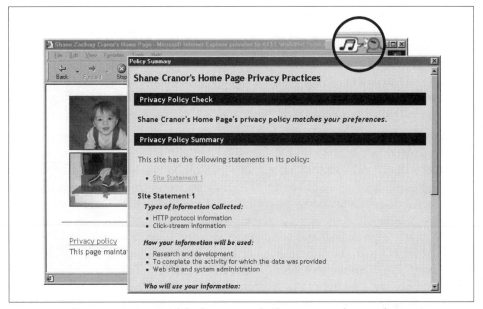

Figure 1-2. The AT&T Privacy Bird displays a green bird icon at sites that match a user's privacy preferences; users can click on the bird to obtain a summary of the site's privacy policy

Another P3P user agent, the Microsoft Internet Explorer 6 web browser, automatically checks P3P compact policies at sites that set cookies. Users can configure IE6 to filter cookies that do not have compact policies or that have compact policies that do not match their preferences. IE6 displays an "eye" symbol in the bottom right corner of the browser window when cookies are blocked. Users can also select the "Privacy Report" option from the View menu to have IE6 fetch a site's P3P policy and generate and display a human-readable version.

In May 2002 Netscape released the preview version of its Netscape Navigator 7 software, which includes P3P functions similar to those found in IE6. Users can configure Netscape to filter cookies on the basis of their P3P compacy policies. They can also select Page Info from the View menu and go to the Privacy tab to have Netscape fetch a site's P3P policy and generate and display a human-readable version.

While the IE6 and Netscape P3P implementations are good first steps that are helping stimulate P3P adoption, they make cookie-filtering decisions based on compact policies only; they do not base these decisions on full P3P policies. Hopefully, in the future Microsoft and Netscape will offer configuration options that take advantage of full P3P policies.

Chapter 12 discusses a variety of ideas for P3P user agents. For example, a P3P user agent might be built into an electronic wallet or other software that includes a data repository that stores data users frequently exchange with web sites. The data in this repository might be identified by the standard names defined in the P3P base data schema. Before automatically filling out a form or submitting data on behalf of a user, a P3P-enabled electronic wallet might fetch the relevant P3P policy and compare it with the user's preferences. If a site does not have a P3P policy or has a policy that does not match the user's preferences, the wallet can alert the user. The wallet might also automatically create and fill out forms with requested data, annotating the forms with the site's data practices.

P3P also has a standard language for encoding a user's privacy preferences, called *A P3P Preference Exchange Language* (APPEL). APPEL files specify what actions the user agent should take, depending on the types of disclosures made by a web site. APPEL files are used by P3P user agents—they are not intended to be sent to web sites. APPEL is not designed to be read by end users either; it is useful mostly for organizations—such as privacy advocacy groups, privacy seal providers, or governmental privacy agencies—that don't like the default settings that come with P3P user agents and want to develop their own "canned" P3P configuration files to distribute to users. It also enables users who have found a configuration setting they like to export it from one user agent and import it into another. However, not all P3P user agents include the ability to import and export APPEL files. The APPEL files themselves are encoded in XML, just like P3P policies. The details of writing APPEL files are discussed in Chapter 13.

P3P-Enabling a Web Site

P3P-enabling a web site is usually a fairly easy process, from a technical standpoint. However, it may require web site operators to take a more detailed look at their data practices than they have done previously and to coordinate policies and practices across the hosts in their domains. Here is an overview of the steps required to P3P-enable a web site. Part II of this book details this entire process.

1. Create a privacy policy.
2. Analyze the use of cookies and third-party content on your site.
3. Determine whether you want to have one P3P policy for your entire site or different P3P policies for different parts of your site.
4. Create a P3P policy (or policies) for your site.
5. Create a policy reference file for your site.
6. Configure your server for P3P.
7. Test your site to make sure it is properly P3P-enabled.

Most P3P-enabled web sites end up with one P3P policy reference file on each of their servers and one or more P3P policies on a central server. They may also configure their servers to send a P3P compact policy whenever they set cookies.

P3P policies include the following information:

- Contact information for the business, organization, or person who owns the site
- Whether individuals can find out what personal data a site keeps about them in its databases
- How to resolve privacy-related disputes with the site (customer service desk, privacy seals, relevant privacy laws, etc.)
- The kinds of data collected
- How collected data is used, and whether individuals can opt-in or opt-out of any of these uses
- Whether/when data may be shared and whether there is opt-in or opt-out
- Policies for periodic purging of collected data

A variety of software tools are available to assist web site developers in P3P-enabling their sites. Some of these are described later in this book; however, for the most up-to-date lists of P3P tools, see *http://p3ptoolbox.org/tools/* and *http://www.w3.org/P3P/implementations/*.

Why Web Sites Adopt P3P

Since Microsoft released their P3P-enabled IE6 web browser in 2001, an increasing number of web sites have adopted P3P. A December 2001 survey by the Progress and

Freedom Foundation found that 23% of the most popular web sites and 5% of a random sample of the top 5,625 domains that collect personally identifiable data were P3P-enabled.[*] The authors of the report concluded: "This seems to be a fairly rapid rate of adoption, given the newness of the product and the fact that relatively few consumers have installed IE6."

By April 2002, about a third of the top 100 web sites had adopted P3P. Early adopters of P3P come from a variety of sectors and include:

- News and information sites, such as CNET and About.com
- Search engines, such as Yahoo! and Lycos
- Advertising networks, such as DoubleClick and Avenue A
- Telecommunications companies, such as AT&T
- Financial institutions, such as Fidelity
- Computer hardware and software vendors, such as IBM, Dell, Microsoft, and McAfee
- Retail stores, such as Fortunoff and Ritz Camera
- Government agencies, such as the U.S. Federal Trade Commission, the U.S. Department of Commerce, and the U.S. Postal Service
- Nonprofit organizations, such as the Center for Democracy and Technology
- Academic institutions, such as Vanderbilt University eLab

Sites outside the U.S. have also started adopting P3P, including commercial sites and the web sites of several data protection commissioners (for example, the Ontario Information and Privacy Commissioner and the Data Protection Commissioner of Bavaria, Germany).

Many early adopters P3P-enabled their web sites to show their support for the P3P effort and demonstrate their corporate leadership on privacy issues. They were motivated both by a desire to show customers that they respect their privacy and by a desire to demonstrate to regulators that the industry is taking voluntary steps to address consumer privacy concerns. While P3P addresses only a narrow set of privacy issues, it complements other efforts to improve privacy protections, including laws, technology tools, and privacy seal programs.

Some companies have started using privacy as a way of distinguishing their brand—they include privacy messages in their advertising and feature privacy-related aspects of their products. By adopting P3P, they further strengthen the message that they respect consumer privacy. In addition, by adopting P3P, they enable consumers to

---

[*] William F. Adkinson, Jr., Jeffrey A. Eisenach, and Thomas M. Lenard, "Privacy Online: A Report on the Information Practices and Policies of Commercial Websites" (Progress & Freedom Foundation, March 2002), *http://www.pff.org/publications/privacyonlinefinalael.pdf*. The web sites surveyed for this report were determined based on October 2001 Nielson/NetRatings data.

quickly locate and get a brief summary of their privacy policies, and to take advantage of any opportunities to remove themselves from marketing and mailing lists.

Some companies have adopted P3P in anticipation that it may soon become a standard that consumers look for at the web sites they visit. If consumers become accustomed to being able to request a privacy report from their web browser or to seeing a happy privacy-bird icon, they may grow suspicious of sites that are not P3P-enabled. In the future, P3P-enabled search engines may make it easy for consumers to identify P3P-enabled web sites.

Some companies have already found that their web sites do not function correctly when viewed using the latest web browsers if their sites are not P3P-enabled. By default, IE6 looks for P3P compact policies associated with third-party cookies (discussed in Chapter 2) on web sites. Third-party cookies are automatically blocked when they don't have compact policies. Thus, targeted advertising, page counters, and other features that rely on third-party cookies may not work unless companies P3P-enable their sites.

Finally, many web sites have adopted P3P because the individuals who run them value their personal privacy and want the companies they work for to take steps to give individuals more control over their personal information.

CHAPTER 2

The Online Privacy Landscape

Over the past few years, Internet users have grown increasingly aware of online privacy issues. When I started doing research in this area in the early 1990s, most of my friends and acquaintances were only mildly interested in what I was doing. Now, my neighbors ask me how they can avoid junk email, my auto mechanic tells me that he is concerned about his privacy when he trades stocks online, and my mother-in-law asks for advice on blocking cookies. Not only is online privacy getting increasing coverage on the front page of many newspapers, it's showing up on the comics page as well.

From my own experiences, as well as evidence from surveys, many people have a lot of interest in and concern about online privacy issues but little knowledge about the real risks and what legal protections exist. Even business decision-makers have little information with which to make privacy-related decisions. To provide some context for better understanding why P3P was created and how it should be used, this chapter presents an overview of the online privacy landscape. It is difficult to do justice to this topic in just one chapter, however. Readers who want to delve more deeply into this topic will find additional information at the web sites referenced in this chapter or in books such as *Database Nation: The Death of Privacy in the 21st Century*, by Simson Garfinkel (O'Reilly).

Online Privacy Concerns

So, what exactly is everyone so concerned about? Frequently, people tell me that they are concerned about what information they may be leaving behind as they surf the Web and who might get access to it. Some people are worried about marketing calls at dinnertime or junk mail or spam, while others are more concerned about Big Brother. I also hear a lot of concerns about hackers stealing credit card numbers, which is really more of a security concern than a privacy concern.

This section examines survey data on privacy concerns, explores how personal information can "leak out" on the Internet, and compares and contrasts online and offline privacy concerns.

Privacy Surveys

Opinion surveys have asked individuals questions related to privacy for many years. Alan Westin, who has been conducting privacy surveys since 1979, conducted one of the first Internet privacy surveys in 1997. This survey of 1,009 American computer users found that while only 28% of Internet users at the time had ever heard the term "cookie" used in reference to web sites, 53% said they were concerned that information about which sites they visit will be linked to their email addresses and disclosed to some other person or organization without their knowledge or consent. Thus, the survey indicated a high level of concern about online privacy before the issue had been widely publicized in the media.

Subsequent surveys found increasing levels of concern about online privacy. In April 1998, Westin found that 81% of Internet users were concerned about online privacy. Six months later, my colleagues and I conducted a similar survey and found that 87% of Internet users were concerned about online privacy in general and 52% were concerned about cookies.

A number of surveys have found that consumers would be more likely to shop online if they were not so worried about privacy issues. The 1998 Westin survey found that improved privacy protection was the factor that would most likely persuade computer users who do not already use the Internet to go online. A 2001 Forrester Research survey found that 34% of Internet users that do not buy online said they would start purchasing from online retailers if they no longer had to worry about privacy. A 2001 Cyber Dialogue survey found that 27% of Internet users had abandoned an online order due to privacy concerns. And a 2001 survey conducted by professors Mary Culnan and George Milne found that 64% of adult Internet users in the U.S. decided not to use or purchase something from a web site because they were uncertain about how their personal information would be used.

Westin's 1997 survey asked web users about their level of interest in a number of hypothetical software products that might be useful for online shopping. While only 26% of web users expressed interest in customized Internet services that would present them with tailored offers for products and services, 65% said they would be interested in a free and easy-to-use product that would allow them to record their preferences about how they want their personal information used by business web sites, in order to have these preferences checked against the actual policies of sites they visit. These survey results suggest that there was considerable consumer interest in P3P-like tools well before the first P3P user agent was available.

Several surveys have asked consumers about whether they read online privacy policies and, if so, whether they understand or trust them. A 2001 Harris Interactive survey of 2,053 adult Internet users in the U.S. found that only 3% of respondents said they reviewed online privacy notices carefully most of the time, while 64% said they have only glanced at privacy notices or did not read them at all. The same survey found that Internet users were most interested in reading privacy notices to learn how personal information is shared or sold to other companies and how they can remove themselves from company databases. In addition, the survey found that 70% of Internet users would prefer that all companies use the same summary or checklist for their privacy policies. This would help address the common criticism that privacy policies are too difficult to read. When readability expert Mark Hochhauser analyzed the privacy policies on 10 popular web sites for *USA Today*, he found that all were written at a college reading level or higher.*

The 2001 Culnan-Milne survey found that individuals were most likely to read privacy notices at sites where they were using a credit card to make a purchase. That survey also found that only 16% of Internet users did not trust companies to follow their privacy policies. In a 1999 Westin survey, 82% of web users said that whether or not a site posted a privacy policy would make a difference in their decision of whether to provide personal information in exchange for a free product or service. Taken together, the survey results suggest that while the presence of privacy policies on web sites improves consumer confidence, few consumers actually read privacy policies.

Other themes that have emerged from online privacy surveys include that consumers are very concerned about having their credit card numbers stolen online, consumers have fewer privacy concerns when doing business with companies whose brands they recognize, and consumers typically assume the worst when no privacy information is available. One question that is difficult to answer from survey data alone, however, is how much privacy concerns actually affect online behavior. Recent surveys suggest that these concerns impact whether an individual will shop online at all, but it is difficult to determine how much these concerns impact which web sites individuals choose to shop at. In addition, it is unclear how much individuals would be willing to pay for better privacy protection, in terms of higher prices, money for purchasing privacy software, or time spent obtaining and configuring privacy software.

What Your Browser Reveals

Most information that web sites obtain about visitors comes from the answers to questions that the visitors themselves type into forms. Except in cases involving computer viruses or security breaches, information cannot be "stolen" from your hard drive or "sucked out of" your computer. Usually, the only data a web site can get from you (other than the data that you type in) is the data that your browser automatically sends to it. Most of this data is pretty innocuous; however, there are cases where your browser may reveal data that you would rather not have revealed. In addition, this data can be used to link together the various bits of information a site has learned about you from the information you have typed in and the links you have chosen.

---

* Will Rodger, "Privacy Isn't Public Knowledge: Online policies spread confusion with legal jargon," *USA Today*, 1 May 2000, 3D, *http://www.usatoday.com/life/cyber/tech/cth818.htm*.

Survey References

An extensive list of privacy surveys from around the world is available from *http://www.privacyexchange.org/iss/surveys/surveys.html*. The following surveys were mentioned in this section:

- Mark S. Ackerman, Lorrie Faith Cranor, and Joseph Reagle, "Beyond Concern: Understanding Net Users' Attitudes About Online Privacy" (Florham Park, NJ: AT&T Labs, April 1999), *http://www.research.att.com/projects/privacystudy/*.

- Mary J. Culnan and George R. Milne, "The Culnan-Milne Survey on Consumers & Online Privacy Notices: Summary of Responses" (December 2001), *http://www.ftc.gov/bcp/workshops/glb/supporting/culnan-milne.pdf*.

- Cyber Dialogue, "Cyber Dialogue Survey Data Reveals Lost Revenue for Retailers Due to Widespread Consumer Privacy Concerns" (New York: Cyber Dialogue, November 2001), *http://www.cyberdialogue.com/news/releases/2001/11-07-uco-retail.html*.

- Forrester Research, "Privacy Issues Inhibit Online Spending" (Cambridge, MA: Forrester, October 3, 2001).

- Louis Harris & Associates and Alan F. Westin, "Commerce, Communication, and Privacy Online" (New York: Louis Harris & Associates, 1997), *http://www.privacyexchange.org/iss/surveys/computersurvey97.html*.

- Louis Harris & Associates and Alan F. Westin, E-Commerce and Privacy, "What Net Users Want" (sponsored by Price Waterhouse and Privacy & American Business. Hackensack, NJ: P & AB, June 1998). *http://www.privacyexchange.org/iss/surveys/ecommsum.html*.

- Opinion Research Corporation and Alan F. Westin, "'Freebies' and Privacy: What Net Users Think" (sponsored by Privacy & American Business. Hackensack, NJ: P & AB, July 1999). *http://www.privacyexchange.org/iss/surveys/sr990714.html*.

- Privacy Leadership Initiative, *Privacy Notices Research Final Results* (conducted by Harris Interactive, December 2001), *http://www.ftc.gov/bcp/workshops/glb/supporting/harris%20results.pdf*.

When you type an address—called a uniform resource locator, or URL—into your browser or click on a link, your browser uses the HyperText Transfer Protocol (HTTP) to fetch the web page or other resource you requested. A typical HTTP request includes information about your web browser and operating system, what language you prefer, what URL you are requesting, and the URL of your previous request (called the *referer*). The request may also include a bit of text called a cookie. Here is a request that my browser generated when I went to *http://buy.com* and did a search on the word "beer."

```
GET /retail/searchresults.asp?qu=beer HTTP/1.0
Referer: http://www.us.buy.com/default.asp
```

```
User-Agent: Mozilla/4.75 [en] (X11; U; NetBSD 1.5_ALPHA i386)
Host: www.us.buy.com
Accept: image/gif, image/jpeg, image/pjpeg, */*
Accept-Language: en
Cookie: buycountry=us; dcLocName=Basket; dcCatID=6773; dcLocID=6773; dcAd=buybasket;
loc=; parentLocName=Basket; parentLoc=6773;
ShopperManager%2F=ShopperManager%2F=66FUQULLOQBT8MMTVSC5MMNKBJFWDVH7; Store=107;
Category=0
```

My computer's IP address was also sent to the web site when the HTTP connection was established.

To see what your web browser reveals about you, visit *http://snoop.cdt.org* or *http://cgi.spaceports.com:81*. (Be patient, it may take several minutes before any information is displayed.)

When web sites receive requests from browsers, they send back the resource requested (if it exists), along with some additional information called *headers*. These headers contain information that your browser may find useful as it displays the requested resource. They can also include other information, such as the location of a web site's P3P policy reference file, and sites may also send a special header that contains a request to set a cookie on your computer.

It is important to understand that a request for a web page generally results in your browser generating several HTTP requests. If the page you are requesting contains images, for example, the initial response from the web site will include the URLs for each image. Your browser will then request each of these URLs in order to get the images. The images might be located on the same web site as the main page; however, it is quite common for some or all of the images to be located on a different web site. Each request that your browser makes will result in information being sent to a web site, and each response will include headers and possibly cookies.

Besides responding to your request, web servers usually save information about the request in a log file. Many web sites store all the information your browser throws at them. Others store only a subset of that information. A small number of web sites take pains to "cleanse" their log data of information that might be used to identify an individual user or computer by removing or truncating IP addresses and other information. Here is an example of a typical log entry that appeared in the log file of one of the web sites I maintain:

```
135.207.6.62 - - [21/Dec/2001:10:49:39 -0500]
"GET / HTTP/1.1" 200 5575 "http://lorrie.cranor.org/"
```

This particular entry was the result of me clicking on a link on my home page. Thus, the referer URL that appears in this log entry is the URL of my home page, *http://lorrie.cranor.org*. The IP address, 135.207.6.62, is the address of the computer I was using at the time. Log entries often include the actual name of the computer that was used to access a site, making it easy to see, for example, if visitors are coming from a particular university or company.

Internet Fundamentals

To understand online privacy issues, it is helpful to have a basic understanding of how the Internet works.

The Internet is an international network of computers. Each computer on the network has a unique numeric address called an *Internet Protocol (IP) address*. This is similar to a phone number. Each computer also has a unique name that is easier for people to remember than a numeric address, and computers can translate easily between this name and the numeric address.

When computers send messages to each other across the Internet, they break up the messages into small bundles of information called *packets* and attach the IP address of both the sending and receiving computer to each packet. A sending computer passes its outgoing packets to a nearby computer, which forwards them to another nearby computer. This process continues until the packets reach the destination address, much as letters sent through the postal mail may be sent from a local post office to a regional post office and then to another local post office once they have reached their destination city. Because each packet contains the address of the sending computer, an acknowledgment can be sent back to that computer once the packet is received, or an error message can be sent if a problem occurs. Once all of the packets associated with a message are received, the receiving computer can put them back together and read the original message.

Internet packets are similar to postcards—they can be read by any computer they pass through on the way to their destination. In addition, receiving computers (and even some of the computers that help forward a message to its destination) may save copies of each message. These copies may be routinely scanned by law-enforcement officers, crackers, or even employers who monitor their employees' email. Even after the originals have been read and deleted, copies of messages may be saved on backup tapes, from which it may be possible to retrieve them years later. By encrypting messages and using encrypted protocols, you can prevent other people from reading your messages (see Chapter 3).

It is often possible to trace the path a message took as it traveled across the Internet and determine where it originated. If a message originated from an Internet service provider (ISP), that ISP may be able to determine which of its users sent the message and what telephone line he used to connect to the ISP.

Some web sites routinely analyze their log files in order to monitor how the site is being used, to bill advertisers, or for other purposes. Other sites save the files in case they need them (for example, if someone breaks into their system, they may use the log files to try to get information about the break-in) but do not routinely examine them. For most sites, the log files are of little or no use after a few days, but the old files usually are not deleted. As a result, lawyers and law-enforcement officers sometimes are able to track down information by requesting access to web logs. They may use this information for a variety of purposes, such as to demonstrate that a parent seeking custody of a child routinely visits adult web sites or to link an employee with anonymous comments critical of her employer. When presented with a court order (subpoena) for these logs, a web site operator is required to comply. Web sites can avoid being subpoenaed only by routinely deleting their log files, including all copies on backup tapes.

Cookies

Cookies are bits of text that web sites sometimes send back in their HTTP headers.[*] When your web browser receives a cookie, it usually stores it on your computer. The next time you go back to the web site that sent you the cookie, your browser will automatically send a copy of the cookie back to that site. Web sites often use cookies to store user identification numbers, information about what you are doing on the site (for example, what you have put in your electronic shopping cart), or information about configuration options you have selected (for example, that you have indicated you are on a low-bandwidth connection).

Some cookies, called *session cookies*, are used only during one browser session. When you close your web browser, your computer deletes them. Other cookies, called *persistent cookies*, may be used over many browser sessions. Web sites often specify expiration dates five or more years in the future, to ensure that their cookies will last as long as you have your computer (unless you delete them).

Here is an example of a web site's request to set a cookie:

```
Set-Cookie: p_uniqid=8MCY1NjWqtcAQzf2yC; path=/;
domain=.lycos.com; expires=Thu, 31-Dec-2037 23:59:59 GMT
```

This cookie contains some sort of unique identification number, and the site is requesting that the cookie be sent back to any computer that the user visits in the *lycos.com* domain (*www.lycos.com*, *hotwired.lycos.com*, etc.). This cookie doesn't expire until the year 2037.

Cookies serve many useful purposes and make it easier for web sites to offer customized services and easy-to-use interfaces. They can even be used to help protect privacy, by storing web site customization information on each user's computer rather than in a centralized database.

Many people are concerned about cookies because they can be used to track individuals without their knowledge or consent. Sites may use cookies to keep track of what parts of the site you return to most often, what searches you run, or what ads you have seen. When you go to a physical store, the store generally has no record of what items you looked at or even picked up and examined before making your selection and checking out. If you pay cash, they may not even have a record of what you

---

[*] For a detailed discussion of how cookies work and an interesting account of their history, see David M. Kristol, "HTTP Cookies: Standards, privacy, and politics," *ACM Transactions on Internet Technology* 1, no. 2 (2001) 151–198, *http://doi.acm.org/10.1145/502152.502153*.

bought. But an online store can observe every click that you make and keep track of which items you looked at but didn't buy, and which items you eventually purchased. On a trip to Beijing a few years ago, I noticed that the sales clerks in all the shops I went into followed me closely as I moved around their stores. They seemed to note every item I examined, and often offered comments on the items they thought I was looking at. I found this very disconcerting, and very much unlike a typical U.S. shopping experience. However, this is exactly what happens when you shop at many web sites. A well-designed user interface can make this online tracking and customization useful to the user, but users may still have concerns about how much of this data will be retained and what else it might be used for.

Another concern about cookies is that they are sometimes used to track users across multiple web sites. Cookies are sent back only to the web site that set them, or to other web sites in the same domain (which are presumably owned and operated by the same company). However, there is a simple trick that many companies use in order to easily share information about users among multiple web sites. As explained earlier, a web page is often composed of many components that must each be requested separately. Many web sites that include advertising get their ads from advertising companies. Instead of hosting these ads on their own web servers, they usually just provide the URL of the ad on the advertising company's server. The URL may be customized to indicate information about the page in which the ad has been embedded. When your browser fetches such a web page, it automatically requests the ad from the advertising company's server. When the advertising company's server responds with the image file that contains the ad, it often also sends back cookies. These cookies, called *third-party cookies*, are sent back any time an ad is requested from that ad company. Since ad companies tend to sell their ads to large numbers of web sites, the ad companies are able to use their cookies in combination with information obtained from referer headers to track users across all of the sites where their ads appear. This allows them to keep track of what ads have already been displayed to users, so that they can be shown a greater variety of ads. It also allows the ad companies to build profiles of users and deliver ads to them that they are more likely to find interesting. Thus, the ad companies may be able to figure out whether you are more interested in sports or music, whether you like to travel, and whether you seem interested in buying a new car—all on the basis of what web sites you have visited.

Many ad companies that profile users do so without identifying individual users. These companies have lots of information about your interests, and they may be able to determine the geographic region in which your computer is located, but they don't actually know who you are. In particular, they usually don't know your name, address, phone number, or email address. But some of these ad companies do have the ability to link your profile to such identifying information. If you register or make a purchase at a site that uses an ad company, the site could share the information you provided to them with the ad company, allowing the ad company to identify your profile. The ad company could then look you up in other databases to get more information about you and link that information to your profile as well.

Because cookies can be used in undesirable ways, many Internet users opt not to let their computers accept them at all; they configure their browsers to reject cookies or use cookie-blocking software (described in Chapter 3). However, many web sites do not function without cookies, and many users find that they want to take advantage of services that rely on cookies. Some P3P user agents, such as Microsoft IE6, offer an alternative to rejecting all cookies or asking the user to consider every cookie on a case-by-case basis—users can configure these tools to block only cookies that do not match their privacy preferences. Thus, the cookies that do not pose privacy concerns can be accepted automatically, and the rest can be blocked unless allowed by the user.

Web bugs

I've heard a lot of excitement and questions about web bugs. The name may sound ominous, but web bugs are actually just cookies that are attached to invisible images in web sites. When a cookie is associated with an ad, you can see the ad (although you may not know that it has a cookie), but when a cookie is associated with a web bug, nothing is visibly displayed on the web page. Web bugs are used for the same reasons that other cookies are used: sometimes they enable services that you may find convenient, and sometimes they are used to track you in ways you'd prefer they wouldn't.

Sometimes people use the term "web bugs" to refer to images (visible or invisible) associated with HTML-formatted email. Embedding an image in HTML-formatted email allows the sender of the email to find out when you open the email. In addition, customized links inside the email may allow a site to track which email recipients click on the links. There are also ways that web bugs can be added to Microsoft Word documents.

Industry groups suggest that the term *web beacon* be used instead of web bug. Thus, many privacy policies use this term. Sometimes the terms *cookie anchor*, *clear gif*, or *tracker gif* are also used. However, privacy advocates and the media tend to use the term web bug.

The Privacy Foundation has a lot more information about web bugs on its web site, at *http://www.privacyfoundation.org/resources/webbug.asp*. They have also created a free Internet Explorer add-on called Bugnosis that identifies web bugs embedded in web sites (*http://www.bugnosis.org*).

Referers

One of the pieces of information that web browsers routinely send to web sites is the HTTP referer. The HTTP referer is the URL of the site you were visiting when you made the current request—i.e., the site that referred you to the current site. While the referer can help sites learn how people are finding out about them and can be useful for tracking down problems, they also make it easier for sites to build profiles of visitors and can be particularly dangerous when the address of the previous site includes confidential account information, credit card numbers, or search strings.

The HTTP specification does not require that referer headers be sent; however, most web browsers send them by default to most web sites.

Online Versus Offline Privacy Concerns

Privacy was an issue long before the advent of computers, but privacy concerns have been magnified by the existence and widespread use of large computer databases that make it easy to compile a dossier containing data about an individual from many different sources. These concerns are further exacerbated now that the World Wide Web makes it easy for new data to be collected automatically and added to databases. Data entered into forms or contained in existing databases can now be combined easily with transaction records as well as a record of an individual's every click through cyberspace. As data-mining tools and services become more widely available, privacy concerns are likely to increase still further.

As growing numbers of people use the Internet for an ever-expanding range of activities, the amount of personal data collected via the Internet is increasing. This phenomenon has raised a variety of privacy-related concerns, including:

- Concerns about the secure storage and transfer of information
- Concerns that individuals' information may be collected without their knowledge or consent
- Concerns that the ease with which information can be collected and processed is leading to an increasing amount of data collection, database matching, and secondary use of data
- Concerns that an individual's information may be transferred across jurisdictional boundaries to locations where it is not protected by the same privacy laws in effect where that individual resides

Most of these concerns are not new; indeed, they all existed well before the advent of the Internet. However, as the Internet becomes more pervasive, these concerns are exacerbated.

Security

Many people are concerned that personal information that they send to web sites may not be transmitted or stored securely. If information is sent without taking any special precautions, it may in fact be intercepted and read as it travels across the Internet. Information about how to send information securely is presented in Chapter 3.

How much of a risk are you taking if you don't take steps to transmit information securely? It's hard to answer this question in absolute terms. Most email sent over the Internet today is not encrypted, and many people send credit card numbers and other sensitive information to web sites without encrypting it. Most of these people never experience a problem as a result. However, there are an increasing number of cases of employers reading their employees' email and hackers intercepting credit card numbers and computer passwords. Today, the risk of having your credit card number stolen online is probably not much greater than the risk of having your credit card number stolen by an unscrupulous store clerk or of having your calling card number stolen as you make a call from a crowded airport. Even so, it's easy to reduce the online risk by taking advantage of the security options offered by most ecommerce web sites. However, the risk of having your email read is probably much greater than the risk of having your postal mail read, because it is much easier for someone to read your email without detection—people can automatically scan email to find messages that hold a particular interest to them, and in some cases reading someone else's email is perfectly legal.

Even if information is transmitted securely, there are still risks that it will not be properly secured by the receiving web site. Just as physical records can be stolen, electronic records also can be stolen. However, thieves may not have to physically enter the location where records are kept to steal electronic records. Unfortunately, there's no easy way for you to determine whether the web sites you visit practice good security, and even web sites that take reasonable precautions are not impenetrable.

Security Versus Privacy

Data *security* and data *privacy* are two closely related concepts that are often confused. Data privacy is centrally concerned about data collection and use. Thus, corporate privacy policies explain a company's policies about what kinds of data it collects and how it will use that data. Conversely, in the context of privacy policies, data security describes how privacy policies are enforced. If a company has committed to keeping personal data confidential, it should use security tools ranging from encryption software to locks on the machine room door to secure the data and protect it from people who are not supposed to have access to it.

A great privacy policy is not very useful if a company doesn't also have a comprehensive and effective security system in place. For example, an online bookstore may promise in its privacy policy to keep purchase records confidential, but someone may break into their computer system, copy their customer database, and create a web site listing the names of all the customers who ordered books on alcohol addiction.

Likewise, great security is not all that helpful if the company has a policy of selling your data to the highest bidder. For example, the online bookstore might do an excellent job of protecting its systems from break-ins, but it may routinely sell its customer database—including purchase information—to companies who profile individuals based on their book purchasing habits.

Fair Information Practice Principles

Fair information practice principles are sets of guidelines for keeping personal data private. A number of different sets of these principles have been developed over the past 30 years or so. Some have been developed by government agencies or international organizations; others have been developed by industry or consumer groups. Some have subsequently become the basis of privacy laws.

The Organization for Economic Co-operation and Development (OECD) Guidelines on the Protection of Privacy and Transborder Flows of Personal Data (*http://www.oecd.org/dsti/sti/it/secur/prod/PRIV-en.HTM*) are, perhaps, the best-known set of fair information practice principles. These guidelines, codified in 1980, are the principles on which many other guidelines and data-protection laws are based. The OECD Guidelines include the following eight principles:

Collection Limitation Principle
> There should be limits to the collection of personal data, and any such data should be obtained by lawful and fair means and, where appropriate, with the knowledge or consent of the data subject.

Data Quality Principle
> Personal data should be relevant to the purposes for which it is to be used and, to the extent necessary for those purposes, should be accurate, complete, and kept up-to-date.

Purpose Specification Principle
> The purposes for which personal data is collected should be specified not later than at the time of data collection and the subsequent use limited to the fulfillment of those purposes or such others as are not incompatible with those purposes and as are specified on each occasion of change of purpose.

Use Limitation Principle
> Personal data should not be disclosed, made available, or otherwise used for purposes other than those specified in accordance with the Purpose Specification Principle, except with the consent of the data subject or by the authority of law.

Security Safeguards Principle
> Personal data should be protected by reasonable security safeguards against such risks as loss or unauthorized access, destruction, use, modification, or disclosure of data.

Openness Principle
> There should be a general policy of openness about developments, practices, and policies with respect to personal data. Means should be readily available of establishing the existence and nature of personal data, the main purposes of their use, as well as the identity and usual residence of the data controller.

Individual Participation Principle
> An individual should have the following rights: a) to obtain from a data controller, or otherwise, confirmation of whether or not the data controller has data relating to him; b) to have data relating to him communicated to him within a reasonable time, at a charge (if any) that is not excessive, in a reasonable manner, and in a form that is readily intelligible to him; c) to be given reasons if a request made under subparagraphs (a) and (b) is denied and to be able to

challenge such denial; and d) to challenge data relating to him and, if the challenge is successful, to have the data erased, rectified, completed, or amended.

Accountability Principle

A data controller should be accountable for complying with measures that give effect to the principles stated above.

The term *data subject* refers to the person about whom data has been collected. The term *data controller* refers to the entity (usually a company but sometimes a person or organization) that controls the collection, storage, and use of personal data.

Most of the other sets of principles contain variations on these eight principles. The Council of Europe Convention for the Protection of Individuals with regard to Automatic Processing of Personal Data, ratified in 1985, is based closely on these principles.* In addition, in 1998, the U.S. Federal Trade Commission (FTC) identified five core privacy protection principles based on the OECD guidelines: Notice/Awareness, Choice/Consent, Access/Participation, Integrity/Security, and Enforcement/Redress.†

As companies draft privacy policies, they often find it useful to consider the fair information practice principles and how they address each of them.

Opt-in and Opt-out

Two terms often used in discussions of choice and consent are opt-in and opt-out. *Opt-in* refers to situations in which individuals explicitly request that their personal information be used for a particular purpose; for example, individuals may ask to be placed on a mailing list. *Opt-out* refers to situations in which individuals request that their personal information not be used for a particular purpose; for example, individuals may ask that their information be removed from a mailing list. Companies that place individuals on mailing lists only if they explicitly request it are said to have opt-in practices. Companies that place individuals on mailing lists by default but remove them upon request are said to have opt-out practices.

Privacy Laws

Privacy laws vary greatly throughout the world. Some countries have no privacy laws, others have privacy laws that apply only to narrow sectors, and still others have comprehensive privacy laws that apply broadly. Some privacy laws are aimed at protecting people from governmental incursions into their privacy, while others are aimed at limiting the ability of businesses to collect and use personal data. The

---

* The Convention is available on the Council of Europe web site, *http://www.coe.fr*, as ETS #108.

† U.S. Federal Trade Commission, "Privacy Online: A Report to Congress" (June 1998), *http://www.ftc.gov/reports/privacy3/*.

extent to which privacy laws are enforced also varies. The privacy laws of the European Union (E.U.) and the U.S. are reviewed here. The *Privacy Law Sourcebook*, by Marc Rotenberg (EPIC), is a good reference on privacy laws around the world. In addition, the Privacy Exchange web site (*http://www.privacyexchange.org*) has pointers to many data-protection authorities and national privacy laws.

European Union

For many years most E.U. countries have had fairly comprehensive privacy laws modeled after the Council of Europe Convention. However, the laws originally varied quite a bit from country to country. In 1995, the E.U. passed Directive 95/46/EC, the Directive on Protection of Personal Data (*http://europa.eu.int/smartapi/cgi/sga_doc?smartapi!celexapi!prod!CELEXnumdoc&lg=EN&numdoc=31995L0046*), aimed at harmonizing the European privacy laws. The Directive prescribes a framework for privacy laws based on the OECD principles. This framework also prohibits data transfer to countries lacking "adequate" privacy protections. Each E.U. member country was required to adopt laws consistent with the Directive within three years of its passage.

Many European countries were slow to meet the deadline required by the Directive, and enactment and enforcement of the new laws has proceeded slowly. Nonetheless, a comprehensive, harmonized legal regime for privacy protection is now in place in Europe. Under the European laws, notice must be given about how data will be used at the time it is collected, and there are many restrictions on transferring data to other parties and using personal data for other "secondary" purposes. For sensitive data, such transfers or secondary use can occur only under limited conditions to which the data subject has specifically agreed (opted-in). For other types of data, it is usually sufficient for the data controller to provide a way for data subjects to opt out of secondary uses or transfer. National (and in some countries state) data-protection authorities—usually headed by a privacy or data-protection "commissioner"—supervise the implementation of data-protection laws.

United States

The U.S. does not have a comprehensive privacy protection framework like the E.U. Directive. Instead, the U.S. has a "patchwork" of sector-specific privacy laws that apply to narrow industry sectors. In addition, in recent years the U.S. has relied heavily on voluntary self-regulation in the online privacy area. Thus, although U.S. companies in many sectors are not required to have privacy policies, an increasing number are adopting these policies and posting them on their web sites. Companies that post inaccurate or misleading policies risk an investigation by the FTC.

Safe Harbor

Because U.S. privacy protections are considered inadequate in the eyes of the European authorities, the U.S. Department of Commerce worked with the E.U. to develop a "Safe Harbor" framework, in which U.S. companies can voluntarily treat European citizens' data in a manner consistent with the E.U. Directive (*http://www.export.gov/safeharbor/*). U.S. companies that voluntarily comply with this framework are automatically considered to provide adequate data protection. When a company volunteers to comply with Safe Harbor, it also puts itself under the jurisdiction of the U.S. Federal Trade Commission or other agencies that have the ability to take legal action against them should they fail to comply.

Children's Online Privacy Protection Act (COPPA)

Enacted in 1998, COPPA requires web sites directed at children under age 13 to obtain parental consent before collecting personal information from children. There are a few exemptions—for example, sites are allowed to collect a child's email address in order to respond to an email message from the child. In addition, children's sites must post privacy policies and allow parents to find out what information has been collected about their children. The FTC has extensive information about complying with COPPA on its web site, at *http://www.ftc.gov/bcp/conline/edcams/kidzprivacy/*.

Graham-Leach-Bliley Act

This law, which took effect in 2001, restricts the disclosure of personally identifiable financial information by financial institutions. Financial institutions must provide written or electronic privacy policies that explain what kinds of information they collect, to whom the information will be disclosed, and consumer opt-out rights. In addition, financial institutions must give consumers the ability to opt out of having their data disclosed to unaffiliated third parties (subject to a long list of exceptions) and are prohibited from making disclosures of certain information for marketing purposes. This law also requires a number of security and confidentiality safeguards. The FTC has extensive information about Graham-Leach-Bliley on its web site, at *http://www.ftc.gov/privacy/glbact/*.

Other U.S. privacy laws

A variety of other sector-specific U.S. privacy laws exist. At the national level, these laws include:

- The Fair Credit Reporting Act (1970)
- Privacy Act of 1974
- Family Education Rights and Privacy Act (1974)
- Right to Financial Privacy Act (1978)
- Privacy Protection Act of 1980
- Cable Communications Policy Act of 1984
- Electronic Communications Privacy Act (1986)

- Video Privacy Protection Act of 1988
- Telephone Consumer Protection Act of 1991
- Driver's Privacy Protection Act of 1994
- Communications Assistance for Law Enforcement Act of 1994
- Telecommunications Act of 1996
- Health Insurance Portability and Accountability Act of 1996

In addition, many U.S. states have their own privacy laws. A good reference on U.S. privacy laws is *Compilation of State & Federal Privacy Laws*, by Robert Ellis Smith (Privacy Journal). The Privacy Leadership Initiative provides a brief overview of U.S. state and federal privacy laws on its web site, at *http://www.understandingprivacy.org/content/library/laws.cfm*.

A number of bills have been proposed at the state and national level to encourage the use of P3P. In February 2002, the Virginia legislature adopted a bill encouraging all state and local government agencies and members of the General Assembly to P3P-enable their web sites.[*]

Privacy Seals

One of the problems with web site privacy policies is that consumers often do not know whether they can trust them. Privacy seals help address this problem by certifying that a web site's privacy policy is accurate. Seal providers generally have a set of baseline requirements that companies that want their seals must follow. They use routine or random audits, list seeding, and other techniques to verify that the site practices match stated policies. In addition, seal providers generally assist individuals in resolving privacy-related disputes with web sites that have their seals.

One of the first online seal programs was developed by an organization called TRUSTe (*http://www.truste.org*), which was founded by the Electronic Frontier Foundation and the CommerceNet Consortium. The TRUSTe seal program has evolved over time, as the organization has gained experience. As of this writing, the TRUSTe trustmark is awarded to sites that adhere to the FTC's privacy principles and agree to comply with ongoing TRUSTe oversight and consumer-resolution procedures. TRUSTe also offers a Children's Seal for sites that target children and comply with the COPPA requirements, an eHealth Privacy Seal for healthcare web sites, and an E.U. Safe Harbor Privacy Seal. TRUSTe is also developing a seal program for Japanese web sites. The TRUSTe seals are shown in Figure 2-1.

Another well-known online seal program is BBBOnLine program (*http://www.bbbonline.org*). Owned by the Council of Better Business Bureaus, BBBOnLine

---

[*] HJ 172 Incorporate Privacy Preference Project (P3P) and government web sites, *http://leg1.state.va.us/cgi-bin/legp504.exe?ses=021&typ=bil&val=hj172*.

Figure 2-1. The TRUSTe seals

provides two different privacy seals: a regular privacy seal and a kid's privacy seal. To receive one of these seals, companies must demonstrate that their privacy practices meet an extensive list of requirements, agree to participate in the BBBOnLine dispute-settlement procedures, and undergo and annual audit. BBBOnLine also has an E.U. Safe Harbor Program and a Japanese seal program. The BBBOnLine seals are shown in Figure 2-2.

Figure 2-2. The BBBOnLine seals

P3P-enabled web sites can indicate that they have privacy seals in their P3P policies. Some P3P user agents, such as IE6 and the AT&T Privacy Bird, display these seals when a user requests more information about a site's privacy policy. In addition, P3P provides a field that could be used by seal providers in the future to provide a digital certificate for verifying the authenticity of a seal.

Chief Privacy Officers

Many companies have recently appointed Chief Privacy Officers to oversee their corporate privacy policies. Along with these new positions have come new programs to train CPOs and professional organizations for CPOs. The International Association of Privacy Officers (*http://www.privacyassociation.org*) was recently formed as a result of a merger of two privacy officer associations.

CPOs play a variety of roles, including drafting privacy policies, overseeing employee education programs on privacy-policy compliance, monitoring new developments in privacy regulation, advising business units on privacy-related aspects of new products or services, and responding to questions and concerns about privacy policies.

Privacy-Related Organizations

A large number of privacy-related organizations exist. Most of these organizations have web sites that provide educational information about privacy-related issues. Some actively lobby for more privacy laws, some promote self-regulation as an alternative to privacy laws, and some remain neutral as to whether more privacy regulation is needed. Some of these organizations are funded by individuals and some by industry groups. Some are not really organizations, but actually consulting firms, companies, or even individuals that sell privacy-related products and services. I have found that most of the factual information provided by privacy-related organizations is pretty accurate, regardless of their agenda; however, most provide information with one spin or another, depending on their underlying motivations and who is funding them. Do try to find out who is behind an organization whose information you use, and try to check out the information provided by groups on all sides of the issue.

The following web sites are devoted to privacy-related issues:

American Civil Liberties Union (ACLU) — *http://www.aclu.org*
Center for Democracy and Technology — *http://www.cdt.org*
Computer Professionals for Social Responsibility — *http://www.cpsr.org*
Consumer Privacy Guide — *http://www.consumerprivacyguide.org*
Electronic Frontier Foundation — *http://www.eff.org*
Electronic Privacy Information Center — *http://www.epic.org*
Health Privacy Project — *http://www.healthprivacy.org*
Junkbusters — *http://www.junkbusters.com*
Online Privacy Alliance — *http://www.privacyalliance.org*
Privacy and American Business — *http://www.pandab.org*
PrivacyExchange — *http://www.privacyexchange.org*
The Privacy Forum — *http://www.vortex.com/privacy.html*
Privacy Foundation — *http://www.privacyfoundation.org*
Privacy International — *http://www.privacy.org/pi*
Privacy Journal — *http://www.privacyjournal.net/*
Privacy Leadership Initiative — *http://www.understandingprivacy.org*
Privacy.org — *http://www.privacy.org*
Privacy Rights Clearinghouse — *http://www.privacyrights.org*
Privacy Times — *http://www.privacytimes.com*
Roger Clarke's Dataveillance and Information Privacy Pages — *http://www.anu.edu.au/people/Roger.Clarke/DV/index.html*
Yahoo Internet Privacy News — *http://headlines.yahoo.com/Full_Coverage/Tech/Internet_Privacy*

CHAPTER 3
Privacy Technology

Online privacy tools perform many functions. Tools are available for encrypting files and email, establishing secure channels to web sites, and establishing encrypted "tunnels" between two computers on the Internet. These tools prevent eavesdropping and protect data from unauthorized access. In addition, anonymity tools are available that prevent online communications from being linked back to a specific individual and prevent eavesdroppers from learning with whom an individual is communicating. Some tools allow users to build anonymous, yet persistent, relationships with web sites, thus allowing sites to track user behavior or provide customized services without building identifiable user profiles.

As web sites have exploited web browser features to track individuals' browsing behavior, tools have been developed to disable these features, and some browsers have built in additional user controls. For example, a variety of tools are available that can block or give users more control over the use of cookies (for more information on cookies, see Chapter 2). In addition, many of the anonymity and cookie-blocking tools also block the automatic transmittal of the HTTP Referer header, which tells web sites the address of the last site the user visited. A set of identity management tools have been introduced as well that help people manage their online identities and protect their privacy.

Related to these privacy tools are a number of security tools, including personal firewalls and virus-detection software, which are beyond the scope of this book.

This chapter is not really about P3P, but it is included in this book to provide more background on privacy technology. While the role of P3P is to make users aware of web site privacy practices and to make it easier for users to make informed choices about when to provide data to web sites, many other privacy tools exist that are designed to actually suppress the transmission of data or restrict access to data or computers. These tools are actually quite complementary to P3P tools. In situations where data transfer is necessary to facilitate a transaction (for example, I must provide my credit card number and address if I want to buy something on credit and have it delivered to my house), P3P tools can help users understand how their data will be used. Encryption tools might be used to secure the data when it is actually transferred over the Internet. In situations where data transfer is not really necessary, anonymity tools might be used to make sure no data is transferred.

This chapter provides a brief overview of the various technological tools that can help people protect their online privacy. There are entire books dedicated to exploring this topic in more detail; for example, see *Web Security, Privacy & Commerce*, by Simson Garfinkel with Gene Spafford (O'Reilly) and *Privacy Defended: Protecting Yourself Online*, by Gary Bahadur, William Chan, and Chris Weber (QUE). The web site *http://www.privacytoolbox.org* also has more information about privacy-related technologies.

 When selecting security and privacy software tools and services, be careful. Many companies offer security tools that do not live up to their marketing claims. If it sounds too good to be true, it just might be. Be especially suspicious of tools that claim to use proprietary encryption algorithms or that guarantee absolutely unbreakable security. Generally, the most reliable encryption algorithms are those that have been published and have undergone years of public scrutiny. Likewise, open source tools can more easily be analyzed by security experts for possible problems. Look for reviews of privacy and security products by reputable security experts.

Encryption Tools

Whenever sensitive information is stored on a computer or transmitted over the Internet, it should be protected using strong encryption. A detailed discussion of encryption algorithms and products is beyond the scope of this book. However, I will touch briefly on some basic types of encryption products that are useful for helping individuals protect their privacy.

Encryption algorithms are based on mathematical functions that are relatively easy to compute if you know the secret number contained in the encryption key but very difficult to compute otherwise. If somebody wants to decrypt a file but doesn't have the key, she can try every possible key until she finds the right one. This is called a *brute force attack*. If the key is not many digits long, a computer can try every possible key pretty quickly. But if you make the key long enough, it will take even the fastest known computers many years to try every possible key. Thus, the probability of discovering the key you used within your lifetime would be very small. As computers have gotten faster, longer keys have been necessary to avoid brute force attacks. Until recently, many people used 56-bit encryption keys (that is, keys composed of 56-digit binary numbers). However, there are now supercomputers that can find 56-bit keys in a matter of days.* Security experts currently recommend the use of 128-bit keys.

---

* A 56-bit encryption key has 2^{56} possible combinations. In 1998, the DES Cracker computer built by the Electronic Frontier Foundation searched 88 billion keys every second and found a 56-bit key in 56 hours. In 1999, the DES Cracker was used in conjunction with a worldwide network of PCs to find a 56-bit key in just 22 hours. For more information about the DES Cracker, see *http://www.eff.org/descracker/*.

Many encryption tools still use keys that are much shorter than 128 bits. In fact, because of legal restrictions on exporting strong encryption from the U.S. (lifted in 1999), some commercial software developers use 40-bit encryption. A brute force attack can uncover a 40-bit key in less than a minute (or in a few seconds, if you use a supercomputer). These keys may be sufficient to protect your files from casual snoopers, but they are clearly insufficient for any applications that require real security.

Public Key Cryptography

In traditional cryptographic systems, messages are encrypted using a secret key and decrypted using the same secret key. If a person wants to encrypt the files on his computer so that only he has access to them, such a system is adequate. However, if he wants to send a secret message to a friend, he has to first share the secret key with her. But unless the two friends have the opportunity to meet face-to-face in a private place, there may not be a secure channel on which to transmit the key.

Public key cryptography systems avoid this problem by using a pair of keys rather than a single secret key. Each key pair has a *public key* and a *private key*. Any message encrypted with the public key can be decrypted only with the corresponding private key, and vice versa. A person can send his public key to anyone or even publish it in a directory without compromising his private key. Thus, if Bob wants to send a secret message to his friend Alice, he must first ask her for her public key or look it up in a directory. Bob can use Alice's public key to encrypt a message that only she will be able to decrypt.

Bob might also use his own private key to digitally *sign* his message to Alice, so that she knows that it was not forged. If Alice uses Bob's public key to successfully decrypt a message, she knows that the message must have been encrypted using Bob's private key.

Applied Cryptography by Bruce Schneier (John Wiley & Sons) has become a classic introduction to cryptography. Most computer security books also include chapters on cryptography.

File Encryption

Even if you are not planning on sending files over the Internet, when you are storing sensitive information on your computer you may want to encrypt it to protect it from nosey coworkers or family members as well intruders (electronic or physical). If your computer is connected to the Internet, a virus or worm could potentially copy any of your files and transmit them to others. If you store files on a shared computer, other users and system administrators may be able to gain access to your files. By encrypting your files, you prevent them from being read by anyone who does not know the encryption key.

A variety of commercial software packages can be used for file encryption. Be wary of those that come with word-processor or spreadsheet programs—they often use very weak encryption algorithms. There are also a number of shareware and free encryption programs, some of which offer good strong encryption.

Pretty Good Privacy (PGP) is one of the best-known encryption programs. It was originally developed by Philip Zimmermann and distributed for free. The PGPi project home page (*http://www.pgpi.org*) has pointers to the latest free version as well as to a variety of PGP-related products. A commercial version is available as well (*http://www.pgp.com*).

Email Encryption

As email travels across the Internet, it may pass through many points along the way where it can be intercepted and read. Server administrators may read email stored on a server, and some companies routinely scan the email of all their employees (there are even products marketed specifically for this purpose!). You can use encryption to protect the email you send from being read by anyone other than the intended recipient.

Encryption capabilities of popular mail programs

Recent versions of many popular email programs include the ability to send and receive encrypted email, to sign email messages with digital signatures, and to encrypt saved email messages. Microsoft Outlook, Microsoft Outlook Express, Netscape Messenger, Eudora Light, and Eudora Pro can all send signed and/or encrypted messages.

Plug-in programs are available that add PGP support to email programs including Microsoft Outlook, Microsoft Outlook Express, Microsoft Exchange, Lotus Notes, Netscape Messenger, Pegasus Mail, Claris Emailer, Elm, Pine, Zmail, and Emacs. The PGPi project web site has a good list of PGP plug-in programs.

Web-based encrypted email

Many people do not use email programs on their own computers but instead rely on web-based email services that allow them to access their email from any web browser. A number of these services, such as *http://www.hushmail.com*, *http://www.ynnmail.com*, *http://www.ziplip.com*, and *http://www.zixmail.com*, allow users to send and receive encrypted email. These services use a variety of techniques for encrypting email, including providing Java™ applet encryption programs and SSL connections established by a web browser (see the next section for information about SSL). These services are convenient because they do not require users to download special software or purchase digital certificates. However, most are much more vulnerable to attack than other types of encrypted email.[*]

---

[*] Bruce Schneier reviewed several web-based encrypted email programs and discussed their vulnerabilities in the August 15, 1999, issue of his *Crypto-Gram* newsletter. See *http://www.counterpane.com/crypto-gram-9908.html#Web-BasedEncryptedE-Mail*.

Encrypted Network Connections

Email and file encryption are useful for protecting your data in storage and when it is being transmitted via email, but additional steps are necessary to protect the communications between your computer and other computers on the Internet. If you fill out forms on web sites or use programs such as *telnet* to log in to remote computers, you may be sending sensitive data across the Internet. This section introduces two protocols for transmitting encrypted data over the Internet. In addition, there is a variety of software on the market that allows users to create secure tunnels between their computers and other computers on the Internet or to establish *virtual private networks* (VPNs). VPNs allow data exchanged between computers to remain private—as if it were traveling on a corporate intranet—even though it is really traveling on the public Internet.

Secure Sockets Layer

The Secure Sockets Layer (SSL) is a general-purpose protocol for transmitting encrypted data over the Internet. It is used by all of the major web browsers for securely transmitting data to web sites that support SSL. The SSL protocol provides for encrypted data transmission as well as authentication of clients and servers. Web sites that use SSL transmit digital certificates that browsers can use to authenticate them.

When you use your web browser to fill out online forms, it is a good idea to check to see whether SSL is being used. Without SSL, the data you submit will be sent across the Internet in plain text for all to see. Internet Explorer displays a closed padlock icon in the bottom-right corner of its window when SSL is in use. Netscape Navigator 4 displays a closed padlock icon in the bottom-left corner of its window to indicate that SSL is in use and an open padlock icon to indicate that SSL is not in use. (Previous versions of Netscape Navigator displayed keys and broken keys.) Clicking on the Netscape lock icon or double-clicking on the Internet Explorer lock icon brings up additional security information, as shown in Figure 3-1.

Even if a web site uses SSL, your data may not be well protected if the site does not use a strong encryption algorithm. Some versions of web browsers use weak, 40-bit encryption. However, 128-bit strong encryption versions are also available, and some financial web sites require visitors to have a browser capable of 128-bit encryption in order to access their services. To better protect your data and to take advantage of these secure financial services, download a strong-encryption version of your favorite web browser. The latest releases of most web browsers include strong encryption by default.

Once you have a web browser capable of 128-bit encryption, you may want to check to see if the sites you visit actually use strong encryption. After clicking on the Netscape lock icon, you can click on the "Open Page Info" button to find out the strength of the encryption the web site you are visiting is using. You can get this information from Internet Explorer by hovering your mouse over the lock icon.

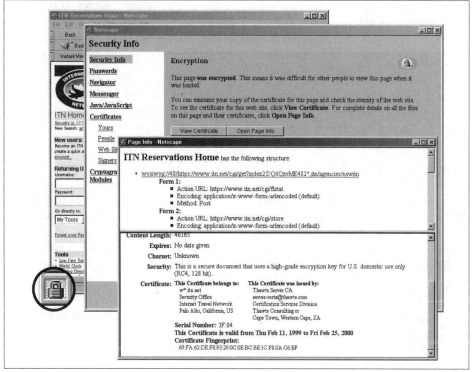

Figure 3-1. Netscape Navigator 4.6 displays a small, closed padlock icon in the bottom-left corner when SSL is in use; clicking on this icon brings up a Security Info window from which a Page Info window can be opened to find out what kind of encryption is being used as well as information about the site's certificate

Both Netscape and Internet Explorer also have the ability to warn users about potentially dangerous situations, such as when they enter and leave web sites secured with SSL and when they are about to submit unencrypted forms. Users can control whether warnings are displayed in each of several situations.

Secure Shell

Secure Shell (SSH) is a program that allows users to log into other computers on a network using secure variations on standard Unix commands. It also allows for secure X Window System connections and secure forwarding of TCP connections such as HTTP and POP connections.

If you use a Unix system, use the SSH replacements for *telnet*, *rlogin*, *rsh*, and *rcp* to ensure that your passwords and data are transmitted securely. If you frequently open X connections over the Internet, consider using SSH to establish secure X connections as well. Once SSH is configured on your system, it will be invoked automatically whenever you open an X connection, and all data transmitted over X connections will be secured.

If you frequently use a Windows system to connect over the Internet to other systems (for example, to a computer at your office), SSH may be useful for establishing secure *telnet* sessions, accessing a corporate intranet via a web browser, or securely accessing POP mail servers. However, you might also want to consider VPN systems that offer more comprehensive solutions.

A free version of SSH is available from OpenSSH (*http://www.openssh.org*). Commercial versions of SSH can be obtained from Data Fellows (*http://www.datafellows.com*) and SSH Communications Security (*http://www.ssh.org*).

Anonymity and Pseudonymity Tools

P3P was designed primarily for interactions that require some amount of personal data to be exchanged. However, Internet users often engage in interactions with web sites that do not require any exchange of personal information. Users who simply want to browse web pages may have no need to reveal personal information, but information is revealed automatically by their browsers. (The kinds of information that can be revealed automatically are discussed in Chapter 2.) A number of tools have been developed to help Internet users surf the Web anonymously. These anonymizing agents focus on minimizing the risk that requests to web sites can be linked to IP addresses from which users can be identified.

Anonymizing Proxies

A *proxy* is a server that sits in between a web client and the web site to which the client is sending a request. Proxies were originally developed to store cached copies of fetched documents and supply them to clients to reduce the number of requests to remote servers. Proxies act as intermediaries. Some proxies simply take requests from clients and forward them on to servers, then take responses from servers and pass them back to clients. Other proxies may modify a client's request or a server's response before forwarding it. For example, a proxy may strip out information that might identify a client, or it might remove banner ads from content returned by a server. Requests to web sites may be forwarded through multiple proxies before they reach their destinations.

Anonymizing proxies are services that submit requests to web sites on behalf of users, as shown in Figure 3-2. Because all requests are submitted by a proxy, the only IP address revealed to the web sites is that of the proxy.

Users of anonymizing proxy services are not anonymous to the proxy or to their own ISPs, who may log their users' web activities. Before using an anonymizing proxy service, users should read the service's policy to find out what information the service logs and to whom it may disclose that information. Users should also realize that the service may be compelled to share its log files with law-enforcement officers, even if there is no mention of this in the service's policy. And, of course, an unscrupulous

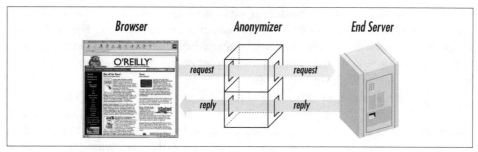

Figure 3-2. How requests and responses pass through an anonymizing proxy

service may not actually follow its policy at all! In addition, users must disable the use of Java and JavaScript to ensure their anonymity when using most anonymizing proxies. Some anonymizing proxies claim to automatically block potentially hostile Java and JavaScript programs, but most require users to disable them in their browsers.

One of the best-known anonymizing proxy services is the Anonymizer (*http://www.anonymizer.com*), a commercial service that offers both fee-based services and a free service supported by advertising. Other anonymizing proxies that were operational as of this writing include *http://rewebber.de, http://www.idzap.com, http://www.ponoi.com, http://www.safeweb.com, http://www.magusnet.com/proxy.html*, and *http://hyperarchive.lcs.mit.edu/telecom-archives/secret-surfer.html*.

Mix Networks and Similar Web Anonymity Tools

Several anonymity tools have been developed around the concept of *mix networks*. A mix network is a collection of routers—called *mixes*—that use a layered encryption technique to encode the path that communications should take through the network.[*] In addition, mix networks use techniques such as buffering and message reordering to further obscure the correlation between messages entering and exiting the network.

To better illustrate how mix networks work, let's imagine a hypothetical secure parcel delivery service called SPS. SPS customers can send parcels to anyone in the world without revealing their identities to the recipient, SPS, or any other party. SPS has a network of branch offices around the world. Parcels are sent from office to office, until finally they are sent in the postal mail to their destinations. To send a secure parcel, a customer goes to a local SPS office and selects a set of branch offices through which to route her package. To maximize security, she can spin a dial and randomly select offices—of course, this will usually result in an indirect route for the package, but SPS never promises prompt delivery!

---

[*] The concept of mixes was first introduced by David Chaum. See David Chaum, "Untraceable electronic mail, return addresses, and digital pseudonyms,"*Communications of the ACM* 24, no. 2 (1981):84–88, *http://doi.acm.org/10.1145/358549.358563*.

Once the customer selects her route, she picks up a set of nesting metal boxes and a special lock for each office she has selected for her route, as shown in Figure 3-3. The locks slip onto the boxes like the combination locks used on gym lockers. Once locked, they can be unlocked only by employees of the designated office. The customer marks the package with the address of the recipient. Then she places it inside the smallest metal box and locks it with the lock of the last office on the route she selected. She marks the outside of the box with the name of that office. She then places the locked box inside a slightly bigger metal box and locks it with the lock of the next-to-last office on the route she selected. Then she marks the outside of the box with the name of that office. She continues this process until she has used up all the locks and boxes. She pays the clerk and deposits her locked and boxed parcel in a bin for delivery.

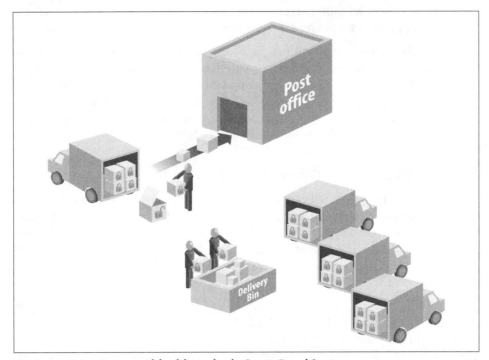

Figure 3-3. Preparing a parcel for delivery by the Secure Parcel Service

When a truck full of parcels arrives at an office, the clerk unloads the truck and unlocks the boxes around each parcel. If a parcel contains yet another locked box, the clerk puts it in a delivery bin, mixing it in with the parcels brought in to that branch office by customers. Otherwise, the clerk sends it to the post office for delivery to the final recipient. The truck is then reloaded with waiting parcels from the delivery bins until there is no more room. If there are not enough parcels to fill the truck, the clerk puts locks on empty boxes and places them on the truck. If there are too many parcels, some have to wait for the next truck to arrive. Because the new parcels brought in are mixed with the already waiting parcels, parcels are not necessarily shipped out in the order in which they arrive.

Clearly, this is not a very efficient way to run a shipping business, but it does achieve the desired security results.

- By allowing customers to select random routes and place their parcels in locked nested boxes corresponding to these routes, SPS ensures that when a parcel arrives at a branch office, that office knows only the branch it came from and the branch to which it is headed. It has no way of knowing the identity of the sender or the recipient. (The clerks at the first office on the route may be able to learn the identity of the sender, and the clerks at the last office may be able to learn the identity of the recipient, but nobody can learn the identity of both the sender and the recipient.)

- By mixing the parcels that arrive with those already waiting to be delivered and by filling delivery trucks with empty parcels when there are not sufficient parcels waiting to be delivered, SPS ensures that parcels cannot be traced simply by observing the traffic into and out of the branch offices.

Mix networks are very similar to our hypothetical parcel delivery service. Instead of locking parcels in metal boxes, senders encrypt their communications using the public keys of each mix on the route. The mixes store the messages they receive and, at designated intervals, randomly forward a message to its destination. If no message is waiting to be sent, the mix randomly generates a message to send. Mixes can also pad messages so that every message in the network is the same length (in our parcel delivery service example, people might be able to gain information by observing that lighter parcels are generally closer to their final recipients than heavier parcels; requiring all messages to be the same length in the mix network avoids this problem). Unlike anonymizing proxies, mix networks provide anonymity without requiring that users trust the servers that forward requests.

A number of mix networks and related web anonymity systems have been developed as research prototypes and commercial services. Unfortunately, most are no longer available as of this writing.*

Anonymous Email

A variety of services are available for sending anonymous email. These services offer varying degrees of anonymity and a number of different types of interfaces. Electronic Frontiers Georgia maintains a list of anonymous remailer services and related information and tools at *http://anon.efga.org/Remailers/*.

---

* Ian Goldberg discusses the reasons why it has been difficult for anonymity services to become viable businesses in a paper he presented at the 2002 Privacy Enhancing Technologies Workshop: "Privacy-enhancing technologies for the Internet, II: Five years later."

Anonymous remailers are similar to anonymizing proxies: they strip off identifying information from email headers and forward the email message to its destination. Your email address will be unknown to the recipient of your email; however, it may not be unknown to the remailer operator. If you use a remailer for an illegal activity, the operator may be subpoenaed to reveal your email address. Some remailer operators have decided to shut down their services rather than be forced to respond to such subpoenas. To better protect their anonymity, remailer users often encrypt their messages and send them through a chain of remailers. Only the first remailer in the chain knows the user's real email address, and users can take steps to hide their addresses even from that remailer.

Most remailers support a variety of features, including the ability to accept encrypted messages that contain instructions for processing and the ability to send replies back to an anonymous sender.

Filters

Filters are tools that selectively block email messages, web pages, newsgroups, HTML cookies, HTML headers, specific words contained in web pages or emails, or other content. Filters may be used by parents to prevent their children from accessing adult content or by individuals to block unwanted email. They may also be used to prevent web sites from sending cookies or to prevent children from providing personal information to strangers. The focus of this section is on using filters to help protect privacy.

Cookie Cutters

Cookie cutters are utility programs that prevent your computer from exchanging cookies with web sites. Some cookie cutters block all cookies, others can be configured to selectively block certain cookies, and still others remove the cookies after the fact. Some cookie cutters are part of Internet privacy suites that include other software, such as personal firewalls, virus detectors, or web site ad removers. Cookie-cutter software available as of this writing includes *http://www.adsubtract.com, http://www.anonymizer.com/services/washer.shtml, http://www.thelimitsoft.com/cookie.html, http://www.junkbusters.com/ht/en/ijb.html, http://www.kburra.com/cpal.html, http://www.guidescope.com, http://www.idcide.com, http://www.privsoft.com,* and *http://www.intelytics.com/personalSentinel/.*

Child-Protection Software

Adults should know better than to provide personally identifying information to strangers they meet in chat rooms, but children may not. Some parents use filtering software to prevent their kids from typing in their names and home phone numbers (or parents' credit card numbers) and sending them to web sites or chat rooms. They may also subscribe to services that restrict the email addresses with which their children may correspond.

Many child-protection software tools and kids' Internet services have features that parents can use to help protect a child's privacy. The GetNetWise web site (*http://www.getnetwise.org*) has an extensive list of child-protection software. You can search this site for tools that have privacy-protection features built in.

Identity-Management Tools

Since 1999, at least a dozen companies have announced new services and tools that help people manage their online identities and protect their privacy. Most of these tools allow users to store information in secure personal data stores and use it in conjunction with automatic form-filling features. Some restrict automatic form-filling to sites that have policies that match a user's privacy preferences. Some have mechanisms that allow users to opt-in to automatically sharing information with marketers of products or services in which they have expressed interest—sometimes anonymously, and sometimes in exchange for discounts, coupons, or monetary compensation. These services and tools are often referred to as *infomediaries*, a term coined by John Hagel.[*]

Unfortunately, most of the tools introduced in this category have been short-lived, so any specific information I might provide about them would likely be out of date by the time this book is published.

Other Tools

Every week, new online privacy–related tools seem to emerge on the market. Here are a few that don't fall readily into the categories of tools discussed in this chapter.

A number of tools, such as Window Washer (*http://www.webroot.com/washer.htm*) and CyberScrub (*http://www.cyberscrub.com*), can be configured to automatically clean up the files left behind on your computer by web browsers and email programs. They remove all traces of what web sites you visited, what files you viewed, and what files you deleted. In addition to helping you protect your privacy from others with whom you may share a computer, removing these files frees up disk space and often improves system performance.

The McAfee Privacy Service (*http://www.mcafee.com*) contains a suite of privacy-related tools and services that includes ad and cookie blockers, encryption tools,

---

[*] John Hagel and Marc Singer, *Net Worth: Shaping Markets When Customers Make the Rules* (Boston: Harvard Business School Publishing, 1998).

tools to remove residual files from your computer, and tools to prevent children from sending personal information to web sites. The suite also includes tools to filter adult content, restrict access to chat rooms, manage passwords, secure networked computers, and protect against computer viruses.

Zero-Knowledge Systems (*http://www.freedom.net*) offers a number of privacy- and security-related products, including ad and cookie blockers, personal firewalls, and other tools to enhance web privacy and security.

The Online Privacy Store (*http://onlineprivacystore.com*) offers a wide selection of privacy and security tools for sale.

CHAPTER 4

P3P History

The story of how P3P came to be is quite long. Those who just want to get down to business and use P3P may want to skip this chapter, but those who are interested in understanding how and why P3P was developed should keep reading. It took over five years to develop P3P. This chapter was written to offer some insights into what happened along the way. These insights will help you understand some of the reasons that P3P turned out the way it did. Details of some of the design decisions made in the process of developing P3P are discussed further in Chapter 11.

The Origin of the Idea

The ideas behind P3P have been around for some time. The concept of providing technical tools that allow users to control the conditions under which their personal information will be released or their solitude interrupted has emerged in a variety of contexts over the past 10 years. For example, the idea of using technical mechanisms to control when a caller's phone number is revealed emerged during the caller identification (caller ID) debates of the early 1990s.[*] In 1994, Ross Mitchell and Judith Wagner Decew introduced the term "dynamic negotiation" and proposed that it be used to determine when to send the caller's number.[†] Around the same time, a group of German researchers began work on "reachability management" systems that allow call recipients to use Newton MessagePads to control the conditions under which they may be interrupted by phone calls (*http://www.iig.uni-freiburg.de/dbskolleg/themen/the21_e.html*). The system also allows callers to control the conditions under which their identities may be revealed to call recipients. More recently,

---

[*] Joel Reidenberg and others discussed various technical rules for privacy. See, for example, Joel R. Reidenberg, "Rules of the Road for Global Electronic Highways: Merging the Trade and Technical Paradigms," *Harvard Journal of Law & Technology* 6 (1993):287–305.

[†] Ross E. Mitchell and Judith Wagner Decew, "Dynamic Negotiation in the Privacy Wars," *Technology Review* 97, no. 8 (1994):70–71.

some phone companies have started offering services that allow customers to block incoming calls when caller ID information is not provided.

In 1995, Deirdre Mulligan, Janlori Goldman, and Daniel Weitzner, at the Center for Democracy and Technology (CDT), began discussing the idea of using the Platform for Internet Content Selection, or PICS (*http://www.w3.org/PICS/*), as a tool to help Internet users protect their privacy. They worked with PICS cochair Paul Resnick to present the idea to the Federal Trade Commission in November 1995. Developed by the W3C, PICS is a system for labeling web content according to a set of criteria called a *rating system*. While PICS rating systems could be used to capture virtually any type of information about web content, PICS was being applied mostly to rate the content of web pages according to their suitability for children. Indeed, the PICS effort was launched primarily as a nonlegislative alternative to the U.S. Communications Decency Act and other, similar legislation. A variety of PICS rating systems were proposed that included rating scales for sex, nudity, violence, adult language, and other factors that might make a web site unsuitable for children. But, as Resnick demonstrated at the June 1996 FTC Workshop on Consumer Privacy on the Global Information Infrastructure,* PICS can also be used to rate web sites according to their information practices. Fordham University Law Professor Joel Reidenberg wrote a PICS rating system based on the Canadian Standards Association privacy standard to demonstrate this idea.† Resnick also proposed that PICS be extended to allow people to negotiate with web sites over information practices.

There was much enthusiasm for the idea of "PICS for privacy" at the FTC workshop, although some of the privacy advocates present warned that the model would need to be supplemented by enforcement mechanisms and laws. Then–FTC Commissioner Christine Varney was particularly enthusiastic about the idea. In the fall of 1996, the PICS cochairs (Resnick and Jim Miller) worked with CDT to garner industry support for pursuing this effort.

Resnick and Miller realized that PICS for privacy would need to have support from businesses—especially online marketers—to be successful, so they approached the Direct Marketing Association (DMA) with the idea. This was actually the beginning of my involvement in the P3P effort. During my second week at AT&T Research, Resnick (who was also working for AT&T Research at the time) and Miller asked me to help them prepare a demo of a privacy rating system for PICS. Later that week, the three of us presented the demo at a DMA meeting in Manhattan.

---

* Resnick's comments can be found in the transcript of session two of the June 4, 1996, workshop, beginning on page 79. These comments are followed by an interesting discussion among the panelists. The transcript is available from the workshop web site, at *http://www.ftc.gov/bcp/privacy/wkshp96/privacy.htm*.

† See the appendix of Joel Reidenberg's paper "Information Privacy Rules Through Law and Technology," presented at the 19th International Conference of Privacy Data Protection Commissioners in September 1997 (*http://www.privacy.fgov.be/conference/pt4_2.html#part6*).

The DMA leaders were intrigued, but they expressed concerns about using a PICS-like model in which unacceptable content is blocked without providing feedback to the web site. However, the idea of extending PICS to allow for some form of negotiation between user and web site appealed to them. This negotiation offered a new option in the opt-in versus opt-out debate—an explicit choice mediated by a software user agent. Several weeks after our presentation, the DMA agreed to support the new privacy technology effort.

The Internet Privacy Working Group

In mid-November 1996, CDT convened the Internet Privacy Working Group (IPWG) to further explore the development of a PICS-like privacy tool. Initial participants included America Online, AT&T, the Business Software Alliance, the Center for Media Education, Citicorp, the Coalition for Advertising Supported Information and Entertainment, the Consumer Federation of America, the DMA, Disney, The Dun & Bradstreet Corp., the Electronic Frontier Foundation, TRUSTe, IBM, the Interactive Services Association, MCI, Microsoft, the National Consumers League, and the W3C. The group first drafted a mission statement, which stated that IPWG's objective was to "outline a framework for privacy on the Internet through the implementation of fair information practice policies and the development of technical specifications" and to "craft policies and technical tools that give users the ability to make choices about the flow of personal information while supporting seamlessness, the free flow of information, and the development of global commerce."

IPWG appointed a "vocabulary subcommittee" to develop a draft privacy vocabulary—a standard set of terms that web sites could use to describe their privacy practices. The subcommittee produced several drafts of a privacy vocabulary and worked with the W3C to develop a demonstration privacy tool for the June 1997 FTC privacy workshop. By this time the technology had been given a name: the Platform for Privacy Preferences, or P3 for short. The acronym was later changed to P3P, after the W3C received notification that the name P3 was trademarked.

Tim Berners-Lee and Deirdre Mulligan demonstrated the early P3P prototype at the June 11, 1997, FTC workshop. This prototype implementation was developed by an MIT student with assistance from several W3C staff members and myself. While it succeeded in demonstrating P3P concepts, the complicated user interface left many in the audience with the impression that P3P would be far too complicated for most Internet users to understand. A script for the prototype presentation can be found at *http://www.w3.org/Talks/970612-ftc/ftc-sub.html*. This prototype is discussed further in Chapter 14.

While P3P was focused on negotiating agreements about web site privacy practices, if was often suggested that P3P should also include mechanisms for transferring data according to these agreements. There was growing interest in tools that would allow users to fill out online forms automatically, and some IPWG members felt that P3P should include these tools so that all data transfers would be performed under P3P control. On the other hand, other IPWG members were reluctant to associate a privacy-protection tool with a tool that made it easier for web sites to collect personal information. No consensus on this issue was reached within IPWG.

W3C Launches the P3P Project

In May 1997, P3P was officially launched as a W3C project. The initial plan was for the W3C to pursue the technical work necessary to develop P3P while the policy work proceeded within IPWG, but eventually the W3C ended up doing most of the policy work within two policy-oriented P3P working groups. IPWG's involvement during the rest of the project was minimal, although many of the IPWG members were also W3C members and participated in the W3C working groups.

The official W3C P3P kickoff meeting was held at the W3C's Boston site in June 1997. Over the next two years, a series of working groups were convened by the W3C. Initially, W3C management planned to launch a number of short-term working groups in series that would each develop a small piece of the P3P specification. However, this strategy resulted in a lack of continuity and a lot of duplication of effort each time a working group was created. Ultimately, the specification was not finished until the W3C decided to charter a single working group with the mission of completing the entire specification.

P3P working group members represented over a dozen W3C member companies and organizations, as well as invited experts from academia and government. Throughout the P3P design process, data-protection authorities and privacy advocates played an important role. Representatives from several data-protection authorities joined P3P working groups or attended working group meetings and participated in the process directly. These included representatives from the French CNIL, the Ontario Information and Privacy Commission, the Privacy Commissioner of Schleswig-Holstein, and the Hong Kong Privacy Commissioner's Office. In addition, several experts from academia as well as representatives from CDT and TRUSTe participated in the development of P3P. While many of the other working group members were official representatives of the companies that employed them, most considered themselves to be privacy advocates as well. These individuals often rejected proposed solutions that would have served to benefit their companies if they personally believed that they were not consistent with the interest of protecting privacy. While these individuals were accountable to their employers, most of them did not consult with their employers on every decision that had to be made, and many of them indicated frequently that their comments represented their personal opinions.

While the P3P working group members were trying to develop P3P as a tool that would help protect privacy, concerns were being raised that P3P might be used in privacy-invasive ways. I felt that it was important to document the intent of the working group and to provide some guidelines about how to use P3P in a way that would help users protect their privacy, so in 1998 I drafted a set of "P3P Guiding Principles" and sought buy-in on them from the working group members.[*] These principles were initially published as a signed W3C Note and later added to the P3P specification as an appendix. Here is a summary of the guiding principles:

Information Privacy

Service providers should preserve trust and protect privacy by applying relevant laws and principles of data protection and privacy to their information practices.

Notice and Communication

Service providers should provide timely and effective notices of their information practices, and user agents should provide effective tools for users to access these notices and make decisions based on them.

Choice and Control

Users should be given the ability to make meaningful choices about the collection, use, and disclosure of personal information. Users should retain control over their personal information and decide the conditions under which they will share it.

Fairness and Integrity

Service providers should treat users and their personal information with fairness and integrity.

Security

While P3P itself does not include security mechanisms, it is intended to be used in conjunction with security tools. Users' personal information should always be protected with reasonable security safeguards, in keeping with the sensitivity of the information.

The Evolving P3P Specification

The details of the P3P specification changed regularly as it was developed. During the first two years of development, the P3P vocabulary was expanded from the initial IPWG draft and then revised several times. Cookie-like persistent identifiers were added to the specification by one working group and later removed by another. A complicated protocol for communication between user agents and web sites was developed and modified several times.

The P3P Specification Working Group was chartered in July 1999 with the mission of finishing the P3P 1.0 specification. The group made significant changes to the

---

[*] I discuss some of the motivations behind the P3P Guiding Principles in a paper I originally wrote for the DIMACS workshop on Design for Values: Ethical, Social and Political Dimensions of Information Technology. See Lorrie Faith Cranor, "Bias and Responsibility in 'Neutral' Social Protocols," *Computers and Society*, September 1998, pp. 17–19, *http://lorrie.cranor.org/pubs/dimacs-values.html*.

The World Wide Web Consortium

The World Wide Web Consortium (W3C) is a group of over 500 companies, universities, and nonprofit organizations that work together to develop common protocols that promote the continued evolution and interoperability of the World Wide Web.

Most of the work of the W3C is carried out within the many working groups that are chartered to work on developing interoperable protocols or "recommendations" for a particular area or application. Most working group members participate in working groups on behalf of their employers. However, working groups often include "invited experts" who are invited by the group's chair to participate because of the expertise they can bring to the group. W3C member companies volunteer their employees to participate in working groups of interest to each company.

W3C working groups typically hold their discussions on private mailing lists and conference calls (and periodic face-to-face meetings) and produce public "working drafts" about every three months. Members of the public are invited to provide feedback on these drafts. Once a working group has nearly completed a specification, it releases a public "last call" working draft and provides a deadline for comments. The working group must respond to every substantive comment that it receives. After completing a last-call period and addressing the comments, the working group issues a public "candidate recommendation" working draft. This draft is accompanied by a set of "exit criteria" that indicate the kinds of implementations necessary to demonstrate that the specification can be implemented in an interoperable manor. Once the exit criteria are met, the group issues a "proposed recommendation" draft for consideration by the W3C membership. W3C members are given several weeks to review this draft and cast ballots either indicating their support for the draft or raising specific concerns. The W3C Director reviews the ballots and, once satisfied that the major concerns have been addressed, issues the specification as an official W3C Recommendation.

The W3C web site contains a list of member organizations and more information about the W3C's goals, activities, and processes. See *http://www.w3.org*.

---

specification over the first few months. These changes came about mostly due to a consensus among working group members that the P3P draft specification was too complicated to be adopted. The specification contained features whose details had not been fully worked out, that were likely to conflict with other web protocols, and that appeared quite difficult to implement. Furthermore, representatives from companies that were considering adopting P3P on their web sites expressed concerns about the feasibility of implementing P3P in large organizations with many web sites and multiple customer databases. Their concerns covered not only technical and logistical issues, but also policy implications.

During the summer of 1999, features were removed from P3P one by one, and the protocol for reaching a P3P agreement was progressively simplified. When the working group met at a face-to-face meeting at the beginning of October, the group decided to take the final step and remove the negotiation and agreement concept from P3P altogether. By removing this concept, the group made it possible for web sites to implement P3P without adding any special software to their servers. Existing servers could be configured to advertise the locations of their P3P policies, and user agents could fetch these policies using standard web protocols. Furthermore, without the requirement that they attempt to negotiate an agreement, user agent tools could simply present privacy information to users in an easy-to-understand format, without necessarily evaluating it or using it to make decisions.

While there was much debate about the usefulness of many of the features that were removed from the P3P specification, there were a small number of removed features that most members of the working group agreed should eventually be returned, if possible. The group proposed that these features be considered for future versions of P3P. These features include mechanisms that would:

- Allow sites to offer a choice of P3P policies to visitors
- Allow visitors (through their user agents) to explicitly agree to a P3P policy
- Allow for nonrepudiation of agreements between visitors and web sites
- Allow user agents to transfer user data to web sites under a P3P agreement

As someone who participated in the P3P project from the beginning and shared the original vision of P3P as a negotiation protocol, I was somewhat disappointed that these features were dropped from P3P 1.0. On the other hand, as the project developed it became clear to me that P3P was suffering from too many requirements and too many features and that we were losing sight of what could realistically be implemented and deployed.

A lot of really smart computer scientists worked on the P3P project and proposed all sorts of clever features that would allow for complex negotiation, multiple (and extensible) methods for transferring data, a new state-management mechanism to replace cookies, and more. But in the end, potential adopters told us that all they really wanted to do was make their human-readable privacy policies available in a machine-readable format.

In hindsight, the P3P project was hampered by a lack of agreement on requirements. The development of the specification would have gone more smoothly if more time was spent at the beginning developing and building consensus on a set of requirements for P3P. Furthermore, given the policy and social implications of P3P, a public vetting of the requirements early on would have been useful. W3C process has evolved significantly since the launch of the P3P project, and if the project were being initiated in 2002, I think it would be managed in a very different way.

Negotiation

The use of the term "negotiation" within P3P evolved throughout the project. Originally, many of the participants envisioned a system that would allow web sites and user agents to haggle over privacy practices by engaging in a series of offers and counteroffers. This multi-round negotiation was later replaced with a single-round negotiation, in which the site has to make all of its offers up front. If more than one offer is made, the user agent chooses which one to accept, if any.

Paul Resnick and I spent a lot of time examining the negotiation aspect of P3P in 1997. We concluded that usually web sites and user agents would come to the same agreement, regardless of whether a single-round or multi-round negotiation process was used. We proved that under certain assumptions this is always the case, and we pointed out situations (under different assumptions) where this would not be the case. One case where multi-round negotiation may lead to a different outcome is when a web site adds time delays before making offers after the first round. Users who do not want to wait through these delays may decide to take the first offer instead of waiting for a more preferable, subsequent offer.[*]

Negotiation was eventually removed altogether, to simplify P3P implementation. The complete removal of negotiation changed the way that a lot of people thought about P3P. With negotiation, many people thought of P3P as a tool for getting web sites to do business under user-specified privacy terms. Without negotiation, P3P became simply a tool for informing users about web site privacy practices. In practice, even if the technical mechanism to support negotiation existed in P3P, I don't think it would be used, except to offer explicit trade-offs between privacy and something else (discounts, enhanced services, etc.).[†] I am not sure why a site would offer a better privacy policy only to users who negotiate unless those users were willing to offer something in exchange.

Automatic Data Transfer

The relationship between P3P and automatic data-transfer mechanisms was controversial from the beginning. While it can be argued that tools that facilitate data collection are contrary to the goals of privacy protection, it can also be argued that the best way to protect privacy is to integrate privacy-protection tools with the tools that people use to transfer their data. Thus, users of such combination tools will have the opportunity to be reminded of privacy considerations at the time when they are most relevant: when the data transfer is about to take place.

When they launched the project in 1997, W3C management decided that data-transfer mechanisms should be included as part of P3P. This was prompted in part by two W3C submissions: Netscape's Online Profiling Specification (OPS) and Microsoft's Privacy and Profiling submission. The well-timed OPS press release generated a huge

---

[*] Lorrie Faith Cranor and Paul Resnick, "Protocols for Automated Negotiations with Buyer Anonymity and Seller Reputations," *Netnomics* 2, no. 1 (2000):1–23, *http://www.si.umich.edu/~presnick/papers/negotiation/*.

[†] Esther Dyson describes P3P in *Release 2.1: A Design for Living in the Digital Age* (New York: Broadway Books, 1998), pp. 257–261. She envisions people using P3P to negotiate for privacy and discounts.

---

amount of media coverage just after Memorial Day. As a result, OPS became better known than P3P, and there was much confusion about what the differences were between the two technologies. The OPS submission (*http://www.w3.org/Submission/1997/6/*) focused mostly on data exchange, while P3P was focused more on privacy negotiations. Some of the ideas from OPS were folded into P3P, but the OPS specification was never independently advanced after it was submitted to the W3C.

Many P3P working group members initially felt that the data-transfer mechanism could be a selling point for P3P. The details of the mechanism evolved for about two years. From the beginning, the P3P specification called for a user data repository where users could store values for P3P data elements. Later, a source attribute was added to P3P data elements to indicate whether an element would be collected by the web site (perhaps using an HTML form) or transferred by the agent (using P3P data-transfer methods or an automatic form-filling feature). If an element was to be transferred using P3P methods, the agent would retrieve the data from the user's repository (or prompt the user to enter it) and send it to the site.

The data-transfer mechanism raised a number of technical problems. Because the data was to be transferred in an HTTP header, there was a risk that it might be truncated by servers or proxies that had hardcoded limits on header lengths (4,000-byte limits are common). To fix this problem would likely have required the invention of a new HTTP method that would allow P3P data to be transferred as content. There were also problems surrounding how to refer to data elements in multiple languages. Moreover, this mechanism raised concerns about unnecessary data transfer. If data transfer was automatic and easy, much more data would likely be transferred than if users were required to type in any data to be sent to web sites.

Because of these problems, the data-transfer mechanism was eventually removed from the P3P specification and replaced with a statement about how P3P can interoperate with other data-transfer software, such as electronic wallets and automatic form-fillers. By interoperating with these external mechanisms, P3P notifies users about privacy at the critical point before a data transfer takes place.

The Patent Issue

In October 1997, Drummond Reed, cofounder of Intermind Corporation, notified the W3C that Intermind had received notice of allowance from the U.S. Patent and Trademark Office for a patent "pertaining to the use of metadata for automated, intelligent communications relationships." In July 1998, Intermind announced that it had received notice of allowance for a second patent, this one directly related to P3P. This was the first time any of the members of the W3C working groups (other than W3C staff members) had any knowledge that there might be an intellectual-property problem associated with P3P. In August 1998 Intermind proposed licensing terms to W3C members that would require both vendors of P3P software and web sites that used P3P to pay royalties to Intermind. By the time the second patent was issued, in

January 1999, P3P working group members had become extremely concerned about the situation and the way it had been handled by both Intermind and the W3C. Several companies that had been actively involved in the P3P project dropped out of the working groups, and others deferred their P3P implementation plans. Several news articles predicted the patent issue would likely spell the end for P3P.

After mounting pressure from its members, the W3C decided to convene a working group to develop a patent policy aimed at preventing similar problems from occurring in the future. In May 1999, the W3C issued a press release announcing that it would research the "validity and applicability of this patent" and requested assistance from the web community in identifying relevant prior art (*http://www.w3.org/1999/05/P3P-PatentPressRelease.html*).

In October 1999, W3C published an analysis, written by attorneys from the law firm of Pennie & Edmonds, LLP, of the relationship between P3P and the Intermind patent .[*] The attorneys found that the only similarity between P3P and the Intermind patent "is that both involve transfer of data structures from a server to a client and both relate broadly to controlling communications." However, they pointed out that Intermind told the patent office that what distinguished its claimed "control structure" from preexisting technology was a communications object abstraction that contains all of the information necessary to completely define a client/server communication relationship. Because P3P does not use such a control structure, the attorneys concluded that, in their opinion, "the use of P3P would not infringe any claim" of Intermind's patent.

Two weeks before the W3C's patent analysis was published, Reed addressed a meeting of the International Security, Trust, and Privacy Alliance (ISTPA) and announced that Intermind had changed its name to OneName Corporation, had changed its business plan, and was preparing to offer a royalty-free license to use its patent in P3P implementations. In March 2000, I received a letter from OneName stating, "As a result of these changes [to our business plan], we can now assure you that, in spite of positions that Intermind may have taken in the past, OneName has no intention of charging a royalty or preventing the use of this technology by the P3P project."

Feedback from Europe

In January 1998, the European Commission issued an opinion on P3P.[†] This opinion stated that P3P "must be applied within the context of a framework of enforceable data protection rules, which provide a minimum and nonnegotiable level of

---

[*] B. Rein, G. Stephens, and H. Lebowitz, "Analysis of P3P and US Patent 5,862,325," W3C Note 27-October-1999, *http://www.w3.org/TR/P3P-analysis/*.

[†] European Commission Working Party on the Protection of Individuals with regard to the processing of Personal Data, Opinion 1/98, Platform for Privacy Preferences (P3P) and the Open Profiling Standard (OPS), *http://www.epic.org/privacy/internet/ec-p3p.html*.

privacy protection for all individuals." The opinion suggested that the P3P vocabulary be expanded to include information about remedies, should web sites fail to comply with their stated privacy policies. This suggestion was taken into consideration, and a disputes section with a remedies subsection was added to the P3P vocabulary. The opinion also raised concerns about how defaults would be set in P3P user agents as well as whether these agents might transfer data to web sites without user consent. The decision to remove the concept of automatic data transfer from P3P reduced this concern somewhat; however, the choices implementers make about defaults remain very important.

In August 2000, representatives from the P3P working groups gave presentations at the privacy summer school in Kiel, Germany. Following the presentations, the Privacy Protection Commissioners of Berlin, Brandenburg, Hamburg, Northrhine-Westphalia, Schleswig-Holstein, and Zurich held a press conference and issued a statement supporting the P3P effort but reiterating that P3P is useful only in conjunction with privacy laws (see the sidebar "Privacy Commissioners' Press Release").

Finishing the Specification

After the P3P Specification Working Group simplified the specification, the P3P last-call period began. A W3C last-call period usually lasts a few weeks, but the P3P last-call period lasted six months, in order to give sufficient time to vet P3P in both the technical and policy communities. The working group revised the specification several times during the last-call period, based on the feedback received, and on May 10, 2000, published a working draft that addressed all of the major issues raised during the last-call period. These changes included some vocabulary additions and changes in the mechanisms for associating P3P policies with web content.

In July 2000, the W3C held a P3P Interoperability Session to test-drive the emerging P3P implementations and introduce P3P to the world. Vendors demonstrated several prototype P3P user agents and policy-generator tools. In a feedback session following the demonstrations, the working group collected a number of additional issues to address in the specification. Most of these issues concerned the performance of the P3P protocol and issues related to finding the right P3P policy for images and other content embedded in web pages.

The working group worked with P3P software implementers to resolve the performance issues that were raised. IE6 developers became actively involved in the working group during this period, and they were instrumental in a number of specification revisions, including the addition of compact policies. The working group published a revised working draft on October 18, 2000, that went through a shorter, two-week last-call period that resulted in only a few additional public comments.

On December 15, 2000, the working group published the P3P 1.0 specification as a "Candidate Recommendation." In W3C lingo, this is a stable draft that will be changed only to correct errors or address implementation issues; suggestions for new

Privacy Commissioners' Press Release

The following is an English translation of an excerpt from a press release issued on August 29, 2000, by the Independent Centre for Privacy Protection Schleswig-Holstein, Germany. For the full release, see http://www.datenschutzzentrum.de/somak/somak00/ p3pe_pm.htm.

On the occasion of presenting the upcoming new P3P standard at the summer school in Kiel the Privacy Protection Commissioners of Berlin, Brandenburg, Hamburg, Northrhine-Westphalia, Schleswig-Holstein and Zurich state as follows:

...Among European Privacy Protection Commissioners the consensus grows: P3P technology is useful for online privacy, but not sufficient on its own because P3P offers only a basic standard for privacy protection. Under any circumstances, additional, effective privacy monitoring and precise laws to protect Internet users are required. P3P allows a great part of the model European privacy protection act to be translated into "bits and bytes." Privacy protection is more difficult in the USA where citizens have to get by without the backing of laws and Privacy Protection Commissioners.

In Germany P3P has to be implemented as soon as possible and on its basis a comprehensive privacy concept has to be developed in order to adequately realize the Teleservices Data Protection Act. P3P 1.0 is a first step in the right direction. With P3P 1.0 the development in this area has not yet come to an end, but additional features have to be integrated. In the long run the use of P3P and other privacy tools could be an advantage in market competition for German Internet business, as the Teleservices Data Protection Act incorporates a higher degree of privacy protection compared to other European countries. According to surveys from many countries, customers will prefer web sites where a maximum of privacy protection is technically guaranteed.

P3P is an important building block of a new privacy protection concept that increasingly focuses on transparency and market-economic elements. P3P provides the Privacy Protection Commissioners new possibilities for co-operation with the industry and to make effective privacy protection in Europe a competitive factor. In the future consumers should be given more and more opportunities to create demand for privacy protection through their consumer behavior. This should make it clear to companies that European privacy protection is an advantage and that privacy-invasive sites don't have a chance in the market in the long run.

---

features are deferred for consideration in a later version of the specification. The Candidate Recommendation included a set of exit criteria for the working group to meet before advancing the specification to the next step in the W3C process. The exit criteria focused on demonstrating that the specification could be implemented.

Over the next several months, implementers began to build P3P user agents and policy-generating software that complied with the Candidate Recommendation draft. In addition, over 100 web sites became P3P-enabled. The feedback from these implementers proved quite valuable, and a number of relatively minor changes to the specification were made to address the concerns that were raised. In September 2001, a new Last Call specification was issued that incorporated all of these changes. By January 2002, all of the exit criteria had been met, and the working group issued the specification as a "Proposed Recommendation." The Proposed Recommendation was reviewed by the W3C membership, and on April 16, the W3C Director issued the P3P 1.0 Recommendation.

As web site interest in P3P increased, the W3C began a series of workshops to teach webmasters how to P3P-enable their sites. The Internet Education Foundation organized much of the P3P outreach in the U.S. and developed a web site of P3P resources at *http://p3ptoolbox.org*.

Legal Implications

People often ask how P3P fits into various legal frameworks. P3P is complementary to almost all legal frameworks. In countries with minimal legal privacy protections, P3P provides individuals with information on what commitments, if any, companies will make with respect to their privacy. P3P user agent tools can make it easy for individuals to take advantage of any opt-outs that companies provide. In countries that have more comprehensive legal privacy protections, the structured notice provided by P3P is useful for individuals who want to better understand how their information will be used. In addition, P3P policies include fields in which web sites can declare the privacy laws they follow and the privacy seal programs in which they participate. This makes it easier for individuals to find out what privacy protections they might have when visiting a particular web site (or to discover that some of the sites they frequent don't protect their privacy). This is especially important because of the international nature of the World Wide Web; individuals often end up visiting web sites located outside of their own countries that may have completely different privacy laws.

As the P3P specification was being finalized, a number of individuals and companies suggested that either the W3C make an explicit statement that P3P policies are not legally binding or that web sites post P3P policies that they then disavow. The P3P Coordination Group (the chairs of the P3P working groups and the W3C staff involved in the P3P project) issued the following statement in response to a letter from BITS, The Technology Group for The Financial Services Roundtable (*http://lists.w3.org/Archives/Public/www-p3p-public-comments/2001Dec/0010.html*):

> P3P is a protocol and machine-readable vocabulary through which services (Web sites) and user agents (users) can communicate about the service's privacy policy. The operation of this protocol will result in users receiving and using information about a site's privacy practices. However, W3C, as a technical standards setting body, is not competent to declare what the legal status of these statements should or should not be, especially given the fact that W3C develops technical standards with global reach. That determination must be up to legal and regulatory authorities in the proper jurisdiction.

Users, however, can be expected to make decisions based on the content of P3P statements. Therefore, the proper functioning of P3P depends on organizations implementing P3P to make sure that all policies are consistent with both the practices of that organization and the human readable policy found on that Web site. For example, if for some reason a site's P3P statements contradicted the human readable privacy notice, users would not be able to know what the site's policy actually is and would be unable to make an informed choice about the privacy relationship into which they are entering.

In an 1999 essay, Joseph Reagle anticipated this issue when he wrote, "In American culture—at least—there is an odd convention, particularly among children and politicians, whereby someone can negate the meaning of their statement by crossing their fingers behind their back. Can one do the same with metadata?"* On a number of occasions, I have described a site that would disavow its own P3P policy as having a "just-kidding" policy. If such sites are designed so as to appear to P3P user agents to have valid P3P policies, these just-kidding policies serve to undermine the P3P effort. In some jurisdictions, such policies might be considered legally "deceptive" as well. Sites that don't want to stand behind the statements in a P3P policy should simply opt not to have such a policy.

Criticism

Some privacy advocates say that the existence of P3P may be detrimental, because they believe it will stall proposed privacy legislation. They disagree with the entire premise of P3P—they do not believe that making it easier for consumers to access and understand web site privacy policies will improve the general state of data privacy. Instead, they would like to see efforts focused primarily on privacy legislation. P3P supporters say that P3P will enable consumers to make meaningful choices based on privacy. In addition, they argue that greater consumer awareness of privacy policies will motivate businesses to become more privacy-friendly and will call attention to areas where privacy protections are lacking. Much has been written by those on both sides of this debate (see the upcoming sidebar "Papers on P3P").

Corporations also have differing views on P3P. While many have embraced P3P, some have raised concerns that it may "precipitate a decrease in the flow of marketing information, even where the intended use is benign." Two Citibank employees raised this and other concerns about P3P in a 1998 white paper (not necessarily representative of official Citibank policy):

> P3P allows a user to dictate under what sort of conditions she is willing to give out personal information. If Citibank does not agree to whatever conditions the user puts forth, the user may opt to not transact with the bank at all—thus putting the onus on the bank to tighten the privacy protection until users are willing to transact i.e., to the lowest common denominator.

---

* Joseph Reagle, "Eskimo Snow and Scottish Rain: Legal Considerations of Schema Design" (W3C Note 10-December-1999), *http://www.w3.org/TR/md-policy-design/*.

There is a concern that P3P would let ordinary users see, in full gory detail, how their personal information might be misused by less trusted or responsible web site operators. Such knowledge may cause users to resist giving out information altogether. Some individual business groups have done focus studies on users, and ... concluded that most users would prefer to give out only information needed for the transaction and that they do not like the idea of someone monitoring their browsing behavior.

Fortunately, an increasing number of businesses have decided that transparency, rather than incomprehensible privacy policies, is the best way to build trust with consumers.

Papers on P3P

Karen Coyle, "A Response to 'P3P and Privacy: An Update for the Privacy Community'" (May 2000), *http://www.kcoyle.net/response.html*.

Lorrie Faith Cranor, "Agents of Choice: Tools That Facilitate Notice and Choice About Web Site Data Practices," in *Proceedings of the 21st International Conference on Privacy and Personal Data Protection* (September 13–15, 1999), *http://lorrie.cranor. org/pubs/hk.pdf*.

Lorrie Faith Cranor, "The Role of Privacy Advocates and Data Protection Authorities in the Design and Deployment of the Platform for Privacy Preferences," in *Proceedings of the Twelfth Conference on Computers, Freedom and Privacy* (April 16–19, 2002), *http://lorrie.cranor.org/pubs/p3p-cfp2002.html*.

Lorrie Faith Cranor and Rigo Wenning, "Why P3P is a Good Privacy Tool for Consumers and Companies," (April 2002), *http://www.gigalaw.com/articles/2002/cranor-2002-04.html*.

Electronic Privacy Information Center and Junkbusters, "Pretty Poor Privacy: An Assessment of P3P and Internet Privacy" (June 2000), *http://www.epic.org/reports/prettypoorprivacy.html*.

Deirdre Mulligan, Ari Schwartz, Ann Cavoukian, and Michael Gurski, "P3P and Privacy: An Update for the Privacy Community" (March 2000), *http://www.cdt.org/privacy/pet/p3pprivacy.shtml*.

Garbriel Speyer and Kenneth Lee, "White Paper: Platform for Privacy Preferences Project (P3P) & Citibank" (October 1998), *http://www.w3.org/P3P/Lee_Speyer.html*.

PART II

P3P-Enabling Your Web Site

This part of the book provides webmasters with all of the information they need to use P3P on their sites.

- Chapter 5, *Overview and Options*, describes the components of P3P-enabled web sites and gives an overview of the steps that should be taken to P3P-enable a web site.

- Chapter 6, *P3P Policy Syntax*, defines all of the terms of the P3P vocabulary and explains how they are used.

- Chapter 7, *Creating P3P Policies*, is a tutorial on gathering information about a site's data practices and creating a P3P policy.

- Chapter 8, *Creating and Referencing Policy Reference Files*, explains how to create a P3P policy reference file and describes the methods for setting up your web site so that P3P user agents can find your policy reference file.

- Chapter 9, *Data Schemas*, explains how P3P data elements are defined and used, describes the elements of the P3P Base Data Schema, and explains how to create a new P3P data schema.

- Chapter 10, *P3P-Enabled Web Site Examples*, provides examples of P3P policy and policy reference file components suitable for a variety of common web activities, as well as examples of P3P policies from several real web sites.

CHAPTER 5

Overview and Options

P3P was designed to offer web sites a wide variety of deployment options. Depending on your web site's privacy policy, you may want to write a single P3P policy for the entire site or several policies for different parts of the web site. The P3P policy reference file indicates which policies apply to which parts of your site. Depending on how you manage your web site, you may want to use one of three techniques to help user agents find your policy reference file—the well-known location method, the header method, or the link tag method. In addition, you may choose to use a P3P compact policy to transmit a compact version of your P3P policy in an HTTP header whenever you set a cookie.

This chapter provides an overview of the options available for deploying P3P on a web site. The rest of Part II discusses these options in depth. Chapter 6 provides definitions of all the terms used in a P3P policy, Chapter 7 provides a tutorial on creating P3P policies, and Chapter 8 explains how to create P3P policy reference files and set up your server for P3P. Chapter 9 details P3P data schemas, and Chapter 10 provides examples of P3P-enabled web sites.

P3P-Enabled Web Site Components

P3P-enabling a web site primarily involves creating and deploying P3P XML files and optionally configuring web servers to issue P3P response headers. Here is an overview of the files and HTTP responses involved in P3P-enabling a web site. Each of these components is discussed in more detail later in this book.

P3P policy
> A P3P policy is an XML document that describes a web site's privacy practices. Every P3P-enabled web site must have at least one P3P policy, either in a standalone file or included in a policy reference file.

Policy reference file
> A P3P policy reference file is an XML file that tells user agents which P3P policy applies to which URLs and cookies on a web site. Policy reference files may also

contain P3P policies and data schema. Every P3P-enabled web site must have at least one policy reference file.

Data schema

A P3P data schema defines data elements that may be referenced by a P3P policy. It may also define data structures that can be used to define data elements. The P3P specification defines a P3P Base Data Schema that includes elements that represent data such as the user's name, the user's business address, and HTTP protocol information. P3P-enabled web sites need to include data schema files only if their policies reference new data elements not already defined in the P3P Base Data Schema or elsewhere.

Human-readable privacy policy

A human-readable privacy policy is a privacy policy written in a natural language (English, French, German, Chinese, etc.). Every P3P-enabled web site must have a human-readable privacy policy that is consistent with the P3P policy that references it. In addition, some disclosures in a P3P policy place further requirements on the human-readable privacy policy. For example, a site that uses the NON-IDENTIFIABLE element must explain how it anonymizes data, and a site that use the stated-purpose, legal-requirement, or business-practices retention elements must explain its retention policy. Sites that provide individuals with access to their own data must also explain how that access is provided.

Opt-in or opt-out policy

An opt-in or opt-out policy is a natural-language statement about how an individual can exercise opt-in or opt-out options offered by the web site. Every P3P-enabled web site that offers opt-in or opt-out options must have an opt-in or opt-out policy. This policy might provide instructions for opting in or opting out, contact information, or a web form that individuals can use to opt-in or opt-out. The opt-in or opt-out policy may be included in the human-readable privacy policy.

Compact policy

A compact policy is an abbreviated version of a P3P policy that describes the privacy practices associated with cookies. Compact policies are added to the HTTP response headers served with cookies. They are optional for P3P-enabled web sites, but some P3P user agents use them extensively.

P3P header

P3P-enabled web sites may serve HTTP response headers that include the URL of a P3P policy reference file. These headers may also include a compact policy.

Some of the files mentioned here can be combined on a web site. For example, a P3P policy file can contain one or more policies. In addition, it can contain P3P data schema. Alternatively, a P3P policy may be included in a policy reference file rather than in its own file. In addition, an opt-in or opt-out policy may be included in a human-readable privacy policy.

Web sites that include multiple hosts (for example, *www1.example.com*, *www2.example.com*, etc.) may place a single P3P policy and human-readable privacy policy in a central location. Generally, there will be one policy reference file on each host, although in some circumstances sites may have multiple policy reference files on each host or may have one policy reference file in a central location.

P3P Deployment Steps

Some of the first questions webmasters ask when they are considering deploying P3P on their sites are "How long is this going to take?" and "How difficult is this going to be?" The answers to these questions, of course, depend on the details of the web site. A small company that already has a privacy policy posted on its site should be able to deploy P3P in a few hours. Large companies may need to have their attorneys spend time reviewing their P3P policies, and they may need to figure out the best way to deploy P3P on a large number of servers around the world. Companies that provide third-party web services, such as advertising agencies and content distribution networks, may have some more complicated decisions to make as well.

I have seen P3P deployed on an active commercial web site in as little as 10 minutes. The webmaster for that site was visiting my office and was able to start with one of my example policy and policy reference file sets, make the necessary changes for his site, remotely log in to his live server, publish the files, and use the W3C P3P Validator to verify that everything worked.

To help you estimate how much work is required for P3P deployment on your web site, here is an outline of the basic steps involved. These will be discussed in more detail in the rest of this chapter and in the following three chapters.

1. Create a privacy policy. The privacy policy needs to include enough details to be useful for creating a P3P policy. If you have already created a detailed policy for your site, you've done most of the difficult work. However, as you create your P3P policy, you may discover some issues in your privacy policy that you need to revisit. If you don't yet have a privacy policy or your policy does not go into much detail about the kinds of data your site collects or how this data is used, you will probably have to get your company's lawyers or policymakers involved in articulating your company's privacy policy.

2. Analyze the use of cookies and third-party content on your site. Privacy policies describe the kinds of data a company may collect, but they generally do not go into much detail about the ways in which cookies are used. Cookies can enable otherwise unidentifiable data to be linked to identifiable data, sometimes unintentionally. They may also enable data to be shared in unanticipated ways. It is important to analyze how cookies are used on your web site and how they interact with other cookies and with HTML forms. It is also important to identify any content or cookies on your web site that web browsers may treat as third-party

content (because it is served from a different domain than the page in which it is embedded).

3. Determine whether you want to have one P3P policy for your entire site or different P3P policies for different parts of your site. If you already have multiple privacy policies for your site, you will probably want to have multiple P3P policies as well. For example, some sites have different policies associated with different types of services they offer. Even if you have a single, comprehensive policy for your entire site, you may want to have multiple P3P policies. For example, your site's privacy policy might include a statement like "We do not collect personally identifiable information from visitors except when they fill out a form to order a product from us." You may wish to create two P3P policies—one for use on part of your site where there are no forms and the other for use on the parts of the site where visitors fill out forms to order products.

4. Create a P3P policy (or policies) for your site. You can use one of the P3P policy generator tools (described later in this chapter) to easily create a P3P policy without having to learn XML. You will need a detailed understanding about the kinds of data your site collects and how it is used, but most of this should be documented in your site's privacy policy.

5. Create a policy reference file for your site. Most policy-generator tools will help you create a policy reference file. This file lists all of the P3P policies on your site and the parts of your site to which they apply. In most circumstances, you will have just one policy reference file for your entire site. However, if you have a very large number of policies on your site, or if you don't want to provide information that would reveal the structure of your site (perhaps due to security considerations, if parts of your site are password-protected), you may want to have multiple policy reference files.

6. Configure your server for P3P. On most sites, this can be done by simply placing the P3P policy and policy reference files on the web server in the proper locations. However, because of how they are set up, some sites may find it advantageous to configure their servers to send a special P3P header with every HTTP response. Some sites may find it useful to add special P3P LINK tags to their HTML content. Some sites also send compact versions of P3P policies with HTTP Set-Cookie responses (this is especially important for sites that serve third-party cookies).

7. Test your site to make sure it is properly P3P-enabled. You can use the W3C P3P Validator to test your site and report back a list of any problems it finds. Of course, this tool cannot verify that your P3P policy matches your privacy policy or that either policy conforms with your actual practices. However, it can make sure that your policy and policy reference files are syntactically correct and that you've configured everything properly. You can try the W3C P3P Validator at *http://www.w3.org/P3P/validator/*.

Developing a Privacy Statement

The following is an excerpt from Roger Clarke's Privacy Statements web page (http:// www.xamax.com.au/DV/PStatemts.html), used with permission.

It is advisable that your organization first develops a Privacy Statement within the context of a broad strategy relating to privacy and other consumer matters. The following steps then need to be taken:

- Determine the scope you want your Privacy Statement to have. In particular, the statement might be a complete customer charter covering terms and conditions, and addressing transactions undertaken over the counter, and by telephone and mail; or it might be restricted to privacy, and to the specific context of Internet communications.
- Consult relevant laws, Codes of Conduct, and corporate policies that affect your organization's dealings with its customers.
- Consider current Government policies, emergent privacy principles, and draft legislation.
- Determine your organization's intentions in relation to data collection, data storage, data usage, and data disclosure.
- Define the approach your organization takes, or intends to take, in relation to privacy-related questions and complaints from the public, from public interest representatives and advocates, from industry associations, and from regulatory bodies.
- Express your organization's intentions in a draft Privacy Statement.
- Undertake consultation with representatives of the organization's clientele, privacy advocates and regulatory bodies.
- Promulgate your organization's Privacy Statement, on your web-site, and through other channels.

A well-designed Privacy Statement is of course a significant opportunity to gain coverage through appropriate media, in order to project the organization's desired image to its clientele, and to project an image of corporate responsibility to regulatory bodies.

Creating a Privacy Policy

Some companies have had privacy policies for many years; however, since the mid-1990s, an increasing number of companies have adopted privacy policies and posted these policies on their web sites. In the U.S. this push for privacy policies has been driven largely by the FTC's frequent reports on the number of web sites with privacy policies and by industry self-regulatory efforts. If your company doesn't yet have a privacy policy, now is the time to consider writing one. If you're reading this book, you probably already knew that—but just to be clear, If you want to use P3P on your web site, you must have a privacy policy for your web site! You may want to write a privacy policy that covers your entire business rather than just your web site, but at minimum you must have a web site privacy policy if you want to P3P-enable your site.

Because a privacy policy is a commitment from your company, you should think about it the way you think about any other contract into which your company enters. Don't commit to terms you don't intend to meet, and make sure the appropriate managers and legal council sign off on it before you publish it. After you write a privacy policy, it's a good idea to review your internal corporate processes to ensure that they are consistent with your policy and to put procedures in place to make sure that all employees are aware of it and follow it. You may want to undergo a periodic privacy audit to make sure your company is following its policy. You can conduct a self-audit or hire a consulting firm that specializes in privacy audits.

You might also consider using software tools that can help automate the process of monitoring your own web site with respect to privacy. See, for example, Intelytics Site Sentinel (*http://www.intelytics.com/site/index.jsp*), the PrivacyWall family of products from Idcide (*http://www.idcide.com*), the WebCPO product from Watchfire (*http://www.watchfire.com*), and the Tivoli products from IBM (*http://www.tivoli.com*). Also, the Zero-Knowledge P3P Analyzer (*http://p3p.zeroknowledge.com*) helps sites track their P3P compact policies. These tools won't guarantee that you don't make a mistake, but they will make it easier to spot problems quickly.

 Anyone who can edit files on your web server might be running applications that set cookies or collect data from web site visitors. Make sure that you communicate with all of these people, so that you understand their data practices and they understand your corporate privacy policy.

So how do you get started? The first thing to do is to determine which people in your company need to be involved in preparing and approving a privacy policy. This will probably include some high-level managers and attorneys and might also include representatives from the teams within your company that are responsible for running your web site and for collecting and maintaining personal data (on customers, employees, or anyone else). It is also helpful to review privacy policies from similar companies as well as any privacy guidelines that are relevant to your industry. Many industry associations have drafted such guidelines and have them available on their web sites.

Your team of privacy-policy drafters first needs to determine the scope of your new policy—will it be a comprehensive policy, a policy for just your web site, or a policy for some subset of your business? Next, review your current practices. What would your policy look like if you were to simply document your current information practices? Now, look toward the future. If your company is interested in earning a reputation for protecting customers' privacy, you may want to commit to improving your practices by reducing the amount of data you collect, how long you keep it, or how widely you share it. You may also want to improve your security precautions or offer your customers more choices about how their data is used (opt-in or opt-out options). On the other hand, you may anticipate new products or services that your company may offer that will require data practices that are not adequately addressed by documenting only current practices. This is where your company needs to make some policy choices and decide what sort of privacy policy you are willing to commit to and follow. While it is possible to change your company's policy as your business changes, you should plan to do so only occasionally, because doing it properly is a huge amount of work. In addition, you should plan on asking your customers for their informed consent before using data collected under an old policy in ways that are described only in the new policy.

Your policy should include enough detail to answer the questions you will have to answer to create a P3P policy. This will be covered in detail in the next chapter, but here's a basic outline of the information you should provide:

- The name and contact information for your company or organization.
- A statement about the kind of access you provide to individuals regarding information you hold about them.
- A statement about the privacy laws with which you comply, the privacy seal programs in which you participate, and other mechanisms available to your customers for resolving privacy disputes. This statement may also describe what remedies you offer should a privacy-policy breach occur.
- A description of the kinds of data you collect. If your web site uses cookies, be sure to mention this and to explain how the cookies are used.
- A description of how collected data is used and whether individuals can opt-in or opt out of any of these uses.
- Information about whether data may be shared with other companies and, if so, under what conditions and whether or not consumers can opt-in or opt-out of this.
- Information about your site's data-retention policy, if any. Do you make any commitments about purging records on a regular basis?
- Information about how consumers can take advantage of opt-in or opt-out opportunities.

P3P doesn't cover web site security practices, but most privacy policies include a statement about the site's commitment to security. In addition, web sites with content aimed at children often describe their policy with respect to children's data. When drafting a privacy policy, it's also useful to refer back to the fair information practice principles, introduced in Chapter 2.

Some online resources that may be helpful as you draft your privacy policy include:

- The Direct Marketing Association's guide to creating privacy policies (*http://www.the-dma.org/library/privacy/creating.shtml*)
- The Online Privacy Alliance Guidelines for Online Privacy Policies (*http://www.privacyalliance.org/resources/ppguidelines.shtml*)

- The Better Business Bureau's sample privacy notice (*http://www.bbbonline.com/ privacy/sample_privacy.asp*)
- The TRUSTe Privacy Resource Guide (*http://www.truste.org/bus/pub_ resourceguide.html*)
- The Privacy Leadership Initiative's Privacy Manager's Resource Center (*http:// understandingprivacy.org/content/pmrc/*)
- The Privacy Diagnostic Tool (PDT) Workbook from the Information and Privacy Commission/Ontario (*http://www.ipc.on.ca/english/resources/pdt/pdt.pdf*)

Once you have figured out what your policy should be, take some time to draft it in a way that will make it readily understandable to the general public. If it is a lengthy policy, include a short summary at the beginning, and use language that avoids jargon and legalese. You may want to write it as a series of questions and answers or include headings to highlight each of the major points. For example, the Better Business Bureau suggests using the following headings:

- Our Commitment to Privacy
- The Information We Collect
- How We Use Information
- Our Commitment to Data Security
- Our Commitment to Children's Privacy
- How to Access or Correct Your Information
- How to Contact Us

If your web site includes content in multiple languages, make sure you post your policy in each of these languages.

Analyzing the Use of Cookies and Third-Party Content

A thorough analysis of the use of cookies and third-party content on your web site can be tedious and time-consuming, but it is a good idea to do this to make sure that the statements you make in both your human-readable privacy policy and your P3P policy are accurate and that all the content on your web site will be covered by P3P policies. To conduct this analysis, you will first need to create a list of all of the web servers in your domain (or domains), including those on your internal intranet. Depending on the size and complexity of your web site, you may want to examine each server, ask the administrator of each server to respond to a survey, or use automated software tools to discover where and how cookies and third-party services are being used on your web site. After you complete your analysis, you may find that you need to change some of your practices or adjust your privacy policy.

What Needs to Be Included in an Online Privacy Policy?

From "The ABC's of Privacy," by the Direct Marketing Association. Reprinted with permission.

Your organization's privacy policy is a vital link between you and your customers or stakeholders. The following "ABC's of Privacy" cover the questions consumers are asking. Your online privacy policy should answer them.

About Me

What information do you collect about me and my family and is it secure?

It is important that you disclose to your online customers what information you collect from them while they visit your site and how you assure the security of that information. Consumers want to know if you collect their domain names and e-mail addresses, or keep records about pages they visited on your site. If you combine the information given to you by the consumer with information from other sources, tell the consumer. If you have a site that is frequented by children, urge them to get a parent's permission before collecting any identifiable data online. If they are 12 and under, get a parent's consent first before collecting or using data.

Benefits

How do you use the information collected, and how does it benefit me?

Consumers need to know how your organization uses the information that is collected about them on your Web site. They may or may not be comfortable with some of your information collection practices. They need to know if information about them is used to improve or customize your Web site content or customer service, or for marketing purposes, or if it is distributed to third parties for marketing purposes.

Choices

What choices do I have about your use of information about me?

Customers want to have choices over how information about them is used. Part of this empowerment involves providing consumers with a way to remove themselves from the marketing process. An example of this might be an e-mail address for consumers to request that information collected from them is not used to develop marketing lists.

Cookies

Cookies (introduced in Chapter 2) can be used either to store data directly or as a key that allows data collected on separate occasions to be linked together. Several ways that cookies that do not actually contain personally identifiable information may be linked to such information are explained below. To understand how this linkage occurs, it is important to keep in mind some basic information about how cookies work. Cookies are *set* by a web site by including a `Set-Cookie` header in an HTTP response. This header indicates not only the name and value of the cookie, but also when it expires and a domain and path. Web browsers automatically check to see whether they have any cookies with matching domains and paths before they make a request. If they find a matching cookie, they *replay* that cookie by adding to the request a header with the cookie's name and value.

Web sites that keep personally identifiable customer data set cookies that contain unique identifiers. These cookies generally contain long strings of numbers and letters that are meaningless to the user but that the web site can use to look up a customer's records. In some cases, the site may add information about a user's use of the web site each time he visits. Because this information gets linked to personally identifiable information via a cookie containing a unique identifier, the P3P policy for the cookie must declare the unique identifier, the personally identifiable information, and the site usage information.

Sites often use more than one cookie. Some of these cookies may contain or be linked to personally identifiable information, while others may not. Imagine, for example, a site that sets a cookie containing a unique identifier (linked to personally identifiable information) and an anonymous cookie that stores only information about a user's preferences at that web site. If a web browser replays both cookies as part of the same HTTP request, the unique ID cookie can be linked to the anonymous cookie. This, in turn, allows the anonymous cookie to be linked to personally identifiable information. This linking is possible because most web servers store in their server logs information about all the cookies replayed with a request. Thus, the two cookies are recorded together in the server logs. If you want to declare in your P3P policy that your cookies are not linked to identifiable data, you need to make sure that they are never replayed in the same request as cookies that are linked to identifiable data or form submissions that contain identifiable data. Alternatively, you can take precautions to make sure such cookies are not logged in your server log files or otherwise recorded together.

 Do you really need to declare data that is theoretically linked to cookies even if you do not make use of the linked data? A good rule of thumb is that if your web site architecture looks the same as it would look if you were making use of the linked data, you should declare the linked data, regardless of whether you actually use it. If you want to be able to claim that the data is not linked, you will need to take steps to make sure it doesn't get linked.

Ensuring that anonymous cookies are never replayed with cookies linked to identifiable data can be difficult, especially for a site that is distributed over many servers or administered by many individuals. This can be even more difficult if your domain includes servers that are administered for your company by a third party. To understand what data might be linked to a particular cookie, you must be aware of the set of URLs to which that cookie might be replayed and of all of the cookies that might be replayed to that set of URLs.

Identifying the set of URLs to which a cookie might be replayed is straightforward—it is determined by the domain and path attributes of the Set-Cookie header. To minimize unexpected problems, you should restrict the cookie as much as possible, ideally to the URLs directly related to a single application. If the cookie is replayed to URLs that you do not administer, you may not be able to control the kinds of data to which it might be linked or the ways that it might be used. However, the commitments you make in your P3P policy apply wherever that cookie might be replayed—even if it is replayed to servers that are not P3P-enabled.

Identifying the other cookies that might also be replayed to the URLs to which a particular cookie can be replayed can be a difficult problem. Anyone who is posting content on a web server may create applications that set cookies that can be replayed to every URL on that server. Even worse, anyone who is posting content on any web server in your domain may create applications that set cookies that can be replayed to every server in your domain. Thus, preventing other cookies from being replayed with a particular cookie requires constant vigilance and good communication between all web site administrators in a domain. You should consider using automated tools, such as one of the web site monitoring programs mentioned in the last section, which can produce alerts when new cookies are detected.

Unless you are extremely careful, if your web site uses cookies that are replayed with every web request across your domain, these cookies will be linked with all of the online data you collect. In that case, it is a good idea to declare a single policy for your entire site that includes all the cookies on your site.

Third-Party Content

IE6 considers images, frames, and other content served from a different domain than the page in which it is embedded to be third-party content. One typical case of third-party content is a banner advertisement embedded in an HTML page. If the banner ad is served from the advertising company's domain, it is considered third-party content. Companies use a variety of services—to monitor web site usage, process payments, distribute content, or provide customized services, for example—that require objects to be embedded in their web pages as third-party content. Some companies own more than one domain name (*example.com* and *example.net*, for example). When content from one domain is embedded in an HTML page from another, it appears to browsers that third-party content is being served (when I talk about third-party content in this book, I am referring to content that appears to browsers to be third-party content, regardless of whether it actually *is* third-party content).

An entire web site can sometimes appear to be third-party content, when the site gets "framed" by another site. Some search services place their own logos and links at the top of a web page and then embed another web site in an HTML frame below it. To the user, the embedded site may appear to be the first-party site, but to the browser, the search engine is the first-party site and the embedded site is third-party content.

Something similar may happen when a user uses a web-based email service to read an email that contains a web page. Web-based email services often display email messages in a frame. If someone emails you a web page (for example, a news article from an online news service), that web page becomes framed content. If the web page includes image links, your browser will fetch the images from the news service. If the news service has a different domain name than your email service, those images, and any cookies associated with them, are considered to be third-party.

There are several reasons that you need to be aware of both third-party content on your site and situations in which your site may be viewed in a third-party context.

- For your site to be fully P3P-enabled,[*] all of the third-party content in it should be P3P-enabled as well. You may need to discuss P3P with your third-party service providers and ask them to P3P-enable their content. If the third party is acting as your agent and does not use any of the data it collects from your customers for any purposes beyond what is stated in your privacy policy, the third party can create a policy reference file that references your P3P policy. However, if the third party makes other uses of the data it collects, it will need to develop its own P3P policy. Chapters 8 and 10 provide additional information and examples related to associating policies with third-party content.

- By default, IE6 blocks third-party cookies that do not have P3P compact policies. If there are cookies associated with any of the third-party content on your site, it is important that the cookies have compact policies and that corresponding full P3P policies be placed on the third-party site. Depending on the policy associated with these cookies and each user's settings, the third-party cookies may still be blocked by some browsers. If the cookie is critical to an application, you should make sure your application can detect whether the cookie was blocked and behave in a useful way even if the cookie is blocked. You may need to work with your third-party service providers to make sure blocked third-party cookies don't "break" applications.

- When third-party content or a link to third-party content is embedded in an HTML page, web browsers fetching this content send a referer header containing the URL of the page in which the content or link is embedded. Any personal information that is encoded in the URL of the referring page is thus transferred to the third party. In some cases, this data transfer takes place by agreement between the first-party and third-party sites. In other cases, the transfer is inadvertent. In either case, such transfers may need to be mentioned in the first party's P3P policy (unless the third party is really just a different domain owned by the same company or is a service provider acting as an agent).

---

[*] A particular URL on your site is considered P3P-enabled if it is properly associated with a valid policy and policy reference file. However, if that URL is an HTML page in which images or other content are embedded, some P3P user agents may display warnings or block cookies if the embedded content is not P3P-enabled as well.

One Policy or Many?

The simplest way to deploy P3P on a web site is to translate the site's human-readable privacy policy into a single P3P policy and associate that policy with all of the site's content. However, some sites may find it advantageous to create multiple P3P policies.

Sites that have content that is created and maintained by multiple entities not all bound by the same policies should offer separate P3P policies corresponding with each entity's policy. For example, in an online shopping mall, each store might have its own privacy policy. In this case, each store should have its own P3P policy. In addition, companies that have different privacy policies for each of their business units should have multiple P3P policies. Sites that allow individuals to create their own web pages—for example, universities that allow students to post their own personal web pages—should be cautious about advertising a sitewide privacy policy unless they can be sure that it will be followed by all of the individuals with pages on that site.

Sites that handle data in different ways depending on the part of the site in which it was collected may want to post multiple P3P policies. For example, a site that has an area especially for children might want to post a special P3P policy for that area that reflects the site's policy for handling data from children (in the U.S. there are legal restrictions on the collection of data from children—see Chapter 2 for more information). Alternatively, sites may write their P3P policies to include all of their data practices for all parts of the site. Thus, if a site collects data for completing the current transaction on one page and for research and development on another, the site could declare both data-collection purposes in a single P3P policy posted on both pages.

The advantage of posting separate policies is that web site visitors are given only the data-collection information relevant to the pages they request. Thus, visitors need not be concerned about data collection that occurs several clicks into a site when they are viewing a site's home page, where minimal data-collection occurs. However, some sites may prefer to present a consistent policy across the entire site, so that visitors are not surprised when they download a page that requests additional data. Furthermore, sites that choose to post multiple policies must be careful to associate the correct policy with each page as pages are updated over time. As P3P-aware web site management systems are created, tools may be developed that make it easier to ensure that the correct P3P policy is associated with each page.

If your site uses cookies, you should also declare a P3P policy for the cookies on your site. You can either declare the same policy for cookies as you do for the rest of your site or declare a different policy for cookies (or even a different policy for each cookie your site uses). Again, site management is simpler if you use the same policy for cookies as you do for the rest of your site. However, declaring different policies for cookies depending on their function allows users to make cookie-acceptance decisions separately for each cookie—thus, even if users object to some of the cookies on your site, they may not set their browser to reject all of them.

If you decide to declare different policies for cookies depending on their functions, be very careful that you fully understand the function of each cookie and the environment in which it may be replayed. As discussed in the previous section, if you set a cookie so that it will be replayed with any request to your web site, any application developer who works on your site might decide to take advantage of it and use it. If you set the cookie so that it can be returned to multiple hosts in your domain, the cookie may end up being used by applications running on computers of which you may not even be aware. Likewise, your cookies may be replayed with (and thus linked to) other cookies of which you are not aware. If you cannot be sure about where your cookies might be replayed or to what they might be linked, it is best to declare a single policy for all your cookies (and possibly your entire web site). In fact, this is what I recommend for most web sites.

Generating a P3P Policy and Policy Reference File

If your privacy policy is fairly simple (or if you happen to enjoy writing XML), you may want to write your P3P policy and policy reference file by hand in XML, perhaps using one of our example policies from Chapter 10 as a starting point. However, most people will probably opt to use a P3P policy-generator program.

A popular policy-generator program is the P3P Policy Editor from IBM, which was developed by one of the authors of the P3P specification—Martin Presler-Marshall—and some of his colleagues. It features a drag-and-drop interface, shown in Figure 5-1, that lets you edit P3P policies by dragging icons representing P3P data elements and data categories into an editing window. The tool also has pop-up windows that let you set the properties associated with each data element (purpose, recipient, etc.) and fill out general information about the site's privacy practices. As you add each data element, you can view the XML that has been created, as well as a corresponding human-readable version of the policy. There is also a useful Errors tab that indicates problems with your policy, such as leaving out information in required fields. The editor comes with good documentation and a set of templates for typical web sites. This tool can also create policy reference files. It is available for free download from the IBM Alphaworks web site at *http://www.alphaworks.ibm.com/tech/ p3peditor/*.

The P3P Policy Editor runs on Windows, AIX, Solaris, and Linux platforms and requires users to first install Java 1.2.2 or Java 1.3. Novice Windows users may have difficulty installing this software and using the drag-and-drop interface, but experienced Windows users should find the tool fairly easy to install and use. Unlike some of the easier-to-use questionnaire-driven tools, this tool offers users the flexibility to create any valid P3P policy. Once you learn how to use it, you can create new P3P

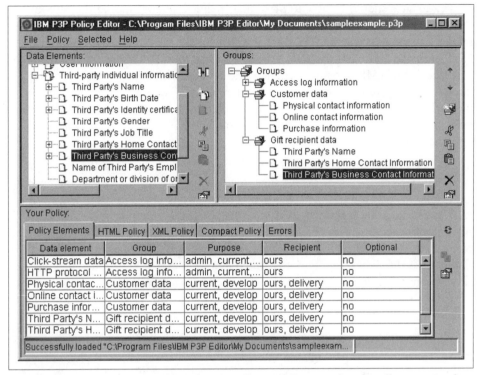

Figure 5-1. The IBM P3P Policy Editor features a drag-and-drop interface that allows users to drag data elements from the left column into groups they create in the right column

policies and edit existing ones very quickly. However, to use this tool effectively, you need to have a good understanding of P3P policies (after you read Chapters 6 and 7 of this book, you should be well prepared to use the P3P Policy Editor to develop your own P3P policy).

 You can download the Java 2 Runtime Environment Standard Edition Version 1.3 from *http://java.sun.com/j2se/1.3/jre/*. Make sure you download the version that is appropriate for the operating system running on your computer.

Helping User Agents Find Your Policy Reference File

The P3P specification designates */w3c/p3p.xml* as the well-known location for policy reference files. P3P user agents automatically check this location for a policy reference file at every site they visit.

Most web sites should be able to place their policy reference files at the well-known location without a problem. However, for sites that do not want to do this, two alternatives are offered: sites can be configured to send a special P3P header with every HTTP response, or LINK tags that give the location of the policy reference file can be embedded in HTML documents. Using one of these alternatives also gives sites the option of using more than one policy reference file, which allows sites that have more than a few dozen policies (for example, content-distribution networks that have a different policy for each customer) to avoid having an extremely large policy reference file.

The HTTP header alternative is most useful for sites that have decided to use multiple policy reference files. It allows sites to send a pointer to the policy reference file applicable to each request. The down side of using the HTTP header instead of the well-known location is that there may not be a way for a user agent to know a site's policy before requesting a resource. Thus, some user agents may suppress cookies, referer headers, or other information until they receive the P3P response header. Sites that use the HTTP header alternative for content that may be embedded in a web site should consider using a HINT element (discussed in Chapter 8) in the policy reference file for the site in which the content is embedded. The HINT element tells web browsers where to look for policy reference files.

The HTML LINK tag alternative was designed primarily for sites in which content providers have access to only a designated area of the web server (which does not include the /w3c directory) and do not have the ability to configure the server to send extra HTTP response headers. For example, students who want to provide privacy policies on personal home pages hosted on a university server, or individuals or organizations with sites that do not have their own domains, may want to use this alternative. This alternative has the same drawbacks as using the HTTP header. In addition, sites that choose to use this alternative must add a LINK tag to every HTML document within the site that is covered by the P3P policy, which may be a time-consuming task. Also, if visitors request non-HTML documents (images, PostScript or PDF files, etc.) directly without following a link from an HTML document on that site, their user agents may be unable to find the policy reference file when LINK tags are used.

Combination Files

Throughout most of this book, I assume that your site will have separate files for your policy reference file and for each of the policies on your site. However, you can put policies in the same file as a policy reference file, or put multiple policies in a single file. A policy reference file may also reference a policy contained in a different policy reference file.

Web site administration may be easier if these files are separate, as they can be updated independently and set with different expiry intervals. In addition, a company with multiple web servers may want to have policy reference files on each server that all point to a central policy file. Furthermore, if a company has many policies in a single file but most users access only parts of the site covered by one or a small number of these policies, user agents will have to download unneeded policies.

The advantage of combining a policy reference file with policies or combining multiple policies in a single file is that it reduces the number of HTTP requests necessary before a user agent can evaluate a site's policy. For companies with only one or a small number of web servers, it generally makes sense to combine policy and policy reference files.

Compact Policies

P3P-enabled web sites have the option of providing short summaries of their policies with respect to cookies in P3P HTTP response headers that accompany Set-Cookie headers. These compact policies are designed as an optimization to allow for cookie processing to proceed before a full P3P policy is evaluated. Sites can use compact policies only if they set cookies and if the cookie-related statements in their full P3P policies do not include mandatory extensions (discussed in Chapter 6). The details of writing compact policies are discussed in Chapter 7. The P3P HTTP header is discussed in Chapter 8.

> While compact policies are entirely optional for P3P-enabled web sites, IE6 relies heavily on them. This browser makes cookie-blocking decisions based solely on compact policies. By default, IE6 blocks "third-party" cookies that do not have compact policies.

A site that uses compact policies has a policy reference file and a full P3P policy, just like any other P3P-enabled web site. In addition, the site configures its web server to include a P3P header with all of its responses that contain Set-Cookie requests (or with every response). Here is an example of what such a server response might look like:

```
HTTP/1.1 200 OK
P3P: policyref="http://cookie.example.com/w3c/p3p.xml",
     CP="NON DSP ADM DEV PSD OUR IND PRE NAV UNI"
Content-Type: text/html
Content-Length: 8934
Server: Netscape-Enterprise/3.6 SP3
Set-Cookie: lubid=010033443C463628000C0000; path=/;
domain=.example.com; expires=Thu, 31-Dec-2003 23:59:59 GMT
Set-Cookie: pref=no-frame; path=/; expires=Thu, 31-Dec-2003 23:59:59 GMT
```

Note that the compact policy applies to all cookies set in this HTTP response. In this case, it applies to two cookies. If the HTTP response includes scripts that set cookies, the compact policy applies to these cookies as well.

Compact policies must be sent as part of a P3P HTTP header. To do this, you must be able to get your web server to issue this header. Depending on what server you use, you can do this by configuring files on your server (Appendix B provides instructions for several popular web servers) or by inserting an HTML META element into your HTML content with the http-equiv attribute set to P3P and the content attribute set to the P3P header you want issued. Here is an example of such a META element:

```
<META http-equiv='P3P'
content='policyref="http://cookie.example.com/w3c/p3p.xml",
    CP="NON DSP ADM DEV PSD OUR IND PRE NAV UNI"'>
```

Some servers look for http-equiv and generate headers accordingly. However, if your server does not do this, you won't get a P3P header. User agents are not required to support http-equiv, and most currently ignore it. Make sure you test out this feature on your server.

If you decide to use compact policies, you need to be careful about what expiration date you place on your cookies, as the compact policy applies for the lifetime of the cookie. Many web sites are in the habit of placing very long expiration dates on their cookies—for example, 30 years—so that they essentially never expire. However, these sites may not be prepared to say that their privacy policies won't change for 30 years. If a site sets a cookie with a compact policy and decides to change its policy before the cookie expires, it must reset the cookie when the user returns to the web site by issuing a new Set-Cookie header. Keeping track of which cookies have been reset and when can be quite a hassle.

You should also be aware that compact policies provide a simplified representation of a site's policy that may cause the site's data practices to appear more privacy-invasive than they actually are. For example, imagine a site that has online contact information and clickstream information linked to cookies. Say the site uses the online contact information internally but shares clickstream information with other parties. A compact policy for this site would simply state that the site collects online contact and clickstream information and shares data with other parties. The compact policy is not granular enough to indicate that only the clickstream information is shared. If you decide to use compact policies on your site, make sure you examine them carefully and are comfortable with the statement they make.

The Safe Zone

It is impossible to make an HTTP request for anything, including a P3P policy, without revealing some information (for example, an IP address) and risking that it might be used in a privacy-invasive way. The P3P specification defines a *safe zone* to allow P3P policies to be requested with less risk. Minimal data collection takes place in the safe zone, and any data that is collected is used only in nonidentifiable ways.

The P3P specification recommends that P3P user agents help implement the safe zone by suppressing the transmission of data unnecessary for the purpose of finding a site's policy—such as the HTTP referer header, cookies, and user agent information—until after the policy has been fetched.

The P3P specification further states that, to serve a P3P policy file or policy reference file, servers should not require the receipt of an HTTP referer header, cookies, user agent information, or other information unnecessary for responding to the request. If user agents send any of this information in the process of requesting a P3P policy file or policy reference file, servers should not use the information in an identifiable way.

There are two important practical implications of the safe zone for web sites:

- You need to make sure that the HTTP referer header and cookies are not essential to serving your P3P policy and policy reference files.
- If you do any data mining on your web server logs that results in identifying individuals or households, you need to make sure that you exclude data requests for P3P files.

 As part of its safe-zone implementation, IE6 does not do authentication on safe zone requests. Therefore, IE6 may not be able to fetch P3P files from web sites that require authentication. This problem occurs mostly on corporate intranet sites.

Testing Your Web Site

After you have P3P-enabled your web site, don't forget to test it to make sure everything is working properly. Use the W3C P3P Validator (*http://www.w3.org/P3P/validator/*) to check your P3P files for proper syntax and make sure they are all installed in the correct location. This validator will allow you to check the syntax of individual P3P policy files or to enter a URL and check to make sure it is properly P3P-enabled by identifying and checking the relevant policy reference and policy files. The validator checks only a single URL, not your entire site, so make sure you validate URLs on different parts of your site, especially if you have more than one P3P policy. Also be sure to test your site from outside your corporate intranet.

In addition to the W3C P3P Validator, new tools are being developed to help web sites develop and test their P3P implementations. Check the Web for the latest information on P3P tools.[*]

You may also want to browse your web site using one or more P3P user agents with various user preference settings, to see how visitors that use P3P will view your site.

---

[*] The P3P implementation page at *http://www.w3.org/P3P/implementations/* lists P3P user agents as well as P3P generators and validators. *http://p3ptoolbox.org* also lists P3P tools.

Some of the web site privacy self-assessment tools have features that can help you see how P3P user agents will respond to your site's policy. You should check the human-readable language produced by the P3P user agents and self-assessment tools against the language in your human-readable privacy policy and make sure that you have not made any errors in translating your policy into P3P.

The TEST Element and TST Token

Once you P3P-enable your web site, you are making a public commitment about your site's privacy practices. Many companies would rather not make such a commitment until they have fully tested and reviewed their P3P policies. While you are still testing your policy, you may want to include the TEST element in your full P3P policy and the TST token in your compact policy (discussed in Chapter 6). This will let P3P user agents know that your policy is still being tested. The W3C P3P Validator can validate policies with the TEST token. IE6 ignores compact policies with the TST token. The AT&T Privacy Bird treats sites with the TEST element as if they have no P3P policies but provides a policy summary with a note that it is for testing purposes only.

P3P Policy Syntax

P3P policies are machine-readable representations of web site privacy policies that use the standard P3P privacy vocabulary. Whether you are a P3P user, a web site operator, or a P3P implementer, it is important that you understand the vocabulary with which P3P policies are written. This chapter describes all of the components of a P3P policy and defines all the terms used in the P3P vocabulary. Chapter 7 explains how to put these components together into a P3P policy.

A P3P policy consists of a series of assertions that a web site makes about its privacy practices. Policies contain two main types of assertions: general assertions that apply generally to a site's data practices, and data-specific assertions (grouped together into *statements*) that apply to the way the site handles particular kinds of data. For example, a site might make a general assertion that it allows individuals to access their information in the site's databases and a data-specific assertion that it collects financial data to complete transactions.

This chapter begins by explaining the XML syntax used in P3P policies. In the next two sections, general and data-specific assertions are introduced. Then I explain how the P3P vocabulary can be extended and discuss some of the technical details of a P3P policy file. A quick-reference guide to all of the components of a P3P policy is provided in Appendix A.

XML Syntax

P3P policies are encoded using a computer-readable language called XML. If you use a policy generator to create your P3P policy, there is no need for you to learn to read and write XML yourself. However, it is useful to have a basic understanding of XML so that you can better understand both the examples in this book and the P3P policies you create.

An XML document contains a single XML *element*, which in turn may contain other XML elements. Elements are made up of one or more *tags*. All XML tags begin with a left angle bracket (<) and end with a right angle bracket (>).

Elements that do not contain other elements are represented by a single XML tag that ends with a slash character. For example:

```
<ELEMENT/>
```

Elements that contain other elements are represented by a pair of XML tags that surround one or more other XML tags. For example:

```
<BIG-ELEMENT>
  <element/>
</BIG-ELEMENT>
```

Notice that the opening tag does not contain a slash, while the closing tag contains a slash at the beginning (self-contained elements have the slash at the end).

Some elements have text, called *character data* (or *PCDATA*), between their opening and closing tags. For example:

```
<ELEMENT>
 character data
</ELEMENT>
```

PCDATA is associated with the tags that surround it but is not itself part of a tag.

Some elements may also have *attributes*, which provide additional information related to the element. For example, this element has a single attribute:

```
<element attribute-name="attribute-value"/>
```

The P3P specification lists and defines the XML elements and attributes that are permitted in P3P files. A P3P policy file contains a POLICIES element with a variety of attributes and subelements. A P3P policy reference file contains a META element with an xmlns attribute and a variety of subelements.

XML files may contain comments that help make them easier to read. Comments do not change the meaning of the computer-readable XML. XML comments are tags that begin with the string <!-- and end with the string -->. Here is an example of a comment:

```
<!-- This is a comment -->
```

General Assertions

There are five types of general assertions that web sites might make in their P3P policies: location of human-readable policies and opt-out mechanisms, indication that the policy is for testing purposes only, web site identification and contact information, access information, and information about dispute resolution. They must appear in a P3P policy in the order presented here. The five types of general assertions are described in the following sections.

Assertions in a P3P Policy

General assertions:

- Location of human-readable policies and opt-out mechanisms — `discuri` and `opturi` attributes of `<POLICY>`
- Indication that this policy is for testing purposes only — `<TEST>` (optional)
- Web site contact information — `<ENTITY>`
- Access information — `<ACCESS>`
- Information about dispute resolution — `<DISPUTES>` (optional)

Data-specific assertions:

- Consequence of providing data — `<CONSEQUENCE>` (optional)
- Indication that no identifiable data is collected — `<NON-IDENTIFIABLE>` (optional)
- How data will be used — `<PURPOSE>`
- With whom data may be shared — `<RECIPIENT>`
- Whether opt-in and/or opt-out options are available — required attribute of `<PURPOSE>` and `<RECIPIENT>`
- Data-retention policy — `<RETENTION>`
- What kind of data is collected — `<DATA>`

Policy Attributes

All P3P-enabled sites are required to have human-readable privacy policies in addition to their P3P policies. These policies must be consistent with the P3P policies but may convey additional information or clarification. The URL for a human-readable privacy policy is called a *disclosure URL*. A disclosure URL is represented in the P3P syntax with the `discuri` attribute of the `POLICY` element. The value of this attribute is a URL.

If a site offers visitors an opportunity to opt into or opt out of any data practices, the site must also include a human-readable explanation of how to do this. This explanation can be part of the human-readable privacy policy or at a separate URL called an *opt-out URL*. The opt-out URL is required when sites have opt-out mechanisms. It is also required when sites have opt-in mechanisms, because users must be able to change their minds and opt-out later. There may be an opt-out form at the URL indicated by the opt-out URL, or there may be instructions for opting out via telephone, postal mail, or another channel. The opt-out URL is represented in the P3P syntax with the `opturi` attribute of the `POLICY` element. The value of this attribute is a URL.

In addition to the `discuri` and `opturi` attributes, the `POLICY` element has a `name` attribute, which is used in a policy reference file to refer to the policy. The value of the `name` attribute should not include any spaces. If more than one policy is included in a single file, each must have a unique name.

Here is an example of the opening tag of a P3P POLICY element:

```
<POLICY name = "general-p3p-policy"
   discuri = "http://www.example.com/privacy.html"
   opturi ="http://www.example.com/opt-out.html">
```

This tag indicates that the policy has been assigned the name "general-p3p-policy" and that the site has a human-readable privacy policy at *http://www.example.com/privacy.html* and an opt-out policy at *http://www.example.com/opt-out.html*.

Test Policy Indicator

P3P policies may contain TEST elements to indicate that they have been written for testing purposes only and should not be considered valid P3P policies. Web sites may want to deploy test policies while they are testing their P3P configurations. The TEST element doesn't take any attributes—it just looks like this:

```
<TEST/>
```

Web Site Contact Information

A P3P policy contains an ENTITY element that provides contact information for the legal entity (a business, person, organization, government agency, etc.) that is responsible for the privacy practices described in the policy. For example, O'Reilly & Associates is the entity associated with the web site at *http://www.ora.com/* and Lorrie Cranor is the entity associated with the web site at *http://lorrie.cranor.org*.

An ENTITY element must contain the name of the entity and at least one piece of contact information (postal address, email address, telephone number, fax number, etc.) The ENTITY element may contain any elements from the business data set (described in Chapter 9). Some self-regulatory guidelines require specific types of contact information to be included.

Here is an example of an ENTITY element:

```
<ENTITY>
  <DATA-GROUP>
    <DATA ref="business.name">O'Reilly &amp; Associates</DATA>
    <DATA ref="business.contact-info.postal.street">90 Sherman Street</DATA>
    <DATA ref="business.contact-info.postal.city">Cambridge</DATA>
    <DATA ref="business.contact-info.postal.stateprov">MA</DATA>
    <DATA ref="business.contact-info.postal.postalcode">02140</DATA>
    <DATA ref="business.contact-info.postal.country">USA</DATA>
    <DATA ref="business.contact-info.online.email">help@oreillynet.com</DATA>
    <DATA
     ref="business.contact-info.telecom.telephone.telephonenum.intcode">
     1</DATA>
    <DATA
     ref="business.contact-info.telecom.telephone.telephonenum.loccode">
     800</DATA>
    <DATA
     ref="business.contact-info.telecom.telephone.telephonenum.number">
     998-9938</DATA>
  </DATA-GROUP>
</ENTITY>
```

This example includes quite a bit of contact information for the web site. All of the information is included as XML data between the opening and closing DATA tags. Notice that the site's telephone number is split between three tags, as required by the P3P specification.

Access to Identified Data

The access disclosure allows web sites to explain their policies about allowing people to access the identified data the site has collected from them. Some companies refuse to allow individuals to access their records. Others allow access to contact information or billing information and provide opportunities for individuals to report errors and have them corrected. Some companies allow individuals to access their entire records and sometimes even to remove their records from the companies' databases. Access is one of the core fair information practice principles. Companies that collect identified data should provide some form of access if they want their data practices to be considered privacy-friendly.

Access is represented in the P3P syntax with the ACCESS element. The P3P vocabulary defines six access disclosures:

`<nonident/>`
> Web site does not collect identified data. Sites that do not collect identified data may make this disclosure.

`<all/>`
> All identified data. Sites that provide access to all identified data that they collect may make this disclosure.

Identified Data

In privacy regulations, guidelines, and papers about privacy, a variety of terms are used to describe information that identifies an individual to varying degrees. The terms *personal information*, *personally identifiable information* (PII), and *customer identifiable information* are used frequently in the U.S. with slightly varying definitions. The term *customer proprietary network information* (CPNI) is formally defined in U.S. telecommunications regulations. The terms *identified*, *identifying*, and *identifiable* are often used as well. The definitions of these terms differ in whether they include otherwise non-identifiable data if it is stored in certain ways, used in certain ways, or combined with certain other data.

The P3P specification generally uses the term *identified data* to refer to data that a data collector can use to *reasonably* identify an individual. Thus, this definition applies to information, such as a full name, that can identify an individual on its own, as well as to data that identifies an individual when used in combination with other data. However, the coverage of this term is limited to combinations of data performed by a single data collector using a reasonable amount of effort. Thus, if a data collector has data that could be used to identify someone if it were combined with other data obtainable only from another source, the data will generally not be considered identified (if the other source is a public directory, however, the data probably would be considered identified). Of course, this definition does leave some gray areas that are open to interpretation.

Note that the NON-IDENTIFIABLE element (discussed later in this chapter) uses the term "identifiable" with a very broad definition that includes any data that *could* be used to identify an individual.

`<contact-and-other/>`

Identified contact information and other identified data. Sites that allow people to access identified contact information and certain other identified information may make this disclosure. These sites need not provide access to all such information.

`<ident-contact/>`

Identified contact information. Sites that allow people to access some or all of the identified contact information (e.g., name, address, phone number) collected from them may make this disclosure.

`<other-ident/>`

Other identified information. Sites that allow people to access information other than identified contact information (e.g., subscription information, account information, preferences) may make this disclosure.

`<none/>`

None. Sites that do not allow individuals to access any of their own information should make this disclosure.

Sites provide access through a variety of mechanisms, including a web site, a telephone number, or postal mail. They can allow individuals a range of access, including finding out what information is stored about them, correcting incorrect information, or withdrawing information. The access disclosure does not indicate the type of access or how it is provided. However, sites that disclose that they provide some kind of access are expected to provide further details about that access in their human-readable privacy policies.

Here is an example of an access disclosure that indicates that the site does not collect identified data:

```
<ACCESS><nonident/></ACCESS>
```

Sites that make this disclosure should not collect name, address, or other personally identifying information. Sites can make this disclosure even if they collect some identifiable information, such as IP addresses, as long as they do not use this information to identify individuals (and could not reasonably use this information to identify individuals, even if they wanted to, without obtaining additional information from other parties).

Dispute Resolution

P3P policies should include information about what visitors can do if they have a privacy-related dispute with a web site. A web site can provide information for contacting a customer service representative, privacy seal program, or other organization that will help resolve the dispute, or it can reference an applicable law under which the dispute may be resolved or a court where a legal complaint may be filed. Optionally, the site can make a declaration about the remedies that may be available should a privacy-policy breach occur.

Dispute-resolution procedures are represented in a P3P policy with a DISPUTES-GROUP element, which can contain one or more DISPUTES elements. Each DISPUTES element must have a resolution-type attribute that takes one of the following values:

service

> Customer service. Sites should use this disclosure to indicate that they have customer service representatives that individuals can contact to attempt to resolve their disputes. The sites must provide contact information for the customer service representatives in the short-description or LONG-DESCRIPTION field or at the service URL.

independent

> Independent organization. Sites should use this disclosure to describe an independent organization that individuals can contact to attempt to resolve their disputes. This is where a site would indicate that it has a seal from a privacy seal provider. The site must provide the name of the independent organization in the short-description or LONG-DESCRIPTION field and a URL for information on contacting the organization in the service field.

court

Court. Sites should use this disclosure to indicate that individuals can file legal complaints against them to resolve disputes. The site must provide in the service field a URL with information about the appropriate legal forum, but need not reference a particular law.

law

Applicable law. Sites should use this disclosure to indicate that disputes arising in connection with their privacy statements will be resolved in accordance with an applicable law. The site must indicate the name of the applicable law in the short-description or LONG-DESCRIPTION field or provide information about the applicable law at the service URL.

In addition to the resolution-type, each DISPUTES element must have a service attribute, which indicates one of the following: the URL of the customer service web page or independent organization, or the URL for obtaining information about the relevant court or applicable law.

 The term *service* is used for two different purposes in the DISPUTES element: it is one of four possible values for the resolution-type attribute, and it is also the name of a mandatory attribute.

A DISPUTES element can also have a short-description attribute that provides either a short, human-readable description of the appropriate legal forum, applicable law, or third-party organization, or contact information for customer service. The short-description may be no more than 255 characters long. For a longer, human-readable description, a DISPUTES element can take a LONG-DESCRIPTION subelement.

A DISPUTES element can optionally take a verification attribute. The value of this attribute can be a URL or digital certificate that can be used for verification purposes. The DISPUTES element is designed to give users an added degree of confidence that a web site will actually abide by its P3P policy. However, there is a risk that the assurance made in the DISPUTES element itself may be bogus. In the future, independent organizations such as privacy seal providers might issue digital certificates that can be used to automatically authenticate these assertions. If this happens, the digital certificate could be included in or referenced by the verification attribute. User agent implementers could then add features to their implementations that would use the verification information.

A DISPUTES element can have an IMG subelement that indicates the URL of a relevant logo and, optionally, its width and height. The IMG element must also have an alt attribute, which provides a short textual alternative for the logo.

A DISPUTES element should have a REMEDIES subelement that specifies the possible remedies in case a site does not live up to the commitments it makes in its policy. The P3P vocabulary defines three types of remedies:

```
<correct/>
```
Errors or wrongful actions arising in connection with the privacy policy will be remedied by the site. This means that the site will correct any errors but will not necessarily provide monetary compensation.

```
<money/>
```
If the site violates its privacy policy, it will pay the individual an amount specified in the human-readable privacy policy or the amount of damages.

```
<law/>
```
Remedies for breaches of the policy will be determined based on the law referenced in the DISPUTES element.

Here is an example of a DISPUTES-GROUP with four DISPUTES elements:

```
<DISPUTES-GROUP>
  <DISPUTES resolution-type="independent"
    service="http://www.bbbonline.org" short-description="BBBOnline">
    <LONG-DESCRIPTION>BBBOnline Privacy Program</LONG-DESCRIPTION>
    <IMG src="http://www.att.com/CDA/images/privacyseal6.gif"
      alt="BBBOnline Privacy Seal" />
  </DISPUTES>
  <DISPUTES resolution-type="service"
    service="http://www.att.com/privacy/"
    short-description="Customer service">
    <LONG-DESCRIPTION>If you are a consumer with concerns about the
      AT&amp;online privacy policy or its implementation you may
      contact us at 1-888-9-ATT-WEB. If you are a business customer,
      please call 1-877-744-4531.</LONG-DESCRIPTION>
    <REMEDIES><correct/></REMEDIES>
  </DISPUTES>
  <DISPUTES resolution-type="law"
    service="http://www.fcc.gov/csb/facts/csgen.html"
    short-description="Protection of Subscriber Privacy
      (Cable Act, as amended, Sec. 631)">
    <REMEDIES><law/></REMEDIES>
  </DISPUTES>
  <DISPUTES resolution-type="law"
    service="http://www.ftc.gov/bcp/conline/edcams/kidzprivacy/"
    short-description="Children's Online Privacy Protection Act of
      1998, and Federal Trade Commission Rule">
    <REMEDIES><law/></REMEDIES>
  </DISPUTES>
</DISPUTES-GROUP>
```

The first type of dispute resolution listed is the BBBOnLine Privacy Seal, an independent organization. The next one is the site's own customer service department. The last two are privacy laws that apply to this site.

Data-Specific Assertions

There are six types of data-specific assertions that a web site may make in a P3P policy: consequence, non-identifiable, purpose, recipient, retention, and data. All of these assertions are contained within a P3P STATEMENT element. Web sites should group the data elements they collect so that the same policy applies to all elements in a group. A single statement can then represent each group.

For example, a site that collects some data for administrative purposes only (basically, their web logs) and other data in order to process customer orders might have two statements—one pertaining to web logs and the other to order processing. The web-log statement might include the user's IP address and other data stored in the web logs, while the order-processing statement might include each customer's billing and shipping information and the contents of their orders. Here is what these two statements might look like:

```
<STATEMENT>
  <PURPOSE><current/><admin/></PURPOSE>
  <RECIPIENT><ours/></RECIPIENT>
  <RETENTION><indefinitely/></RETENTION>
  <DATA-GROUP>
    <DATA ref="#dynamic.clickstream"/>
    <DATA ref="#dynamic.http"/>
  </DATA-GROUP>
</STATEMENT>
<STATEMENT>
  <PURPOSE><current/><admin/></PURPOSE>
  <RECIPIENT><ours/><delivery/></RECIPIENT>
  <RETENTION><indefinitely/></RETENTION>
  <DATA-GROUP>
    <DATA ref="#dynamic.miscdata">
      <CATEGORIES>
        <physical/><online/><purchase/><preference/>
      </CATEGORIES>
    </DATA>
  </DATA-GROUP>
</STATEMENT>
```

Consequence

A consequence is a human-readable statement that can be shown to a user to explain why a suggested data practice may be valuable in a particular instance even if the user would not normally allow that practice. For example, a site that takes orders for merchandise delivered through the mail might disclose: "We collect your name, billing, and shipping information to process your order and deliver merchandise to you." Likewise, a site that wants to compensate people for providing information might state: "We offer a 10% discount to all individuals who join our Cool Deals Club and allow us to send them information about cool deals that they might be interested in."

A consequence is represented in the P3P syntax as a CONSEQUENCE element. The consequence is described in plain text between the opening and closing tags of the element. CONSEQUENCE is an optional subelement of a STATEMENT.

Here is an example of a CONSEQUENCE element:

```
<CONSEQUENCE>
  We offer a 10% discount to all individuals who join our
  Cool Deals Club and allow us to send them information
  about cool deals that they might be interested in.
</CONSEQUENCE>
```

Non-Identifiable

The NON-IDENTIFIABLE element is an optional subelement of a STATEMENT that may be included when no identifiable data is collected or when any data that is collected is anonymized. When using this element, be very careful that your web site meets the non-identifiable criterion "there is no reasonable way for the entity or a third party to attach the collected data to the identity of a natural person" and that you include a human-readable explanation of how this is achieved at the disclosure URL. Unless your site has no form submissions and keeps no web logs (or takes pains to make sure its web logs are sanitized so that they do not contain IP addresses or other potentially identifying information), you probably don't qualify to use this element. If you anonymize data, you must make sure to remove the original data from all of your logs, backup tapes, etc., and any technique you use to anonymize data must be nonreversible—for example, removing the last seven bits of an IP address and replacing them with zeros. A one-way cryptographic hash function will not be considered nonreversible if the set of possible data values is small enough that all possible hashed values can be generated and compared with the value that someone is attempting to reverse. Web sites have the option of omitting all other elements from STATEMENT elements that contain a NON-IDENTIFIABLE element.

Here is an example statement that contains a NON-IDENTIFIABLE element:

```
<STATEMENT>
  <NON-IDENTIFIABLE/>
  <PURPOSE><admin/></PURPOSE>
  <RECIPIENT><ours/></RECIPIENT>
  <RETENTION><stated-purpose/></RETENTION>
  <DATA-GROUP>
    <DATA ref="#dynamic.clickstream.uri"/>
    <DATA ref="#dynamic.clickstream.timestamp"/>
  </DATA-GROUP>
</STATEMENT>
```

This statement indicates that the requested URL and the time of the request are the only collected data. For this to be accurate, the web site needs to make sure that other information, such as the IP address associated with each request, is not recorded in log files. The site must also include in its human-readable privacy policy an explanation of how it ensures that the data it collects is not identifiable.

Purpose

One of the first questions people usually have about web site privacy policies is "What are they going to do with my data?" Purposes describe the ways a web site uses the data it collects. A purpose is represented in the P3P syntax as a PURPOSE element. Each PURPOSE element contains one or more subelements that describe a site's practices. The P3P vocabulary defines 12 purposes:

`<current/>`

> Completion and support of activity for which data was provided. Information may be used by the site to complete the activity for which it was provided, whether it's a one-time activity (such as returning the results from a web search, forwarding an email message, or placing an order) or a recurring activity (such as providing a subscription service or allowing access to an online address book or electronic wallet). If a site uses information for other purposes in addition to the current activity, it should disclose multiple purposes.

`<admin/>`

> Web site and system administration. Information may be used solely for the technical support of the web site and its computer system. For example, log files that are used for maintaining the web site, diagnosing server problems, or detecting security breaches would be used for this purpose. If the log files are further analyzed for information about site visitors, additional purposes would apply.

`<develop/>`

> Research and development. Information may be used to enhance, evaluate, or otherwise review the site, service, product, or market. This does not include personal information used to tailor content for a specific individual or information used to evaluate, target, profile, or contact an individual.

`<tailoring/>`

> One-time tailoring. Information may be used to tailor or modify the content or design of the site for a single visit. Information must not be used for any kind of future customization beyond the current visit (for example, an online store that suggests other items a visitor may want to purchase, based on the items he has already placed in his shopping basket).

`<pseudo-analysis/>`

> Pseudonymous analysis. Information may be used to create or build a record of a particular individual or computer that is tied to a pseudonymous identifier, without tying identified data (such as name, address, phone number, or email address) to the record. This profile will be used to determine the habits, interests, or other characteristics of individuals *for the purpose of research, analysis, and reporting*, but it will not be used to attempt to identify specific individuals (for example, a marketer may want to understand the interests of visitors to different portions of a web site).

```
<pseudo-decision/>
```
Pseudonymous decision. Information may be used to create or build a record of a particular individual or computer that is tied to a pseudonymous identifier, without tying identified data (such as name, address, phone number, or email address) to the record. This profile will be used to determine the habits, interests, or other characteristics of individuals *to make a decision that directly affects that individual*, but it will not be used to attempt to identify specific individuals (for example, a marketer may tailor or modify content displayed to the browser based on pages viewed during previous visits).

```
<individual-analysis/>
```
Individual analysis. Information may be used to determine the habits, interests, or other characteristics of individuals *for the purpose of research, analysis, and reporting* (for example, a web site for a physical store may want to analyze how online shoppers make offline purchases).

```
<individual-decision/>
```
Individual decision. Information may be used to determine the habits, interests, or other characteristics of individuals *to make a decision that directly affects that individual* (for example, an online store may suggest items that a visitor may want to purchase based on items he has purchased during previous visits to the web site).

```
<contact/>
```
Contacting visitors for marketing of services or products. Information may be used to contact an individual, through a communications channel other than voice telephone, for the promotion of a product or service. This does not include a direct reply to a question or comment or customer service for a single transaction—in those cases, current would be used. In addition, this does not include marketing via customized web content or banner advertisements embedded in sites the user is visiting—these cases would be covered by the tailoring, pseudo-analysis, pseudo-decision, or individual-analysis purposes.

```
<telemarketing/>
```
Contacting visitors for marketing of services or products via telephone. Information may be used to contact an individual via voice telephone call for the promotion of a product or service. This does not include a direct reply to a question or comment or customer service for a single transaction—in those cases, current would be used.

```
<historical/>
```
Historical preservation. Information may be archived or stored for the purpose of preserving social history as governed by an existing law or policy. This law or policy must be referenced in the DISPUTES element and must include a specific definition of the type of qualified researcher who can access the information, where this information will be stored, and specifically how this collection

advances the preservation of history. (Note that this purpose is expected to be used primarily by government web sites.)

`<other-purpose>`*string*`</other-purpose>`

Other uses. Information may be used in other ways not captured by the above definitions. A human-readable explanation should be provided to describe these purposes.

Web sites must disclose all of the purposes that apply to their data practices. Almost all web sites should disclose the `current` and `admin` purposes. Sites should use the `other-purpose` purpose only if they engage in a practice that is not related to the completion and support of the activity for which the data was provided and is not described by any of the other purposes. Most web sites will not need to use `other-purpose` and should avoid doing so unless they have a practice that really cannot be described any other way. Sites that simply want to provide more detailed information about their data uses should use the `consequence` field for that purpose.

People are often confused because they do not see common data uses such as site registration, banking, or purchasing among the P3P purposes. All of these activities are captured by the `current` purpose. In fact, the `current` purpose is designed to represent all of the purposes for which web site visitors think they are providing data (known as *primary* data uses). The other 11 purposes represent the other uses that a site may make of that data. For example, if an online shopper provides data to place an order, the uses of the data related to processing that order are covered by the `current` purpose. However, if the web site also places the shopper on a mailing list to receive the company's catalogs, that is considered a *secondary* data use, and it requires disclosure of the `contact` purpose. At some web sites, some of the purposes other than `current` are actually primary data uses. For example, a web site visitor may provide information specifically to request a catalog. In these cases, the appropriate purpose should be disclosed with an indicator that it is done only on an opt-in basis.

The subtle distinctions between some of the purposes can be confusing. Table 6-1 shows how the six purposes that involve customization or analysis differ. To determine which purpose best describes a particular activity, you should ask the following questions:

Does the activity involve creating a profile of the user?

A profile is a record that links together multiple pieces of data about an individual. Generally, for one-time customizations, no such record is created. For many types of research and analysis, data is aggregated to determine the average characteristics or activities of users and is not stored in profiles. However, some types of analysis require building a profile that links together a variety of data about each user.

How is the user identified?

For activities that do not involve creating profiles, the user may not be identified at all. For other activities, users may be identified by name, government ID, etc., or by a pseudonym not easily linked back to a specific individual.

Does this result in a decision that directly affects the user?

Sometimes analysis is done so that companies can learn about trends and make general decisions about their products and services. Other times, analysis is done to make a decision that will directly impact an individual—for example, what ad to display, what products to feature, or whether to offer credit.

Table 6-1. How purposes that involve customization and/or analysis differ

Purpose	Does this involve creating a profile of the user?	How is the user identified?	Does this result in a decision that directly affects the user?
Research and development	No	User is not identified	No
One-time tailoring	No	User may not be identified at all or may be identified with a pseudonym or with personally identifiable information	Yes
Pseudonymous analysis	Yes	Pseudonym	No
Pseudonymous decision	Yes	Pseudonym	Yes
Individual analysis	Yes	Personally identifiable information	No
Individual decision	Yes	Personally identifiable information	Yes

Each type of purpose (except current) can optionally have a required attribute that explains whether a particular purpose is a required practice for a site. The required attribute takes the following values:

always

The purpose is always required; users cannot opt-in or opt-out of this use of their data. This is the default when no required attribute is present.

opt-in

Data may be used for this purpose only when the user affirmatively requests this use—for example, when a user asks to be added to a mailing list. An affirmative request requires users to take some action to make the request. For example, when users fill out a survey, checking an additional box to request to be added to a mailing list is considered an affirmative request. However, submitting a survey form that contains a prechecked mailing-list request box is not considered an affirmative request. In addition, for any purpose that users may affirmatively request, there must also be a way for them to change their minds later and decline—this must be specified at the opturi.

opt-out

Data may be used for this purpose unless the user requests that it not be used in this way. When this value is selected, the site must provide clear instructions to users on how to opt-out of this purpose at the opturi. Sites should also provide these instructions or a pointer to these instructions at the point of data collection.

Here is an example of a PURPOSE element:

```
<PURPOSE>
  <current/>
  <admin/>
  <develop required="opt-out"/>
  <tailoring required="opt-in"/>
</PURPOSE>
```

In this example, the site uses data for the purpose for which it was provided as well as for web site and system administration. In addition, it may use the data for research and development but allows users to opt-out; and it may use the data for one-time tailoring if users opt-in.

Recipients

A recipients—or domain of use—disclosure defines the parties with which the collected data may be shared. Recipients are represented in the P3P syntax as a RECIPIENT element, which take one or more child elements that describe the types of recipients. A P3P policy need not identify specific data recipients by name. The P3P vocabulary defines six types of recipients:

Ourselves and/or our agents or entities for whom we are acting as an agent. The data is used only by the entity referenced in the privacy policy, its agents, or parties for whom the entity is acting as an agent. For this purpose, an agent is a third party that processes data only on behalf of the entity for the completion of the stated purposes. For example, a delivery service or printing bureau may act as an agent if it uses the data to complete the specified task and does nothing further with it. Many third parties that process data on behalf of a company cannot be considered agents for the purposes of P3P because they use the data for purposes that go beyond the stated purposes. This includes many delivery services, advertising agencies, and credit bureaus. These third parties should be disclosed using one of the other types of recipients.

Delivery services possibly following different practices. The data may be used by entities performing delivery services that may use data for purposes other than completion of the stated purpose. These services may fail to disclose how they use data, or they may explicitly disclose additional data uses. Entities that share data with delivery services that are contractually bound to use the data only for the stated purpose need not disclose this recipient and can use ours instead.

Legal entities following our practices. The data is used by organizations that use data on their own behalf under *equable* practices. The P3P specification defines an equable practice as "a practice that is very similar to another in that the purpose and recipients are the same or more constrained than the original, and the other disclosures are not substantially different. For example two sites with otherwise similar practices that follow different—but similar—sets of industry guidelines." This recipient might be used to describe web sites that share data with partners that have very similar privacy policies.

`<other-recipient/>`

Legal entities following different practices. The data is used by organizations that are constrained by and accountable to the data collector but may use the data in a way not specified in the data collector's practices. For example, a web site may collect data to fulfill an order and share it with a partner who will use it for research and development; the partner's use of the data is different from what the web site disclosed, but the partner is obligated to use the data only according to an agreement it has with the web site. This disclosure does not specify how the data will be used by the organizations to which it is disclosed, only that these organizations are accountable to the data collector. However, it is in the data collector's interest to ensure that the data is not used in a way that would be considered abusive to the users' and its own interests.

`<unrelated/>`

Unrelated third parties. The data is shared with organizations whose data usage practices are not known by the original data collector.

`<public/>`

Public forums. The data may be published in public forums such as bulletin boards, public directories, or commercial CD-ROM directories.

Each recipient can optionally contain one or more `recipient-description` elements containing a description of the recipient. In addition, with the exception of ours, each of these recipients may contain a `required` attribute, which may take the same values as the `required` attribute associated with the purpose elements.

Web sites must disclose all types of recipients relevant to their data practices. However, information may be shared for law-enforcement purposes without disclosing a recipient other than ours. This may occur, for example, if a company's customer records or web logs are subpoenaed or if a financial institution makes routine disclosures to the government to comply with banking laws.

People have asked me whether a members-only chat room, bulletin board, or directory should be considered a public forum in a P3P policy. If the members are bound to follow the site's privacy policy and the site takes responsibility for enforcing this policy, the site might be able to make a reasonable argument for using the ours recipient and not the `public` recipient. However, most sites have only a very limited ability to ensure that members uphold their privacy policies, and thus `public` would be a more accurate description of data recipients for most chat rooms, bulletin boards, and directories, even if they are restricted to members.

Here is an example `RECIPIENT` element that discloses three types of recipients:

```
<RECIPIENT>
  <ours/>
```

```
<delivery>
  <recipient-desciption>
    Federal Express
  </recipient-description>
</delivery>
<public>
  <recipient-desciption>
    Anything you post to our bulletin boards will be available
    to anybody who visits our web site
  </recipient-description>
</public>
</recipient>
```

In this example, the site discloses that data is used by the site and its agents, a delivery company, and a public forum. The site further clarifies that the delivery company it uses is Federal Express and that the bulletin boards on the site are public forums.

Retention

A retention disclosure indicates the type of data-retention policy in effect. While it does not indicate a specific length of time, it does provide some guidelines for when data will be purged. Many of the retention disclosures also require a human-readable retention policy to be posted on the site. Retention is represented in the P3P syntax by the RETENTION element, which takes one of five possible retention policies as a sub-element:

`<no-retention/>`

No retention. Information is not retained for more than a brief period of time necessary to make use of it during the course of a single online interaction. Information must be destroyed following this interaction and must not be logged, archived, or otherwise stored. This type of retention policy would apply, for example, to sites that keep no web server logs, set cookies only for use during a single session, or collect information to perform a search but do not keep logs of searches performed.

`<stated-purpose/>`

For the stated purposes. Information is retained to meet the stated purpose. This requires information to be discarded at the earliest time possible. The site must have a retention policy that establishes a destruction timetable. The retention policy must be included in or linked from the site's human-readable privacy policy.

`<legal-requirement/>`

As required by law or liability under applicable law. Information is retained to meet a stated purpose, but the retention period is longer because of a legal requirement or liability. For example, if a law may allow consumers to dispute transactions for a certain time period, a business may for liability reasons decide to maintain records of transactions. Or a law may affirmatively require a certain type of business to maintain records for auditing or other soundness purposes.

The site must have a retention policy that establishes a destruction timetable. The retention policy must be included in or linked from the site's human-readable privacy policy.

`<business-practices/>`

Determined by site's business practice. Information is retained under a site's stated business practices. The site must have a retention policy that establishes a destruction timetable. The retention policy must be included in or linked from the site's human-readable privacy policy.

`<indefinitely/>`

Indefinitely. Information is retained for an indeterminate period of time. The absence of a retention policy would be reflected under this option. Where the recipient is a public forum, this is the appropriate retention policy.

Here is an example of a retention element:

```
<RETENTION><stated-purpose/></RETENTION>
```

The human-readable retention policy for this site might say:

> We retain your account information for as long as you are an active member of our club. If you ask to have your account deactivated, we will delete all of your account information within three business days. If you do not visit our site for one year, we will also delete your account information.

Data

Perhaps one of the most obvious questions to ask about a web site's data practices is, "What kind of data do they collect?" P3P provides two ways for sites to describe the kinds of data they collect: elements and categories.

Data elements

The P3P specification includes a standard *P3P base data schema* that specifies a common set of data elements of which all P3P implementations should be aware. This set includes information frequently entered into web forms, such as name, address, and phone number, as well as dynamically generated data such as the Referer[*] header field. P3P also includes a mechanism that allows web sites to create their own data schemas to define new sets of data elements (described in Chapter 9). Table 6-2 lists the data elements of the P3P base data schema. Most of these elements also have subelements that can be used to make a more precise statement about the kinds of data collected (for example, year of birth is a subelement of birth date). Because P3P data elements are hierarchical, if a site discloses that it collects a data element that has subelements, the disclosure automatically includes all of the subelements. The complete P3P base data schema is described in Chapter 9.

---

[*] The HTTP specification misspelled the word *referrer*; thus, HTTP has a Referer header. The P3P base data set uses this incorrect spelling too, for consistency with the HTTP specification.

Table 6-2. *The P3P base data schema*

Element name	Category	Explanation
user.name	physical, demograph	User's name
user.bdate	physical	User's birth date (including time of birth)
user.cert	uniqueid	User's identity certificate
user.gender	demograph	User's gender
user.employer	demograph	User's employer
user.department	demograph	Department or division of organization where user is employed
user.jobtitle	demograph	User's job title
user.home-info	physical, online, demograph	User's home contact information—includes postal address, email address, phone/fax/mobile/pager numbers
user.business-info	physical, online, demograph	User's business contact information—includes postal address, email address, phone/fax/mobile/pager numbers
user.login	uniqueid	User's login information—user name and password
thirdparty.name	physical, demographic	Third party's name
thirdparty.bdate	physical	Third party's birth date (including time of birth)
thirdparty.cert	uniqueid	third party's identity certificate
thirdparty.gender	demograph	Third party's gender
thirdparty.employer	demograph	Third party's employer
thirdparty.department	demograph	Department or division of organization where user is employed
thirdparty.jobtitle	demograph	Third party's job title
thirdparty.home-info	physical, online, demograph	Third party's home contact information—includes postal address, email address, phone/fax/mobile/pager numbers
thirdparty.business-info	physical, online, demograph	Third party's business contact information—includes postal address, email address, phone/fax/mobile/pager numbers
thirdparty.login	uniqueid	Third-party's login information—username and password
business.name	demograph	Organization's name
business.department	demograph	Department or division of organization
business.cert	uniqueid	Organization's identity certificate
business.contact-info	physical, online, demograph	Contact information for the organization
dynamic.clickstream	navigation	Clickstream information (usually stored in standard web server logs)
dynamic.http	navigation, computer	HTTP protocol information (usually stored in standard web server logs)—includes user agent information and Referer header
dynamic.clientevents	navigation	Information about a user's interaction with a web browser while visiting a site (collected only if a site uses JavaScript, ActiveX, etc. to explicitly collect this)
dynamic.cookies	*	HTTP cookies

Table 6-2. The P3P base data schema (continued)

Element name	Category	Explanation
dynamic.miscdata	*	Miscellaneous data (described by category)
dynamic.searchtext	interactive	Search terms
dynamic.interactionrecord	interactive	Records about the user's interactions with the site

Each STATEMENT in a P3P policy must contain a DATA-GROUP, which contains one or more DATA elements. The ref attribute of a DATA element is used to reference elements of the base data schema or other data schema. Sites may also use the optional attribute of a DATA element to indicate whether or not they require visitors to submit this data element. A value of no indicates that the data element is not optional (it is required), while yes indicates that the data element is optional. The default is no. When a site indicates in its P3P policy that an element is not required, it should also clearly indicate this on any forms that it might use to request this data element from a user.

When elements from the base data schema are referenced in a P3P policy, they are prepended with a # symbol. Elements defined in other data schemas are prepended with the name of the relevant schema (or, as explained in Chapter 9, the DATA-GROUP can take a base attribute that indicates the name of the schema).

Here is an example of a DATA-GROUP that makes several disclosures about specific data elements:

```
<DATA-GROUP>
  <DATA ref="#user.name"/>
  <DATA ref="#user.business-info.telecom.telephone"/>
  <DATA ref="#dynamic.http.referer"/>
  <DATA ref="#thirdparty.bdate" optional="yes"/>
</DATA-GROUP>
```

By disclosing specific data element names, web sites can make very precise disclosures about the kinds of data they collect. In the future, tools may exist that can tie these disclosures directly to data-transfer mechanisms. However, for sites that collect a wide variety of data or frequently change the kinds of data they collect, a more general disclosure about the categories of data collected may be more practical.

Data categories

Data categories are general descriptions of the kinds of data sites collect. Rather than enumerating every piece of data they collect, sites can provide more general descriptions using data categories. In addition, when sites create new data elements (see Chapter 9), they can use P3P data categories to provide a hint about what kinds of elements they are creating.

Data categories are represented in the P3P syntax with a CATEGORIES subelement of a DATA element. The CATEGORIES element must contain one or more of the 17 category elements defined in the P3P specification.

Generally, when data is referenced by category, the ref attribute of the DATA element takes the value dynamic.miscdata. In addition, the dynamic.cookies data element does not have a predefined category and must be referenced with a specific category.

Here are the 17 P3P data categories:

> Physical contact information. Information that allows an individual to be contacted or located in the physical world. Examples of physical contact information include name, phone number, and postal address.

> Online contact information. Information that allows an individual to be contacted or located on the Internet. Examples of online contact information include email address and personal web site URL.

> Unique identifiers. Nonfinancial identifiers, excluding government-issued identifiers, used for purposes of consistently identifying or recognizing an individual. These include identifiers issued by a web site.

> Purchase information. Information actively generated by the purchase of a product or service, including information about the method of payment.

> Financial information. Information about an individual's finances, including account balance, payment or overdraft history, and information about an individual's purchase or use of financial instruments, including credit or debit information. Information about a discrete purchase by an individual alone, as described in purchase, does not come under this definition.

> Computer information. Information about the computer system that an individual is using to access the network. Examples of computer information include IP address, domain name, browser type, and operating system. Note that information in this category excludes information such as an email address that is generally used to contact or locate an individual on the Internet. By default, most web servers automatically log every request they receive in a format that contains information that falls into this category. Thus, most web sites should disclose that they collect computer information. If the information in server logs is the only computer information a site collects, it may simply disclose the dynamic.http element from the base data set.

`<navigation/>`

Navigation and clickstream data. Data generated by browsing a web site (as opposed to data explicitly entered by a user). This information may include logs of what pages are visited, how long visitors stay on each page, etc. By default, most web servers automatically log every request they receive in a format that contains information that falls into this category. Thus, most web sites should disclose that they collect navigation and clickstream data. If this is the only navigation and clickstream data that a site collects, it may simply disclose the `dynamic.clickstream` element from the base data set. If the site saves the HTTP Referer header in its server logs, it should also disclose the `dynamic.http` data element.

`<interactive/>`

Interactive data. Data actively generated from or reflecting explicit interactions with a service provider through its web site. This information includes queries to search engines or logs of account activity (not web server logs).

`<demographic/>`

Demographic and socioeconomic data. Data about individuals' characteristics. Examples of demographic and socioeconomic data include gender, age, and income.

`<content/>`

Content. The words and expressions contained in the body of a communication. Examples of content include the text of email, bulletin board postings, or chat room communication.

`<state/>`

State management mechanism. Mechanisms for maintaining a stateful session with a user or automatically recognizing users who have previously visited a particular site or accessed particular content. HTTP cookies are the main state management mechanism currently in use.

`<political/>`

Political information. Membership in or affiliation with groups such as religious organizations, trade unions, professional associations, political parties, etc.

`<health/>`

Health information. Information about an individual's physical or mental health, sexual orientation, use or inquiry into health care services or products, and purchase of health care services or products.

`<preference/>`

Preference data. Data about an individual's likes and dislikes. Examples of preference data include musical tastes, favorite sports teams, and answers to opinion questions.

```
<location/>
```
Location data. Information that can be used to identify an individual's current physical location and track him as his location changes—for example, GPS position data.

```
<government/>
```
Government-issued identifiers. Identifiers issued by a government for purposes of consistently identifying the individual—for example, U.S. Social Security Number.

```
<other-category/>string</other>
```
Other. Other types of data not captured by the above definitions. This category should be used only for data that really doesn't fall into any other category, and a human-readable explanation should be provided to describe this data.

Here is an example of a DATA-GROUP that includes category references:

```
<DATA-GROUP>
  <DATA ref="#dynamic.http.referer"/>
  <DATA ref="#dynamic.miscdata">
    <CATEGORIES><physical/><online/><preference/></CATEGORIES>
  </DATA>
  <DATA ref="#dynamic.cookies">
    <CATEGORIES><state/><preference/><uniqueid/></CATEGORIES>
  </DATA>
</DATA-GROUP>
```

This DATA-GROUP references one specific element from the base data schema: #dynamic.http.referer. It also references two other elements that must include category information. This site is declaring that it collects data from three categories. In addition, it uses cookies that store or link data from three categories.

The P3P Extension Mechanism

The P3P working group designed the P3P vocabulary to express the concepts that were generally considered to be important to be able to express in a privacy policy. However, there are many concepts not captured by the vocabulary. These include some concepts that the working group considered but dismissed due to lack of consensus and some concepts the working group members did not even consider. The P3P specification defines an EXTENSION element, which offers a flexible and powerful mechanism for extending the syntax of a P3P policy or policy reference file. The extension mechanism makes it easy to test new concepts and refinements to P3P without breaking existing P3P implementations.

It is important to note that while new vocabulary components can be created easily, they may not be all that useful unless they become widely known. Therefore, those interested in creating extensions may want to work with user agent implementers to make sure their extensions get implemented.

The EXTENION element can be included as a child to most elements in a P3P policy or policy reference file that contain other elements. Thus, it can be included in the POLICY, ENTITY, ACCESS, DISPUTES-GROUP, DISPUTES, REMEDIES, STATEMENT, PURPOSE, RECIPIENT, RETENTION, DATA-GROUP, META, POLICY-REFERENCES, or POLICY-REF elements. The EXTENSION element may also be included in a P3P data schema as a child of a DATASCHEMA element.

Extensions can be either mandatory or optional, indicated by the value of the optional attribute of the EXTENSION element. By default, the value is yes, indicating that the extension is optional. When a P3P user agent encounters an optional extension, it can safely ignore it if it does not understand it. However, when a P3P user agent encounters a mandatory extension that it does not understand, it must assume that it cannot understand the entire P3P policy, data schema, or policy reference file in which the extension is embedded. Generally, this requires that the user agent treat the site as if it has no P3P policy. The requirement that user agents not simply ignore unknown mandatory extensions is important, because it prevents user agents from concluding that a policy matches a user's preferences when the policy includes a mandatory extension that disavows the policy or otherwise modifies its meaning.

A web site may place any valid XML expression between the opening and closing tags of an EXTENSION element. It is recommended that the enclosed extension include a namespace in the form of an xmlns attribute,* to uniquely identify the extension. Extension creators can also place information at the xmlns URL that explains the semantics of their extensions so that user agent developers can implement them appropriately.

Example 6-1 shows an optional P3P policy extension that might be used to indicate whether a web site is compliant with the U.S. Children's Online Privacy Protection Act (COPPA). In this case, the extension consists of a single element with an attribute that can take one of the following values: compliant, non-compliant, or no-children. (COPPA restricts data collection from children under the age of 13—see Chapter 2 for more information.)

Example 6-1. P3P policy with COPPA extension

```
<POLICY . . .
  <EXTENSION optional="yes">
    <COPPA status="compliant"
      xmlns="http://www.example.com/P3P/coppa/"/>
  </EXTENSION>
. . .
</POLICY>
```

---

* For more information on XML namespaces, see T. Bray, D. Hollander, A. Layman (Eds.), *Namespaces in XML* (World Wide Web Consortium, Recommendation, 14 January 1999), *http://www.w3.org/TR/REC-xml-names/*.

Example 6-2 shows another optional P3P policy extension, this one designed to explicitly state the number of days for which a site may retain data before deleting it.

Example 6-2. RETENTION element with retention-time extension

```
<RETENTION>
  <stated-purpose/>
  <EXTENSION optional="yes">
    <retention-time days="17"
      xmlns="http://www.example.com/P3P/retention-time/"/>
  </EXTENSION>
</RETENTION>
```

The retention-time and COPPA extensions are labeled as optional because they do not have any impact on the ability of a P3P user agent to understand the rest of a site's P3P policy. However, for some extensions, it may be critical that a user agent be able to understand them. For example, imagine an extension that was designed to indicate that certain web site data practices apply only to visitors from the European Union, while other practices apply only to visitors not from the European Union. Such a hypothetical extension is shown in Example 6-3.

Example 6-3. STATEMENTS with Safe Harbor extension

```
<STATEMENT>
  <EXTENSION optional="no">
    <SAFE-HARBOR eu-applicable="yes"
    xmlns="http://www.example.com/P3P/safe-harbor/"/>
  </EXTENSION>
  <PURPOSE><current/></PURPOSE>
  <RECIPIENT><ours/></RECIPIENT>
  <RETENTION><stated-purpose/></RETENTION>
  <DATA-GROUP>
    <DATA ref="#user.home-info.postal"/>
  </DATA-GROUP>
</STATEMENT>
<STATEMENT>
  <EXTENSION optional="no">
    <SAFE-HARBOR eu-applicable="no"
      xmlns="http://www.example.com/P3P/safe-harbor/"/>
  </EXTENSION>
  <PURPOSE><current/><profiling/></PURPOSE>
  <RECIPIENT><ours/><other-recipient/></RECIPIENT>
  <RETENTION><indefinitely/></RETENTION>
  <DATA-GROUP>
    <DATA ref="#user.home-info.postal"/>
  </DATA-GROUP>
</STATEMENT>
```

Because the extension in Example 6-3 is mandatory, any user agents that do not understand it will not be able to interpret the site's P3P policy. Sites should be cautious about using a particular mandatory extension until it is implemented in the user agents they expect their visitors to use. Otherwise, user agents may treat them as if they have no P3P policies.

The extensions in the previous examples each contained only one XML element. However, extensions can be defined that contain multiple elements. Example 6-4 shows an extension that provides more detailed information about how an individual can access data held by a site.

Example 6-4. ACCESS element with access-details extension

```
<ACCESS>
  <all/>
  <EXTENSION optinal="yes">
    <access-details
      xmlns="http://www.example.com/w3c/access-details/">
      <online uri="http://www.example.com/access/"/>
      <telephone number="1-800-323-3232"/>
    </access-details>
  </EXTENSION>
</ACCESS>
```

In addition to providing potentially useful information to user agents (and subsequently users), extensions may be employed by P3P policy generators to provide information of use mostly to the policy-generator tools themselves. For example, the IBM P3P Policy Editor uses an extension (shown in Example 6-5) to give a name to each STATEMENT in a POLICY. This allows the editing tool to display labels for each STATEMENT. A person creating a policy with this tool can label each STATEMENT with a descriptive label. If the creator wants to resume editing the policy at a later time, the tool can load the labels back in with the policy, because they were encoded using the EXTENSION tag. As it turns out, this extension has proven useful to P3P user agents too. The IE6 P3P user agent and the AT&T Privacy Bird both take advantage of this extension when displaying a human-readable version of a web site's P3P policy to users.

Example 6-5. STATEMENT with group-info extension

```
<STATEMENT>
  <EXTENSION optional="yes">
    <GROUP-INFO xmlns=
      "http://www.software.ibm.com/P3P/editor/extension-1.0.html" name="Site management"/>
  </EXTENSION>
. . .
</STATEMENT>
```

The Policy File

Now that we've covered all the assertions that can be made in a policy, let's look at the wrappings that are needed to hold it all together. A P3P policy is encoded as a POLICY element. All of the other elements described in this chapter appear somewhere inside the POLICY element. A policy file contains one or more POLICY elements (each with a unique name attribute) that are surrounded by the opening and closing tags of a POLICIES element. In addition to holding all the policies together, the POLICIES element contains information about the lifetime of each policy, and the version of P3P the policies use. Custom data schemas may also appear within a POLICIES element, as discussed in Chapter 9. The POLICIES element may live in a standalone file, or it may appear as part of a policy reference file.

P3P Versions

When the POLICIES element is in a standalone file, it takes an xmlns attribute that indicates the version of P3P being used. Each version of the P3P specification has a unique namespace to identify it. The final P3P1.0 Recommendation namespace is *http://www.w3.org/2002/01/P3Pv1/*. Until a new version of P3P is developed, most P3P-enabled web sites will create policies using this namespace. However, many early-adopter P3P web sites created policies using previous versions of the P3P specification. The version of the specification identified by *http://www.w3.org/2001/09/P3Pv1/* is almost identical to the final Recommendation. There are no differences in the policy syntax, but there are a few differences in the policy reference file syntax: in the older version, the EXTENSION element was not permitted, the scope attribute of the HINT element was called the domain attribute, and the dot value of the domain attribute of the COOKIE-INCLUDE and COOKIE-EXCLUDE elements was not permitted. The version of the specification identified by *http://www.w3.org/2000/12/P3Pv1/* is similar enough that some of the P3P user agents can process policies following that syntax; however, there are a number of syntax differences for both policy and policy reference files.

Language

The xml:lang attribute is used to identify the language of any human-readable fields. Both the POLICY and POLICIES elements can take an xml:lang attribute (META and DATASCHEMA elements can take this attribute as well). Generally, it is best to put the attribute only on the outermost element (POLICIES or META, rather than POLICY), unless your file contains content in multiple languages. Languages are also discussed in Chapter 8.

Here is an example of a policy file with human-readable elements in English:

```
<POLICIES xmlns="http://www.w3.org/2002/01/P3Pv1" xml:lang="en">
. . .
</POLICIES>
```

Here is an example of a policy file with human-readable elements in French:

```
<POLICIES xmlns="http://www.w3.org/2002/01/P3Pv1" xml:lang="fr">
. . .
</POLICIES>
```

This file has one policy in English and one policy in French:

```
<POLICIES xmlns="http://www.w3.org/2002/01/P3Pv1">
  <POLICY name = "policy-en"
    discuri="http://www.example.com/en/privacy.html"
    xml:lang="en">
  . . .
  </POLICY>
  <POLICY name = "policy-fr"
    discuri="http://www.example.com/fr/confidentialite.html"
    xml:lang="fr">
  . . .
  </POLICY>
</POLICIES>
```

Policy Lifetime

As explained in more detail in Chapter 8, a POLICIES element may contain an EXPIRY element that indicates the lifetime of the policy file. If no expiry time is given, the default is one day. The lifetime may be specified as a relative time in seconds, using the max-age attribute, or as a specific date and time, using the date attribute.

Here is an example of a policy file with a 48-hour lifetime:

```
<POLICIES xmlns="http://www.w3.org/2002/01/P3Pv1" xml:lang="en">
  <EXPIRY max-age="172800"/>
  . . .
</POLICIES>
```

And here is an example of a policy file that expires on November 6, 1994 at 8:49:37 GMT:

```
<POLICIES xmlns="http://www.w3.org/2002/01/P3Pv1" xml:lang="en">
  <EXPIRY date=" Sun, 06 Nov 1994 08:49:37 GMT  "/>
  . . .
</POLICIES>
```

Date and Time Formats

The date and time format used in the P3P EXPIRY element is defined in section 3.3 of RFC 2068 (*http://www.ietf.org/rfc/rfc2068.txt*).

Here is an example of the preferred format for date and time:

```
Sun, 06 Nov 1994 08:49:37 GMT
```

All times must be represented in Greenwich Mean Time (GMT).

Weekdays are represented using the following three-letter abbreviations: Mon, Tue, Wed, Thu, Fri, Sat, Sun.

Months are represented using the following three-letter abbreviations: Jan, Feb, Mar, Apr, May, Jun, Jul, Aug, Sep, Oct, Nov, Dec.

CHAPTER 7

Creating P3P Policies

This chapter takes you through the process of creating a P3P policy. Whether you plan to create the policy by hand or use a policy-generator tool, this chapter will help you through the policy-generation process.

Gathering Information About Your Site's Data Practices

As discussed in Chapter 5, the first step in P3P-enabling your web site is to create a privacy policy. We'll assume that you have already completed this step and are ready to move on to creating a P3P policy. Hopefully, most of the detailed information about your site's data practices necessary to create a P3P policy is already contained in your site's privacy policy, but you may need to talk with your company's webmaster or attorneys to clarify some of the details.

P3P policies contain both general information about your site and information about specific types of data that you may collect. The subsections that follow examine the kinds of general and data-specific information that you will need to gather and illustrate this process by example. Detailed definitions of each piece of information contained in a P3P policy are provided in Chapter 6. You will probably refer to these definitions frequently as you create your P3P policy.

The next few pages of this book contain a form that you can fill out to help you develop your site's P3P policy. You may want to photocopy these pages and take notes on them as you find out the answers to the questions they contain. Refer to Chapter 6 or the P3P specification for the definitions of the terms used in this form. Some of these terms have very specific definitions that are not obvious from their names alone.

General Information

1. Policy name: You should give your P3P policy a name that is a single word without any spaces, for example, *policy*, *cookie-policy*, and *catalog_policy* are good names. This name will be used in the name attribute of the POLICY element. If you have more than one policy on your site, the policy name will be used to help identify which policy is being referenced.

   Name:_____

2. URL for site's human-readable privacy policy: P3P-enabled web sites must have human-readable privacy policies posted. The URL of the human-readable policy will be used in the discuri attribute of the POLICY element.

   *http://*_____

3. URL for information about how individuals can opt-in or opt-out: Opt-in/opt-out information might be on your privacy policy page, or it might be on a separate page. This page may provide a form that users can fill out to opt-in or opt-out immediately, or it may provide information about how users can opt-in or opt-out through other means, such as calling an 800 number. The online opt-in or opt-out is, of course, most convenient for your customers and indicates that you respect your customers' privacy preferences. If your site doesn't offer opt-in or opt-out at all, you can omit this field. The URL of the opt-in or opt-out policy will be used in the opturi attribute of the POLICY element.

   *http://*_____

4. Name and contact information for business or organization: name and at least one piece of contact information are required; other contact information is recommended. This information will be used in the ENTITY element.

   Name of business or organization: _____

   Email address: _____

   Web site URL: *http://*_____

   Phone number: _____

   Postal mail address: _____

   _____

   _____

5. Access information: What kind of access does your site provide to allow individuals to find out what data about them you keep in your records? Check one. (Refer to the definitions provided for the ACCESS element in Chapter 6.)

   ❑   Identified data is not collected by this site

   ❑   All identified data

   ❑   Identified contact information and other data

   ❑   Identified contact information

   ❑   Other identified data

   ❑   None (this site collects identified data but does not provide access to it)

6. Dispute resolution: How can consumers resolve privacy-related disputes with your site? (Refer to the `resolution-type` attribute definitions for the `disputes` element in Chapter 6.) Check all that apply, and provide a brief description and URL for each item you check. You may provide more than one dispute-resolution mechanism of a particular type. Optionally, you may provide the URL for an appropriate logo and/or indicate that you will provide one or more remedies should a privacy policy-breach occur.

❑   Customer service

Contact information: _____

URL: *http://*_____

Logo URL: *http://*_____

Remedies: ❑   correct   ❑   money   ❑   law

❑   Independent organization

Name of organization: _____

URL: *http://*_____

Logo URL: *http://*_____

Remedies: ❑   correct   ❑   money   ❑   law

❑ Court

Name of appropriate legal forum: _____

URL with information about appropriate legal forum:

*http://*_____

Logo URL: *http://*_____

Remedies: ❑   correct   ❑   money   ❑   law

❑ Applicable law

Name of law: _____

URL for information about the law:

http:// _____

Logo URL: *http://*_____

Remedies: ❑   correct   ❑   money   ❑   law

Data-Specific Information

P3P allows web sites to create one or more statements that describe their data practices. Each statement describes one or more data elements that are handled with similar practices. If you handle all your data the same way, you need to have only one statement. If you handle each piece of data differently, you may want to have a separate statement for each piece of data. Most web sites will probably be able to group their data practices into a few statements in their P3P policies.

To create a statement, you will need to be able to answer the questions that follow. A template for creating a statement is provided here. Make as many copies of the statement template as you need.

7. Statement name: There is no official statement name attribute in the P3P syntax, but the IBM P3P Policy Editor uses the P3P extension mechanism to provide a name field, which is also used by IE6 and the AT&T Privacy Bird. This name will be displayed to users of some P3P user agents when they examine a summary of your privacy policy.

    Name:_____

8. Non-identifiable: Is it your policy either to not collect data (including web logs) or to anonymize the data referenced in this statement? To be considered anonymized, there must be no *reasonable* way for anyone to attach the collected data to the identity of a natural person. Unless your site has no form submissions and keeps no web logs, or takes pains to make sure the web logs are anonymized, the answer to this question is probably "no." If you say "yes" you must include an explanation in your human-readable privacy policy, and you have the option of omitting the rest of the fields in this statement. If your data is non-identifiable, include a NON-IDENTIFIABLE element in your statement.

    ❑ Yes, data is non-identifiable   ❑ No, data is *not* non-identifiable

9a. Data categories: Check all types of data that apply. (Refer to the data CATEGORIES definitions in Chapter 6.) If you want to provide more detailed information, you may disclose specific data elements (see question 9b) instead of or in addition to the data types listed here. You need to answer either 9a or 9b, but you need not answer both. Check the optional box next to types of data that are optional for the user to provide.

❑ Physical contact information	❑	optional
❑ Online contact information	❑	optional
❑ Unique identifiers	❑	optional
❑ Purchase information	❑	optional
❑ Financial information	❑	optional
❑ Computer information	❑	optional
❑ Navigation and clickstream data	❑	optional
❑ Interactive data	❑	optional
❑ Demographic and socioeconomic data	❑	optional
❑ Content	❑	optional
❑ State-management mechanism	❑	optional
❑ Political information	❑	optional
❑ Health information	❑	optional
❑ Preference data	❑	optional
❑ Location data	❑	optional
❑ Government-issued identifiers	❑	optional
❑ Other: _____	❑	optional

9b. Data elements: Optionally, check all the specific data elements that apply. If you make disclosures about the broad data categories collected, it is not essential that you make explicit disclosures about each data element that you collect. Most of these data elements can be broken down further into subelements (for example, you might collect only year of birth rather than birth date). If you collect only part of an element, indicate that as well. (Refer to Chapter 9 for the complete list of data elements in the P3P base data schema.) Check the optional box next to data elements that are optional for the user to provide.

Data about the user:

- ❑ Name   ❑ optional
- ❑ Birth date   ❑ optional
- ❑ Identity certificate   ❑ optional
- ❑ Gender   ❑ optional
- ❑ Employer   ❑ optional
- ❑ Department or division of organization   ❑ optional
- ❑ Job title   ❑ optional
- ❑ Home contact information   ❑ optional
- ❑ Business contact information   ❑ optional
- ❑ Login information   ❑ optional

Data about a third party (such as a gift recipient):

- ❑ Name   ❑ optional
- ❑ Birth date   ❑ optional
- ❑ Identity certificate   ❑ optional
- ❑ Gender   ❑ optional
- ❑ Employer   ❑ optional
- ❑ Department or division of organization   ❑ optional
- ❑ Job title   ❑ optional
- ❑ Home contact information   ❑ optional
- ❑ Business contact information   ❑ optional
- ❑ Login information   ❑ optional

Data about the user's interaction with the web site:

- ❑ Clickstream data stored in web logs   ❑ optional
- ❑ Last URL requested (HTTP referer)   ❑ optional
- ❑ User agent information   ❑ optional
- ❑ Client events   ❑ optional
- ❑ Search terms   ❑ optional
- ❑ Interaction record or transaction history   ❑ optional

Cookies (indicate one or more data categories associated with these cookies from question 9a above—you must disclose the categories for any data stored in the cookies as well as any data linked via the cookies):

❑ Cookies _____   ❑ optional

10. Data use: For what purposes will this data be used? (Refer to the PURPOSE definitions and required attribute definitions in Chapter 6.) Check all that apply, and for each data use you check, indicate whether it is always required or is performed on an opt-in or opt-out basis.

❑ Completion and support of activity for which data was provided

❑ Web site and system administration

Required: ❑ always   ❑ opt-in   ❑ opt-out

❑ Research and development

Required: ❑ always   ❑ opt-in   ❑ opt-out

❑ One-time tailoring

Required: ❑ always   ❑ opt-in   ❑ opt-out

❑ Pseudonymous analysis

Required: ❑ always   ❑ opt-in   ❑ opt-out

❑ Pseudonymous decision

Required: ❑ always   ❑ opt-in   ❑ opt-out

❑ Individual analysis

Required: ❑ always   ❑ opt-in   ❑ opt-out

❑ Individual decision

Required: ❑ always   ❑ opt-in   ❑ opt-out

❑ Contacting visitors for marketing of services or products

Required: ❑ always   ❑ opt-in   ❑ opt-out

❑ Historical preservation

Required: ❑ always   ❑ opt-in   ❑ opt-out

❑ Telemarketing

Required: ❑ always   ❑ opt-in   ❑ opt-out

❑ Other purposes: _____

Required: ❑ always   ❑ opt-in   ❑ opt-out

11. Data recipients: Who are the data recipients? (Refer to the RECIPIENT definitions in Chapter 6.) Check all that apply, and for each recipient you check, indicate whether it is always required or is used on an opt-in or opt-out basis. Optionally, you may provide a human-readable description of the data recipients as well.

❑ Ourselves and/or our agents or entities for whom we are acting as an agent

Description: _____

❑ Delivery services possibly following different practices

Required: ❑ always   ❑ opt-in   ❑ opt-out

Description: _____

❑ Legal entities following our practices

Required: ❑ always   ❑ opt-in   ❑ opt-out

Description: _____

❑ Legal entities following different practices

Required: ❑ always   ❑ opt-in   ❑ opt-out

Description: _____

❑ Unrelated third parties

Required: ❑ always   ❑ opt-in   ❑ opt-out

Description: _____

❑ Public fora

Required: ❑ always   ❑ opt-in   ❑ opt-out

Description: _____

12. Data-retention policy: Describe the data-retention policy applicable to this data. Unless your retention policy is "no retention" or "indefinitely," you must also describe it in or link to it from your human-readable privacy policy. (Refer to the RETENTION element definitions in Chapter 6.)

   ❑ No retention

   ❑ For the stated purpose

   ❑ As required by law or liability under applicable law

   ❑ Determined by site's business practice

   ❑ Indefinitely

13. Explanation: Optionally, you may provide a human-readable explanation of the data practices described in this statement. Some user agents may show this explanation to users to explain why a data practice may be valuable in a particular instance even if the user would not normally allow the practice. This explanation will be placed in the CONSEQUENCE element.

   _____

   _____

An Example

To help make this more concrete, I will take you through the steps of gathering information and creating a P3P policy for an example web site. I will use the sample privacy policy developed by the Better Business Bureau (*http://www.bbbonline.com/ privacy/sample_privacy.asp*) as a starting point. Let's assume that this privacy policy belongs to a company called Sample Example, which manufactures samples of all sorts of common and unusual products. I've inserted some extra details into the policy provided by BBB so that Sample Example can provide enough information in their human-readable privacy policy to create a P3P policy.

Here is the Sample Example privacy policy that is posted at the fictitious web site *http://www.sample.example.com/privacy.html*:

Our Commitment to Privacy

Your privacy is important to us. To better protect your privacy we provide this notice explaining our online information practices and the choices you can make about the way your information is collected and used. To make this notice easy to find, we make it available on our homepage and at every point where personally identifiable information may be requested.

The Information We Collect

This notice applies to all information collected or submitted on the Sample Example web site. On some pages, you can order products, make requests, and register to receive materials. The types of personal information collected at these pages are: name, address, email address, phone number, credit/debit card information.

On some pages, you can submit information about other people. For example, if you order a gift online and want it sent directly to the recipient, you will need to submit the recipient's address. In this circumstance, the types of personal information collected are: name, address, phone number.

The Way We Use Information

We use the information you provide about yourself when placing an order only to complete that order. We use cookies to provide shopping cart services to you on our web site to make it easier for you to place your order. We do not share the information you provide with outside parties except to the extent necessary to complete that order.

We use the information you provide about someone else when placing an order only to ship the product and to confirm delivery. We do not share this information with outside parties except to the extent necessary to complete that order.

We offer gift cards by which you can personalize a product you order for another person. Information you provide to us to create a gift card is used only for that purpose, and it is disclosed only to the person receiving the gift.

We use return email addresses to answer the email we receive. Such addresses are not used for any other purpose and are not shared with outside parties.

You can register with our web site if you would like to receive our catalog as well as updates on our new products and services. Information you submit on our web site will not be used for this purpose unless you fill out the registration form.

We use non-identifying and aggregate information to better design our web site and to share with advertisers. For example, we may tell an advertiser that X number of individuals visited a certain area on our web site or that Y number of men and Z number of women filled out our registration form, but we would not disclose anything that could be used to identify those individuals.

Finally, we never use or share the personally identifiable information provided to us online in ways unrelated to the ones described above without also providing you an opportunity to opt out or otherwise prohibit such unrelated uses. For information about how to make that choice, see *http://www.sample.example.com/opt-out.html*.

Our Commitment to Data Security

To prevent unauthorized access, maintain data accuracy, and ensure the correct use of information, we have put in place appropriate physical, electronic, and managerial procedures to safeguard and secure the information we collect online.

Our Commitment to Children's Privacy

Protecting the privacy of the very young is especially important. For that reason, we never collect or maintain information at our web site from those we actually know are under 13, and no part of our web site is structured to attract anyone under 13.

How You Can Access Or Correct Your Information

You can access all of your personally identifiable information that we collect online and maintain by calling us at 1-877-EXAMPLE. We use this procedure to better safeguard your information.

You can correct factual errors in your personally identifiable information by sending us a request that credibly shows error. Send your request to us at Sample Example, Office of the CPO, 1 Example Rd., Kensington, MD 20895.

To protect your privacy and security, we will also take reasonable steps to verify your identity before granting access or making corrections.

How to Contact Us

Should you have other questions or concerns about these privacy policies, please call us at 1-877-EXAMPLE or send us an email at *privacy@sample.example.com*.

Sample Example also participates in the BBBOnLine® Privacy Program. Further information about this program is available at *http://www.bbbonline.org*.

Sample Example's privacy policy is pretty thorough and tells us most of what we need to know to create a P3P policy, but we still have a few questions.

We'll start with the general information. We'll give this policy a simple name—*general-policy*. The URL of the site's privacy policy is *http://www.sample.example.com/privacy.html*, and the URL for the site's opt-out information is *http://www.sample.example.com/opt-out.html*.

The human-readable privacy policy includes email and telephone contact information, so that's the information we'll include in the P3P policy as well:

Sample Example, Inc.
privacy@sample.example.com
1-877-EXAMPLE

The human-readable privacy policy states that the company allows access to all personally identifiable information they collect online. Therefore, we can check the *all identified data* box for question 5 in the questionnaire.

The human-readable privacy policy offers two places for consumers to go with concerns about the privacy policy—Sample Example's own customer-service department and BBBOnLine. They provide a phone number and email address for customer service and a URL for BBBOnLine. They may also want to include the URL of the BBBOnLine privacy seal logo in their P3P policy, so that P3P user agents that display disputes logos can display this seal.

Now let's look at the data-specific information. The human-readable privacy policy talks about four groups of data: data about a customer, data about a gift recipient, data about people who fill out the registration form on the site, and data about people who send email to the company. If we talked to their webmaster, we would learn that, like most web sites, Sample Example keeps standard web logs, so we mention this in the P3P policy. That gives us five groups of data, and thus five statements. Let's look at each in more detail.

Our first statement is about customer data. Sample Example describes some specific types of data they collect, such as name, address, email address, phone number, and credit/debit card information. We could enumerate these specific data elements (for everything except the credit/debit card information). However, for added flexibility, we're going to use the data categories *physical contact information*, *online contact information*, and *purchase information* instead. Note that we do not need to mention the *financial information* category because the credit/debit card information collected is associated with a specific purchase and thus is covered under *purchase information*. This data will be used for *completion and support of activity for which data was provided* and for *research and development* (improving the design of the web site). The data recipients are *ourselves and/or our agents* and *delivery services*. While Sample Example does share data with advertisers, they share data only in aggregate form, so they do not need to mention this in their P3P policy. There is no opt-in or opt-out associated with any of these data practices or data recipients. The privacy policy makes no mention of a data-retention policy, and if we were to check with the Chief Privacy Officer, we would find that Sample Example doesn't have one (yet... they are working on drafting one), so for now the retention policy is *indefinitely*. In this case, the collected data is obviously not non-identifiable. We'll include a human-readable explanation for this statement, too: "We collect your contact and billing information so that we can complete your order."

Our second statement is about gift recipient data. This statement is almost the same as our customer data statement; indeed, we could combine the two. However, since the privacy policy makes a point to specifically highlight the fact that Sample Example collects data on gift recipients, we're going to make this a separate statement in the P3P policy. We'll use the name and contact information data elements from the thirdparty data set here, rather than data categories. We will also include a different human-readable statement: "We collect name and contact information for gift recipients so that we can deliver their gifts."

The third statement is about registrant data. The privacy policy is ambiguous about what exactly is collected on the registration page, but if we checked with the webmaster we would find that this page collects the name, online and physical contact information, some demographic information, and some information about each registrant's interests. Thus, the P3P policy should indicate that the data categories *physical contact information, online contact information, demographic and socioeconomic data,* and *preference data* are collected. The site uses this information for *completion and support of activity for which data was provided, research and development,* and *contacting visitors for marketing of services or products.* Sample Example will use the data for marketing to only those customers who have specifically requested this (opted in). This data is shared only with *ourselves and/or our agents.* Again, the retention policy is *indefinitely,* and the data is not non-identifiable. The human-readable explanation for this statement is: "We collect registration information from you so that we can send you catalogs or other requested information and improve our web site."

The fourth statement is about data included in email sent to the company. The privacy policy mentions the return email address of the sender. We can use the *online contact information* category to refer to this, or we can use the specific email address data element from the user's home and/or business contact information. We will also use the *content* category to represent the content of the email message. The only use of this information is *completion and support of current activity,* and the only recipient is *ourselves and/or our agents.* Again, the retention policy is *indefinitely,* and the data is not non-identifiable. The human-readable explanation for this statement is: "We use return email addresses to answer the email we receive. Such addresses are not used for any other purpose and are not shared with outside parties."

Finally, the fifth statement is about web log data. If we talked to the webmaster, we would learn that the web logs include clickstream data, the HTTP referer, and user agent information. The cookies used to maintain shopping carts on the site also show up in the web logs. The site does not, however, collect client events. All of the web log data is used only for *web site and system administration, research and development,* and *completion and support of activity for which data was provided;* the recipients are *ourselves and/or our agents.* The retention policy is *indefinitely,* and the data is not non-identifiable (because this data include IP addresses, which in some cases can be used to identify specific individuals). The human-readable explanation for this statement is: "We maintain standard web logs for web site and system administration and for research and development. This information is not used for any other purpose, nor is it shared with outside parties."

That's pretty much everything we need to know about this web site's privacy practices in order to write a P3P policy. We can fill out this information on our handy forms so that we have it all in one place when we sit down to write the P3P policy.

Turning the Information You Gathered into a P3P Policy

Once you finish gathering the information about your site's privacy practices, the next step is turn this information into a P3P policy. You can create a policy either by manually composing the XML or by using a P3P policy-generator tool. Let's try to create the Sample Example P3P policy using the IBM P3P Policy Editor.

The IBM editor lets us start from scratch or begin with a template. We'll start with a template for sites that collect standard server log data. The first thing to do after creating a new policy using this template is to enter the general information. We can do this by selecting Policy properties from the Policy menu and filling out the information under all five tabs. Figure 7-1 shows how we would fill out the Organization tab with our answers to question 4 in the general information section of our form.

The Web Sites tab allows us to fill in the information from questions 1, 2, and 3 of our form.

The Access tab allows us to indicate the site's access policies (question 5 of our form).

The Assurances tab allows us to add information about one or more mechanisms for resolving disputes with the site about the privacy policy (question 6 of our form). Using the Add button, we can add information about the site's customer service and about the BBBOnLine privacy program.

The Expiry tab allows us to indicate a lifetime for this P3P policy that is different from the 24-hour default. For most policies, including this one, the default will be adequate. This tab also has a checkbox to indicate that a policy is for testing purposes only. It is a good idea to first create a policy with this box checked, then uncheck the box and save the policy again after you have finished testing it.

Now let's add the five statements to our P3P policy. The editor uses the concept of a *group* to represent a P3P statement, so click on the Create Group icon to add the first statement. This icon is the third icon from the top on the far right side of the main policy editor window, as shown in Figure 7-2. If you hover your mouse over it, the words "Create Group" will appear. After you click on this icon, the Groups folder in

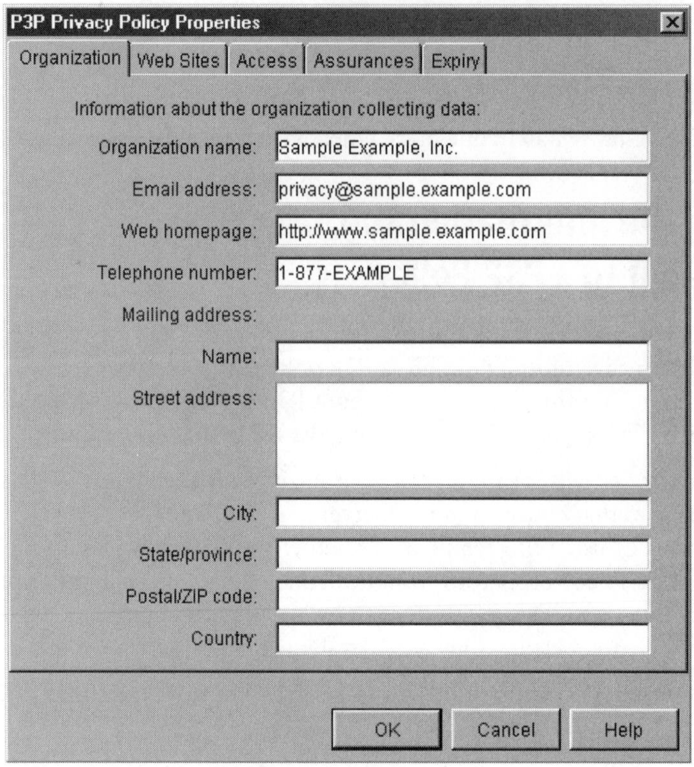

Figure 7-1. Organization properties in the IBM P3P Policy Editor

the right panel will open and New Group will be added to the bottom of the groups list. Right-click on New Group and select Properties from the menu that appears. This brings up the New Group Properties panel, where you can change the name from "New Group" to something more descriptive, like "Customer Data," and type in the human-readable explanation. The New Group Properties panel also has tabs that let you enter purpose, recipient, and retention information for this statement.

When you finish adding properties to the Customer Data statement, you'll need to describe the kinds of data that are covered by this statement. In the left panel of the main policy editor window are folders containing different kinds of data elements. Click on the plus sign to the left of the Broad categories folder to see all the data categories. Click on the "Physical contact information" category and drag it over to the Customer Data group in the right panel. When you release the mouse button, you'll see "Physical contact information" listed under Customer Data in the right panel. Now do the same thing for "Online contact information" and "Purchase information."

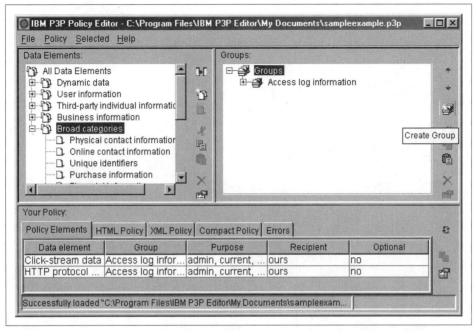

Figure 7-2. Click on the Create Group icon to add a statement to your P3P policy

Repeat this process for the gift recipient statement. Click on the Create Groups icon again to create this group, and fill out the information in the Properties menu. Instead of adding data categories, this time we'll add data elements from the third-party data set. Click on the plus sign to the left of the "Third-party individual information" folder to see the third-party data elements. Drag the "Third Party's Name," "Third Party's Home Contact Information," and "Third Party's Business Contact Information" data elements to the Gift Recipient group in the right panel, as shown in Figure 7-3.

Repeat this procedure to create the registrant data statement and the email statement. Because we started with a template, the web log data statement is already partially created for us. It is at the top of our list of groups in the right panel (labeled "Access log information"). Right-click on it to bring up its Properties panel. Change the human-readable text and make sure all the other information here is correct. If you click on the plus sign to the left of the "Access log information" group, you'll see that it already contains most of the necessary data elements. However, you need to add cookies to this group. Select "HTTP cookies" from "Dynamic data" in the left panel and drag it into the "Access log information" group in the right panel. Then right-click on "HTTP cookies" and check the boxes for the categories of data stored in or linked to the cookies—in this case, *navigation and clickstream*, *state-management*, and *preference* information.

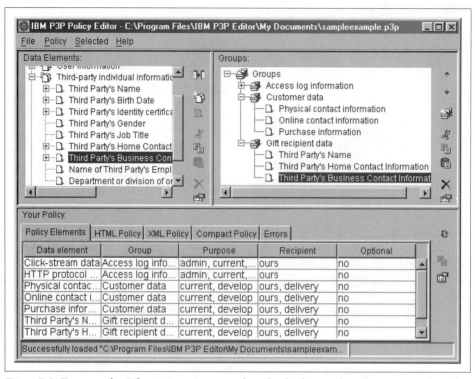

Figure 7-3. To create the Gift recipient statement, drag the third-party data elements into the right panel

When you're done, go to the File menu and save the policy. The editor also generates a natural-language HTML version of this policy. If we were going to use this, we would probably want to edit it, but it is a good way to begin creating a privacy policy if you don't have one. The P3P policy created by the IBM P3P Policy Editor is shown in Example 7-1.

Example 7-1. P3P policy for Sample Example, generated by the IBM P3P Policy Editor

```
<?xml version="1.0"?>
<POLICIES xmlns="http://www.w3.org/2002/01/P3Pv1">
    <!-- Generated by IBM P3P Policy Editor version Beta 1.10 built 2/19/02 2:42 PM -->

    <!-- Expiry information for this policy -->
    <EXPIRY max-age="604800"/>

<POLICY
    discuri="http://www.sample.example.com/privacy.html"
    name="policy">
```

```
    <!-- Description of the entity making this policy statement. -->
    <ENTITY>
<DATA-GROUP>
<DATA ref="#business.contact-info.telecom.telephone.intcode">1</DATA>
<DATA ref="#business.contact-info.telecom.telephone.loccode">877</DATA>
<DATA ref="#business.contact-info.telecom.telephone.number">
  EXAMPLE</DATA>
<DATA ref="#business.contact-info.online.email">
  privacy@sample.example.com</DATA>
<DATA ref="#business.contact-info.online.uri">
  http://www.sample.example.com</DATA>
<DATA ref="#business.name">Sample Example, Inc.</DATA>
    </DATA-GROUP>
    </ENTITY>

    <!-- Disclosure -->
    <ACCESS><all/></ACCESS>

    <!-- Disputes -->
    <DISPUTES-GROUP>
        <DISPUTES resolution-type="service" service="http://www.sample.example.com/
        privacy.html" short-description="Sample Example Customer Service">
            <LONG-DESCRIPTION>If you have any questions or concerns about our privacy
            policy please email privacy@sample.example.com or call
            1-877-EXAMPLE.</LONG-DESCRIPTION>
    <!-- No remedies specified -->
        </DISPUTES>
        <DISPUTES resolution-type="independent" service="http://www.bbbonline.org"
         short-description="BBBOnline">
            <LONG-DESCRIPTION>BBBOnline Privacy Program</LONG-DESCRIPTION>
            <IMG src="http://www.bbbonline.com/privacy/images/privacy.gif"
             alt="BBBOnline Privacy Seal"/>
    <!-- No remedies specified -->
        </DISPUTES>
    </DISPUTES-GROUP>

    <!-- Statement for group "Access log information" -->
    <STATEMENT>
        <EXTENSION optional="yes">
            <GROUP-INFO xmlns="http://www.software.ibm.com/P3P/editor/extension-1.0.html"
             name="Access log information"/>
        </EXTENSION>

    <!-- Consequence -->
    <CONSEQUENCE>
We maintain standard web logs for web site and system administration and for
research and development. This information is not used for any other purpose, nor
is it shared with outside parties.</CONSEQUENCE>
```

Example 7-1. P3P policy for Sample Example, generated by the IBM P3P Policy Editor (continued)

```
    <!-- Use (purpose) -->
    <PURPOSE><admin/><current/><develop/></PURPOSE>

    <!-- Recipients -->
    <RECIPIENT><ours/></RECIPIENT>

    <!-- Retention -->
    <RETENTION><indefinitely/></RETENTION>

    <!-- Base data schema elements -->
    <DATA-GROUP>
    <DATA ref="#dynamic.clickstream"/>
    <DATA ref="#dynamic.http"/>
    <DATA ref="#dynamic.cookies"><CATEGORIES><navigation/><preference/>
     <state/></CATEGORIES></DATA>
    </DATA-GROUP>
</STATEMENT>

    <!-- Statement for group "Customer data" -->
    <STATEMENT>
        <EXTENSION optional="yes">
            <GROUP-INFO xmlns="http://www.software.ibm.com/P3P/editor/extension-1.0.html"
name="Customer data"/>
        </EXTENSION>

    <!-- Consequence -->
    <CONSEQUENCE>
We collect your contact and billing information so that we can complete your order.
</CONSEQUENCE>

    <!-- Use (purpose) -->
    <PURPOSE><current/><develop/></PURPOSE>

    <!-- Recipients -->
    <RECIPIENT><ours/><delivery/></RECIPIENT>

    <!-- Retention -->
    <RETENTION><indefinitely/></RETENTION>

    <!-- Base data schema elements -->
    <DATA-GROUP>
    <DATA ref="#dynamic.miscdata"><CATEGORIES><physical/></CATEGORIES></DATA>
    <DATA ref="#dynamic.miscdata"><CATEGORIES><online/></CATEGORIES></DATA>
    <DATA ref="#dynamic.miscdata"><CATEGORIES><purchase/></CATEGORIES></DATA>
    </DATA-GROUP>
</STATEMENT>

    <!-- Statement for group "Gift recipient data" -->
    <STATEMENT>
        <EXTENSION optional="yes">
```

Example 7-1. P3P policy for Sample Example, generated by the IBM P3P Policy Editor (continued)

```
            <GROUP-INFO xmlns="http://www.software.ibm.com/P3P/editor/extension-1.0.html"
name="Gift recipient data"/>
        </EXTENSION>

    <!-- Consequence -->
    <CONSEQUENCE>
We collect name and contact information for gift recipients so that we can deliver
their gifts.</CONSEQUENCE>

    <!-- Use (purpose) -->
    <PURPOSE><current/><develop/></PURPOSE>

    <!-- Recipients -->
    <RECIPIENT><ours/><delivery/></RECIPIENT>

    <!-- Retention -->
    <RETENTION><indefinitely/></RETENTION>

    <!-- Base dataschema elements. -->
    <DATA-GROUP>
    <DATA ref="#thirdparty.name"/>
    <DATA ref="#thirdparty.home-info"/>
    <DATA ref="#thirdparty.business-info"/>
    </DATA-GROUP>
</STATEMENT>

    <!-- Statement for group "Registrant data" -->
    <STATEMENT>
        <EXTENSION optional="yes">
            <GROUP-INFO xmlns="http://www.software.ibm.com/P3P/editor/extension-1.0.html"
name="Registrant data"/>
        </EXTENSION>

    <!-- Consequence -->
    <CONSEQUENCE>
We collect registration information so that we can send you catalogs or other
requested information and improve our ewb site.</CONSEQUENCE>

    <!-- Use (purpose) -->
    <PURPOSE><contact required="opt-in"/><current/><develop/></PURPOSE>

    <!-- Recipients -->
    <RECIPIENT><ours/></RECIPIENT>

    <!-- Retention -->
    <RETENTION><indefinitely/></RETENTION>

    <!-- Base data schema elements -->
    <DATA-GROUP>
    <DATA ref="#dynamic.miscdata"><CATEGORIES><physical/></CATEGORIES></DATA>
```

```
        <DATA ref="#dynamic.miscdata"><CATEGORIES><online/></CATEGORIES></DATA>
        <DATA ref="#dynamic.miscdata"><CATEGORIES><demographic/></CATEGORIES></DATA>
        <DATA ref="#dynamic.miscdata"><CATEGORIES><preference/></CATEGORIES></DATA>
        </DATA-GROUP>
</STATEMENT>

        <!-- Statement for group "Email data" -->
        <STATEMENT>
            <EXTENSION optional="yes">
                <GROUP-INFO xmlns="http://www.software.ibm.com/P3P/editor/extension-1.0.html"
name="Email data"/>
            </EXTENSION>

        <!-- Consequence -->
        <CONSEQUENCE>
We use return email addresses to answer the email we receive. Such addresses are
not used for any other purpose and are not share with outside parties.</CONSEQUENCE>

        <!-- Use (purpose) -->
        <PURPOSE><current/></PURPOSE>

        <!-- Recipients -->
        <RECIPIENT><ours/></RECIPIENT>

        <!-- Retention -->
        <RETENTION><indefinitely/></RETENTION>

        <!-- Base data schema elements -->
        <DATA-GROUP>
        <DATA ref="#dynamic.miscdata"><CATEGORIES><content/></CATEGORIES></DATA>
        <DATA ref="#dynamic.miscdata"><CATEGORIES><online/></CATEGORIES></DATA>
        </DATA-GROUP>
</STATEMENT>

<!-- End of policy -->
</POLICY>
</POLICIES>
```

Writing a Compact Policy

Compact policies summarize the P3P policies that apply to cookies. Compact policies are included in P3P HTTP headers, which are discussed in Chapter 8. If you serve more than one cookie with a particular HTTP response, your compact policy must cover all of the cookies served on that response.

The easiest way to write a compact policy is to start with a full policy and run it through a tool such as the IBM P3P Policy Editor that will convert it into a compact policy automatically. You can also create a compact policy manually.

With the Sample Example policy from the previous section loaded into the IBM P3P Policy Editor, select Save Compact Policy As from the File menu. The editor will save the following compact policy:

```
CP="ALL DSP CURa ADMa DEVa CONi OUR DELa IND PHY ONL PUR COM
NAV DEM CNT STA PRE"
```

Optionally, you can prune this compact policy and remove the tokens that do not apply to cookies. However, sites should do this only if they are certain that their cookies cannot be linked to the other data they collect.

To manually convert a full policy to a compact policy, start with a full policy that describes the information practices associated with cookies. Examine the statements and write down all of the corresponding PURPOSE, RECIPIENT, RETENTION, and CATEGORIES fields. Include the required attribute when it appears in any purpose or recipient element. Also write down the access field and the remedy fields (if any). If the policy includes the DISPUTES-GROUP, NON-IDENTIFIABLE, or TEST element, indicate that as well. Remember, you cannot use compact policies if the site's full policy uses mandatory extensions or if the site does not use cookies.

Once you have written down all of this information, look up these fields in Table 7-1 and write down the corresponding compact tokens. Remove any duplicate tokens, and that's your compact policy. If you have more than one instance of a given purpose or recipient with different values of the required attribute, it is a good idea to simplify further by including just one instance with the "worst-case" value for the attribute. For this purpose, consider always worse than opt-out and opt-out worse than opt-in. Thus, if you have <contact required="opt-out"/> and <contact required="opt-in"/>, you can reduce it to <contact required="opt-out"/>.

Note that this process aggregates the statement elements, possibly resulting in less precise information than can be conveyed in a full P3P policy. In some cases, the site might be viewed in a more favorable light if the user reviewed the full policy instead. Depending on the user's preferences, the user agent may or may not have enough information to make a decision about accepting cookies based on examining only the compact policy. If the user agent needs more information, it can fetch the full policy. (IE6 is configured so that all information needed to act on user cookie preference settings can be obtained from compact policies.)

IE6 makes cookie-filtering decisions on the basis of compact policies. Under the default setting, only third-party cookies are subject to possible blocking. However, other cookies may be blocked when users change their cookie settings.

For information on the IE6 cookie settings and what kinds of compact policies cause cookies to be blocked or restricted, see Appendix C. Note that some of the beta releases of IE6 behave slightly differently than what is documented in Appendix C.

Table 7-1. Compact policy tokens

Type of element or attribute	Policy element or attribute	Compact policy token
PURPOSE	\<current/>	CUR
	\<admin/>	ADM
	\<develop/>	DEV
	\<tailoring/>	TAI
	\<pseudo-analysis/>	PSA
	\<pseudo-decision/>	PSD
	\<individual-analysis/>	IVA
	\<individual-decision/>	IVD
	\<contact/>	CON
	\<historical/>	HIS
	\<telemarketing/>	TEL
	\<other-purpose/>	OTP
required	always	a
	opt-in	i
	opt-out	o
RECIPIENT	\<ours/>	OUR
	\<delivery/>	DEL
	\<same/>	SAM
	\<unrelated/>	UNR
	\<public/>	PUB
	\<other-recipient/>	OTR
RETENTION	\<no-retention/>	NOR
	\<stated-purpose/>	STP
	\<legal-requirement/>	LEG
	\<business-practices/>	BUS
	\<indefinitely/>	IND
CATEGORIES	\<physical/>	PHY
	\<online/>	ONL
	\<uniqueid/>	UNI
	\<purchase/>	PUR
	\<financial/>	FIN
	\<computer/>	COM
	\	NAV
	\<interactive/>	INT
	\<demographic/>	DEM
	\<content/>	CNT
	\<state/>	STA
	\<political/>	POL
	\<health/>	HEA
	\<preference/>	PRE
	\<location/>	LOC
	\<government/>	GOV
	\<other-category/>	OTC
NON-IDENTIFIABLE	\<NON-IDENTIFIABLE/>	NID
DISPUTES	\<DISPUTES/>	DSP

Table 7-1. Compact policy tokens (continued)

Type of element or attribute	Policy element or attribute	Compact policy token
ACCESS	<nonident/>	NOI
	<all/>	ALL
	<contact-and-other/>	CAO
	<ident-contact/>	IDC
	<other-ident/>	OTI
	<none/>	NON
REMEDIES	<correct/>	COR
	<money/>	MON
	<law/>	LAW
TEST	<TEST/>	TST

Avoiding Common Pitfalls

I've examined many P3P policies created by early adopters of P3P and have observed a number of common errors. Here are some of the most frequent errors and how you can avoid them:

- Some policies don't mention web logs. However, almost every site keeps web logs. Unless you know for a fact that your site keeps no web logs, make sure you mention them in your P3P policy. Several examples of how to do this are given at the end of Chapter 9.

- Some policies do not disclose all of the data associated with cookies. It is not sufficient to describe only the data stored in a cookie; you must also describe the data linked to the cookie. So, for example, if the cookie contains a unique identifier that is used as a database key, all of the types of information in that database must also be described. You must also be aware of how this data will be used by all of the sites in your domain to which the cookie might be sent.

- Some policies disclose the contact purpose unnecessarily. The contact purpose need be disclosed only if the site may contact visitors for marketing. If the site contacts visitors only in response to their emails or as part of performing the service the visitor requested (unless the requested service is marketing), the contact purpose is not necessary.

- Sites should make sure that if they indicate that opt-in or opt-out choices are available, they disclose an opturi that actually explains how to opt-in or opt-out. I've seen some sites point to a statement that says that it is possible to opt-out but does not provide instructions on how to do it. I've also seen sites that incorrectly write an email address or phone number in the opturi field instead of providing a URL. A mailto URL is also not a valid opturi, as it provides no information about opt-out options.

- Finally, I've seen many sites that have created P3P policies and posted them on their web sites without testing them. Take a careful look at the policy you have created and check to see how one or more P3P user agents interpret it. Make sure the policy that you post says what you intend it to say.

 The W3C has a public mailing list for individuals who have questions about implementing P3P on their web sites. This is a good place to read about how other sites have solved problems they've faced when implementing P3P and to ask any questions you have. To subscribe, email *www-p3p-policy-request@w3.org* with "subscribe" in the subject line. The mailing list archive is available at *http://lists.w3.org/Archives/Public/www-p3p-policy/*.

CHAPTER 8

Creating and Referencing Policy Reference Files

P3P was designed to give webmasters flexibility in determining how to apply P3P policies to their web sites. As discussed in Chapter 5, a site might have one policy that covers the entire site or multiple policies covering different parts of the site. To declare where their policies are located and what parts of the site they cover, P3P-enabled web sites use a special file called a *policy reference file*. The policy reference file acts as an index to the site's P3P policies. Once a user agent has fetched a site's policy reference file, it can use that file to determine the locations of all of the site's policies, until the policy reference file expires. Thus, user agents need not fetch a new policy reference file for every requested resource.

This chapter explains how policy reference files are created and discusses the options for referencing these files on a web site. It also explains the procedures for changing a policy or policy reference file and discusses the details of applying policies to cookies, forms, applets, and other types of content.

Creating a Policy Reference File

Like P3P policies, P3P policy reference files are XML files. These files can be created either by hand or with a P3P policy-generator tool that is also capable of creating policy reference files. If you plan to use a policy-generator tool to create a policy reference file, you may not need to concern yourself with the syntax details explained in this section. However, it is still important for you to understand how policy reference files are used to apply P3P policies to cookies, forms, and other types of objects.

Policy Reference File Syntax Overview

A *policy reference* is used to associate a P3P policy with a set of URLs or cookies. Each policy reference file contains one or more policy references. The policies themselves can also be placed in a policy reference file, or they can be placed in separate files.

Policy reference files are enclosed in META elements. The META element takes an xmlns attribute to indicate the P3P version. Optionally, it can also take an xml:lang attribute to indicate the language of any human-readable fields in the file. The META element contains a POLICY-REFERENCES element that contains all the policy references. Optionally, the META element can also contain extensions as well as a POLICIES element that contains the P3P policies themselves.

The POLICY-REFERENCES element contains an optional EXPIRY element, references to one or more P3P policies, and optionally hints and extensions. Expiry, policy references, and hints are described in this chapter. Extensions are described in Chapter 6.

Example 8-1 is an abbreviated policy reference file containing examples of all of the required and optional elements. The elements must appear in the order shown here.

Example 8-1. Abbreviated policy reference file

```
<META xmlns="http://www.w3.org/2002/01/P3Pv1" xml:lang="en">
  <EXTENSION>
    . . .
  </EXTENSION>
  <POLICY-REFERENCES>
    <EXPIRY max-age="172800"/>
    <POLICY-REF about="#policy1">
      <INCLUDE>/</INCLUDE>
      <INCLUDE>/news/*</INCLUDE>
      <EXCLUDE>/news/top/*</EXCLUDE>
    </POLICY-REF>
    <POLICY-REF about="#policy2">
      <INCLUDE>/news/top/*</INCLUDE>
    </POLICY-REF>
    <POLICY-REF about="/P3P/policies.xml#policy3">
      <INCLUDE>/photos/*</INCLUDE>
      <INCLUDE>/ads/*</INCLUDE>
      <COOKIE-INCLUDE/>
    </POLICY-REF>
    <HINT scope="http://www.example.org" path="/mypolicy/p3.xml" />
    <EXTENSION>
      . . .
    </EXTENSION>
  </POLICY-REFERENCES>
  <POLICIES>
    <POLICY discuri="http://www.example.com/disc1" name="policy1">
      . . .
    </POLICY>
    <POLICY discuri="http://www.example.com/disc2" name="policy2">
      . . .
    </POLICY>
  </POLICIES>
  <EXTENSION>
    . . .
  </EXTENSION>
</META>
```

This example includes three extensions: one at the beginning, one at the end, and one inside the POLICY-REFERENCES element. The POLICY-REFERENCES element also contains the optional EXPIRY element and three POLICY-REF elements. Each of the POLICY-REF elements is used to associate a specific P3P policy with a set of URLs or cookies, using INCLUDE, EXCLUDE, COOKIE-INCLUDE, and COOKIE-EXCLUDE elements. The HINT element indicates the location of a policy reference file for third-party content. This example also includes a POLICIES element that contains two P3P policies. P3P policies can be placed in their own files or in a policy reference file.

Policy and Policy Reference File Lifetime

The EXPIRY element indicates the lifetime of a policy or policy reference file. When a user agent fetches a policy reference file, it can rely on the policy references in that file until the file expires. Thus, if the user requests other pages at the site or returns to the site later, as long as the policy reference file has not expired, the user agent need not fetch it again. Once the policy reference file expires, the next time the user goes to the site, the user agent will generally request the policy reference file again. Likewise, when a user agent fetches a policy file, it need not fetch that file again until it expires. So, for example, if a user agent checks a site's policy and finds that it will expire in three days, the agent need not check the policy again if the user returns to that site in less than three days. After three days have passed, the user agent must recheck the policy the next time the user goes to that site.

Policy files and policy reference files each have their own EXPIRY elements. However, it is not possible to have different lifetimes associated with each policy in a single policy file.

It is important to note that regardless of policy and policy reference file lifetimes, once data is collected under a particular policy, that policy is assumed to apply for as long as the data is retained (unless the data collector has obtained informed consent to change the policy). Thus, the expiration time applies only to the collection of new data. Sites can declare either an absolute or a relative date and time of expiry. Absolute expiry times are stated in Greenwich Mean Time (GMT). Relative expiry times are given in seconds from the time the response was sent from the origin server.* The minimum acceptable expiry time is 86,400 seconds, or 24 hours. A policy reference file that contains no EXPIRY element has a default lifetime of 24 hours.

Policies and policy reference files need not expire at the same time. However, if either the policy or the policy reference file for a particular URL has expired and a user agent is unable to download a nonexpired version of that file, it will assume that the URL is not covered by a P3P policy.

---

* The P3P specification requires user agents to use the Pragma: no-cache HTTP request header when requesting P3P policies and policy reference files, to ensure that they accurately calculate relative expiry times.

Unless a site is phasing out a privacy policy or is concerned about performance issues and wants to reduce the frequency of policy reference file downloads, the default 24-hour EXPIRY value is usually reasonable. (The procedures for phasing out or changing a policy are discussed at the end of this chapter.) If you are using the default, you need not include the EXPIRY element at all, and you won't ever have to worry about your policies or policy reference files expiring. If you want to explicitly set the expiry time in your policy reference file, you must use either a date or max-age attribute (but not both).

Here is an example of an absolute expiry time:

```
<EXPIRY date="Sun, 07 Jan 2008 08:49:37 GMT"/>
```

And here is an example of a relative expiry time (in this case, two days):

```
<EXPIRY max-age="172800"/>
```

 Unless you have a good reason not to, use the default 24-hour expiry time on all of your P3P policies and policy reference files by omitting the EXPIRY element.

Policy References

Each policy reference is contained within a POLICY-REF element. This element takes one attribute, about, and contains a number of other elements. The about attribute indicates the URL of the referenced P3P policy. URLs are interpreted relative to the URL of the policy reference file itself. So, if a policy reference file is in the */w3c/* directory of *http://www.example.com* and the value for the about attribute is policy1.xml, the policy must be located at *http://www.example.com/w3c/policy1.xml*. However, if the value for the about attribute is /policy1.xml, the policy must be located at *http://www.example.com/policy1.xml*. The value of the about attribute can also be a full URL, or a reference to a policy contained inline in the policy reference file. References to inline policies begin with the # character.

Example 8-1, earlier in this chapter, references three policies. The first reference is to *policy1*, a policy that is included inline in this policy reference file. The second reference is to *policy2*, which is also included in this policy reference file. The third reference is to *policy3*, which is located in a separate policy file on the web site.

Associating Policies with Web Site Content

You must explicitly declare the parts of your web site to which your P3P policy (or policies) applies. The P3P specification allows each unique URL to have its own P3P policy. Images, sounds, applets, and other objects embedded in a web site that have their own URLs can also have their own policies. Cookies can also have P3P policies associated with them.

The INCLUDE and EXCLUDE elements are used within a POLICY-REF element to indicate the content to which a particular policy applies. Each INCLUDE element specifies a relative URL or set of relative URLs to which the policy applies. The EXCLUDE element specifies a relative URL or set of relative URLs to which the policy does not apply. These URLs should be excluded from the set defined by any INCLUDE elements that appear within the same POLICY-REF.

All INCLUDE and EXCLUDE URLs must be relative URLs—thus, they must refer only to content on the server that referenced the policy reference file. Usually, this is the server where the policy reference file lives; however, it is possible for a server to reference a policy reference file hosted on a different server. For example, *www.example.com* may serve a P3P header referencing a P3P policy reference file at *http://www.example.net/ p3p.xml*. If this policy reference file includes the line <INCLUDE>/stuff/*</INLCUDE>, it will apply a policy reference to the */stuff* directory on *http://www.example.com*.

The wildcard character * (the asterisk) is used to specify sets of URLs in INCLUDE and EXCLUDE elements. The wildcard can replace any string of zero or more characters.

 The asterisk is a legal character in a URL. Therefore, in a URL that contains an asterisk that is not intended to be a wildcard, you must replace the asterisk with the escape sequence %2A.

Here is an example of a policy reference that applies *policy1* to a site's home page. Notice that this policy applies to only a single page, because no wildcard is used.

```
<POLICY-REF about="#policy1">
  <INCLUDE>/</INCLUDE>
</POLICY-REF>
```

Here is an example that applies *policy2* to the entire site. The wildcard expands the coverage of the policy to the entire site.

```
<POLICY-REF about="#policy2">
  <INCLUDE>/*</INCLUDE>
</POLICY-REF>
```

And here is an example that applies *policy3* to the entire site, except the main home page:

```
<POLICY-REF about="#policy3">
  <INCLUDE>/*</INCLUDE>
  <EXCLUDE>/</EXCLUDE>
</POLICY-REF>
```

Wildcards can appear anywhere in a URL. Here is an example of a policy reference that applies *policy4* to any JPEG or PDF file on the site:

```
<POLICY-REF about="#policy4">
  <INCLUDE>/*.jpg</INCLUDE>
  <INCLUDE>/*.pdf</INCLUDE>
</POLICY-REF>
```

The patterns matched by INCLUDE and EXCLUDE are case-sensitive. If your web site allows files to be requested with either uppercase or lowercase letters interchangeably, you will need to account for this. For example, you might need to include both <INCLUDE>/*.jpg</INCLUDE> and <INCLUDE>/*.JPG</INCLUDE> in your policy reference file (depending on your server, you might also need to account for JpG, jPG, etc.).

Within a given policy reference, all of the INCLUDE elements must appear first, followed by any EXCLUDE elements. A policy reference may also contain additional elements, in the following order: COOKIE-INCLUDE, COOKIE-EXCLUDE, METHOD, and EXTENSION. These elements are described later in this chapter.

P3P user agents process policy references in the order in which they appear. Once a user agent finds a policy reference that applies to a particular URL, it does not examine the other policy references in the file.

Example 8-2 shows a policy reference file with three POLICY-REF elements. Imagine that a user agent was interested in learning what policy applied to the file */special/dogs/labs.html*. The user agent would start by examining the first POLICY-REF element. This element applies *policy-general.xml* to the entire web site, with the exception of the */special/* directory. Because the file in which we are interested is in the excluded directory, the user agent would move on to the next policy reference. This one applies *policy-cats.xml* to all the files in the */special/cats/* directory. The file in which we are interested is not in that directory, so we continue to the third policy reference. This one applies *policy-dogs.xml* to all files in the */special/dogs/* directory, which is where the file in which we are interested is located. If the web site in this example had any other files or directories in the */special/* directory, this policy reference file would not assign any P3P policies to them.

Example 8-2. A policy reference file with INCLUDE and EXCLUDE elements

```
<META xmlns="http://www.w3.org/2002/01/P3Pv1">
  <POLICY-REFERENCES>
    <POLICY-REF about="/P3P/policy-general.xml">
      <INCLUDE>/*</INCLUDE>
      <EXCLUDE>/special/*</EXCLUDE>
      <EXCLUDE>/extra-special/*</EXCLUDE>
    </POLICY-REF>
    <POLICY-REF about="/P3P/policy-cats.xml">
      <INCLUDE>/special/cats/*</INCLUDE>
    </POLICY-REF>
    <POLICY-REF about="/P3P/policy-dogs.xml">
      <INCLUDE>/special/dogs/*</INCLUDE>
    </POLICY-REF>
  </POLICY-REFERENCES>
</META>
```

Associating Policies with Third-Party Content

Some web pages include images, sounds, frames, or other content that is provided by a third party and thus cannot be referenced by a URL relative to that site's policy reference file. Some sites may want to associate their own P3P policies with this "embedded" content. Others may want to associate a P3P policy on the third-party site with this content. However, to prevent malicious sites from making false claims about the privacy policies of other sites, the P3P specification does not allow sites to declare policies for third-party content. P3P does provide a mechanism that sites can use to "hint" at the location of the policy reference file associated with third-party content. P3P user agents will first check the well-known location on the third-party site for the policy reference file, and if no policy reference file can be found (or if the policy reference file does not declare a policy for the content of interest), it will then check the location declared in the relevant hint. If the site does not declare the location of the hinted policy reference files in an HTTP header or LINK tag (discussed later in this chapter), the hint is not valid. Thus, the HINT element is most useful for hinting at where to find policy reference files that are declared using an HTTP header or LINK tag.

A site may include one or more HINT elements in its policy reference file, to hint at the locations of policy reference files on other sites. The HINT element has two attributes, scope and path. The scope attribute describes the URLs to which the hint applies. The path attribute gives the location of the policy reference file on those hosts. The HINT element goes inside the POLICY-REFERENCES element, after any POLICY-REF elements.

The value of the scope attribute must be a URL that does not contain a path, query, or fragment component. Thus, it cannot contain any slashes, other than the double slash before the hostname. It may contain the * wildcard only at the beginning of the hostname. For example, legal values for scope include:

```
http://www.example.com
http://www.example.com:81
http://*.example.com
```

The value of the path attribute is a relative URL that is interpreted relative to the scope attribute. The path attribute must not be an absolute URL.

Here are some examples of hints that a web site might declare:

```
<HINT scope="http://www.example.org" path="/mypolicy/p3p.xml" />
<HINT scope="http://www.example.net:81" path="/w3c/prf.xml" />
<HINT scope="http://*.shop.example.com" path="/w3c/prf.xml" />
```

The first hint states that there is a policy reference file at *http://www.example.org/mypolicy/p3p.xml* that declares policies for *http://www.example.org*. The second hint states that there is a policy reference file at *http://www.example.net:81/w3c/prf.xml* that declares policies for *http://www.example.net:81*. The third hint states that there is a policy reference file in the location */w3c/prf.xml* on every host in the *example.com* domain with a URL of the form *http://*.shop.example.com*.

Associating Policies with Cookies

The COOKIE-INCLUDE and COOKIE-EXCLUDE elements are used to associate P3P policies with cookies. Since cookies are not referenced by URL, a slightly different syntax is used. The COOKIE-INCLUDE and COOKIE-EXCLUDE elements have four attributes: name, value, domain, and path. P3P uses the same definitions for these attributes as are used in the cookie specification,* except that the * wildcard character is also permitted to replace a string of zero or more characters, and the absence of an attribute indicates that any value for that attribute is acceptable. (Thus, setting an attribute value to * is equivalent to omitting the attribute.) Here are the important things to know about each attribute:

- The name attribute is a string that matches the cookie's Name attribute in an HTTP Set-Cookie or Set-Cookie2 response header.

- The value attribute is a string that matches the cookie's Value attribute in an HTTP Set-Cookie or Set-Cookie2 response header.

- The domain attribute is a string that matches the cookie's Domain value in an HTTP Set-Cookie or Set-Cookie2 response header. By setting the value of the domain attribute in a COOKIE-INCLUDE to ".", you can match cookies that are sent back only to the host that set them (indicated by omitting the domain attribute from the Set-Cookie or Set-Cookie2 response header).

  Cookie domain values begin with the dot character (.) and indicate that the cookie should be sent back to any host whose name follows a set of domain-matching rules. As a result of these rules, if the domain is .foo.com, the cookie will be sent back to any host within the *foo.com* domain.

  Note that sites declare cookie policies only for cookies that are set or sent back to that site. User agents will ignore COOKIE-INCLUDE elements that declare policies for other cookies.

- The path attribute is a string that matches the cookie's PATH attribute in an HTTP Set-Cookie or Set-Cookie2 response header. Cookies that omit the PATH attribute have the default path of the request URL that generated the response. The path attribute of a COOKIE-INCLUDE is matched against this default value if a cookie omits the path attribute.

Here is an example policy reference that associates *policy5* with every cookie that is sent back only to the site that set it:

```
<POLICY-REF about="#policy5">
  <COOKIE-INCLUDE domain="." />
</POLICY-REF>
```

---

* See "HTTP State Management Mechanism," D. Kristol and L. Montulli, (Request for Comments 2965, October 2000), *http://www.ietf.org/rfc/rfc2965.txt.*

And here is an example policy reference that associates *policy6* with cookies in the *example.com* domain that include the word "nice" in their names and are associated with resources in the */goodstuff* directory:

```
<POLICY-REF about="#policy6">
  <COOKIE-INCLUDE name="*nice*"
  domain=".example.com" path="/goodstuff" />
</POLICY-REF>
```

> Policies associated with cookies must cover all data that is stored in or linked via those cookies. They must also reference all purposes associated with data stored in or enabled by the cookies. Thus, it is not sufficient to create a policy for a cookie that describes only the data that is actually stored in the cookie if the cookie is used as a mechanism to link together other data. For example, if a cookie is used to identify a registered user to a site, all data associated with that user's record and all purposes for which that record may be used must be disclosed in the policy for that cookie.

Cookie policies can sometimes be a little confusing, as the scope of a cookie policy is not simply a URL or set of URLs. Cookies can be set on one host and sent back to a different host in the domain which may use them for a different purpose than the host that set them. The host setting a cookie (and declaring its policy) must make sure that the policy for the cookie covers all of the uses that any host in the domain might have for that cookie. In addition, sites need to be careful that they don't set multiple conflicting policies for the same cookie. A domain-level cookie—for example, one with domain=".example.com"—can be sent back to any host in the *example.com* domain. Thus, any site in the domain that has a <COOKIE-INCLUDE domain=".example.com" /> in its policy reference file would apply a policy to that cookie. For sites that apply the same policy to every cookie they set, this is not a problem. But sites that want to apply different policies depending on how each cookie is used must be very careful, especially if they use domain-level cookies.

Also note that each cookie has its own expiration date, which may be different from the expiration date associated with the corresponding policy or policy reference file. If a cookie's P3P policy expires before the cookie itself expires, user agents may attempt to fetch a new policy after the original one expires. If a compact policy is set with a cookie, the policy associated with the cookie must have a lifetime as long as the cookie itself.

Distinguishing HTTP Methods

The METHOD element is used in the rare cases where it is necessary to restrict the application of a policy reference to HTTP requests that use a particular method. HTTP methods are used to inform an HTTP server as to the kind of response that is requested. The HTTP/1.1 specification defines the following methods: OPTIONS, GET, HEAD, POST, PUT, DELETE, TRACE, and CONNECT. Additional methods may also be defined. Most web pages are requested using the GET method. Forms are often submitted using the POST method.

By default, a P3P policy reference applies to requests for a resource regardless of HTTP method used. However, some web sites may want to apply different policies depending on the method used. For example, a site might log more information for DELETE requests than for GET requests. Sites can restrict the application of a policy reference to a particular HTTP method by including a METHOD tag in a policy reference, and they can include multiple METHOD tags to indicate that a policy reference applies to multiple methods.

Here is an example policy reference that applies only when the GET and HEAD methods are used:

```
<POLICY-REF about="#policy8">
  <INCLUDE>/catalog/*</INCLUDE>
  <METHOD>GET</METHOD>
  <METHOD>HEAD</METHOD>
</POLICY-REF>
```

Most sites will probably not have any need to use the METHOD element.

Embedded Content, Forms, and Applets

Anything that can be referenced with a URL can have a P3P policy. Thus, images, sound files, HTML forms, and applets can all have their own P3P policies, which are not necessarily the same policies that apply to the HTML pages in which they are embedded.

HTML forms can be a little tricky, because they typically have at least two URLs. People usually think of the form's URL as the URL of the HTML page that contains the form fields where people type in information. However, the form also has an *action* URL, which is the URL that gets invoked when the form is submitted (usually by clicking a submit button). Sometimes action URLs are on completely different web sites from the form fields. The P3P policy that covers the HTML page containing the form usually needs to cover only clickstream data. However, the P3P policy that covers the action URL must cover whatever data might be typed into the form and submitted.

When an HTML page contains an applet or JavaScript code, things can get even more complicated. To what extent must the P3P policy for the HTML page cover these embedded pieces of code? What about downloadable applications that have their own URLs? In general, the policy for a URL must cover actions that the user agent is expected to perform as a result of requesting that URL. These are actions that could take place without the user explicitly invoking them. Here are some examples:

- An HTML page includes JavaScript code that tracks how long the page is displayed and whether the user has moved the mouse over a certain object on the page. When the user goes to another page, the JavaScript code sends the information back to the server. Because this information transfer takes place automatically, without any explicit action from the user, it must be covered by the P3P policy that is applied to the HTML page.

- Another HTML page includes JavaScript code that does the same thing as the last example, except that information is not sent back to the server unless the user clicks a submit button. In this case, the P3P policy that is applied to the HTML page need not cover the submitted data. However, the URL to which the data is submitted should have a P3P policy that covers this data.

- An HTML page contains a link to download an electronic mail program. After users click on the link and download the program, they must run an installation program, start the email program, and use it before any data other than clickstream data gets transferred. The data transfers that result from using the email program need not be covered by the policy for the download URL or the HTML page in which the link is embedded.

Some web sites pass on information to advertising networks or other third parties by embedding this information in the URLs for embedded images. Thus, when the user's browser requests the image, the information is automatically transferred to the third party. A variation on this is a site that automatically redirects users to a third-party site and passes information in the redirect URL. In both of these cases, the first site must disclose this data transfer in its P3P policy. P3P policies can be applied to URLs that result in a redirect message.

Multiple Languages

Web sites that offer content in multiple languages may want to offer their P3P policies in multiple languages as well. The machine-readable XML syntax is the same, regardless of language. However, sites may want to offer human-readable fields, such as CONSEQUENCE, in a language appropriate to the user.

Sites that separate their content into directories according to language can apply a different policy to each directory. For example, a site that offers content in French and English might put its English content in a /en directory and its French content in a /fr directory. It might then have a policy reference file that declares policies as follows:

```
<POLICY-REFERENCES>
  <POLICY-REF about="/P3P/policy-en.xml">
    <INCLUDE>/en/*</INCLUDE>
  </POLICY-REF>
  <POLICY-REF about="/P3P/policy-fr.xml">
    <INCLUDE>/fr/*</INCLUDE>
  </POLICY-REF>
</POLICY-REFERENCES>
```

Alternatively, sites can use the HTTP `Accept-Language` header to determine which language each user prefers and deliver an appropriate policy. Sites that use this mechanism can have multiple policies referenced by the same URL that are identical except for the language of their human-readable elements. These sites should use the HTTP `Content-Language` header to indicate which language has been used for each policy.

Regardless of how many languages a site uses, it can also include an `xml:lang` attribute in `POLICY`, `POLICIES`, `META`, and `DATASCHEMA` elements to indicate the language of human-readable fields. For example, to indicate an English policy, a site would include `xml:lang="en"`; to indicate a French policy, it would include `xml:lang="fr"`.

 For more information on language tags, see *http://www.w3.org/ International/O-HTML-tags.html*.

Referencing a Policy Reference File

Policy reference files tell user agents where to find P3P policies. But how do user agents know where to find the policy reference file itself? P3P provides three mechanisms that sites can use to help user agents find their policy reference files: the well-known location, the P3P HTTP header, and the P3P HTML `LINK` tag. Most sites use the well-known location mechanism; however, under some circumstances, the other mechanisms may be preferable for a particular site.

Sites can use more than one mechanism, but they must be careful not to declare conflicting policies. The P3P 1.0 specification specifies that the well-known location mechanism always takes precedence over the other mechanisms. However, if user agents find conflicting policies for a particular page due to use of multiple mechanisms other than the well-known location, they may assume that any of the policies apply.

The Well-Known Location

Sites use the well-known location mechanism by simply placing their policy reference files at the location */w3c/p3p.xml*. User agents trying to locate a site's policy reference file will first make an HTTP GET request for this special file. So, for example, a user agent looking for a policy reference file on *http://www.example.com* would request *http://www.example.com/w3c/p3p.xml*.

The well-known location method is easy for most web sites to administer—it doesn't require any special server configuration, and it requires the creation of only one file. It also enables user agents to locate policy reference files and policies prior to requesting any content (in the interest of improving performance, some user agents may make requests for policy reference files and content in parallel, but the well-known location gives them the option of waiting until a policy is located and evaluated before requesting content).

The well-known location method does have some drawbacks, however. For sites that have a large number of policies (hundreds or thousands), a single policy reference file at the well-known location will be very big and thus will take a relatively long time to transmit. This is a problem that a site that hosts content for multiple companies might have—for example, an online shopping mall or a content-distribution network. In addition, for sites that are run by people who have access to only certain directories on a web server, it may not be possible to create a file at the well-known location. The HTTP header and HTML LINK tag mechanisms, respectively, can address these two problems.

Some URLs end with a colon followed by a number, indicating that they should be fetched from a specific *port* indicated by that number. P3P considers different ports on a single host to be different sites. Thus, requests for a policy reference file at the well-known location on one port do not provide information about the policy that applies to URLs on the same host but at a different port. For example, a request to *http://www.example.com/w3c/p3p.xml:80* would not give any information about policies that apply to *http://www.example.com/:443*. The default HTTP port is port 80, while the default SSL port is port 443. Thus, separate policy reference files may be needed for SSL (secure) requests and for regular requests on the same server.[*]

HTTP Headers

In a typical HTTP request, a web client sends a web server one or more HTTP headers asking for a web page or other information. The web server responds with a code to indicate a successful response or an error, information about the type of information being returned, and, if possible, the requested information. Thus, a successful request for the web page *http://www.example.com/sample.html* might look this:

```
GET sample.html HTTP/1.1
Host: www.example.com
. . .
```

And the server response might look like this:

```
HTTP/1.1 200 OK
Content-Type: text/html
. . .
CONTENT OF SAMPLE.HTML
```

---

[*] In some cases, a site may use the same policy reference file for content at different ports. For example, if a site serves the same content in response to requests to multiple ports and applies the same policies to this content regardless of port, a single policy reference file would be appropriate.

The P3P specification defines a new HTTP header that can be added to any standard HTTP request. Web sites that want to associate a P3P policy reference file with content can configure their servers to insert this HTTP header into all of their responses. Optionally, they can include different policy references in response to different requests. The P3P HTTP header has the following format:

```
P3P: policyref="URL"
```

The P3P header can also include a compact policy instead of, or in addition to, a policy reference. A P3P header that includes both a policy reference and a compact policy has the following format:

```
P3P: policyref="URL", CP="COMPACT POLICY TOKENS"
```

If Example.com uses the P3P header instead of the well-known location, an interaction might begin something like this:

Client request:

```
GET sample.html HTTP/1.1
Host: www.example.com
. . .
```

Server response:

```
HTTP/1.1 200 OK
P3P: policyref="http://www.example.com/prf.xml",
CP="NON DSP CUR ADM DEV PSD IVDo OUR IND PHY PRE NAV UNI"
Content-Type: text/html
. . .
CONTENT OF SAMPLE.HTML
```

Client request:

```
GET prf.xml HTTP/1.1
Host: www.example.com
. . .
```

Server response:

```
HTTP/1.1 200 OK
P3P: policyref="http://www.example.com/prf.xml"
Content-Type: text/html
. . .
CONTENT OF POLICY REFERENCE FILE
```

For detailed instructions on how to configure several popular web servers to add the P3P header, see Appendix B.

If you are using scripts to generate content or set cookies, you may be able to have your scripts insert P3P headers directly, without changing your server configuration. To do this, you need to change the part of the script that outputs the HTTP header to add a statement that prints the P3P header.

Depending on what server you use, you may also be able to issue P3P headers by inserting an HTML META element into your HTML content, with the http-equiv attribute set to P3P and the content attribute set to the P3P header you want issued. Here is an example of such a META element:

```
<META http-equiv="P3P"
content='CP="NON DSP ADM DEV PSD CUSo OUR IND STP PRE NAV UNI"'>
```

Some servers look for http-equiv and generate headers accordingly. However, if your server does not do this, you won't get a P3P header. Make sure you test this feature on your server before relying on it.

Testing Headers

If you use P3P HTTP headers to reference your policy reference file or to provide a compact policy, it is important that you test your site to make sure the headers are actually served on the pages where you are expecting them.

The W3C P3P validator's integrated testing feature will help you test your headers. Step 2 of the validator's report will indicate whether a policy reference file can be retrieved using the header method. It will also report any compact policies it discovers.

Make sure you use the validator to test multiple URLs on your site—when servers are not configured properly, they sometimes include the P3P headers for some URLs but not others. (If you test your site only with a user agent, you may not be able to determine whether a header has been omitted from some URLs, as user agents may cache policy reference files. If you test a URL with a P3P header before testing a URL with the header omitted, the user agent may apply the cached policy reference file to the second URL if it contains a valid policy reference for that URL.)

If you suspect a problem with your header configuration and need more information to track it down, click on the "HTTP headers" link in step 2 of the validator's report. This link will list all of the headers that your server is returning.

If your site includes redirects, tracking down header problems may be more complicated. The GNU *wget* utility is a useful tool for locating header problems (it's useful for a lot of other things, too!). It is available as a free download from *http://www.gnu.org/software/wget/*. To see all of the headers that are sent to your client when you request a URL—including all redirects—use the command wget -S URL.

A similar utility, called cURL, is available as a free download from *http://curl.haxx.se* and is included in some Linux and BSD distributions.

Embedded Link Tags

A simple way to associate a P3P policy with an HTML web page is to embed a special HTML tag called a LINK tag in the HTML code for that page. Using this method requires no changes to web server configuration. Thus, it is useful for people that use space on servers over which they don't have administrative control. If this method is used, all HTML pages on a site that are covered by a P3P policy have to be modified to include the LINK tag. Using this method, a P3P policy cannot be associated with non-HTML content—such as images, audio files, or PDF documents—unless a user agent fetches this content after first fetching an HTML file (the policy reference file linked from the HTML file can declare policies for the entire site).

Sites that want to associate their content with a policy reference file using the LINK tag must embed the tag in the HEAD area of each HTML document. The LINK tag takes the following form:

```
<LINK rel="P3Pv1" href="URL">
```

where URL indicates the location of the P3P policy reference file. Thus, if Example.com maintains a P3P policy reference file at *http://www.example.com/p3p-prf.xml*, they might post the following web page:

```
<HTML>
<HEAD>
  <LINK rel="P3Pv1" href="http://www.example.com/p3p-prf.xml">
  <TITLE>Sample Page</TITLE>
</HEAD>
<BODY>
<P>This is a sample page.</P>
</BODY>
</HTML>
```

The LINK tag may also be embedded in XHTML documents.

Avoiding Policy Reference Conflicts

With only one exception, an unexpired policy reference in a policy reference file is considered valid, regardless of which of the above methods are used to discover the policy reference file. The one exception is that policy reference files found at the well-known location always take precedence over policy reference files found through other means. Here are the ways that a user agent might discover a policy reference file that contains a policy reference for a particular resource:

- At the well-known location
- Referenced by an HTTP header returned with the requested resource
- Referenced by a LINK element embedded in the requested resource
- Referenced by an HTTP header returned with a previously requested resource on the same host
- Referenced by a LINK element embedded in a previously requested resource on the same host

User agents may also discover policy reference files using HINT elements from previously fetched policy reference files. However, these hints are valid only if the hinted policy reference file is also referenced using one of the other mechanisms.

In addition, policy references for cookies can be found in a policy reference file referenced in any of these ways on any host that sets the cookie or to which the cookie can be replayed.

Thus, sites that use mechanisms other than the well-known location to reference their policy reference files risk inadvertently associating multiple policies with the same URL or cookie. Unless one of these files is at the well-known location, user agents may consider any or all of them to be valid. Because it is generally not possible for a site to simultaneously honor multiple policies, and because sites have no way of knowing which policy a particular user agent is considering valid, sites should try to avoid this situation. To prevent policy conflicts, sites should set up administrative procedures that limit the number of people who are permitted to post P3P policies and policy reference files. In addition, sites can have special directories on each host in their domains where all P3P policies and policy reference files are stored. Site administrators should write their policy reference files so that they cover only URLs and cookies under their administrative control.

P3P Policies in Policy Reference Files

Some sites may want to include their P3P policies in a policy reference file. This reduces the number of round trips required for a user agent to locate and fetch a P3P policy. However, a combination file may be more difficult for distributed web sites to maintain, and if a site has a large number of policies, putting them all in a single policy reference file may result in a very large file.

To include a policy in a policy reference file, simply add a POLICIES element after the POLICY-REFERENCES element in the policy reference file. Then include one or more POLICY elements within the POLICIES element, as shown in Example 8-3. Each policy must have a name attribute that is unique to that policy reference file. Note that the POLICIES element should not have xmlns attributes when included in a policy reference file, as it inherits the xmlns attribute from the META element in which it is contained.

Example 8-3. An abbreviated policy reference file containing policies

```
<META xmlns="http://www.w3.org/2002/01/P3Pv1" xml:lang="en">
  <POLICY-REFERENCES>
    <EXPIRY max-age="172800"/>
    <POLICY-REF about="#policy1">
      <INCLUDE>/text/*</INCLUDE>
    </POLICY-REF>
    <POLICY-REF about="#policy2">
      <INCLUDE>/graphics/*</INCLUDE>
    </POLICY-REF>
  </POLICY-REFERENCES>
  <POLICIES>
    <EXPIRY max-age="172800"/>
    <POLICY discuri="http://www.example.com/disc1" name="policy1">
      . . .
    </POLICY>
    <POLICY discuri="http://www.example.com/disc2" name="policy2">
      . . .
```

Example 8-3. An abbreviated policy reference file containing policies (continued)

```
    </POLICY>
  </POLICIES>
</META>
```

Changing Your P3P Policy
or Policy Reference File

From time to time, web sites may need to change the content or coverage of their privacy policies. This will probably require changes to P3P policies or policy reference files. While these changes can be implemented technically by simply replacing these files with new files, web sites should be careful that the changes do not violate commitments made in the old files. In particular, they should be cautious about how they handle data collected under the old policy, and they should be careful to abide by the old policy for as long as a user agent that fetched that policy might believe that the old policy is in effect.

When a site makes a statement in a P3P policy about how it will use data, that assertion is not time-limited. While the site may not agree to apply the policy to new data collected after the policy expires, it must agree to continue applying the policy to data collected when that policy was in effect or to get informed consent to do otherwise. Thus, the site cannot retroactively change the policy that applies to data without consent. So, for example, if a site collects data with the promise not to share it with other companies, the site cannot later decide to share that data unless it first notifies the individuals about whom it has data and asks them for permission to share their data. In some cases, the company may annotate its database as to which users have given permission for sharing and which have not. In other cases, the company may remove from its database altogether those users who have not given permission.

The EXPIRY element of a policy or policy reference file indicates a period of time during which a user agent can safely assume that the policy or policy reference file has not changed. Thus, if a user agent fetches a policy on May 1 with an expiry time of five days, the user agent need not refetch the policy if the user returns to the site on May 3. If a site uses an absolute expiry time, once that time is reached, it is a simple matter of posting a new policy or policy reference file. However, if a site uses a relative expiry time (as most sites do), changing a policy or policy reference file may be a two-step process. Once the site has determined when it wants the new policy or policy reference file to go into effect, it should change the relative expiry time to an absolute time corresponding to when the change becomes effective. Then, at the expiry time, the site should post the new policy or policy reference file. The new file might once again use a relative expiry.

If the new policy or policy reference file is compatible with the old one, such that a user agent that is relying on the old file will not be misled about the site's current practices, the site can simply update the file without worrying about the expiry time.

For example, if policy coverage is extended to areas of the site not previously covered by any policy, the new policy reference file is considered compatible with the old one. Likewise, if the new policy is more protective of user data than the old one, the policies are considered compatible.

Even if new and old policies are not compatible, sites can choose to ignore expiry considerations and instead delay implementing changes described in the new policy. So, for example, if the old policy commits to not sharing data with other companies, and the new policy declares that data can be shared, a site that uses a two-week expiry period might post a new policy but wait more than two weeks before sharing data. Any data collected during the first two weeks that the new policy is posted would be treated as if it were collected under the old policy. For sites that use the default one-day expiry period or short relative expiry periods, this is the easiest and most practical way to proceed.

Avoiding Common Pitfalls

I've discovered many early P3P-enabled web sites that did not get their policy reference files quite right. Here are some of the most frequent errors and how you can avoid them:

- One of the most common errors I have seen is a site that includes the line `<INCLUDE>/</INCLUDE>` in its policy reference file when it wants to apply a policy to the entire site. This statement applies the policy only to the home page. The correct way to apply a policy to an entire site is with `<INCLUDE>/*</INCLUDE>`. I have also seen sites that use a \ character instead of a / character inside the INCLUDE element. The \ character is incorrect.

- It is easy to get confused about the absolute URL to which a relative URL is relative. Relative URLs in the about attribute are evaluated relative to the policy reference file (which is often in the /w3c directory). Relative URLs in INCLUDE and EXCLUDE elements are evaluated relative to the root of the host to which they are applied. To avoid some of this confusion, you can always begin your relative URLs with a / character, to indicate that they are relative to the root of the host to which they are applied.

- Don't forget to include the name of the policy in the about attribute. The policy name is in the name attribute of the POLICY element. Add a pound sign (#) to the end of the URL for the policy file, then add the policy name. Thus, if a policy named "policy" was found in a file at *http://www.example.com/w3c/policyfile.xml*, the about attribute would have the value *http://www.example.com/w3c/policyfile. xml#policy*. URLs cannot contain spaces unless they are properly escaped, so do not put a space in your policy name.

- If you want to apply your policy to cookies on your site, don't forget your COOKIE-INCLUDE elements. P3P user agents will not apply any policy to your cookies unless you have COOKIE-INCLUDE elements.

- Don't put your policies and policy reference files on parts of your web site that are password-protected or require authentication—P3P user agents usually cannot authenticate themselves and thus will not be able to fetch these files automatically. If you have a password-protected site that you want to P3P-enable, it is best to put your P3P files outside the password-protected area.

- If you have a secure server addressed with a URL like *https://www.example.com/* and you are using the well-known location, make sure that a request to *https://www.example.com/w3c/p3p.xml* will return your policy reference file. If the policy reference file is not accessible with an *https* request, P3P user agents won't be able to find it.

- If you are using the HTTP header method or compact policies, make sure you test your site to make sure your server is actually serving the necessary headers for all the URLs that are supposed to have them (see the sidebar "Testing Headers"). If your site uses CGI scripts, make sure that the headers are served on the script-generated pages, too. And if you set cookies when sending HTTP redirect responses, make sure that the headers are served with the redirect responses.

CHAPTER 9

Data Schemas

P3P provides a variety of ways for describing the data that web sites collect. Data elements can be described by their name, their category, their structure, and the data set to which they belong. In this chapter, I discuss each of these ways of describing data elements and introduce all of the elements of the P3P Base Data Schema. I also explain how to create your own data schemas.

If you plan to use a P3P editor to help you P3P-enable a web site and you aren't planning on creating your own data schema, it is not essential that you understand most of the material in this chapter. However, the tables and the definitions of the P3P Base Data Schema elements may serve as a useful reference.

Sets, Elements, and Structures

A P3P data schema is used to define data elements that may be referenced in P3P policies. The P3P specification includes the P3P Base Data Schema, a standard set of data elements that all P3P implementations should know about. In addition, the P3P extension mechanism may be used to define a new data schema. Other data schema languages exist (for example, XML Schema, which uses an XML-based syntax), but P3P uses its own schema language, which was developed prior to the standardization of XML Schema.

A P3P data schema is encoded either using an XML DATASCHEMA element in a stand-alone XML file or within a POLICIES element in a policy or a policy reference file.

Data schemas use the DATA-DEF element to define *data elements* and *data sets*. Data elements are individual pieces of data, such as first name and home postal code. Data sets are groups of data that contain multiple data elements, and sometimes other data sets as well. For example, the home postal address data set contains data elements for street address, city, state, country, and postal code. In P3P policies, the DATA element is used to refer to both data elements and data sets that are collected by a web site. A reference to a data set is an indication that a site may collect all of the elements in that set.

Data schemas use the DATA-STRUCT element to define *data structures*. Data structures allow data set "templates" to be created that can be reused with multiple data sets. For example, a postal address data structure can be used to describe both the home postal address data set and the business postal address data set. Data structures are referenced only in data schemas—a web site cannot reference a data structure from a P3P policy.

Fixed and Variable Categories

Every data element can be described by one or more *data categories*. Most data elements are defined in a data schema as belonging to a specific *fixed* data category indicated by the data schema. Whenever these elements are referenced in a P3P policy, their data categories are implied. Web sites cannot override the predefined data categories. However, some data elements are defined in a data schema as *variable* elements. These elements do not have predefined data categories. Web sites must declare a data category each time they reference a variable data element.

Data structures can also have either fixed or variable categories. If a data structure has a fixed data category, data elements described by that structure inherit that structure's category. If the structure has a variable category, data elements that use that structure can be defined as belonging to any fixed category, or they may be defined as variable-category.

P3P Base Data Schema

The P3P base data schema contains a common set of data elements, sets, and structures about which all P3P implementations must be aware. The base data schema includes a variety of structures on which the base data elements are defined. These structures can also be reused when defining new data schemas.

I describe the data elements and structures of the base data schema in the following sections. Each element and structure is defined with a name, a category, a structure, and a short display name (a short text string that can be displayed to a user to describe a data element). I use an asterisk to indicate variable category elements and types.

The Base Data Structures

This section introduces the structures defined in the base data schema.

Dates

The date structure, shown in Table 9-1, specifies a date and all of its parts. The date structure and its substructures are defined as variable-category. This allows them to inherit the category of the data element to which they are applied; for example, a birthday data element might be in the demographic and socioeconomic data category, while a credit card expiration date might be in the purchase information category. Note that the date structure contains two substructures, ymd and hms. This allows for easy reference to all date information (date.ymd) or to all time information (date.hms) without requiring that date and time information be referenced together.

Table 9-1. The date structure

date	Category	Structure	Short display name
ymd.year	*	*unstructured*	year
ymd.month	*	*unstructured*	month
ymd.day	*	*unstructured*	day
hms.hour	*	*unstructured*	hour
hms.minute	*	*unstructured*	minute
hms.second	*	*unstructured*	second
fractionsecond	*	*unstructured*	fraction of second
timezone	*	*unstructured*	time zone

Names

The personname structure, shown in Table 9-2, specifies information about a person's name.

Table 9-2. The personname structure

personname	Category	Structure	Short display name
prefix	demograph	*unstructured*	name prefix
given	physical	*unstructured*	given name (first name)
family	physical	*unstructured*	family name (last name)
middle	physical	*unstructured*	middle name
suffix	demograph	*unstructured*	name suffix
nickname	demograph	*unstructured*	nickname

Certificates

The certificate structure, shown in Table 9-3, specifies identity certificates (for example, X.509).

Table 9-3. The certificate structure

certificate	Category	Structure	Short display name
key	uniqueid	*unstructured*	certificate key
format	uniqueid	*unstructured*	certificate format

Login information

The `login` structure, shown in Table 9-4, specifies login information for computer systems and web sites that require authentication.

Table 9-4. The login structure

login	Category	Structure	Short display name
id	uniqueid	*unstructured*	login id
password	uniqueid	*unstructured*	password

Telephone numbers

The `telephonenum` structure, shown in Table 9-5, specifies the parts of a telephone number.

Table 9-5. The telephonenum structure

telephonenum	Category	Structure	Short display name
intcode	physical	*unstructured*	international telephone code
loccode	physical	*unstructured*	local telephone area code
number	physical	*unstructured*	telephone number
ext	physical	*unstructured*	telephone extension
comment	physical	*unstructured*	telephone optional comments

Contact information

The `contact` structure, shown in Table 9-6, specifies contact information. Each of the substructures of `contact` can be used separately to specify postal, telecommunications, or online information.

Table 9-6. The contact structure

contact	Category	Structure	Short display name
postal	physical, demograph	postal	postal address information
telecom	physical	telecom	telecommunications information
online	online	online	online address information

Postal mailing addresses

The `postal` structure, shown in Table 9-7, specifies the parts of a postal mailing address.

Table 9-7. The postal structure

postal	Category	Structure	Short display name
name	physical, demograph	personname	name
street	physical	*unstructured*	street address

Table 9-7. The postal structure (continued)

postal	Category	Structure	Short display name
city	demograph	*unstructured*	city
stateprov	demograph	*unstructured*	state or province
postalcode	demograph	*unstructured*	postal code
country	demograph	*unstructured*	country name
organization	demograph	*unstructured*	organization name

Telecommunication numbers

The telecom structure, shown in Table 9-8, specifies a set of telecommunications numbers.

Table 9-8. The telecom structure

telecom	Category	Structure	Short display name
telephone	physical	telephonenum	telephone number
fax	physical	telephonenum	fax number
mobile	physical	telephonenum	mobile telephone number
pager	physical	telephonenum	pager number

Online addresses

The online structure, shown in Table 9-9, specifies a set of online addresses.

Table 9-9. The online structure

online	Category	Type	Short display name
email	online	*unstructured*	email address
uri	online	*unstructured*	home page address

URIs

The uri structure, shown in Table 9-10, specifies a URI composed of an authority, a stem, and a querystring. The authority is the part of the URI that includes the name of the computer being accessed. The stem is the portion of the URI after the authority, up to and including the first "?" character in the URI. The querystring is the part of the URI after the first "?". For URIs that do not contain a "?", the stem is the entire URI and the querystring is empty. So, a typical URI might take the form *http://authority/stem?querystring*. (Remember, for our purposes, a URI is usually a URL.)

Table 9-10. The uri structure

uri	Category	Type	Short display name
authority	*	*unstructured*	URI authority
stem	*	*unstructured*	URI stem
querystring	*	*unstructured*	query-string portion of URI

IP addresses

The `ipaddr` structure, shown in Table 9-11, specifies an IP address. Some web sites use a reduced form of a visitor's IP address rather than the entire address. Storing only a subset of the address information gives visitors to the site some degree of anonymity. While these "stripped" IP addresses or hostnames may not be impossible to associate with individual users, they are significantly more difficult to associate than full IP addresses and hostnames. Therefore, the P3P specification allows sites to indicate whether they collect full or partial hostnames and IP addresses.

The `hostname` element represents either a simple hostname or a full hostname, including the domain name. The `partialhostname` element represents the information of a fully-qualified hostname that has had at least the host portion removed from the hostname. For example, *research.att.com* would be a `hostname`, and *att.com* would be a `partialhostname`.

The `fullip` element represents the information of a full IP Version 4 or IP Version 6 address. The `partialip` element represents an IP Version 4 address that has had at least the last seven bits of information removed. This removal must be done by replacing those bits with a fixed pattern for all visitors (for example, all 0s or all 1s).

Table 9-11. The ipaddr structure

ipaddr	Category	Type	Short display name
hostname	computer	*unstructured*	complete host and domain name
partialhostname	computer	*unstructured*	partial hostname
fullip	computer	*unstructured*	full ip address
partialip	computer	*unstructured*	partial ip address

Access log information

The `loginfo` structure, shown in Table 9-12, represents information typically stored in web server access logs. The requested resource in an HTTP request is captured by the `uri` field. The time at which the server processes the request is represented by the `timestamp` field. Server implementations are free to define this field as the time the request was received, the time the server began sending the response, the time the server finished sending the response, or some other convenient representation of the time the request was processed. The `other` data fields represent other information commonly stored in web server access logs. `other.httpmethod` is the HTTP method (e.g., GET, POST) in the client's request. other.bytes indicates the number of bytes in the response body sent by the server. other.statuscode is the HTTP status code on the request (for example, 200 for a successful page load or 404 for a page not found).

Table 9-12. The loginfo structure

loginfo	Category	Type	Short display name
uri	navigation	uri	URI of requested resource
timestamp	navigation	date	request timestamp
clientip	computer	ipaddr	client's IP address or hostname
other.httpmethod	navigation	*unstructured*	HTTP request method
other.bytes	navigation	*unstructured*	data bytes in response
other.statuscode	navigation	*unstructured*	response status code

Other HTTP protocol information

The httpinfo structure, shown in Table 9-13, specifies information carried by the HTTP protocol that is not generally included in server access logs (but is often logged separately). The useragent field represents the information in the HTTP User-Agent header and all HTTP Accept headers. This information includes information about the type and version of the user's web browser, the types of files the user's browser is able to process, and the language the user prefers. The referer field represents the HTTP Referer header, which gives information about the previous page visited by the user. Note that this field name is misspelled in the same way as the corresponding HTTP header.

Table 9-13. The httpinfo structure

httpinfo	Category	Type	Short display name
referer	navigation	uri	last URI requested by the user
useragent	computer	*unstructured*	user agent information

The user Data Set

The user data set, shown in Table 9-14, includes general information about a user. This set includes specific data elements (such as user.gender) as well as other data sets (such as user.name). When all of the sets are expanded, the complete user data set actually includes 112 elements, which are enumerated in Table 9-15.

Table 9-14. The user data set

user	Category	Structure	Short display name
name	physical, demograph	personname	user's name
bdate	physical	date	user's birth date

Table 9-14. The user data set (continued)

user	Category	Structure	Short display name
cert	uniqueid	certificate	user's identity certificate key
gender	demograph	*unstructured*	user's gender
employer	demograph	*unstructured*	user's employer
department	demograph	*unstructured*	department or division of organization where user is employed
jobtitle	demograph	*unstructured*	user's job title
home-info	physical, online, demograph	contact	user's home contact information
business-info	physical, online, demograph	contact	user's business contact information
login	uniqueid	login	user's login information

Web sites may disclose that they collect any of the individual elements in the user data set. However, they may also disclose that they collect sets of elements. For example, a site that collects user.name may collect any or all of the following: user.name.prefix, user.name.given, user.name.family, user.name.suffix, and user.name.nickname. An element may be truncated before any dot to produce a data set. For example user, user.home-info, user.home-info.telecom, and user.home-info.telecom.telephone are all data sets.

User agents can automatically generate a description of a data element to display to a user by concatenating (separated by commas or another appropriate character) the short display names assigned to the element and the sets to which it belongs. For example, user.home-info.telcom.pager.loccode would have the short display name "user's home contact information, telecommunications information, pager number, local phone area code." While this name is descriptive, it is also somewhat unwieldy and not very friendly. "Area code of user's home pager" might be a more useful description. Thus, user agents can optionally ignore the short display names and use their own words to describe data elements to a user.

All of the data elements in the user and related data sets are listed in the tables in this chapter. To expand out an element in the user data set, start with the element name—say, user.home-info—and look up the structure associated with that element in Table 9-13 (in this case, contact). Table 9-5 shows us that there are three data elements in the contact structure. In this case, let's select the postal element. We will add this to our data element name to get user.home-info.postal. If we want to be more specific than that, we can look up the structure for the postal element, which is the postal structure. According to Table 9-6, the postal structure has seven data elements. Let's select postalcode. Now our data element becomes user.home-info.postal.postalcode. Because postalcode is an unstructured element, we can't provide any more detail than that.

Note that currently there is no standard identity certificate for users to supply for user.cert. We don't expect this data element to be used until such certificates become common.

Web sites that use user.bdate might consider being more specific and declaring user.bdate.ymd instead. The full user.bdate element includes the time of birth, to the nearest second. Unless your site is providing horoscope readings, you probably don't collect information that specific. In addition, for sites that just collect age information, user.bdate.ymd.year can be used.

Table 9-15 lists all the elements of the user data set.

Table 9-15. The elements of the user data set

user.name	user.name.prefix
user.name.given	user.name.family
user.name.middle	user.name.suffix
user.name.nickname	user.bdate
user.bdate.ymd	user.bdate.ymd.year
user.bdate.ymd.month	user.bdate.ymd.day
user.bdate.hms	user.bdate.hms.hour
user.bdate.hms.minute	user.bdate.hms.second
user.cert	user.cert.key
user.cert.format	user.gender
user.employer	user.department
user.jobtitle	user.home-info
user.home-info.postal	user.home-info.postal.name
user.home-info.postal.name.prefix	user.home-info.postal.name.given
user.home-info.postal.name.family	user.home-info.postal.name.middle
user.home-info.postal.name.suffix	user.home-info.postal.name.nickname
user.home-info.postal.street	user.home-info.postal.city
user.home-info.postal.stateprov	user.home-info.postal.postalcode
user.home-info.postal.country	user.home-info.postal.organization
user.home-info.telecom	user.home-info.telecom.telephone
user.home-info.telecom.telephone.intcode	user.home-info.telecom.telephone.loccode
user.home-info.telecom.telephone.number	user.home-info.telecom.telephone.ext
user.home-info.telecom.telephone.comment	user.home-info.telecom.fax
user.home-info.telecom.fax.intcode	user.home-info.telecom.fax.loccode
user.home-info.telecom.fax.number	user.home-info.telecom.fax.ext
user.home-info.telecom.fax.comment	user.home-info.telecom.mobile
user.home-info.telecom.mobile.intcode	user.home-info.telecom.mobile.loccode
user.home-info.telecom.mobile.number	user.home-info.telecom.mobile.ext

Table 9-15. The elements of the user data set (continued)

user.home-info.telecom.mobile.comment	user.home-info.telecom.pager
user.home-info.telecom.pager.intcode	user.home-info.telecom.pager.loccode
user.home-info.telecom.pager.number	user.home-info.telecom.pager.ext
user.home-info.telecom.pager.comment	user.home-info.online
user.home-info.online.email	user.home-info.online.uri
user.business-info	user.business-info.postal
user.business-info.postal.name	user.business-info.postal.name.prefix
user.business-info.postal.name.given	user.business-info.postal.name.family
user.business-info.postal.name.middle	user.business-info.postal.name.suffix
user.business-info.postal.name.nickname	user.business-info.postal.street
user.business-info.postal.city	user.business-info.postal.stateprov
user.business-info.postal.postalcode	user.business-info.postal.country
user.business-info.postal.organization	user.business-info.telecom
user.business-info.telecom.telephone	user.business-info.telecom.telephone.intcode
user.business-info.telecom.telephone.loccode	user.business-info.telecom.telephone.number
user.business-info.telecom.telephone.ext	user.business-info.telecom.telephone.comment
user.business-info.telecom.fax	user.business-info.telecom.fax.intcode
user.business-info.telecom.fax.loccode	user.business-info.telecom.fax.number
user.business-info.telecom.fax.ext	user.business-info.telecom.fax.comment
user.business-info.telecom.mobile	user.business-info.telecom.mobile.intcode
user.business-info.telecom.mobile.loccode	user.business-info.telecom.mobile.number
user.business-info.telecom.mobile.ext	user.business-info.telecom.mobile.comment
user.business-info.telecom.pager	user.business-info.telecom.pager.intcode
user.business-info.telecom.pager.loccode	user.business-info.telecom.pager.number
user.business-info.telecom.pager.ext	user.business-info.telecom.pager.comment
user.business-info.online	user.business-info.online.email
user.business-info.online.uri	user.login
user.login.id	user.login.password

The thirdparty and business Data Sets

The base data schema also includes two data sets based on the user data set: the thirdparty and business data sets.

The thirdparty data set allows web sites to indicate that they collect data about third parties. This may be useful, for example, for sites that allow users to order gifts and send them directly to the recipient, or to provide information about a spouse or business partner. The thirdparty data set is identical to the user data set, except that all of the elements begin with the thirdparty prefix (for example, thirdparty.name. given).

The business data set features a subset of the user data set relevant to businesses and organizations. This data set is designed primarily to be used as part of the ENTITY element, but it may also be applicable to business-to-business interactions. This data set is used in the ENTITY element even when the legal entity operating a web site is an individual. The components of the business data set are shown in Table 9-16.

Table 9-16. The business data set

business	Category	Structure	Short Display Name
name	demograph	*unstructured*	organization name
department	demograph	*unstructured*	department or division of organization
cert	uniqueid	certificate	organization identity certificate
contact-info	physical, online, demograph	contact	contact information for the organization

The dynamic Data Set

The dynamic data set, shown in Table 9-17, contains a set of commonly collected data elements that are generated as part of or describe a user's web-browsing behavior.

Table 9-17. The dynamic data set

dynamic	Category	Structure	Short Display Name
clickstream	navigation	loginfo	clickstream information
http	navigation, computer	httpinfo	HTTP protocol information
clientevents	navigation	*unstructured*	user's interaction with a resource
cookies	*	*unstructured*	use of HTTP cookies
miscdata	*	*unstructured*	miscellaneous non-base data schema information
searchtext	interactive	*unstructured*	search terms
interactionrecord	interactive	*unstructured*	server stores the transaction history

These elements each require a bit of explanation about how they are used.

The dynamic.clickstream element is used by almost all web sites. It represents the combination of information typically found in web server access logs: the IP address or hostname of the user's computer, the URL of the requested resources, the time the request was made, the HTTP method used in the request, the size of the response, and the HTTP status code in the response. Sites that maintain standard server access logs should disclose that they collect dynamic.clickstream. Sites that maintain non-standard logs may wish to disclose only the individual data elements that they actually store.

Most sites also store in their log files information about visitors' user agents as well as the value of the HTTP Referer header field. Sites that log this information should also disclose that they collect dynamic.http. Sites need not try to list all categories of data that might inadvertently be stored in their logs as a result of storing the referer (which might contain personal information that a user enters into a form, for example).

The dynamic.clientevents element represents data about how the user interacts with a web browser while interacting with a site. For example, an application may collect information about whether a user moves a mouse over a certain image on a page or brings up the help window in a Java applet. Events that are covered by other elements in the base data schema are excluded from dynamic.clientevents. For example, requesting a page by clicking on a link is part of the user's interaction with her browser while viewing a page, but merely collecting the URL on which the user has clicked does not require declaring this data element; dynamic.clickstream covers that event. Items covered by this data element are typically collected by client-side scripting languages, such as JavaScript, or by client-side applets, such as ActiveX or Java applets. Behind the scenes, most data represented by dynamic.clickevents are actually events and data defined by the Document Object Model (DOM) Level 2 Events.*

Sites that use the HTTP cookie mechanism should disclose that they collect the dynamic.cookies element. This is a variable-category element, so sites must also disclose the category of data they store in or link via cookies.

Sites that collect additional data not described by any of the elements in the base data schema (or any of the extension data schemas the site uses) should disclose that they collect the dynamic.miscdata element. This is a variable-category element, so it must be accompanied by one or more data categories.

Sites that collect search queries from users in order to perform searches on the users' behalf should disclose that they collect the dynamic.searchtext element. Sites need not try to list all categories of data that might inadvertently be collected as a result of storing general search queries. However, if a search engine is intended to search for a specific type of data, such as health or medical information, a corresponding category disclosure may be necessary.

Sites that store records of their interactions with users that go beyond records of HTTP interactions may disclose the dynamic.interactionrecord element. For example, sites that store records of account transactions should disclose this data element.

Writing a P3P Data Schema

The P3P specification defines the syntax for defining data schemas. This syntax is used for the normative definition of the P3P base data schema. You can also use it to create your own data schema.

---

* Tom Pixley, Ed., *Document Object Model (DOM) Level 2 Events Specification. Version 1.0*, (W3C Recommendation, 13 November 2000), *http://www.w3.org/TR/DOM-Level-2-Events/*.

Sites may want to create their own data schemas in order to explicitly declare data elements not covered by the P3P base data schema. Companies that collect similar types of data might want to get together and create a data schema for their industries—for example, clothing retailers might create a data schema for information about clothes sizes, or financial institutions might create a data schema for information about payment methods. IBM created its own data schema to represent some of the data elements collected frequently by IBM web sites, including information about an individual's IBM computer system and information used to register for services on the IBM web site. Of course, it is never essential that a site create a new data schema in order to use P3P. Whatever data the site collects can always be represented using broad categories.

A data schema is encoded as an XML DATASCHEMA element. This element can stand by itself in a P3P data schema file, or it can be embedded in a POLICIES element in a policy or policy reference file. A DATASCHEMA contains a series of data definitions, data structure definitions, and extensions. Data definitions are encoded in DATA-DEF elements, while data structure definitions are encoded in DATA-STRUCT elements. The P3P specification does not impose any requirements on the order in which DATA-DEF and DATA-STRUCT elements appear, although for readability it is helpful to place DATA-STRUCT elements before the DATA-DEF elements that reference them.

DATA-DEF and DATA-STRUCT elements have mandatory name attributes that represent the name of the data element or structure being defined. If the data element or structure is based on a previously defined structure, the structref attribute is used to reference that structure. In addition, data schema creators can use the short-description attribute or the LONG-DESCRIPTION element to provide a description of the data element or structure that can be displayed to users.

Data schema creators can optionally assign categories to the elements and structures they create using the CATEGORIES element. When a CATEGORIES element is present in a DATA-DEF or DATA-STRUCT, a fixed-category element is defined; otherwise, a variable-category element is defined.

The following rules govern the use of categories in data schemas:

- DATA-STRUCT elements can optionally include category definitions. If a structure definition includes categories, all uses of that structure in data definitions and data structures pick up those categories. If a structure contains no categories, the categories for that structure may be defined when it is used in another structure or data element. Otherwise, a data element using that structure is a variable-category element. Any uses of a variable-category data element in a policy require that its categories be listed in the policy.

- A DATA-DEF with an unstructured type is a variable-category data element if no categories are defined in the DATA-DEF and has exactly those categories listed in the DATA-DEF if any categories are included.

- A DATA-DEF or DATA-STRUCT with a structured type that has no categories defined on that structure produces a variable-category data element/structure if no categories are defined in the DATA-DEF or DATA-STRUCT. If the DATA-DEF or DATA-STRUCT does have categories listed, those categories are applied to that data element and all of its subelements. In other words, categories are pushed down into subelements when defining a data element to be of a structured type, and the structured type does not define any categories.

- A DATA-DEF using a structured type that has categories defined on that structure picks up all the categories listed on the structure. In addition, categories may be listed in the DATA-DEF, and these are added to the categories defined in the structure. These categories are defined only at the level of that data element and are not pushed down to any subelements.

- A DATA-STRUCT that has no categories assigned to it and is using a structured subtype that has categories defined on the subtype picks up all the categories listed on the subtype.

- A DATA-STRUCT that has categories assigned to it and is using a structured sub-type replaces all of the categories listed on the subtype.

- There is a "bubble-up" rule for categories when referencing data elements: data elements must, at a minimum, include all categories defined by any of their children. This rule applies recursively, so, for example, all categories defined by data elements foo.a.w, foo.a.y, and foo.b.z must be considered to apply to data element foo.

- A DATA-STRUCT cannot be defined with some variable-category elements and some fixed-category elements. Either all of the subelements of a category must be in the variable category, or all of them must have one or more assigned categories.

Example 9-1 is a data schema that might be used by a web site that sells clothes and shoes. It defines a garment structure that includes size, gender, color, style, designer, and country properties. It then creates three data elements that use this structure: shirt, pants, and shoe. Notice that the garment.country structure references the postal.country structure from the P3P base data schema. However, we have overridden the category assigned to postal.country by including a CATEGORIES element in the DATA-STRUCT.

Example 9-1. Garment data schema

```
<DATASCHEMA xmlns="http://www.w3.org/2002/01/P3Pv1">
  <DATA-STRUCT name="garment.size"
    short-description="size">
    <CATEGORIES><demographic/></CATEGORIES>
  </DATA-STRUCT>
  <DATA-STRUCT name="garment.gender"
    short-description="gender">
    <CATEGORIES><demographic/></CATEGORIES>
    <LONG-DESCRIPTION>Gender for which garment is intended
      </LONG-DESCRIPTION>
  </DATA-STRUCT>
  <DATA-STRUCT name="garment.color"
    short-description="color">
    <CATEGORIES><preference/></CATEGORIES>
  </DATA-STRUCT>
  <DATA-STRUCT name="garment.style"
    short-description="style">
    <CATEGORIES><preference/></CATEGORIES>
  </DATA-STRUCT>
  <DATA-STRUCT name="garment.designer"
    short-description="designer">
    <CATEGORIES><preference/></CATEGORIES>
  </DATA-STRUCT>
  <DATA-STRUCT name="garment.country"
    structref="http://www.w3.org/TR/P3P/base#postal.country"
    short-description="country of manufacture">
    <CATEGORIES><preference/></CATEGORIES>
  </DATA-STRUCT>
```

Example 9-1. Garment data schema (continued)

```
    <DATA-DEF name="shirt" structref="#garment"
      short-description="shirt"/>
    <DATA-DEF name="pants" structref="#garment"
      short-description="pants"/>
    <DATA-DEF name="shoe" structref="#garment"
      short-description="shoe"/>
</DATASCHEMA>
```

If the web site publishes this schema (say, at *http://www.example.com/w3c/garment-schema/*), it might reference it in its P3P policy by including a DATA-GROUP, like this:

```
    <DATA-GROUP base="http://www.stevesstore.com/w3c/garment-schema/">
      <DATA ref="#shoe.size">
      <DATA ref="#shoe.gender">
      <DATA ref="#shirt">
    </DATA-GROUP>
```

Alternatively, the site could include the schema in the policy file and set the base attribute in the DATA-GROUP to the empty string "". This is shown in Example 9-2.

Example 9-2. Garment data schema embedded in a P3P policy

```
<POLICIES . . .
<DATASCHEMA>
  <DATA-STRUCT name="garment.size"
    short-description="size">
    <CATEGORIES><demographic/></CATEGORIES>
  </DATA-STRUCT>
  <DATA-STRUCT name="garment.gender"
    short-description="gender">
    <CATEGORIES><demographic/></CATEGORIES>
    <LONG-DESCRIPTION>Gender for which garment is intended
      </LONG-DESCRIPTION>
  </DATA-STRUCT>
  <DATA-STRUCT name="garment.color"
    short-description="color">
    <CATEGORIES><preference/></CATEGORIES>
  </DATA-STRUCT>
  <DATA-STRUCT name="garment.style"
    short-description="style">
    <CATEGORIES><preference/></CATEGORIES>
  </DATA-STRUCT>
  <DATA-STRUCT name="garment.designer"
    short-description="designer">
    <CATEGORIES><preference/></CATEGORIES>
  </DATA-STRUCT>
  <DATA-STRUCT name="garment.country"
    structref="http://www.w3.org/TR/P3P/base#postal.country"
    short-description="country of manufacture">
    <CATEGORIES><preference/></CATEGORIES>
  </DATA-STRUCT>
```

Example 9-2. Garment data schema embedded in a P3P policy (continued)

```
  <DATA-DEF name="shirt" structref="#garment"
    short-description="shirt"/>
  <DATA-DEF name="pants" structref="#garment"
    short-description="pants"/>
  <DATA-DEF name="shoe" structref="#garment"
    short-description="shoe"/>
</DATASCHEMA>
<POLICY . . .
  <STATEMENT>
    . . .
    <DATA-GROUP base="">
      <DATA ref="#shoe.size">
      <DATA ref="#shoe.gender">
      <DATA ref="#shirt">
    </DATA-GROUP>
  </STATEMENT>
. . .
</POLICY>
</POLICIES>
```

If the structures and elements defined in the schema are going to be used in only one policy, embedding the schema in the policy makes the policy easier to maintain and reduces the number of requests necessary for a user agent to fetch and interpret the policy. However, when the data elements or structures may be used by multiple policies, it may make more sense to put the data schema in a separate file.

When data schemas are stored in their own files, they must never be changed in ways that could impact the interpretation of P3P policies that reference them. This means that data elements and structures cannot be redefined or removed. However, adding new data or structure definitions is acceptable. This requirement is referred to in the P3P specification as the *persistence of data schemas* requirement.

CHAPTER 10

P3P-Enabled Web Site Examples

This chapter provides various examples of P3P policies and policy reference files to which you may want to refer as you P3P-enable your web site. These examples were designed to represent realistic scenarios that are likely to be applicable to many web sites.

You may also want to look at the policies and policy reference files of some of the web sites you visit for more examples. Just make sure that, when you borrow from the examples in this book or from other web sites, the policies you create accurately reflect your site's privacy policy.

Simple Sites

Many sites, including personal home pages and sites designed primarily to provide information (as opposed to those designed to sell things or provide interactive services), have very simple privacy policies. They tend to collect minimal amounts of data and will generally either commit to using that data in very limited ways or make no commitment that might limit future use of that data. For these simple sites, one P3P policy is probably sufficient for the entire site.

Example 10-1 is a policy reference file for a simple site that has one policy for the entire site. This policy is named *policy* and is located on the host from which the policy reference file was referenced, in a file named *general-policy.xml#policy* in a directory called *privacy*. The policy for this site also applies to all the cookies set by this site.

Example 10-1. Policy reference file for a simple site that has one policy for the entire site

```
<META xmlns="http://www.w3.org/2002/01/P3Pv1" xml:lang="en">
  <POLICY-REFERENCES>
    <POLICY-REF about="/privacy/general-policy.xml#policy">
      <INCLUDE>/*</INCLUDE>
      <COOKIE-INCLUDE/>
    </POLICY-REF>
```

```
    </POLICY-REFERENCES>
</META>
```

If this site did not use cookies, it would leave out the `COOKIE-INCLUDE` tag.

A site may include its policy in its policy reference file. Example 10-2 illustrates how a policy and policy reference file can be combined.

Example 10-2. Policy reference file for a simple site that includes a policy

```
<META xmlns="http://www.w3.org/2002/01/P3Pv1" xml:lang="en">
  <POLICY-REFERENCES>
    <POLICY-REF about="#policy1">
      <INCLUDE>/*</INCLUDE>
      <COOKIE-INCLUDE/>
    </POLICY-REF>
  </POLICY-REFERENCES>
  <POLICIES>
    <POLICY discuri="http://www.example.com/disc1" name="policy1">
      . . .
    </POLICY>
  </POLICIES>
</META>
```

Some personal home pages are hosted on institutional sites. For example, college students often have personal home pages on their university's web site. In this case the university would probably want to exclude student home pages from its own policy reference file, and students could create their own policy reference files to cover the pages they maintain. The student policy reference files would probably be referenced using the `LINK` tag. Example 10-3 is an example of a policy reference file that a student named Shane could use to apply a policy to his home page hosted on a university server. This university would include the statement `<EXCLUDE>/~*</EXCLUDE>` in its policy reference file to exclude student pages.

Example 10-3. Policy reference file for a simple site that has one policy for the entire site

```
<META xmlns="http://www.w3.org/2002/01/P3Pv1" xml:lang="en">
  <POLICY-REFERENCES>
    <POLICY-REF about="/~shane/p3p-policy.xml#policy">
      <INCLUDE>/~shane/*</INCLUDE>
      <COOKIE-INCLUDE/>
    </POLICY-REF>
  </POLICY-REFERENCES>
</META>
```

The "Anything" P3P Policy

Some sites may want to declare a P3P policy that allows them to collect any kind of data and use it for any purpose. I don't advocate this, but Example 10-4 shows what such a policy might look like.

Example 10-4. Policy for a site that may collect any data for any purpose

```
<POLICIES xmlns="http://www.w3.org/2002/01/P3Pv1" xml:lang="en" >
<POLICY name = "anything-policy"
  discuri = "http://www.example.com/privacy/policy.html">
  <ENTITY>
    <DATA-GROUP>
      <DATA ref="#business.name">Example Corp.</DATA>
      <DATA ref="#business.contact-info.online.email">
        privacy@example.com</DATA>
    </DATA-GROUP>
  </ENTITY>
  <ACCESS><none/></ACCESS>
  <STATEMENT>
    <PURPOSE>
      <current/><admin/><develop/><tailoring/>
      <pseudo-analysis/><pseudo-decision/><individual-analysis/>
      <individual-decision/><contact/><historical/><telemarketing/>
      <other-purpose>Any other purpose we want</other-purpose>
    </PURPOSE>
    <RECIPIENT>
       <ours/><delivery/><same/><other-recipient/><unrelated/><public/>
    </RECIPIENT>
    <RETENTION><indefinitely/></RETENTION>
    <DATA-GROUP>
      <DATA ref="#dynamic.miscdata">
        <CATEGORIES>
          <physical/><online/><uniqueid/><purchase/><financial/>
          <computer/><navigation/><interactive/><demographic/>
          <content/><state/><political/><health/><preference/>
          <location/><government/>
          <other-category>Any other type of data</other-category>
        </CATEGORIES>
      </DATA>
      <DATA ref="#dynamic.cookies">
        <CATEGORIES>
          <physical/><online/><uniqueid/><purchase/><financial/>
          <computer/><navigation/><interactive/><demographic/>
          <content/><state/><political/><health/><preference/>
          <location/><government/>
          <other-category>Any other type of data</other-category>
        </CATEGORIES>
      </DATA>
    </DATA-GROUP>
  </STATEMENT>
</POLICY>
</POLICIES>
```

No Data Collection Beyond Web Logs

Many web sites do not use forms, cookies, or any other mechanism to collect user data. However, unless they configure their servers not to keep web logs, they end up collecting some data automatically. This data collection must be disclosed in the sites' P3P policies.

Full web logs

Example 10-5 is a P3P policy for a site with typical web logs. These logs are kept indefinitely and are used to diagnose problems with the web site. They are not shared with other companies; however, they are sometimes analyzed in order to gain insight into how people are using the web site. If the web site will not analyze the logs, or will use the data in the logs only in aggregate form, the develop purpose need not be disclosed.

Example 10-5. Policy for a site with typical web logs and no other data collection

```
<POLICIES xmlns="http://www.w3.org/2002/01/P3Pv1" xml:lang="en" >
<POLICY name="logs-only"
  discuri = "http://www.example.com/privacy/policy.html">
  <ENTITY>
    <DATA-GROUP>
      <DATA ref="#business.name">Example Corp.</DATA>
      <DATA ref="#business.contact-info.online.email">
        privacy@example.com</DATA>
    </DATA-GROUP>
  </ENTITY>
  <ACCESS><nonident/></ACCESS>
  <!-- If the site has a dispute-resolution procedure that it follows,
      a DISPUTES-GROUP should be included here -->
  <STATEMENT>
    <PURPOSE><current/><admin/><develop/></PURPOSE>
    <RECIPIENT><ours/></RECIPIENT>
    <RETENTION><indefinitely/></RETENTION>
    <DATA-GROUP>
      <DATA ref="#dynamic.clickstream"/>
      <DATA ref="#dynamic.http"/>
    </DATA-GROUP>
  </STATEMENT>
</POLICY>
</POLICIES>
```

This policy is very specific about the fact that this site collects only clickstream information and HTTP protocol information. The site could also have a slightly more general policy that would describe the categories of data it collects rather than identifying these data sets. In this case, the following data group could be used in place of the one in Example 10-5:

```
<DATA-GROUP>
  <DATA ref="#dynamic.miscdata">
    <CATEGORIES>
      <computer/><navigation/>
    </CATEGORIES>
  </DATA>
</DATA-GROUP>
```

Sanitized web logs

Some web sites sanitize their web logs and purge them periodically so that they keep only the minimal information they need to diagnose web site problems and compile aggregate statistics on site usage. This allows them to be more privacy-friendly and minimizes the risk that they will have data in their logs that might be requested in a subpoena.

Example Corp. decides to modify their practices so that they keep data only as long as necessary to diagnose web site problems. They believe that two weeks is an adequate time period for this purpose. Furthermore, they decide to sanitize their log files by recording only a partial IP address for each visitor rather than a full IP address and hostname information. They decide not to record HTTP referer information in their logs. Their human-readable privacy policy explains that they aggregate their log data and purge their original logs every two weeks. Any log analysis that they do will only be done with the aggregate data (this data might indicate the number of users who visited each page on the site each day, for example). They can replace the statement in Example 10-5 with the following statement to reflect these changes:

```
<STATEMENT>
  <PURPOSE><current/><admin/></PURPOSE>
  <RECIPIENT><ours/></RECIPIENT>
  <RETENTION><stated-purpose/></RETENTION>
  <DATA-GROUP>
    <DATA ref="#dynamic.clickstream.uri"/>
    <DATA ref="#dynamic.clickstream.timestamp"/>
    <DATA ref="#dynamic.clickstream.clientip.partialip"/>
    <DATA ref="#dynamic.clickstream.other"/>
    <DATA ref="#dynamic.http.useragent"/>
  </DATA-GROUP>
</STATEMENT>
```

Note that the two-week retention period is described in the human-readable privacy policy and represented in the P3P policy by the stated-purpose retention element. Sites do not make specific declarations of exactly how long their retention periods are in their P3P policies.

Basic Forms

When web sites include forms, they must disclose their data practices with respect to the information collected by the forms. They have the option of enumerating the form elements, describing the form elements by category, or enumerating some elements and describing others by category. In general, the more specific a site can be about what data it collects, the less likely a user is to object to the site's data practices. However, enumerating specific data elements can be difficult for sites that contain many forms or include form fields that go beyond the data described by the P3P base data schema.

This section provides some example statements used to describe data collection performed by some common types of forms. These statements would need to be included in addition to a statement regarding web logs in a site's P3P policy.

Email comment form

Many sites include a form to email the webmaster with comments about the web site. Here is an example statement that covers this sort of form when the site commits to use the information submitted via the form only to improve the site, to discard the information on a regular basis, and not to disclose this information to other parties:

```
<STATEMENT>
  <PURPOSE><current/><admin/></PURPOSE>
  <RECIPIENT><ours/></RECIPIENT>
  <RETENTION><stated-purpose/></RETENTION>
  <DATA-GROUP>
    <DATA ref="#dynamic.miscdata">
      <CATEGORIES>
        <content/>
      </CATEGORIES>
    </DATA>
  </DATA-GROUP>
</STATEMENT>
```

Sometimes comment forms include a place for users to submit an email address so that they can receive a response from the site. If the form on this site gives users the option of including an email address, the site might add the following data reference to the above statement:

```
<DATA ref="#dynamic.miscdata" optional="yes">
  <CATEGORIES>
    <online/>
  </CATEGORIES>
</DATA>
```

Order form

Many sites include forms that allow users to order products. These forms typically request information about the item being purchased as well as the purchaser's email address and billing and shipping information. Here is an example statement that such a site might use. This site does not use this information for marketing, research, or any other purposes, and it keeps the information only as long as required by law. This site uses a delivery service with an unknown privacy policy to ship the order.

```
<STATEMENT>
  <PURPOSE><current/><admin/></PURPOSE>
  <RECIPIENT><ours/><delivery/></RECIPIENT>
  <RETENTION><legal-requirement/></RETENTION>
  <DATA-GROUP>
    <DATA ref="#dynamic.miscdata">
```

```
    <CATEGORIES>
      <physical/><online/><purchase/><preference/>
    </CATEGORIES>
  </DATA>
 </DATA-GROUP>
</STATEMENT>
```

If the site wants to be more specific about the data it collects, it might make the following statement instead:

```
<STATEMENT>
  <PURPOSE><current/><admin/></PURPOSE>
  <RECIPIENT><ours/><delivery/></RECIPIENT>
  <RETENTION><legal-requirement/></RETENTION>
  <DATA-GROUP>
    <DATA ref="#dynamic.miscdata">
      <CATEGORIES>
          <purchase/><preference/>
      </CATEGORIES>
    </DATA>
    <DATA ref="#user.name"/>
    <DATA ref="#user.home-info.postal"/>
    <DATA ref="#user.home-info.online.email"/>
    <DATA ref="#user.business-info.postal"/>
    <DATA ref="#user.business-info.online.email"/>
  </DATA-GROUP>
</STATEMENT>
```

If the site allows the purchaser to send the item as a gift to someone else, it might add the following data reference:

```
<DATA ref="#third-party.home-info.postal"/>
```

Mailing list registration form

On some sites, users can register for mailing lists. A site that includes a mailing list registration form might include the following statement in its P3P policy.

```
<STATEMENT>
  <PURPOSE><current/><admin/></PURPOSE>
  <RECIPIENT><ours/></RECIPIENT>
  <RETENTION><stated-purpose/></RETENTION>
  <DATA-GROUP>
    <DATA ref="#dynamic.miscdata">
      <CATEGORIES>
        <online/>
      </CATEGORIES>
    </DATA>
  </DATA-GROUP>
</STATEMENT>
```

If the mailing list is to be used for marketing services or products, the site should also disclose `<contact required="opt-in"/>`.

Search engine

A site that includes a search engine might include the following statement in its P3P policy:

```
<STATEMENT>
  <PURPOSE><current/><admin/></PURPOSE>
  <RECIPIENT><ours/></RECIPIENT>
  <RETENTION><stated-purpose/></RETENTION>
  <DATA-GROUP>
    <DATA ref="#dynamic.searchtext">
      <CATEGORIES>
        <online/>
      </CATEGORIES>
    </DATA>
  </DATA-GROUP>
</STATEMENT>
```

If the site does not record search terms in its log files, it might substitute the following retention element for the one in this statement:

```
<RETENTION><no-retention/><RETENTION>
```

Chat room

A site with a public chat room might include the following statement in its P3P policy. Here we assume that no user ID or password is necessary to participate in the chat room.

```
<STATEMENT>
  <PURPOSE><current/></PURPOSE>
  <RECIPIENT><public/></RECIPIENT>
  <RETENTION><indefinitely/></RETENTION>
  <DATA-GROUP>
    <DATA ref="#dynamic.miscdata">
      <CATEGORIES>
        <content/>
      </CATEGORIES>
    </DATA>
  </DATA-GROUP>
</STATEMENT>
```

Cookies

Web sites that set cookies themselves (first-party cookies) must have COOKIE-INCLUDE elements in their policy reference files. In addition, they must declare the dynamic. cookies data element and indicate the categories of data that are stored in or linked to cookies. If a cookie is used as a way of recognizing users to look them up in a database, the data linked to a cookie may be quite extensive.

Session cookies that ease form filling

Some cookies are used only within the context of a single session. One frequent use of session cookies is to allow users to fill out multiple-page forms more easily. In this case, the cookie temporarily stores a user ID, which is associated with whatever information is being collected by the form. Once the form is completed and submitted, the user ID is no longer needed and is destroyed. The following statement describes this kind of cookie use at a site that is conducting an opinion survey:

```
<STATEMENT>
  <PURPOSE><current/><admin/></PURPOSE>
  <RECIPIENT><ours/></RECIPIENT>
  <RETENTION><no-retention/></RETENTION>
  <DATA-GROUP>
    <DATA ref="#dynamic.cookies">
      <CATEGORIES>
        <state/><uniqueid/><preference/>
      </CATEGORIES>
    </DATA>
  </DATA-GROUP>
</STATEMENT>
```

Cookies that remember passwords

At some sites, users are given the option of storing their passwords in cookies so that they need not enter them each time they return to the site. The following statement describes this kind of cookie use:

```
<STATEMENT>
  <PURPOSE><current/><admin/></PURPOSE>
  <RECIPIENT><ours/></RECIPIENT>
  <RETENTION><stated-purpose/></RETENTION>
  <DATA-GROUP>
    <DATA ref="#dynamic.cookies">
      <CATEGORIES>
        <state/><uniqueid/>
      </CATEGORIES>
    </DATA>
  </DATA-GROUP>
</STATEMENT>
```

Cookies that are used as database keys

Some cookies are used to recognize users so that each of their interactions with a site can be put into a database. The following statement describes the practices of a site that uses these cookies to create a database for determining what ads to show the user at the site (without including any identified data in the database):

```
<STATEMENT>
  <PURPOSE><admin/><pseudo-decision/></PURPOSE>
  <RECIPIENT><ours/></RECIPIENT>
  <RETENTION><stated-purpose/></RETENTION>
```

```
<DATA-GROUP>
  <DATA ref="#dynamic.cookies">
    <CATEGORIES>
      <state/><uniqueid/><interactive/><navigation/><preference/>
    </CATEGORIES>
  </DATA>
</DATA-GROUP>
</STATEMENT>
```

Third-Party Agents

Many sites use third parties as agents to perform various web-related services. These agents may host some of the site's content to reduce the load on its servers, provide search facilities, customize content, or provide other services. However, to be considered an agent for the purposes of a P3P policy, these third parties must abide by the site's privacy policy and use any data they collect only to fulfill the purpose disclosed by the site.

A site might hire a content-distribution network to serve the audio and image files embedded in its pages (e.g., *busy.example.com* might hire *cdn.example.com* to serve its embedded content). CDN is hired under a contract that requires it to act as an agent to Busy. Thus, all the data collected about requests for Busy content from the CDN server is covered under the Busy privacy policy. CDN should include a reference to Busy's P3P policy in its own policy reference file. If CDN's web server is organized hierarchically and CDN has a small number of clients, it might have a policy reference file that looks something like Example 10-6.

Example 10-6. Policy reference file for a content-distribution network

```
<META xmlns="http://www.w3.org/2002/01/P3Pv1" xml:lang="en">
  <POLICY-REFERENCES>
    <EXPIRY max-age="864000"/>
    <POLICY-REF about="http://busy.exmple.com/p3p-policy.xml#policy1">
      <INCLUDE>/busy/*</INCLUDE>
    </POLICY-REF>
    <POLICY-REF about="http://bigsite.exmple.com/p3p-policy.xml#policy">
      <INCLUDE>/bigsite/*</INCLUDE>
    </POLICY-REF>
    <POLICY-REF about="http://news.exmple.com/p3p-policy.xml#ourpolicy">
      <INCLUDE>/news/*</INCLUDE>
    </POLICY-REF>
    <POLICY-REF about="/p3p-policy.xml#policy"> <!-- CDN's own policy -->
      <INCLUDE>/</INCLUDE>
      <INCLUDE>/cdn/*</INCLUDE>
    </POLICY-REF>
  </POLICY-REFERENCES>
</META>
```

Because a third-party agent might have a large number of clients or might not have each client's files separated into their own directories, some agents may want to generate policy reference files for each client rather than using a single policy reference file. Each of these client policy reference files can be referenced via the HTTP header mechanism or an HTML LINK tag. In the latter case, it is also a good idea for each client to use the HINT mechanism in its own policy reference file to hint at the location of the policy reference file that applies to its content that is hosted by CDN. This will allow user agents to find the policy reference files more quickly.

Third Parties with Their Own Policies

Some third parties hired by web sites are not hired in an agent capacity. These parties may perform a service on behalf of a site, but they may also use data collected in the process of performing that service for other purposes. In this case the site must disclose any data sharing that takes place between itself and the third party, and the third party should declare a P3P policy describing its own data practices.

Forms Posted to Other Servers with Different Policies

Some web sites contain forms that are submitted directly to other sites. For example, many web portals have search forms that are submitted directly to search engines hosted on other sites. In these cases, the P3P policy that covers the action URL of the form applies to the search query. This policy generally will be provided by the search engine web site, not the portal site. If the portal site passes additional information to the search engine—for example, by dynamically generating the form with hidden form fields—the portal site must disclose this in its own P3P policy.

Ad Networks That Do Not Qualify as Agents

While some services performed by ad networks qualify these networks as agents, other services do not. For example, some ad networks offer a service that tracks user behavior across many web sites and provides targeted ads based on this information. In these cases, the ad network should have its own P3P policy that describes the type of user profiling it is doing. If the sites on which these ads appear pass any information about their users to the ad network—for example, through the referer—these sites must disclose this in their own P3P policies.

Examples From Real Web Sites

P3P has been implemented on web sites large and small, and many real-world examples are now available that can be helpful to study as you P3P-enable your web site. Here are a few representative examples that illustrate some useful techniques for dealing with common problems. The W3C's P3P web site contains a long list of P3P-enabled web sites at *http://www.w3.org/P3P/compliant_sites/*.

Robroydog.org

Robroy the dog was not the first dog to have his own web site, but he is one of the first dogs to have his own *P3P-enabled* web site. Robroy is a retired greyhound. Since he retired, he has taken up residence with a couple of graduate students and therefore is on a rather restricted budget. He was able to afford a discount domain name registration, but he couldn't pay the bill for any web hosting, so he keeps his web site on a university server. Visitors to *http://robroydog.org/* are automatically redirected to *http://www.cs.unc.edu/~ackerman/robroy/*. Because Robroy does not have access to the */w3c* directory on *www.cs.unc.edu*, he can't use the well-known location mechanism for his P3P policy reference file. Therefore, he embeds a LINK tag in his HTML pages to reference his policy reference file, at *http://www.cs.unc.edu/~ackerman/robroy/w3c/p3p.xml*. Here is the tag he uses:

```
<link rel="P3Pv1" href="w3c/p3p.xml"></link>
```

Notice that he uses a relative URL, which is interpreted relative to the URL of the page in which it is embedded. He could have used an absolute URL, but the relative URL will make it easier for him to maintain his P3P policy should he move his web site to another server later.

Example 10-7 shows Robroy's P3P policy, which was created using the IBM P3P Policy Editor. It's a very basic policy, as Robroy doesn't collect any information other than standard server logs.

Example 10-7. P3P policy for robroydog.org

```
<?xml version="1.0"?>
<POLICIES xmlns="http://www.w3.org/2002/01/P3Pv1">
    <!-- Generated by IBM P3P Policy Editor version Beta 1.10.2 built 3/13/02 11:39 AM -->

    <!-- Expiry information for this policy -->
    <EXPIRY max-age="86400"/>

<POLICY
    discuri="http://robroydog.org/policy.html"
    name="policy1">
    <!-- Description of the entity making this policy statement. -->
    <ENTITY>
    <DATA-GROUP>
    <DATA ref="#business.contact-info.online.email">robroy@robroydog.org</DATA>
    <DATA ref="#business.contact-info.online.uri">http://robroydog.org</DATA>
    <DATA ref="#business.name">Robroydog.org -- Robroy the greyhound</DATA>
    </DATA-GROUP>
    </ENTITY>

    <!-- Disclosure -->
    <ACCESS><nonident/></ACCESS>

    <!-- No dispute information -->
```

Example 10-7. P3P policy for robroydog.org (continued)

```
    <!-- Statement for group "Access log information" -->
    <STATEMENT>
        <EXTENSION optional="yes">
            <GROUP-INFO xmlns="http://www.software.ibm.com/P3P/editor/extension-1.0.html"
                name="Access log information"/>
        </EXTENSION>

    <!-- Consequence -->
    <CONSEQUENCE>
      Our Web server collects access logs containing this information.</CONSEQUENCE>

    <!-- Use (purpose) -->
    <PURPOSE><admin/><current/><develop/></PURPOSE>

    <!-- Recipients -->
    <RECIPIENT><ours/></RECIPIENT>

    <!-- Retention -->
    <RETENTION><indefinitely/></RETENTION>

    <!-- Base data schema elements -->
    <DATA-GROUP>
     <DATA ref="#dynamic.clickstream"/>
     <DATA ref="#dynamic.http"/>
    </DATA-GROUP>
</STATEMENT>

<!-- End of policy -->
</POLICY>
</POLICIES>
```

Robroy's human-readable privacy policy is also a good example of a simple policy for personal web sites.

Privacy Policy for www.RobroyDog.org

This is Robroy the greyhound's website hosted on UNC's Department of Computer Science Web Servers and referred by Gandhi.net. As a dog, I have no reason to collect any information from my visitors, however my web server administrators may collect data in their standard server logs. This information may include, but is not limited to your IP address, referer, information about your web browser, and information about your requests. I will not make use of this information but it may be used by server and system administrators. Questions about this policy should be sent to Robroy@Robroydog.org

This is a *P3P-enabled* site. If you are using a P3P-enabled web browser you should be able to fetch the P3P policy automatically. If not, here is the *P3P policy* and the *P3P policy reference file*.

AT&T

AT&T is a large company with many web servers. The content on these servers is created and maintained by various people in different parts of the company. Rather than undertaking the task of crafting customized P3P policies for each part of the web site, AT&T decided to create one privacy policy for all of its web sites (excluding only the web sites and parts of web sites not under the direct control of AT&T). This policy is shown in Example 10-8.

Notice that the AT&T policy describes several dispute-resolution procedures. AT&T provides information about contacting their own customer-service department as well as information about the Better Business Bureau and three applicable laws.

The AT&T policy has two statements, to distinguish the way clickstream information is handled from the way other personal data is handled. The company commits to not sharing personally identifiable data with other companies for marketing—this is captured in the first statement. The company informs users in the second statement that clickstream data may be shared with online advertising companies.

Example 10-8. P3P Policy for AT&T

```
<?xml version="1.0"?>
<POLICIES xmlns="http://www.w3.org/2002/01/P3Pv1">
    <!-- Generated by IBM P3P Policy Editor version Beta 1.10.2 built 3/13/02 11:39 AM -->

    <!-- Expiry information for this policy -->
    <EXPIRY max-age="86400"/>

<POLICY
    discuri="http://www.att.com/privacy/"
    opturi="http://www.att.com/privacy/consumer/"
    name="general">
    <!-- Description of the entity making this policy statement. -->
    <ENTITY>
    <DATA-GROUP>
     <DATA ref="#business.name">AT&amp;T</DATA>
     <DATA ref="#business.contact-info.online.uri">http://www.att.com/</DATA>
     <DATA ref="#business.contact-info.telecom.telephone.intcode">1</DATA>
     <DATA ref="#business.contact-info.telecom.telephone.loccode">888</DATA>
     <DATA ref="#business.contact-info.telecom.telephone.number">928-8932</DATA>
    </DATA-GROUP>
    </ENTITY>

    <!-- Disclosure -->
    <ACCESS><contact-and-other/></ACCESS>

    <!-- Disputes -->
    <DISPUTES-GROUP>
        <DISPUTES resolution-type="independent" service="http://www.bbbonline.org" short-
description="BBBOnline">
            <LONG-DESCRIPTION>BBBOnline Privacy Program</LONG-DESCRIPTION>
            <IMG src="http://www.att.com/CDA/images/privacyseal6.gif" alt="BBBOnline
Privacy Seal"/>
    <!-- No remedies specified -->
        </DISPUTES>
```

Example 10-8. P3P Policy for AT&T (continued)

```
        <DISPUTES resolution-type="service" service="http://www.att.com/privacy/" short-
description="Customer service">
                <LONG-DESCRIPTION>If you are a consumer with concerns
                about the AT&amp;online privacy policy or its
                implementation you may contact us at 1-888-9-ATT-WEB. If
                you are a business customer, please call
                1-877-744-4531.</LONG-DESCRIPTION>
                <REMEDIES><correct/></REMEDIES>
        </DISPUTES>
        <DISPUTES resolution-type="law" service="http://www.fcc.gov/ccb/ppp/Cpni/" short-
description="Privacy of Customer Information">
                <LONG-DESCRIPTION>Customer Proprietary Network
                Information, Common Carrier Regulation, Section 222 of the
                Telecommunications Act of 1996, the Federal Communications
                Commission's Orders and Rules</LONG-DESCRIPTION>
                <REMEDIES><law/></REMEDIES>
        </DISPUTES>
        <DISPUTES resolution-type="law" service="http://www.fcc.gov/csb/facts/csgen.html"
short-description="Protection of Subscriber Privacy (Cable Act, as amended, Sec. 631)">
                <REMEDIES><law/></REMEDIES>
        </DISPUTES>
        <DISPUTES resolution-type="law" service="http://www.ftc.gov/bcp/conline/edcams/
kidzprivacy/index.html" short-description="Children's Online Privacy Protection Act of
1998, and Federal Trade Commission Rule">
                <REMEDIES><law/></REMEDIES>
        </DISPUTES>
    </DISPUTES-GROUP>

    <!-- Statement for group "General" -->
    <STATEMENT>
        <EXTENSION optional="yes">
            <GROUP-INFO xmlns="http://www.software.ibm.com/P3P/editor/extension-1.0.html"
name="General"/>
        </EXTENSION>

    <!-- Consequence -->
    <CONSEQUENCE>
AT&amp;T uses your personally identifiable information for billing
purposes, to provide services to you, and to inform you of services that may
better meet your needs, but we do not disclose your personally identifiable
information to third parties who want to market products to you, period.
</CONSEQUENCE>

    <!-- Use (purpose) -->
    <PURPOSE><admin/><contact required="opt-out"/><current/><develop/><pseudo-analysis/>
<pseudo-decision/><individual-analysis/><individual-decision/><tailoring/><telemarketing
required="opt-out"/></PURPOSE>

    <!-- Recipients -->
    <RECIPIENT><ours/><other-recipient required="opt-in"/><delivery/></RECIPIENT>
```

Example 10-8. P3P Policy for AT&T (continued)

```
    <!-- Retention -->
    <RETENTION><indefinitely/></RETENTION>

    <!-- Base dataschema elements. -->
    <DATA-GROUP>
    <DATA ref="#dynamic.miscdata"><CATEGORIES><physical/></CATEGORIES></DATA>
    <DATA ref="#dynamic.miscdata"><CATEGORIES><purchase/></CATEGORIES></DATA>
    <DATA ref="#dynamic.miscdata"><CATEGORIES><navigation/></CATEGORIES></DATA>
    <DATA ref="#dynamic.miscdata"><CATEGORIES><interactive/></CATEGORIES></DATA>
    <DATA ref="#dynamic.miscdata"><CATEGORIES><demographic/></CATEGORIES></DATA>
    <DATA ref="#dynamic.miscdata"><CATEGORIES><content/></CATEGORIES></DATA>
    <DATA ref="#dynamic.miscdata"><CATEGORIES><online/></CATEGORIES></DATA>
    <DATA ref="#dynamic.miscdata"><CATEGORIES><computer/></CATEGORIES></DATA>
    <DATA ref="#dynamic.miscdata"><CATEGORIES><preference/></CATEGORIES></DATA>
    <DATA ref="#dynamic.miscdata"><CATEGORIES><uniqueid/></CATEGORIES></DATA>
    <DATA ref="#dynamic.miscdata"><CATEGORIES><government/></CATEGORIES></DATA>
    <DATA ref="#dynamic.miscdata"><CATEGORIES><state/></CATEGORIES></DATA>
    </DATA-GROUP>
</STATEMENT>

    <!-- Statement for group "Clickstream" -->
    <STATEMENT>
        <EXTENSION optional="yes">
            <GROUP-INFO xmlns="http://www.software.ibm.com/P3P/editor/extension-1.0.html"
name="Clickstream"/>
        </EXTENSION>

    <!-- Consequence -->
    <CONSEQUENCE>
We want to make the content on our sites as relevant,
interesting and timely as possible and to do that we use information about
which pages you visit on our site. AT&amp;T uses advertising companies to
deliver ads on some AT&amp;T Web sites. The advertising companies may also
receive some anonymous information about ad viewing by Internet users
on AT&amp;T Web sites. This information cannot be associated with a name
or email address without the customer's permission.
</CONSEQUENCE>

    <!-- Use (purpose) -->
    <PURPOSE><admin/><current/><develop/><pseudo-analysis/><pseudo-decision/><tailoring/>
</PURPOSE>

    <!-- Recipients -->
    <RECIPIENT><ours/><other-recipient/></RECIPIENT>

    <!-- Retention -->
    <RETENTION><indefinitely/></RETENTION>

    <!-- Base dataschema elements. -->
    <DATA-GROUP>
    <DATA ref="#dynamic.cookies"><CATEGORIES><preference/><uniqueid/></CATEGORIES></DATA>
```

Example 10-8. P3P Policy for AT&T (continued)

```
    <DATA ref="#dynamic.clickstream"/>
    <DATA ref="#dynamic.http.useragent" optional="yes"/>
    <DATA ref="#dynamic.http.referer" optional="yes"/>
    <DATA ref="#dynamic.miscdata"><CATEGORIES><navigation/></CATEGORIES></DATA>
    <DATA ref="#dynamic.miscdata"><CATEGORIES><computer/></CATEGORIES></DATA>
    </DATA-GROUP>
</STATEMENT>

<!-- End of policy -->
</POLICY>
</POLICIES>
```

IBM

Like AT&T, IBM is a large company with many web sites. IBM decided to create two P3P policies—one for use on the parts of the site with dynamic content, such as forms and public forums, and the other for use everywhere else. In IBM's P3P policy for dynamic content, the company declared its own data schema to describe data elements frequently collected on IBM forms. This data schema is shown in Example 10-9. The data elements defined by this schema cover information about an individual's IBM computer system, information used to register for services at the IBM web site, information about products purchased and payment methods used at the IBM web site, and content posted to IBM online forums and discussion groups. IBM could have used only the categories given in the P3P specification to describe this data, but it chose to create its own data elements in order to provide more specific information about the data. In the future, IBM webmasters might also use these custom data elements to help standardize forms throughout the business. The details of creating a custom data schema are explained in Chapter 9.

Example 10-9. Data schema defined in IBM P3P policy

```
<DATASCHEMA>

 <DATA-DEF name="ibm" short-description="IBM Data">
  <CATEGORIES><uniqueid/></CATEGORIES>
  <LONG-DESCRIPTION>Custom data elements defined by IBM.
  </LONG-DESCRIPTION>
 </DATA-DEF>

 <DATA-DEF name="ibm.computerinfo" short-description=
  "Computer information">
  <CATEGORIES><computer/></CATEGORIES>
  <LONG-DESCRIPTION>Information about your IBM computer system (for example, a computer
serial number for an IBM personal computer you may have registered online).</LONG-
DESCRIPTION>
 </DATA-DEF>
```

Example 10-9. Data schema defined in IBM P3P policy (continued)

```
<DATA-DEF name="ibm.registration" short-description=
 "Registration information">
 <CATEGORIES><uniqueid/></CATEGORIES>
</DATA-DEF>

<DATA-DEF name="ibm.registration.userid" short-description=
 "IBM User ID">
 <CATEGORIES><uniqueid/></CATEGORIES>
 <LONG-DESCRIPTION>User ID created by registering for an IBM application or service.</
LONG-DESCRIPTION>
</DATA-DEF>

<DATA-DEF name="ibm.registration.password" short-description=
 "IBM Password">
 <CATEGORIES><uniqueid/></CATEGORIES>
 <LONG-DESCRIPTION>Password created by the user when registering for an IBM application
or service.</LONG-DESCRIPTION>
</DATA-DEF>

<DATA-DEF name="ibm.purchaseinfo" short-description=
 "Purchase information">
 <CATEGORIES><preference/><purchase/></CATEGORIES>
 <LONG-DESCRIPTION>Information about products being purchased and payment method.</LONG-
DESCRIPTION>
</DATA-DEF>

<DATA-DEF name="ibm.purchaseinfo.payment" short-description=
 "Payment information">
 <CATEGORIES><purchase/></CATEGORIES>
 <LONG-DESCRIPTION>Information needed to process payment for an online purchase,
including credit card type, number, and expiry information.
</LONG-DESCRIPTION>
</DATA-DEF>

<DATA-DEF name="ibm.postings" short-description=
  "Forum posting content">
  <CATEGORIES><content/></CATEGORIES>
  <LONG-DESCRIPTION>Content posted to public forums or discussion groups.</LONG-
DESCRIPTION>
</DATA-DEF>

</DATASCHEMA>
```

PART III

P3P Software and Design

This part of the book discusses design issues related to both the P3P vocabulary and P3P software. These chapters provide some of the design rationale behind the P3P vocabulary as well as information on how the vocabulary may be translated into P3P user agent interfaces. These chapters are intended primarily for software developers interested in building P3P into their products and individuals who want to develop P3P preference settings. However, these chapters also serve to tie together the concepts introduced in the previous sections of the book and demonstrate how everything comes together in P3P software implementations.

- Chapter 11, *P3P Vocabulary Design Issues*, discusses some of the issues faced while designing the P3P vocabulary and how they were resolved.

- Chapter 12, *P3P User Agents and Other Tools*, gives an overview of the various kinds of P3P tools that might be developed and discusses P3P user agent compliance requirements.

- Chapter 13, *A P3P Preference Exchange Language (APPEL)*, describes the language for encoding user privacy preferences.

- Chapter 14, *User Interface*, provides guidelines and suggestions for designing usable interfaces for P3P user agents.

CHAPTER 11

P3P Vocabulary Design Issues

If you've read Part II of this book, you now know the ins and outs of the P3P vocabulary. However, you may have some questions about why the P3P vocabulary ended up the way it is. There is a lot of history behind the P3P vocabulary—in fact, it is the result of five years of work by dozens of individuals. Many parts of the vocabulary changed numerous times along the way. Some parts were extremely controversial and reflect compromises reached after months of debate.

All along, our goal in developing the P3P vocabulary was to develop a language that captures the core components of privacy policies that can be used as part of automated decision-making. The vocabulary needed to be granular enough to distinguish a wide variety of practices but not so granular that a law degree would be required to understand the differences between practices. As much as possible, we wanted to include multiple-choice fields in order to make the vocabulary useful for automated processing; however, some human-readable fields also proved necessary to provide explanations that might be presented to human users of privacy tools. This chapter discusses some of the challenges that were faced and the trade-offs that were made as the P3P working groups developed the P3P vocabulary.

Rating Systems and Vocabularies

The P3P vocabulary is often described as a privacy *rating system*, but it actually does not convey positive or negative ratings. We use the term *vocabulary* rather than rating system, because it provides a language for talking about privacy rather than a mechanism for evaluating privacy policies. However, it is possible to construct privacy rating systems that evaluate disclosures made using the P3P vocabulary.

We use rating systems all the time, for various purposes. The movie reviewers Roger Ebert and the late Gene Siskel popularized the simple thumbs-up/thumbs-down rating system for movies. Five letter grades (and sometimes pluses and minuses) are used to rate students' achievement in each of their subjects. Five stars are used to rate restaurants, movies, and hotels. The popular Zagat restaurant reviews rate food, service, and décor on separate scales from 0 to 30; they also provide an average dinner price and symbols to indicate information about each restaurant's hours and acceptable payment methods. While all of these rating systems are different, they all have the ability to provide succinct information in a format that makes for easy comparisons.

Some rating systems, like the thumbs-up/thumbs-down system, have a small number of variables and a small number of possible values for each variable. Such systems are very simple but don't provide a lot of information. Sometimes a lot of information is not needed—for example, when selecting a movie, a person who generally finds herself in agreement with the Siskel and Ebert reviews and enjoys all genres of movies may find a thumbs-up sufficient information to select a movie. But a person who doesn't always agree with Siskel and Ebert, or who likes to watch dramas but not horror films, may find this rating system insufficient (fortunately, the thumbs-up/thumbs-down ratings are accompanied by lengthy reviews).

Some rating systems are much more sophisticated, including many variables and many possible values for each. *Consumer Reports* typically provides ratings on a five-point scale on five or more aspects of each product rated. In addition, they provide quantitative information about size, weight, cost, or other factors, and an overall score on a scale of 0 to 100. *The Consumer Reports* ratings are expensive and time-consuming to create. To understand them, readers typically need to read the accompanying explanation of how each rating was derived and what exactly it means. These sophisticated ratings provide much more information than a simple rating system, although they still may not answer every question that a prospective purchaser might have about a product.

In addition to complexity, another factor that differentiates rating systems is the degree to which they are subjective. Some rating systems convey factual information only—size, weight, fuel efficiency, etc. Others, like the thumbs-up/thumbs-down system, are entirely subjective. Many rating systems are hybrid systems. For example, a student's letter grade may be based on the number of points he received on his tests and homework assignments throughout the semester. But while the student's teacher tries to be as objective as possible, the number of points awarded for essay questions is often subjective. The *Consumer Reports* ratings combine measurable ratings on factors such as durability and efficiency with subjective ratings derived from asking testers to provide their opinions on factors such as taste, appearance, or ease of use. Even if a rating system is entirely objective, the decision about what factors to rate or the weighting each receives in a summary score is usually a subjective decision.

Related to rating systems are vocabularies or ontologies* for describing and categorizing things. Many of the previously discussed rating systems use vocabularies for

---

* According to *The Free On-line Dictionary of Computing*, edited by Denis Howe (*http://foldoc.doc.ic.ac.uk*), in the context of information science, an ontology is defined as "The hierarchical structuring of knowledge about things by subcategorising them according to their essential (or at least relevant and/or cognitive) qualities."

providing categorization or descriptive information (movie genre, type of restaurant, etc.) that is not meant to imply a positive or negative rating. In addition, such information is often used by itself, without being accompanied by any sort of rating. For example, directories may list information about restaurants such as name, address, type of food, and hours of operation; library catalogs list information about books such as title, author, publisher, and year of publication; and food nutrition labels list information about calories, fat, protein, and vitamins.

In general, simple rating systems that provide positive or negative judgments are easy to understand and interpret, although users may not fully understand the bias inherent in a subjective rating system and whether or not it matches their own. Complex vocabularies that provide more descriptive information and fewer value judgments convey more information but are more difficult to understand. When used as part of a software tool, a more complex vocabulary requires greater user involvement to configure, unless the user interface is designed to hide some of the complexity. However, a more complex vocabulary provides the opportunity to overlay a simpler, perhaps subjective, rating system that might be preferable to many users. From descriptive information, one can always derive a new set of subjective opinions. For example, if you read a nutrition label, you can make a decision about whether a food product meets the requirements for your personal diet; however, given only someone else's determination that the product is "healthy," you cannot recapture the descriptive information. Likewise, if you are told about a movie's plot, character development, cinematography, and acting, you can make a thumbs-up or thumbs-down decision. But given only someone else's thumbs-down, you cannot recapture the descriptive information about the film. Once opinions replace descriptions, information is lost.*

Early on, a decision was made to make the P3P vocabulary as descriptive and objective as possible. Ratings can certainly be derived from the P3P vocabulary, but they are not inherent in the vocabulary itself. This proved to be an important design decision, as it allowed the vocabulary to be developed without building a consensus on what should be considered "good" or "bad" privacy practice. Along the way, some working group members raised objections to the inclusion in the vocabulary of elements that allowed for the description of activities illegal in certain countries. However, the group decided that the vocabulary should be able to describe all common privacy policies, whether good or bad, legal or illegal. Rating systems can then be developed that derive ratings based on the vocabulary, perhaps even labeling some practices as illegal according to certain laws.

Despite the decision to restrict the P3P vocabulary to descriptive information, we cannot claim that no subjectivity is involved. Our decisions about what fields to

---

* Joseph Reagle and I discuss this point further in our paper "Designing a Social Protocol: Lessons Learned from the Platform for Privacy Preferences," in Jeffrey K. MacKie-Mason and David Waterman, eds., *Telephony, the Internet, and the Media* (Lawrence Erlbaum Associates), *http://lorrie.cranor.org/pubs/dsp/*.

include in the vocabulary and what possible values to allow for each of these fields were not without bias. By seeking out input on the P3P vocabulary from a wide variety of people we hoped to keep this bias to a minimum, but it is clear that there is no universal agreement on what vocabulary should be used when talking about privacy. We designed the P3P vocabulary to be extensible, so that new terms can be added in the future.

The only vocabulary design principle that was formally discussed in the P3P working groups was that the vocabulary should be descriptive rather than subjective, but a number of other principles were discussed in the course of debating various vocabulary issues.* In hindsight, getting consensus on some of these principles up front and listing them in a requirements document probably would have helped the vocabulary design process go more smoothly. Here are two of the most important of these principles:

- The vocabulary should allow enough information to be conveyed that a privacy advocate could configure a software tool to distinguish between sites with acceptable and unacceptable privacy policies and a web site could demonstrate that its policies meet various guidelines or legal requirements.

- Each term in the vocabulary either should be usable as a factor in automated decision-making or should provide information that a user would likely find useful when it is displayed by a software tool.

These principles were often used informally as a litmus test to help decide whether particular elements should be included in the P3P vocabulary.

As the P3P vocabulary emerged as an increasingly complicated set of fields and values, concerns were raised that it would be too complicated for any web users to understand and use. Certainly, the vocabulary contains many terms that are not well known to the average consumer, and there are too many fields to make feasible a configuration script that would question a P3P software user about her preferences over every possible combination of web site practices. To mitigate these concerns, we envision that P3P software will offer configuration options that hide much of the complexity of the P3P vocabulary. Furthermore, we expect this software to have the ability to import "recommended settings" put together by privacy experts or organizations that users trust. For example, privacy advocacy groups or consumer groups might recommend settings that configure privacy tools in ways that they consider privacy-protective. Some recommended settings might focus on offering very high levels of privacy, sometimes at the expense of convenience, while other recommended settings might focus on striking a balance between privacy and convenience. By offering a complex vocabulary that can be overlaid with a much simpler

---

* Joseph Reagle comments on some of the tensions involved in the vocabulary development process in section 3.3 of his essay, *Eskimo Snow and Scottish Rain: Legal Considerations of Schema Design* (W3C Note 10-December-1999), *http://www.w3.org/TR/md-policy-design/*.

user interface or with recommended settings, the P3P vocabulary achieves the goals of being both granular and usable. These ideas are discussed further in Chapter 14.

P3P Vocabulary Terms

I could easily fill a whole book just explaining the vocabulary design decisions made during the five-year P3P development process. Indeed, the P3P Specification Working Group (just one of the nine working groups that contributed to the development of P3P, but the group that worked over the longest duration) held over 150 hours of tele-conferences and exchanged over 3,200 email messages over a period of about two and a half years. In addition to the official conference calls and email exchanges, the more active working group members spent many more hours on the phone and exchanging personal emails with other working group members, in an attempt to better understand each other's perspectives and work out compromise positions to present to the working group. Of course, not all of these discussions were about the P3P vocabulary—other aspects of the P3P specification proved controversial as well—but the P3P vocabulary did occupy a large percentage of the working group's time. In this section, I focus on those decisions about the P3P vocabulary that proved most controversial and those that have been the subject of recurring questions from web site developers and policymakers. Most of these decisions were made by the P3P Vocabulary Harmonization Working Group and the P3P Specification Working Group.

Access

At the beginning of the P3P development process, there was a lot of controversy about whether to include the ACCESS element. Privacy advocates felt strongly that the P3P vocabulary should enable disclosures about the kinds of access that companies provide, as access is one of the core fair information practice principles. However, some industry groups argued against including this element, as many U.S. companies had not committed to providing any sort of access at the time. After the FTC highlighted access in its list of five core privacy protection principles,* objections to the ACCESS element were dropped.

Many questions remain about how companies should implement the access principle. What are reasonable ways of providing access? Providing online access to a person's information may pose a security concern. Must access be provided to derived information, or only to information supplied by the individual? Should individuals be able to correct or withdraw their information? Who is responsible for providing access to data that has been transferred to another party—the entity that collected it, or the party to which it was transferred? The P3P vocabulary does not attempt to

---

* Federal Trade Commission, *Privacy Online: A Report to Congress* (June 1998), *http://www.ftc.gov/reports/privacy3/*.

answer any of these questions. Instead, it allows sites to indicate the extent of the access provided by selecting from six categories of access. This is not completely satisfactory to those who would like more information about the terms under which access is provided, but without standard access terms, providing any more specific information in this field proved difficult.

Non-Identifiable data

As discussed in Chapter 6, the P3P specification uses the term "identified data" to refer to data that a data collector can use to reasonably identify an individual. But just because a piece of data is not *identified* does not imply that it is not *identifiable*. For example, a web site operator that collects no data other than standard web logs that are used only for gathering aggregate statistics on site usage and to diagnose problems can claim that she does not collect any identified data. However, these logs contain IP addresses that often can be used to identify an individual or household, with cooperation from the ISP to which the address is assigned (for example, in response to a subpoena). Thus, while the log data may not be identified, it is identifiable.

Some P3P working group members thought it was important to be able to use P3P to test whether a site collects identifiable data. However, if the P3P vocabulary relied only on the term "identified," this would not be possible. By introducing the NON-IDENTIFIABLE element, we were able to provide a way for sites that actually cannot identify users from the data they collect to say so. Few sites are currently able to take advantage of this vocabulary element, but sites that want to emphasize their private services may take precautions to avoid logging any potentially identifiable data so that they can make this disclosure.

Purposes

The P3P vocabulary includes 12 purposes or uses of data. The current purpose describes primary data uses, the other-purpose purpose describes purposes that are not covered by this set of 12, and the remainder describe various secondary data uses. An alternative approach would be to include a variety of primary data uses as well, such as purchases, authentication, and surveys. However, the working group members felt that distinguishing between secondary data uses was most useful for automated decision-making. While some privacy preferences might be based on primary data uses—for example, I might be willing to disclose some data when I'm doing online banking that I might not be willing to disclose when I'm doing online shopping—primary data uses are more obvious to the user and less easily categorized for automated processing.

Primary data uses

The current purpose seemed pretty straightforward to P3P working group members, until people began to enquire as to whether it applied to recurring activities. Initially defined as "completion and support of current activity," it was clear that this purpose could be applied to activities such as one-time purchases. But what if you were purchasing a subscription that would be delivered in multiple installments? Or what if you were signing up for an online mailing list that would send you messages indefinitely? The group considered distinguishing between current and recurring primary data uses. However, the majority of the working group members felt that this distinction would have little practical use for most users. Thus, only one primary purpose remains. However, its meaning was changed to "completion and support of activity for which data was provided," to make it clear that its application should not be limited to one-time activities.

Marketing

Initially, the P3P vocabulary specified only one marking purpose: contact. Working group members felt that there was no need to distinguish between different types of marketing (telephone, postal mail, email, etc.), because the type of contact data collected by the site would indicate the types of marketing that might be conducted (for example, a site that collected only email addresses could not do telemarketing). However, concerns were later raised that sites might combine information collected online with other databases. Thus, a site might collect your name and email address and infer that you are in the market for a car based on your browsing activity. It could then look up your name in another database to find your phone number and call you with information about sales at your local car dealership. A user who provided his name and email address on the assumption that it would not result in a telemarketing call would thus be making an inaccurate assumption. Working group members also realized that individuals' preferences about marketing tend to vary depending on the marketing channel. In particular, telemarketing tends to be a hot-button issue for many consumers.* Consumers who might not object to some marketing might refuse all marketing if they believed a company might put them on a telemarketing list.

Working group members considered a number of ways of distinguishing marketing methods, including adding a method attribute to the contact element and adding separate purpose elements to represent each of several marketing channels. Concerns were raised that it would not be possible to capture every potential marketing channel in the P3P vocabulary and that new channels were emerging that might not fit the existing categories—for example, instant messaging or sending text messages to cell phones. Therefore, the group decided to single out only telemarketing, as that

---

* In our 1998 study, only 11% of respondents said they were comfortable giving their telephone numbers to a web site, while 44% were comfortable supplying a home address and 76% were comfortable supplying an email address. See Mark S. Ackerman, Lorrie Faith Cranor, and Joseph Reagle, "Beyond Concern: Understanding Net Users' Attitudes About Online Privacy" (April 1999), *http://www.research.att.com/projects/privacystudy/*.

seemed to be the marketing channel that raised the most concerns for users. Thus, the `telemarketing` purpose was added.

Profiling

Many concerns have been raised about web sites collecting data to build user profiles that are later used for a variety of purposes, including targeted marketing and web site customization. Users' preferences about whether they are profiled may vary depending on what kinds of information are included in the profile, who is doing the profiling, how the profile may be used, and whether it may be shared with other companies.

Capturing the concept of profiling in the P3P vocabulary proved challenging. The first decision that had to be made was where the concept best fit into the vocabulary. The purpose section of the vocabulary seemed to be the best choice, but many working group members argued that profiling is rarely, if ever, the reason that data is collected. Companies put data into profiles and in turn use those profiles for various reasons. Some working group members suggested that profiling would be captured more accurately in a vocabulary element that described the form in which data would be stored and the duration over which it would be retained. Others suggested that the key concept was whether data on a particular individual was being linked together. In the end, the consensus of the working group was to include the concept of profiling in one or more purpose elements, as the alternative approaches seemed to add a significant and unnecessary degree of complexity to the vocabulary.

Once the working group decided to include profiling purposes in the vocabulary, it had to determine how many different profiling-related purposes to distinguish. This was a controversial decision that was revisited several times throughout the P3P development process. Ultimately, the working group decided to distinguish these purposes along two axes: whether the profile was tied to identified data ("individual" or "pseudo"), and whether the profile would be used to make a decision that directly affects the individual ("decision" or "analysis"). Thus, four profiling-related purposes were added to the vocabulary: `pseudo-analysis`, `pseudo-decision`, `individual-analysis`, and `individual-decision`.

Recipients

Working group members initially came up with a list of about three dozen types of data recipients, distinguished according to their relationship with the data collector and whether they follow the same privacy policy as the data collector, a different policy, or no policy at all. The different relationships discussed included subsidiaries, parent companies, business partners, agents, and unrelated companies, among others. As the group discussed definitions for each of these recipients, it soon became clear that many of these distinctions were difficult to define clearly and not of much value to individuals reviewing web site privacy policies. The long list of data recipients was eventually divided into four groups:

- The entity referenced in the privacy policy and its agents that operate under the same privacy policy
- Other entities that operate under the same privacy policy
- Other entities that operate under different privacy policies and are accountable to the entity referenced in the privacy policy
- Other entities that have unknown privacy policies and public forums where anyone may access and use the data

These four groups seemed to capture most of the important distinctions between data recipients. Some argued that the third and fourth groups should be combined, as once a company shares data with companies that are not following its privacy policy, it doesn't really matter whether the company doing the sharing knows their policies—the individuals whose data is being shared will not know what these policies are. However, some people felt that the distinction was important, as some individuals may be more comfortable with data being shared with companies that are accountable to the original data collector. In the end, the working group decided to keep both of these groups.

Another distinction that some felt was important was the distinction between sharing data with companies and posting data to public forums. While in both cases individuals have no control over what happens to their data, individuals often voluntarily submit their data to public forums. Thus, companies with bulletin boards and chat rooms on their web sites wanted to make clear that data submitted to these forums was available to the public but that the company was not selling this data. Eventually this category was split in order to make this distinction.

It was also pointed out that companies frequently work with agents whose privacy policies they do not know. Delivery companies and credit card companies are examples of such agents. However, if every company that accepted credit cards for payment or shipped products to customers had to disclose in their P3P policy that they share data with other companies, the P3P RECIPIENTS field would not be very useful. After much discussion, the P3P working group concluded that no special disclosure was needed for companies that share data with credit card companies in order to process customer payments, as those customers already have a relationship with the credit card company (and presumably already had an opportunity to review the credit card company's privacy policy). However, no such relationship exists between customers and delivery services such as FedEx, UPS, or even the United States Postal Service. To address this problem, a special delivery services recipient was added.

Categories

When analyzing a privacy policy, it is important to know what kinds of data may be collected. Individual preference about how data may be used tends to vary greatly depending on the data in question, but coming up with a comprehensive list of data collected on web sites is practically impossible. The P3P working group came up with a basic list of common personal data elements (the P3P Base Data Schema, discussed in Chapter 9) and a mechanism for extending it. However, the list was too long and unwieldy to expect users to be able to express opinions about every data element in it. And even if they could (perhaps with the assistance of a user interface that grouped these elements into a small number of categories), users would constantly encounter new data elements about which they had not yet expressed an opinion. In addition, the task of listing every piece of data collected by a large web site was also deemed nearly impossible.

To address these problems, the P3P working group introduced the notion of data *categories*. Every data element in a P3P policy is described by one or more categories. Most data elements are defined as belonging to a particular category. However, the P3P specification also allows for the definition of variable-category data elements that take different categories depending on how they are used. Web sites now have three ways to describe data in their P3P policies: they can enumerate data elements from the base data schema, they can enumerate new data elements that they have defined in their own data schemas, and they can use a miscellaneous data element (dynamic.miscdata) and declare only the categories of data they collect. Thus, web sites have a choice about how specific they want to be about the data they collect, and user agents are guaranteed to know a little bit about any data element they encounter in a P3P policy, even if they have never seen it before. This means that P3P user agents can allow users to specify preferences about specific data elements or about entire categories of data elements (or some combination thereof).

Identifiers

One of the P3P categories is *unique identifiers*. This category was originally envisioned to cover everything from login IDs to social security numbers to checking account numbers. However, this category seemed to contain too many different elements whose degrees of sensitivity varied greatly.

Some working group members suggested that P3P include two identifier categories—globally-unique and locally-unique identifiers. The globally-unique identifiers category was for identifiers used to uniquely identify an individual in a variety of contexts. For example, a social security number is a globally-unique identifier. Locally-unique identifiers need be unique in only one context. For example, when you select a login ID, it need be unique only on the computer system or web site on which you are setting up an account; it doesn't matter if someone else has the same ID on some other system. Coming up with good definitions to distinguish globally- and locally-unique identifiers proved difficult. Furthermore, some working group members worried that identifiers could easily start off as locally-unique and evolve into globally-unique identifiers. Indeed, the U.S. Social Security Number was once a locally-unique identifier, but over time it has taken on a wide variety of uses. Even something like an airline frequent-flyer number might start off as a locally-unique ID but turn into a globally-unique ID when the airline partners with hotel chains, travel agents, and others who might want to use this ID as an easy way to keep track of customers.

Finally, the P3P working group decided to focus on the identifiers that seemed to be most problematic—government-issued identifiers, such as the Social Security Number, and financial account numbers. A new category was created just for government-issued identifiers, and financial account numbers were included with other financial information in the financial category.

Credit card numbers

Credit card numbers were difficult to categorize, because they are both financial account identifiers and a component of most online purchase records. Initially, the working group was going to classify credit card numbers in the financial category. However, this would have resulted in every web site that accepted credit card payments having to disclose that it collected financial information. Users would not be able to distinguish such sites from banks and other financial institutions that collect much more extensive individual financial information. Therefore, the working group decided that credit card information and other financial account numbers could be classified in the purchase category when they are used only to facilitate a purchase.

What's Not in the P3P Vocabulary

In addition to questions about why we included various elements in the P3P vocabulary or why we use them in particular ways, I often get questions about things that are not in the P3P vocabulary. Two areas that I am frequently asked about are web site ratings and security.

I have heard many suggestions for approaches to using P3P to allow web sites to rate themselves for a variety of purposes. The most common proposal is that web sites should use P3P to indicate whether or not they contain adult content or are appropriate for children. The P3P working group did not consider adding anything along these lines to the P3P vocabulary because it is clearly outside the scope of our charter to develop a vocabulary for privacy. In addition, the W3C had already developed a protocol for web site ratings, the Platform for Internet Content Selection (PICS), discussed in Chapter 4.

Another, more relevant omission from the P3P vocabulary is any mention of security. Data security is a core privacy principle and thus is quite appropriate for the P3P vocabulary. However, the P3P working group decided not to include it, because the group was unable to come up with anything meaningful that web sites could say in their privacy policies about security. Good security is a process, and it cannot be evaluated based only on information about what software is installed on a web site or what type of encryption it uses. In the future, security issues might be addressed as part of a seal program, or web site security auditing standards might be developed. However, there are currently no established criteria by which to measure the level of web site security that can be conveyed succinctly and in a meaningful way to people who are not security experts.[*]

Finally, it is important to remember that P3P includes an extension mechanism that can be used to add new vocabulary elements. Should a consensus develop that additional elements are needed, web sites can use this mechanism to add vocabulary to their P3P policies, and user agent developers may agree to add support for these new elements in their tools. Furthermore, many companies have expressed interest in having the W3C work on a second version of P3P to address some of the issues that P3P1.0 was not able to address.

[*] The topic of web site security disclosures was discussed extensively by the FTC's Advisory Committee on Online Access and Security, on which I served in 2000. This committee was also unable to come up with much guidance on what types of security disclosures would be meaningful for web sites to make. See *http://www.ftc.gov/acoas/*.

CHAPTER 12

P3P User Agents and Other Tools

P3P policies on web sites are not very useful without tools that are able to read them. A P3P user agent is a tool that can fetch and read P3P policies and do "something useful" for users. This might include displaying symbols or text related to a site's privacy policy, determining whether a site's policy matches a user's preferences, or selectively blocking cookies based on a site's policy. P3P user agents can be standalone tools, or they may be built into web browsers, electronic wallets, or other software. P3P user agents can also be designed for personal computers, PDAs, cell phones, or other devices.

Opportunities exist for creating other types of P3P software as well. P3P policy editors and P3P-aware web site management tools can assist web sites in their P3P deployment. Search engines and comparison-shopping services might be enhanced to look for P3P policies, too.

In this chapter, we will explore the different kinds of P3P user agents and other types of P3P tools that might be created. The W3C maintains a list of available P3P tools at *http://www.w3.org/P3P/implementations/*. This chapter concludes with a discussion of requirements for building tools that comply with the P3P specification.

P3P User Agents

A wide range of different kinds of P3P user agents are possible. They can be classified according to whether they are built into a web browser, are added on to a browser, or are standalone software; whether they work on demand or continuously; whether they provide information only or take actions automatically; and the extent to which they are customizable. Furthermore, P3P user agents may be developed for a variety of platforms and may offer a number of different features.

Architecture

Some P3P user agents are built into web browsers or other end-user software applications, others are built into web proxy servers or provided as part of an ISP or other service, and still others are designed as plug-ins or other add-ons. P3P user agents can also be standalone software.

When a P3P user agent is built directly into a browser, it has direct access to all web requests and responses made by the browser. This type of implementation has the ability to alter or suppress HTTP headers as needed and to control the timing of P3P-related requests with respect to content requests. In addition, cookies can easily be suppressed or altered on the basis of their P3P policies.

As of this writing, the Microsoft Internet Explorer 6 (IE6) web browser (introduced in Chapter 1 and described in more detail in Appendix C) and the Netscape Navigator 7 web browser included P3P features, and open source developers were in the process of adding P3P features to Mozilla. In the future, other web browsers may be built with P3P features. In addition, by using Microsoft's Internet Explorer Web Browser Controls, developers could build a new P3P-enabled web browser based on Internet Explorer.*

Web proxy–based P3P user agents are built into proxy servers that intercept all of a user's web requests. Proxies can make P3P requests prior to or simultaneously with forwarding the user's requests to the web site. They can also intercept cookies and suppress or alter them based on P3P policies. Proxy servers can be set up as either remote or client-side proxies. Remote proxies are located somewhere on the Internet and usually are used by many users. Users typically do not have to download any special software to use them. Client-side proxies are run on a user's own computer and are designed for a single user. Remote proxies typically slow down Internet access (unless they take advantage of caching to improve performance) and potentially expose users to additional third-party monitoring of web browsing behavior (see the discussion of anonymizing proxies in Chapter 3). Client-side proxies have fewer potential problems; however, they still may have performance issues, as they may not be able to take advantage of all of a browser's performance optimizations. While proxies typically work with almost any web browser, they usually do not integrate cleanly into a browser's user interface.

Many client-side and remote proxies already exist for other purposes, including caching, anonymity services, and banner ad removal. The addition of a P3P user agent to these proxies may be attractive and can probably be done with minimal performance impact. A P3P user agent could also be built into services provided by an ISP.

The European Community Joint Research Center (JRC) has developed a prototype P3P user agent called the JRC P3P Proxy Service that works as either a client-side or remote proxy (*http://p3p.jrc.it*).

---

* Michael Edwards and Scott Roberts, "Reusing Internet Explorer and the Web Browser Control: An Array of Options" (MSDN Library, July 30, 1998) *http://msdn.microsoft.com/library/default.asp?url=/library/en-us/dnwebgen/html/reusebovw.asp*.

Additional functionality can be added to Netscape Navigator, Mozilla, Opera, and other web browsers by using a browser plug-in, or to the Internet Explorer web browser using a browser helper object.* P3P user agent add-ons should be more efficient than proxy implementations and integrate more readily into the browser's user interface; however, they typically have limitations not shared by browser or proxy implementations. For example, browser helper objects do not have direct access to the headers on HTTP responses that come as a result of a user's browser HTTP requests. Therefore, a browser helper object cannot look for P3P HTTP headers without making duplicate HTTP requests explicitly for this purpose or obtaining header information through some mechanism other than the documented API. In addition, a separate add-on usually must be developed for each browser with which it will be used. Nonetheless, browser add-ons are attractive because they can be developed with easy-to-use interfaces.

The AT&T Privacy Bird (introduced in Chapter 1 and described in more detail in Chapter 14) is an example of a P3P user agent implemented as a browser helper object.

P3P user agents can also be part of standalone software, such as a tool designed specifically for checking the privacy policies at web sites on demand. They can also be hybrid tools that use both proxy and browser helper object mechanisms, for example.

On Demand or Continuous

P3P user agents can be created that continuously monitor a user's interactions with web sites and check the P3P policies for all web resources a user requests. Continuous monitoring allows user agents to provide persistent indicators about site privacy policies (perhaps as symbols in the corner of the browser window) and to take automatic actions based on site policies and user preferences. Because continuous P3P user agents must be aware of a user's interactions with web sites, they must have access to all of the user's web requests.

Simpler user agents check for P3P policies only when a user requests them. These "on-demand" user agents need not be aware of a user's web requests. An on-demand user agent built into a browser or as a browser add-on can have an easy-to-use interface that allows a user to simply click a privacy button to trigger a P3P request. Standalone P3P user agents can include a form that lets a user type in a URL to check for a P3P policy. These user agents might even be web-based, requiring no software downloads.

The AT&T Privacy Bird is an example of a continuous P3P user agent. It is a browser helper object that checks for P3P policies associated with every site a user visits—both for embedded images and other content, and for the surrounding page. It

---

* Dino Esposito, "Browser Helper Objects: The Browser the Way You Want It" (MSDN Library, January 1999) *http://msdn.microsoft.com/library/default.asp?url=/library/en-us/dnwebgen/html/bho.asp.*

displays a symbol in the top-right corner of the browser window to convey P3P-related information.

IE6 and Netscape 7 are examples of both continuous and on-demand user agents. They continuously monitor requests by web sites to set cookies and check for P3P compact policies associated with these cookies; however, they do not continuously check for full P3P policies associated with these web sites. To get information about a site's full P3P policies, a user must explicitly request a privacy report by selecting the appropriate option from the IE6 or Netscape 7 View menus.

The W3C P3P Validator was not designed as a P3P user agent; however, it can be thought of as a very basic on-demand P3P user agent that simply fetches and displays raw P3P policies without translating them into a more human-friendly format.

Information-Only or Automatic Action

Some P3P user agents simply inform users about site policies, while others may take automatic actions, such as blocking cookies or referer headers. Some automatic user agents might block access altogether to web sites that don't match a user's preferences. Others might control access to a user's electronic wallet or data repository on the basis of a site's P3P policy.

The W3C P3P Validator is the simplest kind of information-only user agent, as it presents the raw XML of the P3P policy and indicates whether it is a valid P3P policy. The AT&T Privacy Bird is a much more sophisticated information-only user agent. It compares a site's P3P policy with a user's preferences and displays a symbol that indicates whether the policy matches the user's preferences. It also generates a human-readable "policy summary" from the XML policy.

The IE6 privacy report and Netscape 7 privacy summary features are on-demand, information-only P3P user agents. The privacy report and privacy summary are similar to the AT&T Privacy Bird's policy summary. However, IE6 and Netscape 7 also include automated tools for checking the P3P compact policies associated with cookies and then processing the cookies according to the user's settings. IE6 and Netscape 7 are able to allow cookies as-is or block them. In addition, they have the ability to "downgrade" cookies by turning persistent cookies into cookies that will be deleted at the end of a user's session. IE6 can also "leash" cookies by allowing them to be used only in a first-party context and not in a third-party context (Appendix C describes IE6 cookie filtering in more detail). Netscape 7 can "flag" cookies so that users are alerted with a cookie icon.

The JRC P3P user agent can be configured to block cookies and referer headers based on P3P policies and to deny users access to web sites that do not match their privacy preferences.

Generic or Customized

The degree to which P3P user agents can be customized varies quite a bit. At one extreme are generic user agents that offer users no choices; at the other end are customized user agents that allow users to specify detailed preferences and actions to take based on these preferences. The P3P specification requires that compliant implementations offer users the ability to import preference settings using a documented preference language.

An on-demand P3P user agent that simply displays a P3P policy, perhaps in an easy-to-read format, is an example of a generic P3P user agent. A continuous P3P user agent that displays a privacy "rating" for each site based on its interpretation of the site's P3P policy is also a generic P3P user agent (assuming users are not given any ability to influence the rating—for example, by weighting some aspects of a privacy policy as more important than others). Generic P3P user agents can even take automatic actions based on P3P policies, without giving users an opportunity to determine when these actions should be taken.

The simplest way for a P3P user agent to offer customized features is to provide a small number of settings options. IE6 offers six basic cookie settings, which determine when cookies are blocked, leashed, or downgraded. In addition, users can configure IE6 to make exceptions for cookies from certain sites. Also, users can import custom settings for a wide range of preferences and actions (see Appendix D for details on how to do this). Figure 12-1 shows the IE6 privacy settings panel.

The AT&T Privacy Bird offers three basic privacy settings. The settings panel, shown in Figure 12-2, shows the specific warnings that are triggered by each setting and allows users to further customize their settings by checking or unchecking the corresponding boxes. Users can also import settings files written in a limited version of the APPEL language (described in detail in Chapter 13).

The JRC P3P Proxy Service is fully customizable using the APPEL language.

Other Types of P3P Tools

In addition to user agents, a variety of other types of P3P tools are being developed. P3P editors, generators, and validators have already been created, and web site management tools with P3P features are emerging. P3P search and comparison tools are also envisioned in the future.

Generators and Editors

P3P generators and editors generate policy and policy reference files for web sites. For most web site operators, these tools are a convenient alternative to creating P3P files by hand.

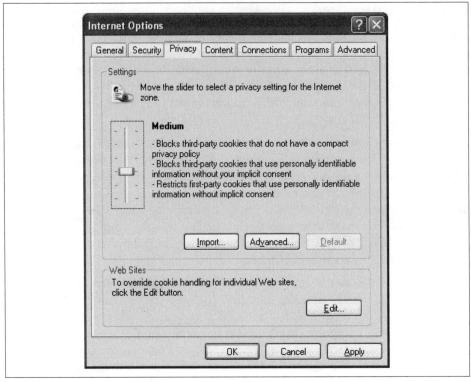

Figure 12-1. The IE6 privacy settings panel allows users to select one of six preset settings, import customized settings, or override settings for particular web sites

As discussed in Chapters 5 and 7, the IBM P3P Policy Editor is a popular tool for generating P3P files. The IBM tool has a drag-and-drop interface that allows policy creators to drag policy components into position and select the appropriate properties for each. You can create almost any legal P3P policy with this tool.

Policy-generator tools that provide questionnaires for policy creators to fill out can be somewhat easier to use than the IBM P3P Policy Editor, but they offer less flexibility. For many web sites, these tools may be adequate. Microsoft provided such a "Privacy Wizard" for earlier versions of the P3P specification. Watch for a future release of an updated version of the Microsoft Privacy Wizard.

Validators

P3P validators are useful for verifying that a web site has been properly P3P-enabled. They can check policy or compact policy syntax and make sure the policies referenced in policy reference files are accessible. Of course, they can't verify that a P3P policy accurately represents a site's practices.

The W3C provides a P3P Validator as a service on its web site (*http://www.w3.org/ P3P/validator/*). The Validator allows you to type in a URL to check whether it has

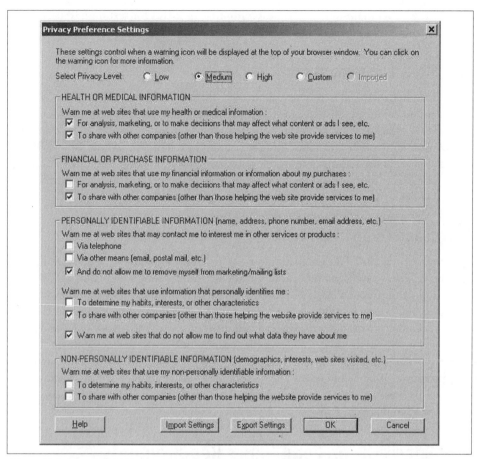

Figure 12-2. The AT&T Privacy Bird privacy settings panel allows users to select one of three pre-set settings, customize their settings, or import settings files written in a simplified version of the APPEL language

been properly P3P-enabled (integrated validation) or to upload an individual P3P policy or policy reference file. The integrated validation feature also allows you to view all the headers that a site sends back in response to a request, so that you can see any P3P headers that might be included. The W3C makes the source code of the Validator available for anyone interested in running the Validator on his own system.

David Grant has a P3P "Compact Policy Translator" service on his web site (*http://www.davidjonathangrant.info/p3p/*). This service allows you to type in a compact policy and have it translated into a human-readable format. In addition, the translator checks for errors, provides information on how the compact policy will be treated by IE6, and provides information on configuring different kinds of web servers to send this policy as an HTTP header. Grant also makes the source code of his service available.

Finally, the W3C maintains a P3P Test Suite that is useful for testing P3P user agent tools (*http://p3ptest-1.w3.org*).

Web Site Management Tools

Tools that help web sites manage their own privacy policies and monitor compliance are beginning to incorporate P3P-related features. As discussed in Chapter 5, several web site monitoring tools have features that you can use to monitor the deployment of cookies and compact policies on your web site and see how P3P user agents will respond to your site's policy. In the future, we may see web site editing tools that include options to generate P3P policies directly from web forms or to update policy reference files as new content is generated.

Search and Comparison Tools

As more sites become P3P-enabled, it would be useful to have P3P features built into search engines. Search engines could weight search results on the basis of a privacy score derived from each site's P3P policy, or they could allow users to indicate their privacy preferences and filter search results on the basis of whether sites match these preferences. Shopping tools that already allow comparison of vendors of a particular product on the basis of price, shipping terms, and customer satisfaction ratings might also include comparisons on the basis of P3P policies in the future. Currently, it is a difficult and tedious process for consumers who are interested in selecting vendors on the basis of privacy policies to do so—the advent of P3P-enabled search and comparison tools could make such selections feasible.

P3P Specification Compliance Requirements

This book focuses primarily on the P3P compliance requirements for web sites. However, the P3P specification includes a variety of requirements that apply to P3P user agents and other P3P software. This section presents a brief overview of these requirements. If you are developing P3P software, you should also read the P3P specification to make sure you understand all of these requirements.

Fetching and Processing P3P Policies and Policy Reference Files

The P3P specification requires that P3P user agents be able to fetch P3P policy reference files at the well-known location and as specified in a P3P HTTP header. User agents that render HTML are also required to be able to fetch policy reference files specified using a P3P HTML LINK tag. P3P user agents are required to be able to parse the policy reference file, determine what policy applies to a given URL or cookie, and fetch that policy.

P3P user agents must not use P3P policy and policy reference files that have expired. However, they are not required to cache these files until they expire.

The P3P specification does not place any requirements on when a P3P user agent fetches P3P files. User agents may fetch these files before fetching requested content, to provide privacy information prior to taking actions that may have privacy implications, but they can also fetch P3P files simultaneously with or after fetching requested content. Regardless, it is recommended that user agents suppress as much unnecessary information as possible (referer and other optional headers, cookies, etc.) until P3P files have been fetched and evaluated.

P3P user agents are not required to take advantage of HINT elements in policy reference files or to fetch or process compact policies. These are optional performance optimizations.

The P3P specification requires user agents to render or act upon only P3P files that are well-formed XML. It recommends that user agents render or act upon only P3P files that conform to the P3P XML schema, but this is not a requirement.

Guiding Principles

The P3P specification includes the P3P Guiding Principles as an appendix (reproduced here as Appendix E). The Guiding Principles include 13 specific recommendations for P3P user agent software:

1. *User agents should provide mechanisms for displaying a service's information practices to users.*

   User agents should include a way for users to get a human-readable representation of a site's P3P policy, or possibly a symbolic representation of key points from the policy.

2. *User agents should provide users with an option that allows them to easily preview and agree to or reject each transfer of personal information that the user agent facilitates.*

3. *User agents should not be configured by default to transfer personal information to a service provider without the user's consent.*

   These two guidelines apply only to user agents that include automatic form fillers or other data-transfer mechanisms. These user agents should not transfer data silently in the background without the user's consent. While there may be a setting that allows the user to select automatic data transfer, the default setting should require user consent before each data transfer. For example, a user agent might fill out a form automatically and provide a submit button that the user must press before any data is transferred.

4. *User agents should inform users about the privacy-related options offered by the user agent.*

P3P user agents should include help files, tutorials, or other information to help users understand their privacy-related options. Because many users are not familiar with privacy terminology and the details of privacy policies, user agents may serve to help educate users in this area.

5. *User agents should include configuration tools that allow users to customize their preferences.*

    Not everyone will want their P3P user agents to behave the same way. P3P user agents should be configurable so that users can select settings that reflect their personal preferences. If the user agent has a feature that judges web site policies or compares them with user preferences, it is especially important that the user be able to customize these preferences. The P3P specification also requires that P3P user agents be able to import user preference files using a documented preference language.

6. *User agents should allow users to import and customize P3P preferences from trusted parties.*

    Setting up detailed preference configurations can be difficult and time-consuming, and it might require more knowledge about privacy policies than most users have. User agents should provide a mechanism for importing preference files, so that these files can be created and distributed by privacy advocates or other parties with expertise in this area that users trust. The P3P specification further requires that "User agents MUST document a method by which preferences can be imported and processed." The APPEL language (described in Chapter 13) was designed for this purpose, but user agent implementers may alternatively specify their own language.

7. *User agents should present configuration options to users in a way that is neutral or biased toward privacy.*

    Because P3P user agents are supposed to assist users in protecting their privacy, they should not be biased against privacy protections. Thus, configuration options should be presented in a neutral way, or they should be presented in a way that is biased toward privacy. For example, any default settings should be neutral or more privacy-protective than other settings.

8. *User agents should be usable without requiring the user to store personal information as part of the installation or configuration process.*

    User agents that have automatic data-transfer capabilities should not require that users store personal information to use the user agent. Users may not want to take advantage of the data-transfer capabilities, or they may want to enter this data at the beginning of each session and not have it stored permanently on their computers. User agents that do not have data-transfer capabilities should not need users to store their personal information.

9. *User agents should act only on behalf of the user according to the preferences specified by the user.*

   The P3P specification actually has a formal requirement that is even stronger than this guideline: "P3P user agents MUST act according to the preference settings selected by the user." This guideline and requirement have a variety of implications. First, the guideline implies that user agents should allow users to specify preferences and that they should act in the user's interests rather than in the interests of web sites or other parties. Then the requirement says that user agents need to make sure they can act according to these preferences. This has the implication, for example, that when user agents encounter P3P policies with syntax errors, whatever they decide to do with these errors must be consistent with the user's preferences. If by ignoring the syntax errors the user agent might mistakenly take an action contrary to the user's preferences, this requirement implies that the user agent should not ignore the syntax error.

10. *User agents should accurately represent the practices of the service provider.*

    User agents usually provide either a human-readable representation of a site's P3P policy or a set of symbols to provide information about the site's P3P policy. Whenever a user agent presents such information, it should present this information accurately, so as not to misrepresent web site policies.

11. *User agents should provide mechanisms for protecting the personal information that users store in any data repositories maintained by the agent.*

12. *User agents should use appropriate trusted protocols for the secure transmission of data.*

13. *User agents should warn users when an insecure transport mechanism is being used.*

    These three guidelines apply primarily to user agents that include automatic data-transfer mechanisms. P3P user agents that transfer data should take appropriate security precautions both while the data is being transferred and while it is being stored on the user's computer. User agents that do not include automatic data-transfer mechanisms may be built into web browsers or other tools that users can use to fill out forms and transfer data themselves. Whenever possible, these tools should warn users when they are transferring data using an insecure mechanism.

CHAPTER 13

A P3P Preference Exchange Language (APPEL)

The P3P 1.0 specification provides a standard syntax for web sites to express their privacy practices, but it does not include a syntax for users to express their preferences about these practices. A P3P Preference Exchange Language (APPEL)* is a separate W3C specification designed to provide a standard language for expressing privacy preferences.† User agents can be P3P-compliant without implementing the APPEL specification.

This chapter provides an overview of the goals of the APPEL specification, instructions for writing APPEL rule sets, and an overview of how P3P user agents evaluate APPEL rule sets. It also includes some APPEL rule set examples and information about alternative P3P preference languages.

APPEL Goals

The primary goal in developing the APPEL language was to facilitate the sharing and installation of user privacy preferences in the form of rule sets. Given the complexity of the P3P vocabulary, P3P working group members believed that most users would set their P3P preferences using a tool that substantially simplified the choices. However, limiting privacy choices to a small number of options selected by user agent developers makes users depend on these developers to select reasonable privacy options. If users are to delegate these choices, it is likely that they would prefer to delegate them to someone they trust to act in their best interest—probably not a commercial software vendor. Therefore, a mechanism is needed to allow other

---

* The APPEL working group members initially weren't sure how to pronounce this acronym, but eventually agreed to pronounce it a-pell, as in the French *appel* (call), not the English *apple*, so as to avoid any associations with a certain computer manufacturer.

† The description of APPEL in this chapter is based on the 15 April 2002 APPEL working draft, available from *http://www.w3.org/TR/2002/WD-P3P-preferences-20020415/*. This working draft has not been finalized as of this writing and is therefore subject to change. The latest draft is available online from *http://www.w3.org/TR/P3P-preferences/*. Use the change log at the end of the latest draft to determine what changes were made.

parties to develop "canned" P3P settings files that users can import into their user agents. This allows privacy advocates and sophisticated users to create P3P settings and distribute them to others.

Giving privacy advocates the ability to create P3P settings files allows them to effectively rate the privacy practices of thousands of web sites without having to visit each one. Privacy advocates can simply encode their rating criteria into an APPEL file and distribute it to users to import into their P3P user agents, or they can set up a web-based tool that allows users to type in a URL and have it rated against an APPEL file. Of course, the APPEL rating criteria are limited to the fields included in the self-reported P3P policy. However, a web-based tool could also factor in other information (e.g., information about the number of privacy complaints filed against a site). User agents could be built that query servers for this additional information and take it into account as well.

Another goal in developing APPEL was to provide a way for users to share their preferences with a variety of agents. For example, a P3P-enabled search engine might rank search results based on how closely each site matches a user's privacy preferences. Such a tool might allow users to select from several preset preference settings or upload their own APPEL files. Furthermore, APPEL gives users who use multiple computers or more than one P3P user agent the ability to easily share their privacy settings across user agents.

As discussed in Chapter 1, the idea for P3P grew out of the W3C's Platform for Internet Content Selection (PICS) project. PICS included a language for encoding user preferences about PICS labels, called PICSRules (*http://www.w3.org/TR/REC-PICSRules/*). Much of the underlying logic of APPEL is borrowed from PICSRules. However, APPEL is necessarily more complex than PICSRules, because while PICSRules was designed to make decisions based on simple attribute-value pairs, APPEL was designed to make decisions based on semistructured XML documents. The APPEL working group explored the possibility of using an existing database query language or a trust management system* rather than defining a new language. The existing languages we explored would have placed a large implementation burden on user agent implementers, and they were not well suited for processing XML. The W3C XML Query (*http://www.w3.org/XML/Query/*) work may eventually result in a language suitable for encoding and processing P3P preferences. This language will probably offer more flexibility than APPEL, and if it becomes a standard browser component, the implementation overhead will be reduced. Anticipating that XML Query may eventually become a suitable language for use in P3P user agents, the APPEL working group focused on developing a special-purpose rule language for P3P that could easily be implemented in P3P user agents under development as the P3P 1.0 specification was being completed.

---

* See, for example, the Keynote Trust Management System (*http://www.cis.upenn.edu/~angelos/keynote.html*).

APPEL Evaluator Engines

APPEL can be implemented in P3P user agents in a variety of ways. P3P user agents that use APPEL for importing preference files may represent APPEL rules internally, using the same XML structures used by the language, or they may use their own representations. However, for simplicity, I assume that user agents represent APPEL rules internally the same way they are encoded in the language. I also assume that each user agent includes a software module called an APPEL evaluator engine. All P3P user agents that comply with APPEL should *appear* to function this way, even if they actually function in a different way internally.

After a user agent fetches a P3P policy, it passes to the APPEL engine the policy, any data schemas it references, and the URL of the requested resource. This information passed to the APPEL engine is referred to as the *evidence*. In addition to the evidence, the APPEL engine is given an APPEL file, in which privacy preferences are represented as a series of one or more rules. The engine evaluates the evidence against each rule in turn; when a match is found, the corresponding rule fires. The engine returns information about the first rule to fire. Optionally, the engine may continue evaluation after a rule fires and return information about all of the rules that fired. The rule evaluation process is described in more detail later in this chapter.

Writing APPEL Rule Sets

APPEL files are called *rule sets* because they are composed of a series of one or more rules. Each rule includes a pattern to be matched against P3P policies and an action to be taken in the event that a match is found (request a resource, block a site, or request a resource but limit the request headers to essential headers only). Rules can match simple patterns—for example, a particular purpose or data element—or they can match more complex patterns—for example, a specific data element used for either or both of two specific purposes and shared in a specific way.

APPEL rule sets are encoded in XML.* As you can see from Example 13-1, the syntax looks very similar to P3P policy syntax, because APPEL rule sets include fragments of P3P policies. Example 13-1 shows an APPEL rule set that includes four rules. The first rule fires at any site in the *example.com* domain, regardless of what P3P policy is in place. The second rule fires if a policy contains the same, other-recipient, public, or unrelated recipient. The third rule fires if a policy contains the health category and the contact, telemarketing, or other-purpose purpose. The fourth rule fires if no other rules fire.

---

* Many of the languages designed to do pattern matching over XML are not themselves encoded in XML. The use of XML makes APPEL fairly easy to read and allows APPEL to be parsed with the same parser used for parsing the P3P policy. However, the syntax for expressing logical connectives (and, or, etc.) in APPEL is somewhat awkward.

Example 13-1. An APPEL rule set with four rules

```
<appel:RULESET xmlns:appel="http://www.w3.org/2002/03/APPELv1"
               xmlns:p3p="http://www.w3.org/2002/01/P3Pv1"
               crtdby="W3C" crtdon="2002-03-15T16:41:21+01:00">

  <appel:RULE behavior="request" prompt="no"
              description="This is a trustworthy site.">
    <appel:REQUEST-GROUP>
      <appel:REQUEST uri="http://*.example.com/*"/>
    </appel:REQUEST-GROUP>
  </appel:RULE>

  <appel:RULE behavior="limited" prompt="yes"
              description="Warning! Data may be shared.">
    <p3p:POLICY>
      <p3p:STATEMENT>
        <p3p:RECIPIENT appel:connective="or">
          <p3p:same/>
          <p3p:other-recipient/>
          <p3p:public/>
          <p3p:unrelated/>
        </p3p:RECIPIENT>
      </p3p:STATEMENT>
    </p3p:POLICY>
  </appel:RULE>

  <appel:RULE behavior="limited" prompt="yes"
              description="Warning! Healthcare data may be used for
              marketing or unknown purposes.">
    <p3p:POLICY>
      <p3p:STATEMENT appel:connective="and">
        <p3p:PURPOSE appel:connective="or">
          <p3p:contact/>
          <p3p:telemarketing/>
          <p3p:other-purpose/>
        </p3p:PURPOSE>
        <p3p:DATA-GROUP>
          <p3p:DATA>
            <p3p:CATEGORIES>
              <p3p:health/>
            </p3p:CATEGORIES>
          </p3p:DATA>
        </p3p:DATA-GROUP>
      </p3p:STATEMENT>
    </p3p:POLICY>
  </appel:RULE>

  <appel:RULE behavior="request"
              description="Privacy policy matches your preferences">
    <appel:OTHERWISE/>
  </appel:RULE>

</appel:RULESET>
```

Like P3P policies, APPEL rule sets can be written manually or with a special-purpose editor. The European Joint Research Center has created an APPEL rule set editor that you can download for free from *http://p3p.jrc.it/downloadP3P.php*. As shown in Figure 13-1, the JRC RuleSet Editor features a graphical user interface for creating rules and specifying the order in which they should appear. The APPEL code is shown at the bottom of the window. Clicking the New Advanced button opens the window shown in Figure 13-2, which allows for the creation of detailed patterns to be matched against P3P policies.

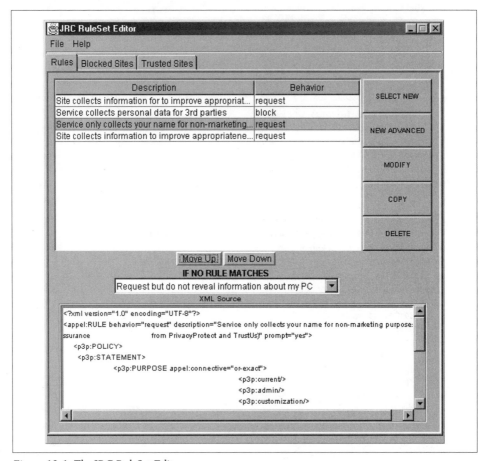

Figure 13-1. The JRC RuleSet Editor

Rule Sets

Each rule set contains a single `appel:RULESET` element, which contains a sequence of one or more rules. The APPEL engine evaluates these rules in the order in which they

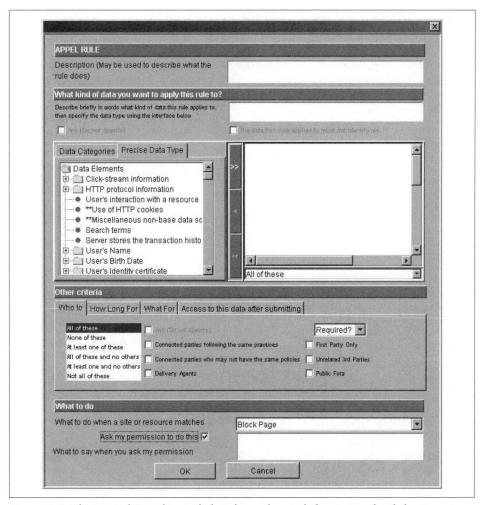

Figure 13-2. The JRC RuleSet Editor includes advanced controls for creating detailed patterns to match against P3P policies

appear. Each rule evaluates to either true or false. Once a rule is found that evaluates to true, evaluation stops and the APPEL engine returns information about the rule that fired (optionally, evaluation may continue and the APPEL engine may return information about all of the rules that fired). The appel:RULESET element has three optional attributes:

crtdby

The name of the rule set's author—generally either a person or an automated tool. This is used primarily for internal documentation, although it could be displayed to a user who is selecting a rule set.

crtdon

> The time and date at which the rule set was created (formatted as per section 3.3 of RFC 2068, explained at the end of Chapter 6, or as per ISO8601*). This is used primarily for internal documentation, although it could be displayed to a user who is selecting a rule set.

description

> A short explanation that the user agent can display when a user is selecting a rule set.

In addition, APPEL rule sets must include XML namespace declarations to indicate both the version of APPEL and the version of P3P being used. Here is an example of an opening tag of an APPEL rule set that includes just these two required attributes:

```
<appel:RULESET xmlns:appel="http://www.w3.org/2002/03/APPELv1"
               xmlns:p3p="http://www.w3.org/2002/01/P3Pv1">
```

Rules

Each appel:RULESET element contains one or more rules, represented by appel:RULE elements. Each appel:RULE element takes a mandatory behavior attribute and seven optional attributes:

behavior

> The action that should be taken if a match is found for the pattern part of the rule—either request, limited, or block.

appel:connective

> A logical connective—either or, non-or, and, non-and, or-exact, or and-exact.

crtdby

> The name of the rule author—generally either a person or an automated tool.

crtdon

> The time and date at which the rule was created (formatted as per section 3.3 of RFC 2068 or as per ISO8601).

description

> A short explanation that can be displayed by the user agent when a rule fires or used to assist in rule file debugging.

prompt

> Whether or not an informational prompt should be displayed to the user when the rule fires (yes or no). The default value is no. It is recommended, but not required, that user agents have the ability to display such prompts. User agents

---

* ISO8601: *Data elements and interchange formats—Information interchange—Representation of dates and times.* International Organization for Standardization. The key points from this document necessary to format dates and times are summarized at *http://www.w3.org/TR/NOTE-datetime/.*

may offer users choices when they display these prompts, (e.g., whether to override the indicated behavior).

persona
> For user agents that support form filling and multiple user data repositories, this string identifies the data repository that should be used if a form is to be filled out automatically.

promptmsg
> A short explanation that the user agent can display when prompting the user to make a decision.

The description and promptmsg attributes are similar; however, there is an important distinction between them. A description is designed to be displayed as part of a passive message to the user or included in descriptive information about a site's policy. A promptmsg is designed to be included in an active user prompt, which will typically require the user to make a decision or take some action. Both attributes are designed to contain text written in a natural language readable by a particular group of users. To support users who speak different languages, rule set creators can create multiple identical rule sets that differ only in the language used for these human-readable messages.

The behavior attribute takes one of three possible values, indicating the action user agents should take after a rule fires:

request
> The user agent should proceed with requesting the resource.

limited
> The user agent should proceed with requesting the resource but should transmit only the minimal HTTP headers necessary for the request—generally, this means that user agents will suppress cookies and referer headers.

block
> The user agent should not request the resource.

Each of these behaviors may be combined with a user prompt if the prompt attribute is set to yes. A promptmsg should be provided in this case.

Pattern Matching

Each APPEL rule contains a pattern to be matched, in the form of a p3p:POLICY element, an appel:otherwise element, an appel:REQUEST-GROUP element, or an appel:REQUEST-GROUP element followed by a p3p:POLICY element.

Matching patterns in policies

Rules designed to match patterns in P3P policies include p3p:POLICY elements. These elements contain snippets of a P3P policy. Each element from a P3P policy appears exactly as it would appear in the policy, except that it is prefixed with p3p: and can optionally take an appel:connective attribute.

Any P3P policy element that is part of the match criteria must appear in the APPEL rule. The element must appear in its proper context—that is, surrounded by its parent element, which must be surrounded by its parent element, etc., all the way up to the POLICY element. So, for example, if you want to create an APPEL rule that will fire when a policy contains the telemarketing purpose, you need to include the telemarketing element, the PURPOSE element, the STATEMENT element, and the POLICY element in the APPEL rule, each prefixed as follows:

```
<p3p:POLICY>
  <p3p:STATEMENT>
    <p3p:PURPOSE>
      <p3p:telemarketing/>
    </p3p:PURPOSE>
  </p3p:STATEMENT>
</p3p:POLICY>
```

You can also specify multiple elements from a P3P policy that will trigger a rule to fire. By default, if multiple elements appear in the rule, they all must appear in the policy for the rule to fire. This can also be represented explicitly by using the and connective. For example, the following pattern matches policies that contain both the telemarketing and contact purposes:

```
<p3p:POLICY>
  <p3p:STATEMENT>
    <p3p:PURPOSE appel:connective="and">
      <p3p:contact/>
      <p3p:telemarketing/>
    </p3p:PURPOSE>
  </p3p:STATEMENT>
</p3p:POLICY>
```

This snippet would have the same meaning even if appel:connective="and" was omitted. Other connectives allow us to specify other logical relationships, such as or and not.

Connectives apply to the subelements of the element to which they are attached. Thus, in the previous example, the connective applies to the p3p:contact and p3p: telemarketing elements. These subelements are referred to as *contained expressions*.

Here are the six APPEL connectives and the rules for applying them:

or

> Matches if at least one of the contained expressions appears in the policy. Always fails if there are no contained expressions. Useful for rules that should fire if "*one or more of the following* is present."

and

> Matches if all of the contained expressions appear at the correct positions in the policy (the default when no connective is given). Always matches if there are no

contained expressions. Useful for rules that should fire if "*all of the following* are present."

non-or

Matches if none of the contained expressions appear in the policy. Always matches if there are no contained expressions. This is the equivalent of negating an or. Useful for rules that should fire if "*none of the following* are present."

non-and

Matches if not all of the contained expressions appear at the correct position in the policy. Always fails if there are no contained expressions. This is the equivalent of negating an and. Useful for rules that should fire if "*the following group as a whole* is *not* present."

or-exact

Matches if at least one of the contained expressions appears in the policy and no other expressions appear in that part of the policy. Always fails if there are no contained expressions. Useful for rules that should fire if "*one or more of the following and nothing else* is present."

and-exact

Matches if all of the contained expressions appear at the correct positions in the policy and no other expressions appear in that part of the policy. Always matches if there are no contained expressions and the policy does not contain any subelements at the corresponding positions. Useful for rules that should fire if "*all of the following and nothing else* are present."

 You can specify a rule that fires at web sites that do not have P3P policies by using a non-or connective in the appel:RULE element:

```
<appel:RULE behavior="behavior"
        appel:connective="non-or">
    <p3p:POLICY/>
</appel:RULE>
```

Sometimes you might want to specify match criteria that include one or more attributes of an element. For example, suppose you want a rule to fire if a policy contains the telemarketing element with the required="opt-out" attribute. This would be represented in an APPEL rule as follows:

```
<p3p:POLICY>
  <p3p:STATEMENT>
    <p3p:PURPOSE>
      <p3p:telemarketing required="opt-out" />
    </p3p:PURPOSE>
  </p3p:STATEMENT>
</p3p:POLICY>
```

Attributes in rules match attributes in policies whenever both their names and values are identical. If an element in a rule has attributes, the corresponding element in the policy must have the same attributes. Any additional attributes found in the corresponding element in the policy are ignored, regardless of what connective is used.

Attribute values in rules may use the * wildcard character to represent any string of zero or more characters (but the wildcard character is not permitted in the ref attribute of the p3p:DATA element or the base attribute of the p3p:DATA-GROUP element).

In attribute values, URLs that contain spaces, punctuation characters, or other special characters must be properly escaped, as per RFC 1738 (*http://www.ietf.org/rfc/rfc1738.txt*).

An APPEL rule can contain at most one of each of the following elements: p3p:POLICY, p3p:STATEMENT, and p3p:DATA-GROUP.

Rules limited to certain URLs

The appel:REQUEST-GROUP element is used to limit the application of a rule to a specific URL or set of URLs. An appel:REQUEST-GROUP element contains one or more appel:REQUEST elements. Each appel:REQUEST element specifies a URL to which the rule should be applied. When a user visits one of these URLs, the APPEL engine will evaluate this rule; otherwise, the rule will be skipped. The * wildcard can be used in a URL to represent any string of zero or more characters and thus specify a range of URLs. Optionally, the appel:REQUEST-GROUP can take an appel:connective attribute.

In appel:REQUEST elements, URLs that contain spaces, punctuation characters, or other special characters must be properly escaped, as per RFC 1738.

APPEL engines are not expected to follow URLs or have any understanding of HTTP redirects. It is up to the user agent that invokes the APPEL engine to supply the appropriate URL for evaluation. Once the user agent discovers that a URL has been redirected, it should evaluate the policy for the URL from which the resource is ultimately available.

This example appel:REQUEST-GROUP element applies a rule to any URL of any site in the *example.com* domain, as well as to the home page of *www.example.net*:

```
<appel:REQUEST-GROUP appel:connective="or">
  <appel:REQUEST uri="http://*.example.com/*"/>
  <appel:REQUEST uri="http://www.example.net/"/>
</appel:REQUEST-GROUP>
```

Catch-all rules

Rules are evaluated in the order in which they appear in a rule set. In some cases, a rule evaluator will get to the end of a rule set without having any rule fire. The appel:OTHERWISE element is placed in the last rule in a rule set and is used to indicate what should happen if no rule fires.

Rule Order

Because APPEL rules are processed in the order in which they appear in the rule set, and the first rule that fires determines the user agent's behavior, rule ordering is significant. Two rule sets that contain identical rules in different orders may produce different results.

Figuring out the order for a rule file can be tricky. I find it easiest to start by writing down all the rules I want to fire when a policy contains something "bad." These rules will generally have limited or block behaviors, and they may have prompts. Then I write down any exceptions to these rules, which usually have the request behavior. For example, I might decide that a policy with the other-recipient recipient is generally bad, but I might make an exception if the only data collected is from the preference or computer category. If there are sites that I want to access regardless of their P3P policies, I also consider them to be exceptions. I then order the rules so that the exceptions appear first, then the bad rules. I order the bad rules with the worst stuff appearing first, so that the first rule to fire will be the one that the user is likely to care about the most. If some of the bad rules have the block behavior and others have the limited behavior, I place all of the block rules before the limited rules. I usually place an appel:OTHERWISE element at the end and give it the request behavior, so that any policy that doesn't include something "bad" will be assumed to be "good."

There are, of course, lots of other ways to approach rule ordering. One of the other authors of the APPEL specification prefers to enumerate all of the good things he is looking for in policies and place those rules first in his rule set. Any policy that is not "good" he assumes to be "bad."

Processing APPEL Rules

This section explains the nitty-gritty details of processing APPEL rules. It is written primarily for APPEL engine implementers. Those readers not implementing APPEL engines may want to skip to the next section.

 Java source code for an APPEL engine is available as a free download from JRC at *http://p3p.jrc.it/downloadP3P.php*.

APPEL Engine Inputs and Outputs

As already discussed, a P3P user agent submits to an APPEL evaluator engine a rule set and various pieces of evidence. The evidence includes:

- The URL of the requested resource
- A P3P policy
- Any data schemas referenced by the P3P policy

It is also useful to pass the APPEL engine the URLs of the P3P policy and data schemas.

After evaluating the rule set against the evidence and finding a rule that fires, the APPEL engine returns:

- A behavior (request, block, or limited)
- The value of the prompt attribute (if the rule that fired had this attribute)
- The value of the description, promptmsg, and persona attributes (if the rule that fired had any of these attributes)
- Optionally, the rule that fired

An APPEL engine can optionally return this information about all of the rules that fired, not just the first.

APPEL Rule Evaluation

An APPEL engine evaluates the pattern part of each rule against the evidence, to determine whether there is a match. A formal definition of a match involving a p3p: POLICY element appears below. (The APPEL engine must also be able to check for matches involving appel:OTHERWISE and appel:REQUEST-GROUP elements.) In this definition, the term *contained expression* refers to any subelement of an XML element or to a text string (called PCDATA) that appears between the opening and closing tags of an XML element and outside the tags themselves. The term *expression* refers to an XML element, its attributes, and its contained expressions.

Several normalization procedures must be done before checking for a match. Normalization procedures and special rules for handling PCDATA, attributes, and DATA elements are described later in this section.

 P3P policies and APPEL rule sets are case-sensitive.

Definition: An expression "E" matches an XML element or PCDATA string "X" in the evidence if and only if all of the following eight rules hold:

1. The names of XML element E and X are identical, or the values of PCDATA string E and X are identical (after both have been normalized).
2. For each attribute in E, there is an attribute with an identical name and value in X (after the attributes in E and X have been normalized and wildcard and DATA element rules have been accounted for).
3. *If E includes an* or *connective*, a match can be found in X for at least one of E's contained expressions by applying these eight rules (this rule always fails if E has no contained expressions).
4. *If E includes an* and *connective or no connective*, a match can be found in X for all of E's contained expressions by applying these eight rules.

5. *If E includes a* non-or *connective,* no match can be found in X for any of E's contained expressions by applying these eight rules.

6. *If E includes a* non-and *connective,* no match can be found in X for at least one of E's contained expressions by applying these eight rules (this rule always fails if E has no contained expressions).

7. *If E includes an* or-exact *connective,* a match can be found in X for at least one of E's contained expressions by applying these eight rules, and X does not contain any expressions for which a match cannot be found in E by applying these eight rules.

8. *If E includes an* and-exact *connective,* a match can be found in X for all of E's contained expressions by applying these eight rules, and X does not contain any expressions for which a match cannot be found in E by applying these eight rules (if E has no contained expressions, this rule holds only if X has no contained expressions).

PCDATA

Some P3P elements can include text strings between the opening and closing tags but outside the tags themselves. These text strings are called PCDATA. The CONSEQUENCE element takes PCDATA. For example:

```
<CONSEQUENCE>This info helps us serve you better.</CONSEQUENCE>
```

The following steps must be taken to normalize any PCDATA in both a rule and the evidence:

1. Remove all XML comments (XML comments begin with <!-- and end with -->).

2. Replace all occurrences of tabs (#x9), line feeds (#xA), and carriage returns (#xD) with spaces (#x20).

3. Replace each contiguous sequence of spaces with a single space.

4. Remove any leading or trailing spaces.

When APPEL rules contain PCDATA that includes the * wildcard character, a string of zero or more characters in the evidence may match the *.

 Some XML parsers treat a block of PCDATA that contains XML comments as two or more separate PCDATA blocks. Such blocks should be merged during the normalization process, or the matching algorithm must treat these blocks as if they had been merged.

Here is an example of some PCDATA:

```
     This  is
<!-- This is a comment -->
   an     example.
```

And here is how it looks after it has been normalized:

```
This is an example.
```

Attributes

Attribute matching involves a string comparison on both the attribute name and attribute value. The following normalization must be done before attempting to match attributes:

- Attributes that have defined default values should be explicitly added to the evidence wherever they have been omitted. Table 13-1 lists the attributes of P3P elements that have default values.

- Characters in URLs that are required to be escaped according to RFC 1738 must be escaped. Escaped characters in URLs that are not required to be escaped according to RFC 1738 must be unescaped, with the exception of literal asterisk characters.

- Literal asterisk characters (those not intended to be wildcards) must be escaped in both the rules and the evidence.

In addition, when APPEL rules contain attributes that use the * wildcard character, a string of zero or more characters in the evidence may match the *.

Table 13-1. Attributes of P3P elements that take default values

Element	Attribute	Default value
DATA-GROUP	base	http://www.w3.org/TR/P3P/base
DATA	optional	no
EXTENSION	optional	yes
same	required	always
other-recipient	required	always
delivery	required	always
public	required	always
unrelated	required	always
admin	required	always
develop	required	always
tailoring	required	always
pseudo-analysis	required	always
pseudo-decision	required	always
individual-analysis	required	always
individual-decision	required	always
contact	required	always
historical	required	always
telemarketing	required	always
other-purpose	required	always

DATA elements

Some extra processing is needed to normalize DATA-GROUP and DATA elements and their attributes:

- The base attribute of the p3p:DATA-GROUP element may be omitted in an APPEL rule when that attribute takes the default value of *http://www.w3.org/TR/P3P/base*. Thus, the default value must be inserted in both the rule and the evidence if it has been omitted.

- When the base attribute of the p3p:DATA-GROUP has the value of the empty string (""), the base is the URL of the local document. This value should be substituted for the empty string in both the rule and the evidence.

- The ref attribute of the DATA element may take as its value a fragment identifier (for example, *#user.name*) or a full URL (for example, *http://www.w3.org/TR/P3P/base#user.name*). If only a fragment identifier is given, the full URL can be derived by appending the fragment identifier to the value of the base attribute of the DATA-GROUP in which the DATA element is contained. This should be done for all fragment identifiers in ref attributes in the rule and in the evidence.

- If a rule includes a CATEGORIES element, each fixed-category DATA element in the evidence must be expanded to contain a CATEGORIES subelement for each of its categories (as defined in the element's data schema). Any improperly declared categories in the evidence should be removed.

- If a variable-category DATA element in the evidence does not contain one or more explicit categories, the policy should not be considered valid.

After the above normalization has been performed, two ref attributes are considered to match if they both have the same base and one fragment identifier is a prefix of the other. For example, *http://www.w3.org/TR/P3P/base#user.name* and *http://www.w3.org/TR/P3P/base#user.name.family* match, regardless of which is part of the rule and which is part of the evidence.

Other Privacy Preference Languages

The P3P 1.0 Specification does not require that P3P user agents use the APPEL language. However, it does mandate that P3P user agents be able to import user preference settings using some documented language. Thus, some P3P user agent implementers have opted to use alternative languages.

Internet Explorer 6

IE6 allows customized privacy settings to be imported using an XML Privacy Import File, which consists of an ordered set of rules that results in a variety of cookie-related actions. The rules are evaluated based on each site's compact policy and domain name and on whether a cookie is used in a first-party or third-party context. Appendix D has detailed instructions for creating IE6 Privacy Import Files.

AT&T Privacy Bird

The AT&T Privacy Bird, Version Beta 1.1, allows users to import and export settings files using a restricted version of APPEL. Its APPEL engine returns a list of the description fields from all limited rules that fired, and these are displayed to the user in the policy summary. If a limited rule fires, the privacy policy mismatch icon (the angry red bird) is displayed; however, no cookies or headers are actually blocked.

Here are the restrictions:

- Rules must use only the limited behavior and the request behavior. The request behavior should appear only in the last rule in the rule set. The blocked behavior must not be used.

- The prompt attribute must not be used (if it is used, it is ignored).

- Rules must not specify matches over CDATA (e.g., in the CONSEQUENCE and ENTITY elements).

- Rules must not specify matches that involve the EXTENSION element.

- Rules must not include the REQUEST-GROUP element.

Example 13-2 is the rule set used by the AT&T Privacy Bird, Version Beta 1.1, when it is set to the medium privacy setting. This rule set should also work with a P3P user agent that uses the complete APPEL syntax.

Example 13-2. The AT&T Privacy Bird's medium setting APPEL rule set

```
<?xml version="1.0"?>
  <appel:RULESET xmlns:appel="http://www.w3.org/2001/02/APPELv1"
                 xmlns:p3p="http://www.w3.org/2000/12/P3Pv1"
crtdby="AT&amp;T Privacy Bird" crtdon="Sun Feb 10 21:47:31 2002" >

    <appel:RULE behavior="limited" description="Site may use health or medical
      information for analysis or to make decisions that may affect what content
      or ads you see, etc." >
    <p3p:POLICY >
      <p3p:STATEMENT >
        <p3p:PURPOSE appel:connective="or" >
          <p3p:pseudo-analysis required="always" />
          <p3p:pseudo-decision required="always" />
          <p3p:individual-analysis required="always" />
          <p3p:individual-decision required="always" />
        </p3p:PURPOSE>
        <p3p:DATA-GROUP >
          <p3p:DATA >
            <p3p:CATEGORIES >
              <p3p:health />
            </p3p:CATEGORIES>
```

```
            </p3p:DATA>
          </p3p:DATA-GROUP>
        </p3p:STATEMENT>
      </p3p:POLICY>
    </appel:RULE>

    <appel:RULE behavior="limited" description="Site may use health or medical
      information for marketing" >
      <p3p:POLICY >
        <p3p:STATEMENT >
          <p3p:PURPOSE appel:connective="or" >
            <p3p:contact required="always" />
            <p3p:telemarketing required="always" />
          </p3p:PURPOSE>
          <p3p:DATA-GROUP >
            <p3p:DATA >
              <p3p:CATEGORIES >
                <p3p:health />
              </p3p:CATEGORIES>
            </p3p:DATA>
          </p3p:DATA-GROUP>
        </p3p:STATEMENT>
      </p3p:POLICY>
    </appel:RULE>

    <appel:RULE behavior="limited" description="Unless you opt-out, site may use
      health or medical information for analysis or to make decisions that may
      affect what content or ads you see, etc." >
      <p3p:POLICY >
        <p3p:STATEMENT >
          <p3p:PURPOSE appel:connective="or" >
            <p3p:pseudo-analysis required="opt-out" />
            <p3p:pseudo-decision required="opt-out" />
            <p3p:individual-analysis required="opt-out" />
            <p3p:individual-decision required="opt-out" />
          </p3p:PURPOSE>
          <p3p:DATA-GROUP >
            <p3p:DATA >
              <p3p:CATEGORIES >
                <p3p:health />
              </p3p:CATEGORIES>
            </p3p:DATA>
          </p3p:DATA-GROUP>
        </p3p:STATEMENT>
      </p3p:POLICY>
    </appel:RULE>

    <appel:RULE behavior="limited" description="Unless you opt-out, site may use
      health or medical information for marketing" >
      <p3p:POLICY >
        <p3p:STATEMENT >
          <p3p:PURPOSE appel:connective="or" >
```

```
              <p3p:contact required="opt-out" />
              <p3p:telemarketing required="opt-out" />
          </p3p:PURPOSE>
          <p3p:DATA-GROUP >
            <p3p:DATA >
              <p3p:CATEGORIES >
                <p3p:health />
              </p3p:CATEGORIES>
            </p3p:DATA>
          </p3p:DATA-GROUP>
        </p3p:STATEMENT>
    </p3p:POLICY>
</appel:RULE>

<appel:RULE behavior="limited" description="Site may share health or medical
    information with other companies (other than those helping the site provide
    services to you)" >
    <p3p:POLICY >
      <p3p:STATEMENT >
        <p3p:RECIPIENT appel:connective="or" >
          <p3p:same required="always" />
          <p3p:other-recipient required="always" />
          <p3p:unrelated required="always" />
          <p3p:public required="always" />
        </p3p:RECIPIENT>
        <p3p:DATA-GROUP >
          <p3p:DATA >
            <p3p:CATEGORIES >
              <p3p:health />
            </p3p:CATEGORIES>
          </p3p:DATA>
        </p3p:DATA-GROUP>
      </p3p:STATEMENT>
    </p3p:POLICY>
</appel:RULE>

<appel:RULE behavior="limited" description="Unless you opt-out, site may
    share health or medical information with other companies (other than
    those helping the site provide services to you)" >
    <p3p:POLICY >
      <p3p:STATEMENT >
        <p3p:RECIPIENT appel:connective="or" >
          <p3p:same required="opt-out" />
          <p3p:other-recipient required="opt-out" />
          <p3p:unrelated required="opt-out" />
          <p3p:public required="opt-out" />
        </p3p:RECIPIENT>
        <p3p:DATA-GROUP >
          <p3p:DATA >
            <p3p:CATEGORIES >
              <p3p:health />
            </p3p:CATEGORIES>
```

Example 13-2. The AT&T Privacy Bird's medium setting APPEL rule set (continued)

```
            </p3p:DATA>
          </p3p:DATA-GROUP>
        </p3p:STATEMENT>
      </p3p:POLICY>
    </appel:RULE>

    <appel:RULE behavior="limited" description="Site may share financial
      information or information about your purchases with other companies
      (other than those helping the site provide services to you)" >
      <p3p:POLICY >
        <p3p:STATEMENT >
          <p3p:RECIPIENT appel:connective="or" >
            <p3p:same required="always" />
            <p3p:other-recipient required="always" />
            <p3p:unrelated required="always" />
            <p3p:public required="always" />
          </p3p:RECIPIENT>
          <p3p:DATA-GROUP >
            <p3p:DATA >
              <p3p:CATEGORIES appel:connective="or" >
                <p3p:purchase />
                <p3p:financial />
              </p3p:CATEGORIES>
            </p3p:DATA>
          </p3p:DATA-GROUP>
        </p3p:STATEMENT>
      </p3p:POLICY>
    </appel:RULE>

    <appel:RULE behavior="limited" description="Unless you opt-out, site may
      share financial information or information about your purchases with other
      companies (other than those helping the site provide services to you)" >
      <p3p:POLICY >
        <p3p:STATEMENT >
          <p3p:RECIPIENT appel:connective="or" >
            <p3p:same required="opt-out" />
            <p3p:other-recipient required="opt-out" />
            <p3p:unrelated required="opt-out" />
            <p3p:public required="opt-out" />
          </p3p:RECIPIENT>
          <p3p:DATA-GROUP >
            <p3p:DATA >
              <p3p:CATEGORIES appel:connective="or" >
                <p3p:purchase />
                <p3p:financial />
              </p3p:CATEGORIES>
            </p3p:DATA>
          </p3p:DATA-GROUP>
        </p3p:STATEMENT>
      </p3p:POLICY>
    </appel:RULE>
```

```
<appel:RULE behavior="limited" description="Site may contact you to interest
   you in other services or products and does not allow you to remove yourself
   from marketing/mailing list" >
   <p3p:POLICY >
     <p3p:STATEMENT >
       <p3p:PURPOSE appel:connective="or" >
         <p3p:contact required="always" />
         <p3p:telemarketing required="always" />
       </p3p:PURPOSE>
     </p3p:STATEMENT>
   </p3p:POLICY>
</appel:RULE>

<appel:RULE behavior="limited" description="Site may share information that
   personally identifies you with other companies (other than those helping
   the site provide services to you)" >
   <p3p:POLICY >
     <p3p:STATEMENT appel:connective="and" >
       <p3p:RECIPIENT appel:connective="or" >
         <p3p:same required="always" />
         <p3p:other-recipient required="always" />
         <p3p:unrelated required="always" />
         <p3p:public required="always" />
       </p3p:RECIPIENT>
       <p3p:DATA-GROUP >
         <p3p:DATA >
           <p3p:CATEGORIES appel:connective="or" >
             <p3p:physical />
             <p3p:online />
             <p3p:government />
           </p3p:CATEGORIES>
         </p3p:DATA>
       </p3p:DATA-GROUP>
     </p3p:STATEMENT>
   </p3p:POLICY>
</appel:RULE>

<appel:RULE behavior="limited" description="Unless you opt-out, site may
   share information that personally identifies you with other companies
   (other than those helping the site provide services to you)" >
   <p3p:POLICY >
     <p3p:STATEMENT appel:connective="and" >
       <p3p:RECIPIENT appel:connective="or" >
         <p3p:same required="opt-out" />
         <p3p:other-recipient required="opt-out" />
         <p3p:unrelated required="opt-out" />
         <p3p:public required="opt-out" />
       </p3p:RECIPIENT>
       <p3p:DATA-GROUP >
         <p3p:DATA >
           <p3p:CATEGORIES appel:connective="or" >
             <p3p:physical />
```

Example 13-2. The AT&T Privacy Bird's medium setting APPEL rule set (continued)

```
              <p3p:online />
              <p3p:government />
            </p3p:CATEGORIES>
          </p3p:DATA>
        </p3p:DATA-GROUP>
      </p3p:STATEMENT>
    </p3p:POLICY>
  </appel:RULE>

  <appel:RULE behavior="limited" description="Site does not allow you to find
    out what data they have about you" >
    <p3p:POLICY >
      <p3p:ACCESS >
        <p3p:none />
      </p3p:ACCESS>
    </p3p:POLICY>
  </appel:RULE>

  <appel:RULE behavior="limited" description="This site collects data for an
    unknown purpose" >
    <p3p:POLICY >
      <p3p:STATEMENT >
        <p3p:PURPOSE >
          <p3p:other-purpose required="always" />
        </p3p:PURPOSE>
      </p3p:STATEMENT>
    </p3p:POLICY>
  </appel:RULE>

  <appel:RULE behavior="limited" description="Unless you opt-out, this site
    collects data for an unknown purpose" >
    <p3p:POLICY >
      <p3p:STATEMENT >
        <p3p:PURPOSE >
          <p3p:other-purpose required="opt-out" />
        </p3p:PURPOSE>
      </p3p:STATEMENT>
    </p3p:POLICY>
  </appel:RULE>

  <appel:RULE behavior="request" >
    <appel:OTHERWISE />
  </appel:RULE>

</appel:RULESET>
```

CHAPTER 14
User Interface

The P3P 1.0 Specification focuses on defining the syntax and semantics of P3P policies and mechanisms for associating them with web resources. It describes a protocol that enables P3P-enabled web sites and P3P user agents to interoperate. However, it says very little about how P3P user agents should communicate with users. The P3P working groups left user interface issues mostly unspecified, because a standardized user interface is not necessary for P3P to work. In addition, it is not at all obvious, even to those of us who have spent over five years working on P3P, what the "right" P3P user interface is. The complexity and flexibility of the P3P vocabulary creates both opportunities and challenges for user interface developers. P3P user agent developers are charged with the task of making P3P both usable and useful, despite its complexity. In this chapter, I discuss some of the approaches P3P user agent developers can take to achieve this goal.

I begin this chapter with five case studies, based on my experiences developing the AT&T Privacy Bird and four earlier prototype P3P user agents. I then discuss strategies for developing privacy preference setting interfaces, user agent behavior, accessibility issues, and protecting privacy.

Case Studies

From the beginning of my involvement in the P3P effort, I was interested in exploring user interface design for P3P user agents. In 1997, I worked with some of the W3C staff members to develop a demo of a P3P user agent for presentation at an FTC workshop. In 1999, I designed a prototype P3P user agent called Privacy Minder that worked as a client-side proxy. In 2000, I worked with a team from Microsoft to develop a browser helper object prototype P3P user agent. In 2001, we extended this initial prototype at AT&T and conducted a usability study. After completing the study, we redesigned the prototype and released a public beta of the AT&T Privacy Bird in February 2002. Each of these projects was a learning experience.

W3C P3 Prototype

The W3C P3 Prototype* was developed in 1997, prior to the official launch of the P3P project at the W3C. At this time, a draft vocabulary had been developed by the Internet Privacy Working Group, but no work had been done on the P3P syntax or protocol. The W3C prototype was a Java implementation developed by David Shapiro as a student project. W3C staff member Joseph Reagle and I developed a PICS rating system to encode the IPWG draft vocabulary. We used this rating system to add PICS privacy labels to a few demonstration web sites. We also developed several sample PICSRules files for encoding user preferences.

The IPWG draft vocabulary included descriptions of 7 types of information and 9 uses of information, and an indicator as to whether identifiable information would be disclosed to other parties. This resulted in 126 data/use/disclosure combinations, represented by a 3-dimensional matrix. To flatten the matrix and prune it somewhat, we came up with 5 disclosure policies that incorporated the purpose of disclosure. This resulted in 14 uses of information—9 ways data could be used by the site that collected it and 5 ways it could be used by other companies. Thus, we ended up with 98 data/use combinations, which could be represented with a 2-dimensional matrix, as shown in Figure 14-1.

Due mostly to the limitations of the GUI development tools we were using, we were unable to represent the matrix in the user interface. We used a tabbed interface, as shown in Figure 14-2, in which each column of the matrix was represented on its own tab. But whether represented in tabbed or matrix form, the number of choices was clearly overwhelming. Therefore, we developed a set of 10 standard settings—6 for adults and 4 for children—with the idea that most users would simply select one of these standard settings rather than dealing with 98 individual choices. We developed a one-line description and a short paragraph for each setting. Advanced users could view the matrix to understand the settings they selected in more detail, or use the tabbed interface to create their own settings.

Here are the adult settings we developed:

- Access all web sites
- Sites may share my information with others
- Sites may share my information as long as I have a chance to review that decision
- Sites may use my information only internally
- Sites may use my information only for the express purpose for which I supplied it
- I want to be close to anonymous

---

* The script of the W3C P3 Prototype demo for the 1997 FTC workshop is available at *http://www.w3.org/Talks/970612-ftc/ftc-sub.html*.

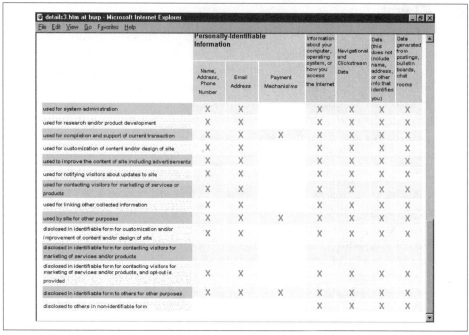

Figure 14-1. A matrix representing user preferences over the IPWG draft vocabulary

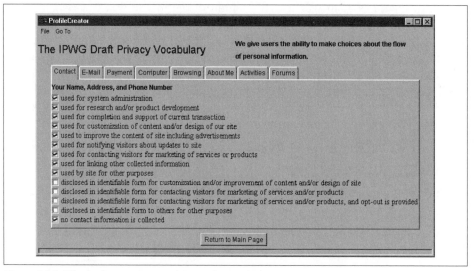

Figure 14-2. The preference setting menu in the W3C P3Prototype

And here are the child settings:

- My child can visit web sites that share personally identifiable information with others

- My child can visit web pages that collect personally identifiable information for internal purposes only
- My child can visit web pages that collect information as long as it cannot be tied to his or her real identity
- I want my child's online privacy to receive the maximum amount of privacy protection

The W3C P3 Prototype evaluated the privacy policy (in the form of a PICS label) behind each site a user visited and compared the site's policy with the user's preference settings. At sites that did not match a user's preference, a window popped up to notify the user of the mismatch and to give her the option of ignoring the mismatch just this once, or every time she returned to the site. The user could also view the site's policy or change her preference settings. However, it soon became clear that an interface that relied only on pop-up windows to provide privacy feedback would quickly annoy users.

The W3C P3 Prototype was a useful demonstration of some of the basic ideas behind P3P, but it also demonstrated that developing an easy-to-use interface for P3P was not going to be an easy task.

Privacy Minder

After an initial draft of the P3P specification was completed in 1999, I designed a prototype P3P user agent called Privacy Minder* to try out the P3P protocol and demonstrate some user interface ideas. This user agent was implemented as a client-side proxy. The code was developed in Java by Stephen Juth and Jennifer Mason. The early versions of the P3P specification included a somewhat complicated protocol for requesting P3P policies and negotiating agreements with web sites. This protocol included a mechanism for automatically transferring data back to the web site after an agreement was reached.

Privacy Minder featured a floating toolbar, shown in Figure 14-3, that includes menus for configuring user settings, symbols to indicate the results of checking a site's P3P policy, and buttons for displaying a site's human-readable privacy policy and accessing the help files.

Figure 14-3. The Privacy Minder toolbar

---

* The documentation and source code for Privacy Minder are available from *http://www.research.att.com/ projects/p3p/pm/*.

The leftmost symbol on the Privacy Minder toolbar indicates whether a site has a P3P policy. For sites that do not have P3P policies, an extra symbol appears to indicate whether or not data is collected through HTML forms on the current web page. A cookie symbol appears at sites that use cookies. The rightmost symbol is the logo of a privacy seal provider, which appears if the site has a DISPUTES element with an image URL in its P3P policy.

Privacy Minder came with four built-in settings and allowed users to import additional settings using an early version of APPEL (however, it did not include a GUI for specifying custom settings). Privacy Minder also included a data repository for users to store data for automatic form filling.

Because the P3P specification on which Privacy Minder was based had the concept of privacy agreements, Privacy Minder was designed to accept or reject agreements based on the user's preferences. Users could also ask for *informational* or *warning* prompts. Informational prompts, shown in Figure 14-4, were designed for situations where a site's policies match a user's preferences but the user wants to explicitly consent to any data transfers. They provide a short synopsis of the site policies and a form automatically pre-filled with the requested data. Warning prompts were designed for situations where a site's policies do not match a user's preferences. They indicate the cause of the mismatch and give users the opportunity to make an agreement despite the mismatch or to cancel their requests.

Privacy Minder's floating toolbar allows status symbols to be displayed without necessitating the use of pop-up windows at every site, and it allows configuration menus to be accessed easily. However, the toolbar can display information about only one web browser window at a time, which is confusing for users who frequently browse with multiple open windows. The toolbar provides information only about the P3P policy of the site the user requests; it does not display information about policies associated with frames, images, and other embedded content. We experimented with the idea of checking the P3P policies on embedded content and replacing graphics with placeholder images when their policies did not match the user's preferences. Due to the complexity of the P3P protocol at the time, we found that checking the policies on all embedded content was time-consuming and significantly delayed page rendering.

AT&T/Microsoft P3P Browser Helper Object

After the P3P specification was revised to eliminate automatic data transfer, negotiation, and agreement, the P3P protocol was greatly simplified. In the spring of 2000, I worked with a team from Microsoft to develop a prototype P3P user agent based on the revised specification. This user agent was implemented as a browser helper object for the Microsoft Internet Explorer 5 web browser. After users install the P3P user agent, a privacy button is added to their IE toolbars. Clicking on this button launches the P3P tool.

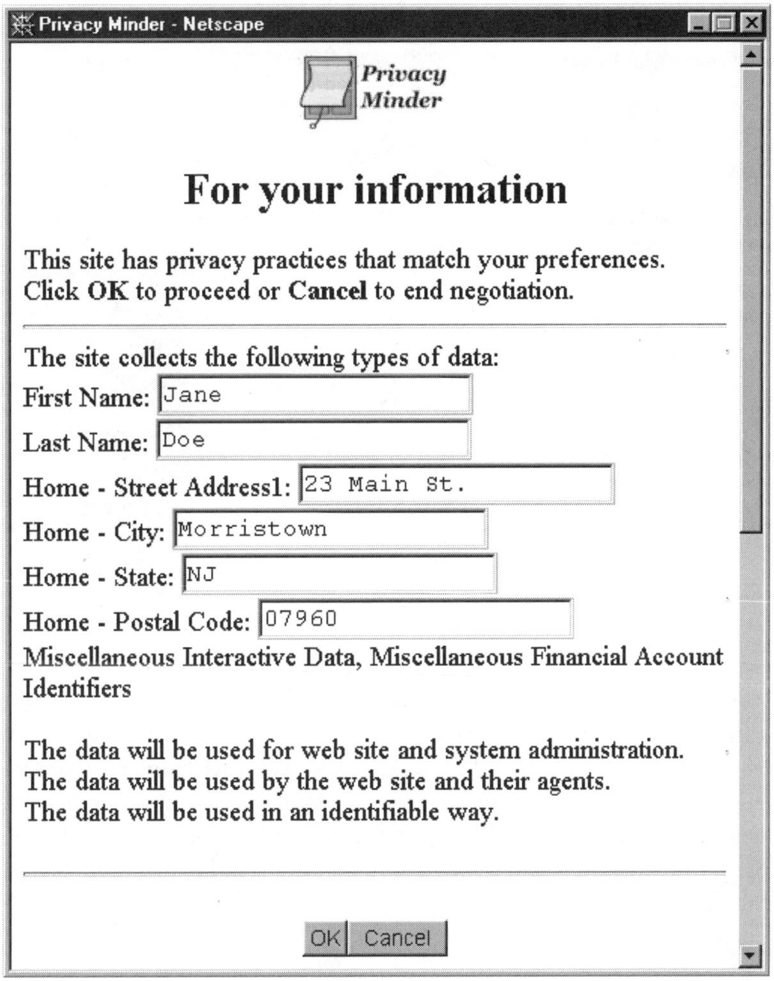

Figure 14-4. Privacy Minder informational prompt

The first time users launch this P3P user agent, they are prompted to select their preference settings using the preference window, shown in Figure 14-5. This user agent has no default preference settings.

My colleague Ellen Isaacs and I spent a lot of time designing the preference window. Our goal was to design a set of choices that could fit entirely on one screen. At this point, the P3P vocabulary had more than 10 different fields, and it would have been nearly impossible to represent all possible choices on one screen. After reviewing privacy survey results (including many of those discussed in Chapter 2), we concluded that those aspects of a privacy policy in which users were most likely to be interested were the type of data collected, how the data would be used, and whether the data would be shared. The survey data also indicated that users felt particularly strongly

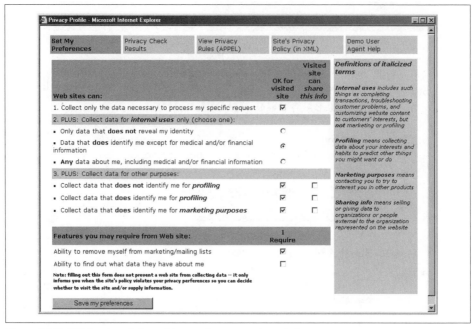

Figure 14-5. P3P browser helper object preference setting window

about telemarketing calls and being put on marketing and mailing lists. We reviewed the data categories and purposes described by the P3P vocabulary and selected those about which users seemed to feel most strongly. We then constructed an interface that allowed users to indicate whether various data practices were acceptable, focusing on those practices about which we believed users would be most likely to have strong opinions. This interface boiled down the thousands of options offered by the P3P vocabulary to 10 choices.

We realized that many of the terms used in the P3P vocabulary would not be familiar to most web users, so we tried to simplify the language in the choices we offered. We also provided definitions for several terms on the right side of the preference window.

Despite our efforts to make settting preferences simple, when we watched people try to use the browser helper object, we discovered that the interface was still confusing. Although many users were confused by the terminology, few noticed the definitions of the terms. Also, checking boxes to indicate what practices were acceptable confused some users. A later version of the interface that asked users to indicate the practices that they found unacceptable seemed to be less confusing.

When users save their privacy settings, the settings are stored as an APPEL rule set. When users select Privacy Check Results, the current site's P3P policy is fetched and compared against this rule set. The results window, shown in Figure 14-6, displays a link to the site's full privacy policy, the logos of any privacy seals indicated in the

DISPUTES section of the site's P3P policy, and a list of any mismatches between the user's settings and the site's P3P policy.

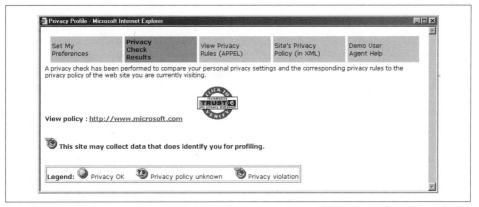

Figure 14-6. The AT&T/Microsoft browser helper object compares a user's preferences with a site's P3P policy and reports any differences; the three "peep hole" symbols are shown at the bottom

My colleague Gary Zamchick developed a set of symbols that were used in the results window, as shown in Figure 14-6. We had planned to display these symbols displayed in the browser toolbar as well, but we were unable to implement this during the short time that we worked on this prototype. Coming up with symbols to represent whether a privacy policy matched a user's preferences was challenging. We explored a variety of symbols that have been associated with the concept of privacy, including eyes, keys, locks, and window shades. We decided to use a closed peep hole to indicate that a site's policies match a user's preferences and an open peep hole to indicate that a site's policies do not match a user's preferences. A peep hole with a question mark was used for unknown policies. We used traffic signal colors—green, yellow, and red—to reinforce the meaning of the symbols. However, the symbols did not prove to be as readily understandable to users as we had hoped.

We tested this user agent informally by observing people using it at a number of public "technology fair" events. I learned a lot from these informal observations that I was able to apply when redesigning the user interface. In addition, we used a panel of consumer advocates as a focus group to discuss the preference setting interface. This group was very vocal about wanting interfaces that allowed users to make their own privacy choices without default settings. However, they also wanted simple interfaces. Trying to satisfy both of these desires simultaneously proved difficult.

AT&T Usability Testing Prototype

In 2001, we continued to work on the browser helper object prototype at AT&T. We did further development work on the user interface and experimented with combining the P3P functionality with the cookie-blocking functionality of the Idcide Privacy Companion software (*http://www.idcide.com/pages/per_intro.htm*). Cathy Mandarino used the Privacy Companion user interface as a starting point and added the P3P features from our previous P3P user agent prototype.

While the development work was in progress, we conducted another focus group with the consumer advocates, showing them slides of our redesigned interface and several alternative sets of icons. Once the prototype was complete, John Baldasare conducted formal usability tests with this prototype in our usability testing lab in Florham Park, New Jersey. We developed a set of P3P-enabled web sites for our test subjects to visit. We asked the subjects to visit these sites and use the prototype to learn about their privacy policies. We observed and videotaped the subjects as they used the prototype, and we recorded interviews with them discussing their experiences with the prototype as well as their attitudes about online privacy issues.

For this version of the prototype, we developed a custom settings window similar to the settings window used in the AT&T/Microsoft browser helper object; however, this time we asked users to indicate unacceptable, rather than acceptable, practices. As shown in Figure 14-7, we used the phrase "warn me at sites that" to make it clear that the tool would warn users but would not prevent sites from engaging in these practices. We also worked on the wording, to minimize the unfamiliar terminology. We provided help files that clarified some of the terms, but we did not include definitions on the settings screen itself. In our usability testing, we found that the phrases "information that does not personally identify me" and "information that does personally identify me" were still confusing to most users.

To make setting preferences easier for users who do not want to consider 13 individual privacy choices, we developed high, medium, and low settings as well. The main settings window, shown in Figure 14-8, offers only these choices. Users can select "custom settings" from this window to access the window for individually configuring each of the 13 privacy settings. The main settings window also allows users to import settings encoded in an APPEL file, and it includes settings for the cookie-blocking features.

In this version of the user agent, a symbol in the browser toolbar indicates whether a site's policies match a user's preferences. This allows users to tell at a glance whether the site displayed in each browser window meets their preferences. Figure 14-9 shows the symbols used in this version of the user agent. We decided to avoid the traditional privacy symbols and instead use symbols that are easily recognizable as conveying positive and negative connotations. This also helped clarify that the tool is providing information to users, rather than actively preventing web sites from engaging in practices users find unacceptable. Gary Zamchick designed a set of hand symbols, again using the green/yellow/red color scheme. The green "thumbs-up" hand indicates a match, the yellow open hand indicates a site that does not have a P3P policy, and the red "thumbs-down" hand indicates a mismatch. In our usability tests, we found these symbols to be easily recognizable and meaningful; however, people seemed to notice the colors more than the shape of the hands, especially when the hands appeared as very small icons in the browser toolbar.

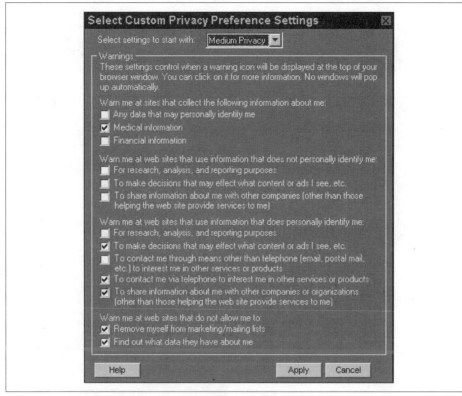

Figure 14-7. Custom privacy preference settings

Clicking on a hand symbol opens a Privacy Policy Detail window, as shown in Figure 14-10. This window provides contact information for the web site and a list of any points where the user's preferences and the site's policies do not match. From this window, users can get a summary of the site's privacy policy (automatically derived from its P3P policy) or change their settings for this particular site (to override cookie-blocking). Users can also click on the Menu button to bring up a menu of all of the tool's functions. The menu can also be accessed by right-clicking on the hand symbol in the toolbar.

One of the biggest problems we identified from the usability tests was that users were confused about how to navigate through the various menus to find what they wanted. Users seemed to have trouble with the right-click concept, but once they figured it out, most forgot that they could also left-click to go right to the Privacy Policy Detail window. The two-tiered approach to both the settings and the policy summary also proved confusing.

Our usability test participants were enthusiastic about the P3P user agent, although many found the user interface somewhat confusing at first. Most did figure out how to use it eventually, however. Most liked the concept of the user agent and said they

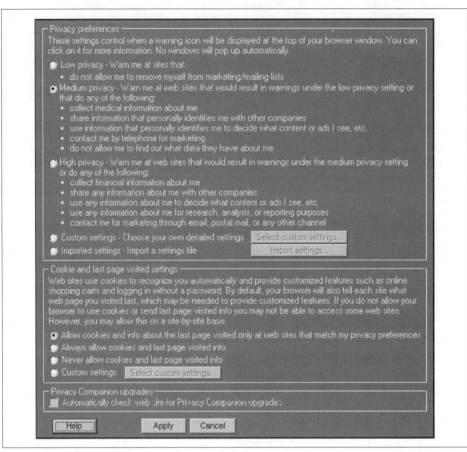

Figure 14-8. All of the standard settings were controlled from this screen; custom settings controls were invoked from this screen

Figure 14-9. Hand symbols were added to the browser toolbar to indicate whether or not a site's P3P policy matched a users preferences

found it to be useful. They liked both the ability to find out about privacy policies easily and the ability to block cookies on the basis of each site's privacy policy.

Unfortunately, the cookie-blocking features were problematic to implement. At the time we did not have the necessary resources to properly integrate the Privacy Companion code with the P3P user agent, so we ultimately we decided to remove the cookie-blocking features from the user agent until more resources become available.

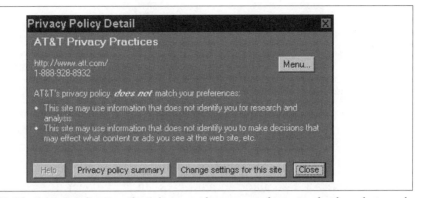

Figure 14-10. The Privacy Policy Detail window provides contact information for the web site and an explanation of any mismatch between the user's preferences and the site's policies

AT&T Privacy Bird

After completing the usability study, we redesigned the prototype P3P tool based on the feedback we received, and Praveen Guduru and Manjula Arjula developed a new implementation. We redesigned the menu flow and combined a number of the windows so that the tool was easier to navigate. We decided to move the hand symbol out of the browser toolbar and into the title bar across the top of the browser window. This enabled the symbol to appear on every browser window—even pop-up windows that did not include the toolbar. However, this meant that the vertical space available for the symbol was very limited. We tried to redesign the hand symbol for the smaller space but found it difficult to make it work well. So we brainstormed more icon ideas, and Gary Zamchick came up with the idea of using a bird symbol in place of the hand symbol.

The bird was appealing because it was cute and somewhat irreverent, but it also had a number of connotations that were appropriate for its function (e.g., bringing to mind phrases such as "a little bird told me"). As shown in Figure 14-11, we used a happy green bird at sites that match a user's preferences, the same green bird with an extra red exclamation point at sites that match a user's preferences but contain embedded content that does not match or does not have a P3P policy, an uncertain yellow bird at sites without P3P policies, an angry red bird at sites that do not match a user's preferences, and a sleeping gray bird when the tool is turned off. The birds also have distinct "bubbles" that are distinguishable by color-blind users and users who do not have color displays, even if the birds themselves are not. After selecting the bird icon, AT&T Privacy Bird seemed an obvious choice as the name for the tool. This was the name we used when we released a public beta of the tool in February 2002.

The bird icon was also appealing because it lent itself readily to accompanying sound effects. Michael Zalot created a set of bird "earcons" to accompany each icon. User

Figure 14-11. The AT&T Privacy Bird icons

feedback on the earcons was mixed. Some users loved them, while others found them very annoying. We added the ability to turn the sounds on and off, but testers of early versions of this software requested the ability to control the sounds for each color of bird individually, so we added this feature as well. It would probably be useful to also provide an option of playing the sounds only when a policy is evaluated (usually, the first time a user visits a site in a 24-hour period).

The AT&T Privacy Bird automatically checks the P3P policy at each web site and displays the appropriate icon. A yellow bird appears and shakes its head from side to side while the P3P policy is being fetched and evaluated.

Because of the confusion users had with the left and right mouse clicks in the previous version of the user agent, we decided to give the left and right mouse click identical functionality in this version. Clicking on the bird reveals a cascading menu that offers both information about the currently visited web site and configuration options. As shown in Figure 14-12, the About This Site menu includes a policy summary, the full P3P policy (from the web site), the site's opt-in/opt-out policy, information about the policies associated with embedded content, and the XML source code of the P3P policy.

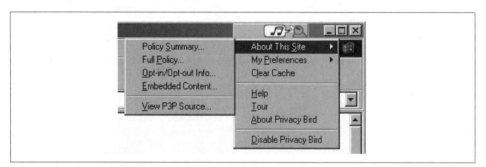

Figure 14-12. The About This Site menu

To reduce some of the navigation confusion, we decided to combine the policy summary and policy detail used in the previous version of the user agent and offer one Policy Summary window. As shown in Figure 14-13, the policy summary begins with a privacy policy check, which indicates any points where a site's policy does not match a user's preferences. Below the check is a summary derived from the site's P3P policy. It includes a bulleted summary of each statement in the policy, as well as information from the ACCESS, DISPUTES, and ENTITY elements, including images of any privacy seals referenced. At sites that use the IBM GROUP-INFO extension (discussed in Chapter 6) for naming statements, the statement name appears at the beginning of each statement.

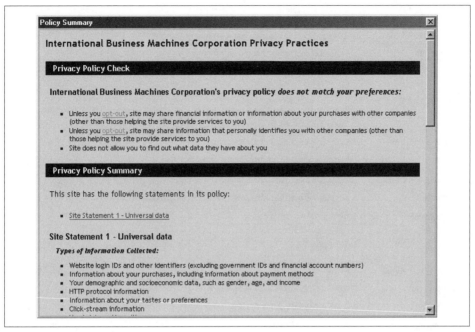

Figure 14-13. A Policy Summary screen

Rather than using the full descriptions of each PURPOSE, CATEGORY, RECIPIENT, and ACCESS element, we developed abbreviated descriptions using language likely to be more readily accessible to users. The category and purpose descriptions we used in the Beta 1.1 version are shown in Tables 14-1 and 14-2, respectively. For purposes for which an opt-out is available, we append the words "unless you opt-out" and provide a hyperlink to the site's instructions for opting out. For purposes that occur only if a user opts-in, we append the words "only if you request this."

Table 14-1. Data categories used in the AT&T Privacy Bird Beta 1.1 Policy Summary

P3P category element	Description
physical	Name, address, phone number, or other contact information
online	Email address or other online contact information
uniqueid	Web site login IDs and other identifiers (excluding government IDs and financial account numbers)
purchase	Information about your purchases, including information about payment methods
financial	Information about your finances, such as account balances, payment or overdraft history, loans, etc.
computer	Information about the kind of computer you are using, the software you are running on it, and its Internet address
navigation	Information about which pages you visited on this web site and how long you stayed at each page
interactive	Information about activities you engaged in at this web site, such as searches you performed or logs of account activity

Table 14-1. *Data categories used in the AT&T Privacy Bird Beta 1.1 Policy Summary (continued)*

P3P category element	Description
demographic	Your demographic and socioeconomic data, such as gender, age, and income
content	The text of email you send to this site, bulletin-board postings, chat room communications, etc.
state	Cookies and related mechanisms
political	Information about your affiliation with groups such as religious organizations, trade unions, professional associations, political parties, etc.
health	Your medical or health care information
preference	Information about your tastes or preferences
location	Information about your current physical location
government	Government-issued identifiers such as social security numbers
other-category	Other unknown types of data

Table 14-2. *Descriptions of purposes in the AT&T Privacy Bird Beta 1.1 policy pummary*

P3P purpose element	Description
current	To complete the activity for which the data was provided
admin	Web site and system administration
develop	Research and development
tailoring	To customize the site for your current visit
pseudo-analysis	To do research and analysis without identifying you
pseudo-decision	To make decisions about what content or ads you see at the web site, etc., without identifying you
individual-analysis	To do research and analysis
individual-decision	To make decisions about what content or ads you see at the web site, etc.
contact	To contact you through means other than telephone (email, postal mail, etc.) to interest you in other services or products
historical	Historical uses
telemarketing	To contact you by telephone to interest you in other services or products
other-purpose	Other unknown uses

One problem with our abbreviated descriptions is that we lose some of the details that some sites may consider critical to the description of their practices. One example of such a detail that has been brought to our attention is the use of the terms "will" and "may." The purpose descriptions in the P3P specification all begin "information may be...." This makes it clear that a site reserves the right to use data in a particular way but does not necessarily use all (or any) of the data for this purpose. In the Policy Summary, our abbreviated purposes are listed under the heading "How Your Information Will be Used." Since the word "may" has been omitted in these abbreviated purposes, it might make sense to change the word "Will" to "May" in the heading.

Our goal was to make the Policy Summary window into a sort of automatically generated privacy "nutrition label." The format is still somewhat verbose to achieve this goal. With additional work, it is likely that the design of the policy summary could be improved significantly.

In addition to displaying the information about the P3P policy for the requested site, we wanted to display information about the policies associated with images, frames, and other embedded content. We added a red exclamation point to the green bird icon to indicate a site that otherwise matches a user's preferences but has embedded content that does not match a user's preferences. As shown in Figure 14-14, we also provided an embedded content window that users can use to get a list of all the embedded content and an indication as to the P3P status of each. Users can get the policy summary or P3P policy file associated with each piece of embedded content. It might be interesting to experiment with visually highlighting each piece of embedded content on the screen when a user selects it, or providing the appropriate P3P icon when a user mouses over it.

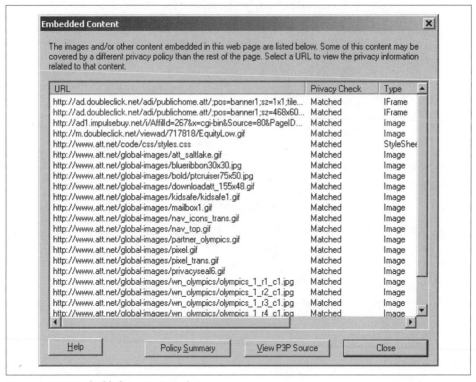

Figure 14-14. Embedded Content window

During our usability tests on the usability testing prototype, we observed that users found the two levels of configuration confusing. Users wanted something simple, like high/medium/low, but they also wanted to understand the meanings of these settings and make more detailed decisions. As shown in Figure 14-15, we decided to combine the simple and custom configurations into a single window that offers the high, medium, and low choices at the top and 12 individual choices below. When a user selects one of the settings at the top, the boxes below that correspond to that setting are automatically checked. Users can customize these settings by checking or unchecking additional boxes. They can also import settings files (perhaps downloaded from a privacy organization's web site) using a limited version of the APPEL language.

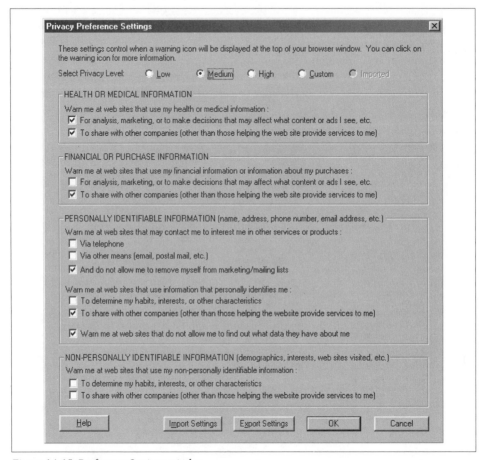

Figure 14-15. Preference Settings window

Table 14-3 explains the 12 choices in detail. These choices are similar to the ones offered in previous P3P user agents, but they were refined based on the feedback we received. To reduce confusion about the meaning of "personally identifiable information" and related terms, we added examples of both identifiable and non-identifiable data. We changed the way we grouped some of the categories and purposes, and we ordered the choices with those about which users are most likely to feel strongly at the top of the list. Beta testers have responded more positively to this version of the preference setting interface than they did to previous versions. One suggestion that has been made is that we consider using the word "alert" rather than "warn," as warn may suggest that something is dangerous when that may not always be the case.

One of the questions we considered when trying to decide what choices to offer was how to handle P3P policies that indicated that a particular purpose was done on an opt-in or opt-out basis, or that a certain data element was optional. We decided to treat optional data the same way as we treat non-optional data, so that users concerned about a particular type of data being used for a particular purpose would be warned about it and would be able to make informed decisions about whether to submit it. For similar reasons, we decided to treat opt-out purposes in the same way that we treat always-required purposes. However, we decided that opt-in purposes should not trigger warnings, as these purposes require that users explicitly agree to them.

Table 14-3. P3P statements that trigger warnings for Privacy Bird Beta 1.1 settings

Preference setting	P3P statements that trigger warning
Warn me at web sites that use my health or medical information for analysis, marketing, or to make decisions that may affect what content or ads I see, etc.	`health` category in combination with any of the following purposes when they have the `required` attribute set to `always` or `opt-out`: `pseudo-analysis`, `pseudo-decision`, `individual-analysis`, `individual-decision`, `contact`, `telemarketing`
Warn me at web sites that use my health or medical information to share with other companies (other than those helping the web site provide services to me)	`health` category in combination with any of the following recipients when they have the `required` attribute set to `always` or `opt-out`: `same`, `other-recipient`, `unrelated`, `public`
Warn me at web sites that use my financial information or information about my purchases for analysis, marketing, or to make decisions that may affect what content or ads I see, etc.	`purchase` or `financial` category in combination with any of the following purposes when they have the `required` attribute set to `always` or `opt-out`: `pseudo-analysis`, `pseudo-decision`, `individual-analysis`, `individual-decision`, `contact`, `telemarketing`
Warn me at web sites that use my financial information or information about my purchases to share with other companies (other than those helping the web site provide services to me)	`purchase` or `financial` category in combination with any of the following recipients when they have the `required` attribute set to `always` or `opt-out`: `same`, `other-recipient`, `unrelated`, `public`
Warn me at web sites that may contact me to interest me in other services or products via telephone	`telemarketing` purpose with `required` attribute set to `always` or `opt-out`
Warn me at web sites that may contact me to interest me in other services or products via other means (email, postal mail, etc.)	`contact` purpose with `required` attribute set to `always` or `opt-out`
Warn me at web sites that may contact me to interest me in other services or products and do not allow me to remove myself from marketing/mailing lists	`telemarketing` or `contact` purpose with `required` attribute set to `always`
Warn me at web sites that use information that personally identifies me to determine my habits, interests, or other characteristics	`individual-analysis` or `individual-decision` purpose with `required` attribute set to `always` or `opt-out`

Preference setting	P3P statements that trigger warning
Warn me at web sites that use information that personally identifies me to share with other companies (other than those helping the web site provide services to me)	`physical`, `online`, or `government` category in combination with any of the following recipients when they have the `required` attribute set to `always` or `opt-out`: `same`, `other-recipient`, `unrelated`, `public`
Warn me at web sites that do not allow me to find out what data they have about me	`access none`
Warn me at web sites that use my non–personally identifiable information to determine my habits, interests, or other characteristics	`pseudo-analysis` or `pseudo-decision` purpose with `required` attribute set to `always` or `opt-out`
Warn me at web sites that use my non–personally identifiable information to share with other companies (other than those helping the web site provide services to me)	any of the following recipients when they have the `required` attribute set to `always` or `opt-out`: `same`, `other-recipient`, `unrelated`, `public`

The Beta 1.1 version of the AT&T Privacy Bird is entirely informational—it does not block cookies or otherwise interfere with a user's browsing experience. There is one case where the software can provide active alerts, however. When a user fills out a form at a web site that does not have a P3P policy or has a policy that does not match the user's preferences, a pop-up box warns the user before the form is submitted. This box gives users the option of viewing a policy summary (at P3P-enabled sites) or asking not to be prompted again at this site. Users can also turn off these active prompts altogether. Such a warning might be even more useful before a user has spent time filling out the forms—for example, the pop-up might appear the first time a user begins typing into one of the form's text boxes. However, this would be more complicated to implement.

Privacy Preference Settings

P3P enables web sites to make a wide variety of declarations about over a dozen aspects of their privacy practices. The APPEL language was designed to allow users to express preferences about any combination of declarations a site might make in its P3P policy. However, APPEL is not designed for use by end users, and rule formulation is known to be a difficult task for users. Even if a tool existed that would make it possible for the average user to create APPEL files, it is unlikely that most people would have the time, patience, inclination, or understanding needed to formulate detailed P3P preferences. Furthermore, even when preferences seem simple—for example, "I don't want anyone to use my data for marketing"—translating these preferences into user agent behavior may not be straightforward. In some cases users may not want to interact with sites whose policies don't match their preferences, while in other cases users may want to proceed with a limited or even a full interaction.

One of the most difficult aspects of designing a P3P user agent is developing an interface for privacy preference settings. User interface designers must find an appropriate level of granularity at which to present the settings and meaningful terminology with which to describe them. In the sections that follow, I discuss ways that the P3P vocabulary can be simplified and how a layered interface can further reduce complexity without limiting functionality. I also discuss several approaches to default settings.

Simplifying the Vocabulary

The P3P vocabulary was designed to distinguish a wide range of data practices; however, as the vocabulary was developed, not a lot of attention was paid to expressing the vocabulary in language readily understandable to the average user. Many of the P3P vocabulary terms borrow terminology from privacy laws and fair information practice principles. While these terms are well known to privacy experts, they are foreign to almost everyone else. In addition, some of the distinctions made in the vocabulary are unlikely to be important to most users—although it is quite likely that the distinctions users find most important will change over time and perhaps even vary across different regions of the world. Thus, it is a challenge for user agent implementers to simplify the language of the P3P vocabulary and find ways of packaging it that will resonate with their users. User agent implementers can focus on a subset of the vocabulary, bundle vocabulary terms together, and use terminology that is likely to be easier for users to understand than the terms used in the P3P vocabulary.

Focusing on a vocabulary subset

User interface designers can make the P3P vocabulary appear simpler by designing interfaces that highlight a subset of the P3P vocabulary that is likely to be of most interest to users. For example, in the AT&T Privacy Bird privacy settings interface, we focused on the data practices that seemed to raise the most concerns for American Internet users: collection of health and financial information, marketing, profiling, and sharing personal data with other companies. We also decided to include the ability to trigger a warning at sites that have no access provisions, because access is getting an increasing amount of attention in the U.S. Although location information is also very sensitive, we did not include a setting that dealt with that information in the AT&T Privacy Bird interface, because we do not anticipate that this user agent will be used much on mobile devices where location information is an issue. However, if I was designing a P3P user agent for a mobile device, I think it would be important to highlight the location category in the user interface.

Bundling vocabulary elements

Some of the distinctions made in the P3P vocabulary are of little importance to many users in practice. To reduce the apparent complexity of the P3P vocabulary, user agent implementers can try to bundle together vocabulary elements that users may think about in similar ways.

In the AT&T Privacy Bird interface, for example, we bundled the six recipients into two groups—sharing and non-sharing—and described the sharing practice as sharing data "with other companies (other than those helping the web site provide services to me)." Sites that disclose only the ours and delivery recipients are considered to be non-sharing, while those that disclose any of the other recipients are considered to be sharing. This grouping makes sense, because most users do not make the kinds of distinctions between different types of sharing that the P3P vocabulary supports. Arguably, the delivery recipient should also be in the sharing group. However, we put it in the non-sharing group because the data is being shared primarily to help the site provide services. Also, it is currently very difficult to ship anything in the U.S. without disclosing data to a delivery company (or the U.S. Postal Service) that might use it for purposes that go beyond making the delivery. Should some of the major delivery companies adopt privacy policies in which they commit to not making secondary use of delivery information, it might then make sense to place delivery in the sharing group.

Another bundle we used in the AT&T Privacy Bird interface was a set of purposes described as "analysis, marketing, or to make decisions that may affect what content or ads I see, etc." We also used the phrase "information that personally identifies me" to describe the physical, online, and government data categories.

Simplifying the language

Because many of the terms used in the P3P vocabulary are not familiar to most Internet users, user agent implementers need to come up with terms that will be more meaningful to users, while accurately describing the P3P vocabulary. Terms such as "pseudonymous analysis" and "individual decision" are meaningless without their accompanying definitions, even to privacy experts. But the definitions are somewhat lengthy to be used verbatim in a user interface. We experimented with a variety of ways of describing these purposes that privacy advocates generally consider to be variations on "profiling." However, the term "profiling" did not appear to be any more meaningful to most users than the vocabulary terms. From a privacy perspective, it is very important to know that these purposes involve building a record about an individual. However, a description of what the record might be used for seemed to resonate better with users. Ultimately, we ended up bundling the profiling purposes with the marketing purposes and some of the most sensitive data groups, and the setting became "Warn me at web sites that use my [data category] information for analysis, marketing, or to make decisions that may affect what content or ads I see, etc." Table 14-3 provides the simplified language used for all of the AT&T Privacy Bird settings. Tables 14-1 and 14-2 detail some of the simplified language used in the Privacy Bird's policy summary.

Layered Interfaces

A common way of reducing the complexity of software user interfaces is to divide the interfaces into two or more *layers*. Many pieces of software feature configuration menus that include only the most commonly used settings and a separate "advanced" menu that includes the less frequently used settings. This is an effective way to hide complicated configuration options from most users, who will never need to access them. One problem with hiding complicated options in an advanced menu, however, is that the advanced menu ends up containing a variety of unrelated options that can be difficult to find, even for expert users.

When we developed the AT&T Usability Testing Prototype, we thought users would appreciate it if we put the complicated privacy settings in a separate "custom" menu and offered only three simple choices on the main configuration screen. However, because users were interested in finding out about the settings behind high, medium, and low, this approach to layering was not very effective. The approach we took in the AT&T Privacy Bird, where we put the simple and custom settings in the same window, seemed much more effective.

The ability to import privacy settings using APPEL or another language adds another layer to P3P user agents. The APPEL language allows for much more detailed configuration options than most GUIs are likely to support.

Another possible approach to developing a user interface for privacy settings is to use a critic-based architecture that periodically prompts users with suggested settings as they use the software.[*] Critics observe how a user interacts with a piece of software and offer suggestions to the user based on their observations.

Default Settings

Despite all of our efforts to develop usable configuration interfaces, it seems that most users rarely change the default settings on many of the software packages they use. Changing the settings can be time-consuming and confusing, and users risk "messing up" their settings and being unable to return their software to the state to which they have grown accustomed.[†] It is thus extremely important that user interface designers make good decisions when defining defaults.

---

[*] The idea of using critics in a P3P user agent is discussed in Lorrie Cranor and Mark Ackerman, "Privacy Critics: UI Components to Safeguard Users' Privacy," in *Proceedings of the ACM Conference on Human Factors in Computing Systems* (CHI'99), short papers (v.2.), pp. 258–259, *http://lorrie.cranor.org/pubs/privacy-critics.pdf*.

[†] Some studies have shown that even experienced users are reluctant to customize software. See, for example, Wendy E. Mackay, "Triggers and barriers to customizing software," in *Proceedings of the Conference on Human Factors and Computing Systems* (1991) p. 153-160, *http://doi.acm.org/10.1145/108844.108867*. However, other studies have shown that when customization is easy many users will customize software, especially software that they use a lot. See, for example, Stanley R. Page, Todd J. Johnsgard, Uhl Albert, and C. Dennis Allen, "User customization of a word processor," in *Proceedings of the Conference on Human Factors and Computing Systems* (1996) p. 340-346, *http://doi.acm.org/10.1145/238386.238541*.

Joseph Reagle and I wrote a paper in which we identified three approaches to defaults, in addition to the approach of simply creating unchangeable settings.* The approaches are:

Option: Leave features that require configuration turned off. In this approach, implementers simply deactivate any features that require special configuration. A user who wishes to use these features must explicitly activate and then configure them. This is the approach that was taken by Microsoft for the "Content Advisor" feature in their Internet Explorer 3.0 software. Parents who wished to use this feature to prevent their children from accessing inappropriate content had to explicitly activate it. At that time they could set a password and select a rating system and settings for their child.

Leaving features turned off may be a good alternative when the features are of interest to a small percentage of users or when they may have adverse impacts on users who are unaware of their presence. In the case of P3P, one could argue that setting defaults that would covertly prevent users from accessing sites that do not match the default privacy settings could have adverse impacts on users, and thus P3P should be turned off by default. On the other hand, P3P might be implemented so that its behavior would be obvious to the user, as would be the mechanisms to change the defaults or disable P3P completely.

When features are left turned off, the chances that they will ever be activated are reduced because many users will never take the time to figure out how to activate them (and some will never even realize they exist).

Option: Leave features unconfigured, but prompt users to configure them before using the software. In this approach, implementers setup their software so that it is not usable until a user configures it. There are many pieces of software that take this approach for their most important settings, although they generally have defaults for their less-important settings that can be reconfigured later.

This alternative has the advantage that users become immediately aware of the existence of features. However, when features take a long time or significant thought to configure, users may grow impatient and give up installing the software or select the simplest configuration options rather than taking the time to select the options they most prefer. This alternative might be useful in P3P if users are initially presented with only a small number of recommended settings.

Option: Configure features with default settings. In this approach implementers decide on some set of default settings for the initial configuration of their software. Users may change these settings later.

This alternative has the advantage that users get the benefits of features without having to take the time to configure them. However, the pre-configured default settings may have a covert impact on the user experience.

---

* See Lorrie Faith Cranor and Joseph Reagle, "Designing a Social Protocol: Lessons Learned from the Platform for Privacy Preferences," in Jeffrey K. MacKie-Mason and David Waterman, Eds., *Telephony, the Internet, and the Media* (Mahwah: Lawrence Erlbaum Associates, 1998), *http://lorrie.cranor.org/pubs/dsp/*. Joseph Reagle and I wrote this paper for the 1997 Telecommunications Policy Research Conference after having spent about six months working on the P3P vocabulary with the Internet Privacy Working Group. I don't think either of us had any idea that the P3P design process was really just at its beginning. Nonetheless, most of the lessons learned in this paper still ring true.

In the case of P3P, pre-configured defaults are likely to be controversial, especially in software not advertised as having any particular biases with respect to privacy. A default that provides minimal privacy protections is likely to be criticized by privacy advocates. However, a default that provides strong privacy protections but blocks access to many Web sites is likely to be criticized by people who don't understand why their Web surfing is being interrupted, as well as by the owners of sites that get blocked frequently. On the other hand, there may be a market for products pre-configured to meet a specific need, for example a product pre-configured with strong privacy defaults and explicitly marketed as "privacy friendly."

If implementers select alternatives in which P3P is enabled by default, Web sites that are not P3P compliant may not be viewable without explicit overrides from users. This could be frustrating for users, but might give sites an incentive to adopt P3P technology quickly. (Although to ease the transition, implementers might include tools that would allow users to access sites with no privacy statements if those sites do not actually collect information other than click-stream data.)

IE6 imposes a default P3P setting that has proven controversial. Because this setting causes some cookies to be blocked, many web sites have been critical of this default. Privacy advocates have criticized the default because it focuses mostly on third-party cookies. On the other hand, this default seems to strike a reasonable balance between business and privacy concerns, and Microsoft's decision to configure IE6 with this default setting probably helped speed up P3P adoption. Nonetheless, privacy advocates have urged Microsoft to abandon default P3P settings in future versions of their software and instead to prompt users to select their own P3P settings.

In designing the AT&T Privacy Bird, we tried to avoid setting defaults for the main privacy settings. We wanted to force users to choose the settings themselves; however, we were concerned that it would be difficult for users to make such choices before they had spent time using and understanding the software. So we decided to offer users only the high, medium, and low options during software installation and to make all of the custom options available after the software was installed. Unfortunately, due to limitations in the installation software we used in Beta 1.1, we were not able to provide much documentation about the high, medium, and low choices until after the software was installed or to present the choices to the user without a suggested option.

User Agent Behavior

The P3P 1.0 Specification describes how user agents should fetch P3P policies, but beyond that, it leaves user agent behavior largely unspecified. Thus, user agents have a wide range of options for using the information they obtain from P3P policies. Chapter 12 described a variety of ways that user agents might behave. Here, I focus on two types of user agent behavior: filtering and informing users.

Filtering

Some P3P user agents may act as filters and block cookies, HTTP headers, form submissions, or even web content at sites that don't match a user's P3P preferences. This can be a very useful feature; however, it may frustrate users if they do not understand what is happening or are unable to control it easily.

To minimize user frustration, the user interface should include some sort of indicator so that users are aware that filtering has occurred. For example, IE6 includes a privacy symbol in the bottom-right corner of the browser window whenever cookies are blocked or downgraded. Users can click on that symbol to get more information about the cookies used by that site or to change their privacy settings. To draw users' attention to this feature, a pop-up appears the first time a cookie is blocked after IE6 is installed.

The ability to override filtering options both on a one-time basis and whenever a user returns to a particular web site is also important. Users often find that they cannot access some web sites or take advantage of certain features when cookies are blocked. Therefore, they appreciate the ability to selectively unblock cookies. Once users have decided not to block a cookie at a particular site, they generally do not want to have to take additional actions every time they visit that site.

To minimize the impact on users' ability to browse the Web, some user agents downgrade cookies instead of blocking them altogether. For example, you can configure IE6 to turn persistent cookies into session cookies or to restrict cookies to being used in a first-party context. IE6 also refrains from blocking cookies that use a special opt-out cookie format.

Providing a user interface for users to control their cookie settings can be a challenge.[*] At the extreme, an interface might allow users to make separate decisions about blocking session cookies, persistent cookies, first-party cookies, and third-party cookies (and also, perhaps, referers and other headers). It might allow users to choose whether cookie-blocking decisions should be made solely on the bases of the policy associated with each cookie or should also take into account the policy of the object with which the cookie is served (if a site's overall policy doesn't match a user's preferences, but the site has a separate policy for cookies that does match a user's preferences, should the cookies be blocked?). Of course, these options can be bundled together so that users are offered only a small number of choices, perhaps with an advanced setting option for those who want to make more detailed decisions themselves.

---

[*] For an interesting analysis of cookie interfaces in popular web browsers, see Lynette I. Millett, Batya Friedman, and Edward Felten, "Cookies and Web browser design: toward realizing informed consent online," in *Proceedings of the SIGCHI conference on Human factors in computing systems* (2001) pp. 46–52, *http://doi.acm.org/10.1145/365024.365034.*

Informing Users

There are a variety of ways that P3P user agents can inform users about privacy policies at the sites they visit. For example, in the case studies, I described our use of symbols, a policy summary, and form submission alerts.

Active versus passive

Active alerts generally take the form of pop-up windows that require users to actively do something (usually click an "OK" button) before they can proceed. Passive alerts can take the form of symbols or other visual queues, sounds, or other indicators that provide information but do not require that a user take action. Active alerts can annoy users when they appear frequently. However, passive alerts can easily be overlooked.

It is unlikely that most users of P3P user agents will want to receive an active alert every time they encounter a web site that does anything that does not match their preferences. Some users may not ever want active alerts, but others may want to receive those alerts at web sites that engage in activities they find particularly troublesome. Some users may want active alerts before form data is submitted to a site that does not match their preferences; others may not want to bother with such alerts after they have already gone through the trouble of filling out the form. Striking the right balance between active and passive alerts can be tricky. It is best to give users some choices about when, if ever, they should receive active alerts.

Symbols

Symbols are a useful way to give users a quick indication about a site's privacy practices. However, coming up with symbols that are instantly recognizable and meaningful is difficult, especially when dealing with an abstract concept like privacy. The limited space available in many user interfaces makes this even more of a challenge.

It would be interesting to try to come up with a set of symbols that would convey more information about a site's policy than simply a match or mismatch. However, for such a symbol set to be useful, it would be important to keep the number of symbols fairly small.

The location of symbols in a user interface can impact how much attention users pay to them. When building a browser-based user agent, the obvious locations for a P3P symbol are in the browser toolbar or title bar, or in the area along the bottom of the browser window. We placed the bird symbol in the title bar because it is the only part of a browser window that never disappears. However, placing a symbol in the browser toolbar allows you to use a larger symbol. In IE6, the P3P symbol is at the bottom of the browser window, where other informational symbols appear. Arguably, this is where a P3P symbol logically belongs. However, the bottom-right corner is generally the last place on a printed page or a computer screen that people who read English as their first language look. One problem with placing the P3P symbol in the title bar is that users who open their web browsers to fit the entire screen or place their browser windows in the top-right corner of the screen sometimes find that the symbol is obscured by other applications. For example, the Microsoft Office toolbar is often fixed in the top-right corner of the screen and places itself in front of other applications. The best solution is probably to allow users to relocate the symbol to the location that works best for them.

Policy representation

P3P policies are encoded in XML syntax and not designed to be read by end users. As already discussed, even the P3P vocabulary terms themselves were not intended for end users. It is the user agent's role to represent a P3P policy in a meaningful way. This might be done by translating every element in the XML policy into terms that users can understand, or it may involve summarizing, pulling out key points, or even representing parts of the policy as symbols.

Recently, there have been a number of efforts to come up with standard and concise formats for representing privacy policies. These efforts have focused on formats that web sites could use for representing their own policies. However, in theory, these standardized policies could be generated automatically from a web site's P3P policy. For example, as shown in Figure 14-16, TrustPage is a privacy policy summary format developed by Privacy Council, a privacy consulting firm. Everything in this summary (except the points about third-party tracking and security) could be generated automatically from a P3P policy.

Explanation of mismatch

Informing users that a site's policy does not match their preferences is somewhat useful, but it is even more useful to inform users exactly where the mismatch occurs. While this is fairly easy for a computer program to determine, it is much harder for a user to figure out. Understanding where a mismatch occurs can help users decide how serious the mismatch is—in particular, whether it is serious enough that they don't want to do business with the web site—and help them tune their settings.

In the AT&T Privacy Bird, we provide a list of mismatches at the top of the policy summary, as shown in Figure 14-13 earlier in this chapter. A user agent might also use a variation on the preference setting menu to show which of the user's specified preferences have not been met, or use symbols or calculate some sort of rating to describe the severity of the mismatch.

Accessibility

One often overlooked aspect of user interface design is making the interface accessible to users who have disabilities or who will be using it under atypical circumstances. This includes people who are blind or who have limited eyesight and will be

Figure 14-16. The Privacy Council's TrustPage is an example of a privacy policy summary format that might be generated automatically by a P3P user agent

using an audio screen reader or unusually large fonts, color-blind users, and users who are deaf or are using a computer with no audio capabilities. It also includes people who may be using software on small devices, such as mobile phones and PDAs. There are a number of simple things that developers can do to make their user interfaces more accessible. However, providing maximum accessibility requires some effort and planning.

The W3C User Agent Accessibility Guidelines (*http://www.w3.org/TR/UAAG10/*) provide a useful overview of the areas on which developers should focus to make their user agents accessible. The Guidelines document includes (and elaborates on) the following 12 principles:

1. Support input and output device-independence.
2. Ensure user access to all content.
3. Allow configuration not to render some content that may reduce accessibility.
4. Ensure user control of rendering.
5. Ensure user control of user interface behavior.
6. Implement interoperable application programming interfaces.
7. Observe operating environment conventions.
8. Implement specifications that benefit accessibility.
9. Provide navigation mechanisms.
10. Orient the user.

11. Allow configuration and customization.

12. Provide accessible user agent documentation and help.

By taking advantage of the hooks already provided in the operating systems and tool-kits they are using, implementers can easily develop software that complies with many of these guidelines.

Developing software that can work with a screen reader requires some extra hooks to be explicitly coded into each application. We developed the AT&T Privacy Bird to work with the JAWS (*http://www.freedomscientific.com*) and Window-Eyes (*http://www.gwmicro.com*) screen readers. We ran into a number of problems as we tried to implement keyboard shortcuts that did not conflict with shortcuts used by either the screen readers themselves or other applications. However, we were eventually able to overcome most of the problems we encountered.

Privacy

When designing a P3P user agent, it is important not to lose sight of the goal of helping users protect their privacy. I've already discussed this in the "Guiding Principles" section of Chapter 12; however, this topic deserves some additional comments. If P3P becomes widely adopted by web sites, it is likely that P3P user agents will become the primary way that users learn about web site privacy policies. The P3P vocabulary is already influencing the way companies write their privacy policies—in fact, representatives from several companies have told me that in the process of creating P3P policies, their companies examined some of their data practices that they had never really considered before. As a result of this process, some companies have, for example, instituted data-retention policies that require them to periodically purge data, or implemented procedures for providing individuals with access to their information. Just as the P3P vocabulary is influencing how web sites think about their privacy policies, it is likely that P3P user agents will influence how users think about privacy. The aspects of privacy policies that user agents highlight in policy summaries or allow users to specify preferences about are likely to be the aspects of privacy policies that users come to think about the most. As users gain a better understanding of what companies do with personal data, they may start questioning corporate data practices, and some companies may be influenced to make their practices more privacy-friendly.

Phil Agre's discussion of research challenges related to protocols for individualized negotiation of personal data handling suggests some important evaluation criteria for P3P implementations:*

---

* Philip E. Agre and Marc Rotenberg, *Technology and Privacy: The New Landscape* (Cambridge: MIT Press, 1997), p. 24.

As opportunities emerge for individuals to customize privacy preferences, research should be conducted to evaluate alternative arrangements. These evaluations should employ a broad range of criteria, including ease of understanding, adequacy of notification, compliance with standards, contractual fairness and enforceability, appropriate choice of defaults, efficiency relative to the potential benefits, and integration with other means of privacy protection. Particular attention should be paid to uniformity of protocols across different industries and applications, so that consumers are not overwhelmed by a pointless diversity of interfaces and contracts.

Above all, it is important that P3P user agent developers strive to develop tools that will have a meaningful, positive impact on users' abilities to protect their own privacy.

There is a danger that P3P user agents may hide some important aspects of privacy policies from users. If users come to think of their P3P user agents as a good source of privacy-related information, but the information provided by these agents is deficient, users may naively believe that their privacy is better protected than it actually is. Thus, it is important that P3P user agent designers be sensitive to privacy issues and that privacy advocates critique P3P user agents and offer suggestions for how they can be improved.[*]

---

[*] For a brief set of principles for privacy protection software, see Harry Hochheiser, "Principles for Privacy Protection Software," in *Proceedings of the Tenth Conference on Computers, Freedom and Privacy* (2000) pp. 69–72, *http://doi.acm.org/10.1145/332186.332250.*

Appendixes

This part of the book provides technical details and material from other sources.

- Appendix A, *P3P Policy and Policy Reference File Syntax Quick Reference*, provides a complete listing of all of the elements of a P3P policy and policy reference file and details the parent and child elements and attributes of each element.

- Appendix B, *Configuring Web Servers to Include P3P Headers*, provides instructions for configuring several popular web servers to issue P3P headers.

- Appendix C, *P3P in IE6*, provides information from Microsoft about the P3P features in the Microsoft Internet Explorer 6 web browser, including details about cookie blocking.

- Appendix D, *How to Create a Customized Privacy Import File for IE6*, provides information from Microsoft about creating customized privacy settings for IE6.

- Appendix E, *P3P Guiding Principles*, contains the set of guiding principles from Appendix 7 of the P3P 1.0 specification.

P3P Policy and Policy Reference File Syntax Quick Reference

This appendix contains a complete alphabetical list of XML elements found in P3P policies and policy reference files, with abbreviated definitions for all of the attributes and elements. The corresponding compact tokens of elements that may be included in compact policies are shown in square brackets.

The child elements for each element are listed in the order in which they are required to appear. Attributes may appear in any order in a P3P policy.

All elements and attributes are labeled according to whether they are mandatory, recommended, optional, or default to a specified value when omitted. Those that include an asterisk before their label may appear more than once, and those that have both an asterisk and the word "optional" may appear zero or more times. A default value is given for each attribute that has a defined default value when that attribute is omitted.

<ACCESS>   mandatory

The ability of an individual to view his or her identified information and address questions or concerns to the site

Parent element

    <POLICY>

Child elements

Must contain exactly one of the following, optionally followed by one or more EXTENSION elements:

[NOI]

    Identifiable data is not used

[ALL]

    Access is given to all identifiable information

[CAO]

    Access is given to identifiable online and physical contact information as well as to other information

`<ident_contact/> [IDC]`
> Access is given to identifiable online and physical contact information

`<other_ident/> [OTI]`
> Access is given to certain other information

`<none/> [NON]`
> No access to identifiable information is given

Attributes
> None

`<CATEGORIES>` optional

Types of data; required for variable-category elements dynamic.miscdata and dynamic. cookies; should not be used in policies for elements with predefined categories

Parent element
> `<DATA>`, `<DATA-STRUCT>`, or `<DATA-DEF>`

Child elements

Must contain at least one of the following:

`<physical/> [PHY]`
> Physical contact information

`<online/> [ONL]`
> Online contact information

`<uniqueid/> [UNI]`
> Unique identifiers

`<purchase/> [PUR]`
> Purchase information

`<financial/> [FIN]`
> Financial information

`<computer/> [COM]`
> Computer information

`<navigation/> [NAV]`
> Navigation and clickstream data

`<interactive/> [INT]`
> Interactive data

`<demographic/> [DEM]`
> Demographic and socioeconomic data

`<content/> [CNT]`
> Content

`<state/> [STA]`
> State-management mechanisms

`<political/> [POL]`
> Political information

`<health/>` [HEA]
> Health information

`<preference/>` [PRE]
> Preference data

`<location/>` [LOC]
> Location data

`<government/>` [GOV]
> Government-issued identifiers

`<other-category>string</other>` [OTC]
> Other types of data

Attributes
> None

<CONSEQUENCE>   optional

Consequences that can be shown to a human to explain a data practice

Parent element   `<STATEMENT>`

Child elements   None

Attributes   None

<COOKIE-INCLUDE> and <COOKIE-EXCLUDE>   optional

Describe the cookies to which a policy applies

Parent element
> `<POLICY-REF>`

Child elements
> None

Attributes
name - *default:* *
> indicates what cookie Name values are acceptable matches

value - *default:* *
> indicates what cookie values are acceptable matches

domain - *default:* *
> indicates what cookie Domain values are acceptable matches

path - *default:* *
> indicates what cookie Path values are acceptable matches

<DATA>
mandatory

Description of data—describes the name and contact information of a data collector when used in an ENTITY element; describes data to be collected when used in a STATEMENT element or as part of a data schema definition

Parent element

<DATA-GROUP>

Child elements

<CATEGORIES> - *optional*

Attributes

ref - *mandatory*

URI reference, where the fragment identifier part denotes the name of a data element, and the URI part denotes the corresponding data schema; when the URI part is not present, the data schema is indicated by the base attribute of the DATA-GROUP that contains the DATA element

optional - *default:* no

Indicates whether the site requires visitors to submit this data element; no indicates that the data element is required, while yes indicates that the data element is not required; used only when contained within a STATEMENT element

<DATA-DEF>
*optional

Defines a data element

Parent element

<DATASCHEMA>

Child elements

<LONG-DESRCIPTION> - *optional*
<CATEGORIES> - *optional*

Attributes

name - *mandatory*

The name of the data element

structref - *optional*

The URI reference for the structure on which the data element is based

short-description - *optional*

A string denoting the short display name of the data element (up to 255 characters)

<DATA-GROUP>
*mandatory

Container for DATA elements

Parent element

<ENTITY> or <STATEMENT>

Child elements

<DATA> - *mandatory*

Attributes

base - *default:* http://www.w3.org/TR/P3P/base
The base URI for URI references in ref attributes; when the attribute value is an empty string (""), the base is the local document

<DATA-STRUCT>   *optional

Defines a data structure

Parent element

<DATASCHEMA>

Child elements

<LONG-DESRCIPTION> - *optional*
<CATEGORIES> - *optional*

Attributes

name - *mandatory*
The name of the data structure

structref - *optional*
The URI reference for the structure on which this data structure is based

short-description - *optional*
A string denoting the short display name of the data structure (up to 255 characters)

<DATASCHEMA>   optional

Contains references to data element and data schema definitions

Parent element

None when it appears in a data schema file; <POLICIES> when it appears in a policy file

Child elements (may appear in any order)

<DATA-DEF> - *optional*
<DATA-STRUCT> - *optional*
<EXTENSION> - *optional*

Attributes

xmlns - *mandatory (when it appears in a data schema file)*
The XML namespace for the P3P policy; for P3P 1.0, the value is http://www.w3.org/2002/01/P3Pv1

xml:lang - *optional*
The language of human-readable elements

<DISPUTES>

Describes dispute-resolution procedures that may be used to resolve disputes about a site's privacy practices

Parent element

<DISPUTES-GROUP> [DSP]

Child elements

<EXTENSION> - *optional*
<LONG-DESRCIPTION> - *optional*
<IMG> - *optional*
<REMEDIES> - *recommended*
<EXTENSION> - *optional*

Attributes

resolution-type - *mandatory*
> Takes one of the following four values: service (customer service), independent (independent organization), court, or law (applicable law)

service - *mandatory*
> The URL of the customer service web page or independent organization, or the URL for information about the relevant court or applicable law

verification - *optional*
> The URL or certificate that can be used for verification purposes

short-description - *optional*
> A short, human-readable description of the name of the appropriate legal forum, applicable law, or third-party organization, or contact information for customer service (up to 255 characters

<DISPUTES-GROUP> [DSP]

recommended

Container for DISPUTES elements

Parent element

<POLICY>

Child elements

<EXTENSION> - *optional*
<DISPUTES> - *mandatory*
<EXTENSION> - *optional*

Attributes

None

<ENTITY>

mandatory

Identifies the legal entity making the representation of the privacy practices contained in the policy; the DATA-GROUP within an ENTITY element must contain a DATA element with attribute ref="#business.name" and at least one DATA element that references a way to contact the entity using an element from the business data set

Parent element   <POLICY>

Child elements   <DATA-GROUP> - *mandatory*

Attributes   None

<EXCLUDE>   optional

Describes the content that is not covered by a particular policy (used in conjunction with INCLUDE)

Parent element   <POLICY-REF>

Child elements   None

Attributes   None

<EXPIRY>   optional default: 24 hours

Indicates the length of time for which the policy is valid

Parent element

    <POLICIES> or <POLICY-REFERENCES>

Child elements

    None

Attributes

date - *optional*

    The absolute expiry time relative to Greenwich Mean Time, formatted according to Section 3.3.1 of the HTTP 1.1. specification

max-age - *optional*

    The relative expiry time in seconds since the response was sent from the origin server, formatted according to Section 3.3.2 of the HTTP 1.1 specification

---

<EXTENSION>   *optional

Describes an extension to the P3P syntax

Parent element

    <POLICY>, <ENTITY>, <ACCESS>, <DISPUTES-GROUP>, <DISPUTES>, <REMEDIES>, <STATEMENT>, <PURPOSE>, <RECIPIENT>, <RETENTION>, or <DATA-GROUP>

Child elements

    Defined by each extension

Attributes

optional - *default: yes*
> Determine whether the extension is mandatory or optional; a mandatory extension is indicated with the no value

---

<HINT>

Gives the location of policy reference files on other sites

Parent element
> <POLICY-REF>

Child elements
> None

Attributes

scope - *mandatory*
> A URL scheme and authority to which the hinted policy reference can be applied; the host part of the authority may begin with the * wildcard

path - *mandatory*
> A relative URL whose base is the URL scheme and authority matched in the scope attribute used to locate the policy reference file on the hinted site

---

<IMG>

An image logo for a dispute-resolution organization or process

Parent element
> <DISPUTES>

Child elements
> None

Attributes

src - *mandatory*
> The URL of the image or logo

width - *optional*
> The width in pixels of the image logo

height - *optional*
> The height in pixels of the image logo

alt - *mandatory*
> A very short textual alternative for the image logo

<INCLUDE>

Describes the content to which a policy applies

Parent element	\<POLICY-REF\>
Child elements	None
Attributes	None

\<LONG-DESCRIPTION\>

optional

Contains a (possibly long) human-readable description of a dispute-resolution organization or procedure

Parent element	\<DISPUTES\>
Child elements	None
Attributes	None

\<META\>

mandatory

Container for P3P policies and policy references

Parent element

None

Child elements

  \<EXTENSION\> - *optional*
  \<POLICY-REFERENCES\> - *mandatory*
  \<POLICIES\> - *optional*
  \<EXTENSION\> - *optional*

Attributes

xmlns - *mandatory*
  The XML namespace for the P3P policy; for P3P 1.0, the value is http://www.w3.org/2002/01/P3Pv1

xml:lang - *optional*
  The language of human-readable elements

\<METHOD\>

optional

Describes the types of HTTP requests to which a policy applies

Parent element	\<POLICY-REF\>
Child elements	None
Attributes	None

\<NON-IDENTIFIABLE\> [NID]

optional

Indicates that no data is collected or no identifiable data is collected

Parent element	`<STATEMENT>`
Child elements	None
Attributes	None

<POLICIES>

Container for P3P policies

Parent element

> `<META>` or none

Child elements

> `<EXPIRY>` - *optional*
> `<DATASCHEMA>` - *optional*
> `<POLICY>` - **mandatory*

Attributes

`xmlns` - *mandatory unless contained within a* `META` *element*
> The XML namespace for the P3P policy; for P3P 1.0, the value is `http://www.w3.org/2002/01/P3Pv1`

`xml:lang` - *optional*
> The language of human-readable elements

<POLICY>

*mandatory

Container for a P3P policy

Parent element

> `<POLICIES>`

Child elements

> `<EXTENSION>` - **optional*
> `<TEST>` - *optional*
> `<ENTITY>` - *mandatory*
> `<ACCESS>` - *mandatory*
> `<DISPUTES-GROUP>` [DSP] - *recommended*
> `<STATEMENT>` - **mandatory*
> `<EXTENSION>` - **optional*

Attributes

`discuri` - *mandatory*
> The URI of the natural-language privacy statement

`opturi` - *optional (mandatory for sites offering opt-in or opting out)*
> The URI of instructions for opting in or opt-out

`name` - *mandatory*
> name of the policy, used to reference the policy in a policy reference file

---

278 | Appendix A: P3P Policy and Policy Reference File Syntax Quick Reference

xml:lang - *optional*
> The language of human-readable elements

<POLICY-REF> *mandatory

Provides the location of a P3P policy and specifies the URLs covered by that policy

Parent element
> <POLICY-REFERENCES>

Child elements
> <INCLUDE> - *optional*
> <EXCLUDE> - *optional*
> <COOKIE-INCLUDE> - *optional*
> <COOKIE-EXCLUDE> - *optional*
> <METHOD> - *optional*
> <EXTENSION> - **optional*

Attributes

about - *mandatory*
> The URL of the P3P policy; if this is a relative URL, it is interpreted relative to the URL of the policy reference file

---

<POLICY-REFERENCES> mandatory

Container for policy references

Parent element
> <META>

Child elements
> <EXPIRY> - *optional*
> <POLICY-REF> - **mandatory*
> <HINT> - **optional*
> <EXTENSION> - **optional*

Attributes
> None

<PURPOSE> mandatory

Purposes for data processing

Parent element
> <STATEMENT>

Child elements

Must contain at least one of the following, optionally followed by one or more EXTENSION elements:

`<current/>` [CUR]
> Completion and support of activity for which it was provided

`<admin/>` [ADM]
> Web site and system administration

`<develop/>` [DEV]
> Research and development

`<tailoring/>` [TAI]
> One-time tailoring

`<pseudo-analysis/>` [PSA]
> Pseudonymous analysis

`<pseudo-decision/>` [PSD]
> Pseudonymous decision

`<individual-analysis/>` [IVA]
> Individual analysis

`<individual-decision/>` [IVD]
> Individual decision

`<contact/>` [CON]
> Contacting visitors for marketing of services or products

`<historical/>` [HIS]
> Historical preservation

`<telemarketing/>` [TEL]
> Contacting visitors for marketing of services or products via telephone

`<other-purpose>`*string*`</other-purpose>` [OTP]
> The use of information not captured by the above definitions; a human-readable explanation should be provided to describe these purposes

Attributes

PURPOSE has no attributes; however, each of the practice elements except `<current/>` can take the following attribute:

required - *default:* always
> Whether the purpose is a required practice for the site; takes one of the following three values: always [a], opt_in [i], or opt_out [o]

`<RECIPIENT>` mandatory

The legal entity, or domain, beyond the service provider and its agents where data may be distributed

Parent element

> `<STATEMENT>`

Child elements

Must contain at least one of the following, optionally followed by one or more EXTENSION elements:

`<ours/> [OUR]`

Ourselves and/or our entities acting as our agents or entities for whom we are acting as an agent

`<delivery/> [DEL]`

Delivery services possibly following different practices

`<same/> [SAM]`

Legal entities following our practices

`<other-recipient/> [OTR]`

Legal entities following different practices

`<unrelated/> [UNR]`

Unrelated third parties

`<public/> [PUB]`

Public forums

Attributes

RECIPIENT has no attributes; however, each of the recipient elements (with the exception of `<ours/>`) can take the following attribute:

required - *default:* always

Whether the recipient is required; takes one of the following three values: always [a], opt_in [i], or opt_out [o]

\<recipient-description\> optional

Describes a recipient element

Parent element   `<ours>`, `<delivery>`, `<same>`, `<other-recipient>`, `<unrelated>`, or `<public>`

Child elements   None

Attributes   None

\<REMEDIES\> recommended

Remedies in case a policy breach occurs

Parent element

`<DISPUTES>`

Child elements

Must contain one or more of the following, optionally followed by one or more EXTENSION elements:

`<correct/> [COR]`

Errors or wrongful actions arising in connection with the privacy policy will be remedied by the site

---

`<money/>` [MON]

> If the site violates its privacy policy, it will pay the individual an amount specified in the human-readable privacy policy or the amount of damages

`<law/>` [LAW]

> Remedies for breaches of the policy statement will be determined based on the law referenced in the human-readable description

Attributes

> None

`<RETENTION>` mandatory

The type of retention policy in effect

Parent element

> `<STATEMENT>`

Child elements

Must contain exactly one of the following, optionally followed by one or more EXTENSION elements:

`<no-retention/>` [NOR]

> No retention

`<stated-purpose/>` [STP]

> For the stated purpose

`<legal-requirement/>` [LEG]

> As required by law or liability under applicable law

`<business-practices/>` [BUS]

> Determined by site's business practices

`<indefinitely/>` [IND]

> Indefinitely

Attributes

> None

`<STATEMENT>` *mandatory (unless a site collects no data)

Container for data practices applied to data elements

Parent element

> `<POLICY>`

Child elements

> `<EXTENSION>` - *optional
> `<CONSEQUENCE>` - optional
> `<NON-IDENTIFIABLE>` [NID] - optional
> `<PURPOSE>` - mandatory (optional if statement is non-identifiable)
> `<RECIPIENT>` - mandatory (optional if statement is non-identifiable)

`<RETENTION>` - *mandatory (optional if statement is non-identifiable)*
`<DATA-GROUP>` - **mandatory (optional if statement is non-identifiable)*
`<EXTENSION>` - **optional*

Attributes

None

`<TEST>` [TST]

Indicates that the policy is for testing purposes only and must not be considered a valid P3P policy

Parent element	`<POLICY>`
Child elements	None
Attributes	None

Configuring Web Servers to Include P3P Headers

This is an edited version of Appendix A of The Platform for Privacy Preferences 1.0 Deployment Guide by Martin Presler-Marshal (IBM), Thomas Deml (Microsoft), and Yuichi Koike (NEC).

When deploying P3P, your site may need to send additional HTTP response headers. The technique for adding HTTP headers to a web server's response varies from server to server.

This section describes how to add HTTP headers to the response for some popular web servers. The choice of web servers here is not meant to imply that P3P can only be used with these servers; we expect that P3P can be deployed with any web server.

Apache and Derivatives

This section covers the Apache Web Server 1.2.x and 1.3.x, as well as servers derived from those versions of Apache. This mechanism will work on all platforms supported by Apache. It will not work on earlier releases (1.1.x, for example), as the headers module was not introduced until Apache 1.2.

Basics

The Apache Web server includes a module called *mod_headers*, which is used to add extra headers to HTTP responses. The configuration directive that is used to add these headers makes use of the normal Apache scoping rules, so headers can be added to an individual file, a set of files matching a regular expression, a set of directories matching a regular expression, or an entire web site.

The headers module is used to add any arbitrary headers to an HTTP response. Thus the Apache web server does not need to "understand" the semantics of P3P headers.

Possible Difficulties

The headers module (*mod_headers*) is an "Extension" module. This means that the source distribution from Apache does not have this module included by default. If you have compiled your own server, you may need to rebuild it to include *mod_headers*. If you are using a binary distribution of Apache, you should check that distribution's documentation to see if *mod_headers* is built in. The IBM HTTP Server distribution of Apache, for example, has *mod_headers* built in.

If you need to rebuild Apache to include the headers module, read the "compiling Apache" instructions from the Apache Web site (*http://httpd.apache.org/docs/install.html*), and make sure that you update the configuration before compiling to include *mod_headers*.

How to Do It

1. Publish the site's policy reference file and privacy policies. Before you put the P3P headers on the content, you should first publish the P3P privacy policies. Copy the policy files to the appropriate part of your server's content tree.

2. Verify that the headers module is being loaded and enabled. If *mod_headers* is compiled as a dynamic shared object (certain binary distributions do this on UNIX platforms, for example), then *httpd.conf* should contain a *LoadModule* directive:

   ```
   LoadModule headers_module path/mod_headers.so
   ```

3. The configuration file also needs an *AddModule* directive to activate the header module:

   ```
   AddModule mod_headers.c
   ```

   The *AddModule* directive is required even if *mod_headers* is compiled into the server (i.e., even if it is not dynamically loaded by a *LoadModule* directive).

4. Decide how the headers will be arranged on the site. If the same compact policy is used on the entire site, then it is usually possible to send the same P3P header for the entire site. On the other hand, if different parts of the site require different compact policies, then separate P3P headers will be required. See "How Directory, Location, and Files sections work" (*http://httpd.apache.org/docs/sections.html*) for instructions on applying different headers to different parts of your site. For this example, we'll assume that we're using one P3P header on the entire site.

5. Create the appropriate scope sections in the server configuration file (*httpd.conf*). This is explained in "How Directory, Location, and Files sections work." For our example, it will look like this:

   ```
   <Location / >
   </Location>
   ```

6. Add the P3P header. To do this, place a Header directive within the section(s) created in the previous step. For our example, the result will look as follows:

```
<Location / >
Header append P3P
  "policyref=\"http://catalog.example.com/P3P/PolicyReferences.xml\""
</Location>
```

For more information on the Header directive, see the documentation for *mod_ headers* (*http://httpd.apache.org/docs/mod/mod_headers.html*).

Microsoft Internet Information Server

This section covers Microsoft Internet Information Server (IIS) on a Microsoft Windows 2000 Server platform.

Basics

The P3P header can be added through the IIS snap-in from the Computer Management console (MMC) on a Microsoft Windows 2000 server. This section assumes that you have already published your site's policy reference file and P3P policy files. It also assumes that you have decided how you will arrange the P3P headers on the site. If the same compact policy is used on the entire site, then it is usually possible to send the same P3P header for the entire site. On the other hand, if different parts of the site require different compact policies, then separate P3P headers are required. For this example, one P3P header is used for the entire site.

Possible Difficulties

None known.

How to Do It

1. Start the IIS snap-in. To access the IIS snap-in from the Start menu, click Programs, Administrative Tools, and then Internet Information Services. The Internet Information Services snap-in appears.
2. Navigate to the web site to which you want to apply the privacy policy.
3. Select the web site and right-click to open the context menu. Select the Properties menu item. The IIS snap-in appears.
4. Select the HTTP Headers property page.
5. Select Add. The Add/Edit Custom HTTP Header dialog box appears.
6. In the Custom Header Name text box, type in P3P. In the Custom Header Value dialog box, type in the contents of the P3P header.

---

iPlanet Web Server

This section covers the iPlanet Web Server (iWS) version 4.1 and 6.0.

Basics

iWS does not provide a way to configure the Web server to send custom response headers. Instead, this must be done by building and installing a server plugin which will add the response headers. iPlanet has provided a document in their knowledge base which documents how to do this.* See the example under "Method 2" in the article for specific instructions.

Possible Difficulties

This requires compiling and installing a NSAPI plugin. In order to do this, you will need access to a C compiler for the platform your server runs on.

How to Do It

See the iPlanet Knowledge Base article for specific instructions.

Jigsaw—The W3C's Web Server

This section covers Jigsaw version 2.1 and later. It covers all platforms supported by Jigsaw.

Basics

Jigsaw has an administration/configuration tool with a GUI, called *JigAdmin*, which allows the administrator to add any HTTP headers to any web resources (files, directories, and CGI scripts).

Possible Difficulties

The JigAdmin configuration does not cover servlets; they must generate their own P3P headers.

---

* iPlanet Knowledge Base: Implementing P3P with iWS 4.1 or iWS 6.0, *http://knowledgebase.iplanet.com/ikb/kb/articles/7747.html*

How to Do It

1. Publish the P3P policies and policy reference files. Before you add the P3P headers on the content, you should first publish the P3P privacy policies and policy reference files. Copy the policy files to the appropriate part of your server's content tree.

2. Use *JigAdmin* to add an HTTP header to a resource using the following procedure:

    a. Double-click the mouse on the target resource in the "Docs space" pane to launch the resource editor.

    b. Select an appropriate frame in the Frames pane—"HTTPFrame" for normal files and directories, or "CGIFrame" for CGI scripts.

    c. Select the "Add frame to selected resource/frame" menu item to launch the Add Frame dialog.

    d. Select "org.w3c.jigsaw.filters.HeaderFilter" in the Class name field in the Add Frame dialog and click OK. Now you will see the HeaderFilter item in the Frames pane in the resource editor.

    e. Select the HeaderFilter item. You will see the header-name and header-value fields in the Attribute pane.

    f. Type the header name and value in the fields. For example, if you put P3P in the header-name field and policyref="http://catalog.example/P3P/ref.xml" in the header-value field, the HTTP header P3P: policyref="http://catalog.example/P3P/ref.xml" will be added to the response of the target resource.

    g. If you want to add more than one HTTP header, repeat steps c-g.

For more information, see the documentation for Jigsaw (*http://www.w3.org/Jigsaw/Doc*).

P3P in IE6

This appendix is an edited version of an October 2001 article written by Aaron Gold-feder and Lisa Leibfried for the MSDN Library titled "Privacy in Internet Explorer 6."* It is reprinted here with permission from Microsoft. This article discusses features of Internet Explorer 6. These features are subject to change in subsequent versions.

The privacy features of Internet Explorer 6 focus on advanced cookie filtering as a major step toward empowering users to protect their privacy. Although solving the cookie problem is not a panacea, it is an industry-leading step in addressing consumer anxiety over privacy concerns. Simply disabling cookies is not a workable solution because many applications depend upon them. Similarly, prompting the user for each cookie download is not feasible because users are typically annoyed with such interruptions.

Advanced cookie filtering works by evaluating a Web site's privacy practices and deciding which cookies are acceptable based on the site's compact policies and the user's own preferences. In the default settings, cookies that are used to collect personally identifiable information and do not allow users a choice in their use are considered "unsatisfactory." By default, unsatisfactory cookies are deleted in the first-party context when the browsing session ends and rejected in the third-party context. In this way, users can choose to enjoy the benefits of cookies, while protecting themselves from unsatisfactory cookies. The full details of cookie filtering are discussed in the sections that follow.

The Internet Explorer 6 technology for understanding a Web site's privacy policy is built upon the P3P Specification. Using Extensible Markup Language (XML), P3P provides a common syntax and transport mechanism that enables Web sites to communicate their privacy practices to Internet Explorer 6 (or any other user agent). Internet Explorer 6 can then inform users of what is happening behind the scenes and assist them by filtering out unsatisfactory cookies.

---

* *http://msdn.microsoft.com/library/default.asp?url=/library/en-us/dnpriv/html/ie6privacyfeature.asp.*

Users can easily adjust the cookie filtering sensitivity of Internet Explorer 6 by using a slider interface with six levels, as shown in Figure C-1. Cookie filtering can also be fully customized in the following ways:

- Accept or deny cookies from specific Web sites
- Import custom cookie filtering settings
- Enable advanced controls for other cookie options

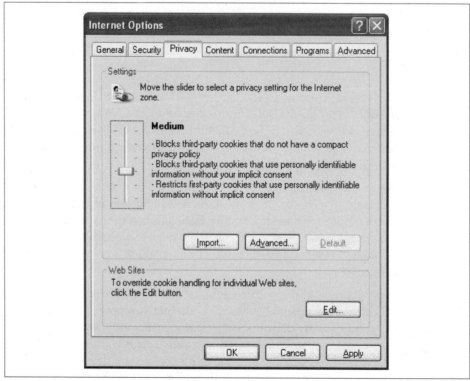

Figure C-1. Internet Explorer 6 privacy tab

Persistent Versus Session Cookies

To discuss how Internet Explorer 6 handles cookies, it is useful to know the difference between persistent and session cookies. Persistent cookies are discarded when they reach their defined expiration time. Cookies that do not have a specified expiration time are regarded as session cookies and are discarded when Internet Explorer is closed.

First- and Third-Party Context

Internet Explorer 6 defines first-party content as that associated with the host domain. Third-party content originates from any other domain. For example, suppose a user visits *www.wideworldimporters.com* by typing this URL in the address bar, and *www.wingtiptoys.com* has a banner ad on this page. If these two sites set cookies, the cookies from *www.wideworldimporters.com* are in a first-party context while the cookies from *www.wingtiptoys.com* are in a third-party context.

Often commercial Web pages are an amalgamation of first- and third-party content. The Internet Explorer 6 privacy features distinguish between first- and third-party content. The underlying assumption is that users have a different relationship with first parties than with third parties. In fact, users might not be aware of the third party or be given a choice in having a relationship with it. For this reason, default privacy settings for third parties are more stringent than for first parties.

The URLs, *www.wideworldimporters.com* and *toys.wideworldimporters.com*, both contain the same minimal domain, *wideworldimporters.com*. Content that shares the same minimal domain as the host domain is considered first-party content. Likewise, cookies set from these domains are considered first-party cookies. Minimal domains must have the same top-level domain (TLD). Some common examples of TLDs are .com, .net, and .org.

P3P and Compact Policies

P3P policies covering the use of cookies can be expressed in a condensed form called compact policies. Essentially, the elements of the P3P policy are mapped to short tokens and aggregated to form a compact policy. The following is a brief example of how this works.

Suppose Blue Yonder Airlines creates a P3P policy with two statements about their data collection practices. In the first statement, Blue Yonder Airlines specifies that it collects demographic information that includes gender, country, and zip code, for pseudonymous analysis (determining user habits and interests without association to a natural person) and that it shares this information with other recipients. The second statement specifies that Blue Yonder Airlines collects online information, specifically an e-mail address, upon the user's affirmative response, which is exclusively used for later contact. Each statement specifies that Blue Yonder Airlines uses cookies to facilitate these transactions. Also included in the policy is the access element which specifies that users have access to the contact information collected from them. Blue Yonder Airlines' full P3P policy might look something like this:

```
<POLICY xmlns="http://www.w3.org/2000/12/P3Pv1"
     discuri="http://www.blueyonderairlines.com/ourprivacypolicy.html"
     opturi="http://www.blueyonderairlines.com/optin.html">
 <ENTITY>
```

```
<DATA-GROUP>
 <DATA ref="#business.name">Blue Yonder Airlines</DATA>
 <DATA ref="#business.contact-info.postal.street">3456 Main St.</DATA>
 <DATA ref="#business.contact-info.postal.city">Tampa</DATA>
 <DATA ref="#business.contact-info.postal.stateprov">Fl</DATA>
 <DATA ref="#business.contact-info.postal.postalcode">77062</DATA>
 <DATA ref="#business.contact-info.postal.country">USA</DATA>
 <DATA ref="#business.contact-info.online.email">molly@blueyonderairlines.com</
DATA>
 <DATA ref="#business.contact-info.telecom.telephone.intcode">1</DATA>
 <DATA ref="#business.contact-info.telecom.telephone.loccode">800</DATA>
 <DATA ref="#business.contact-info.telecom.telephone.number">5550158</DATA>
</DATA-GROUP>
</ENTITY>
<ACCESS><contact-and-other/></ACCESS>
<STATEMENT>
 <PURPOSE><pseudo-analysis/></PURPOSE>
 <RECIPIENT><other-recipient/></RECIPIENT>
 <RETENTION><business-practices/></RETENTION>
 <DATA-GROUP>
  <DATA ref="#user.home-info.postal.country" optional="yes"/>
  <DATA ref="#user.home-info.postal.postalcode" optional="yes"/>
  <DATA ref="#user.gender" optional="yes"/>
  <DATA ref="#dynamic.cookies" optional="yes">
   <CATEGORIES><demographic/></CATEGORIES>
  </DATA>
 </DATA-GROUP>
</STATEMENT>
<STATEMENT>
 <PURPOSE><contact required="opt-in"/></PURPOSE>
 <RECIPIENT><ours/></RECIPIENT>
 <RETENTION><stated-purpose/></RETENTION>
 <DATA-GROUP>
  <DATA ref="#user.home-info.online.email" optional="yes"/>
  <DATA ref="#dynamic.cookies" optional="yes">
   <CATEGORIES><online/></CATEGORIES>
  </DATA>
 </DATA-GROUP>
</STATEMENT>
</POLICY>
```

For each statement element, the category, purpose, and recipient element each have an associated compact form. The access element also has a compact form. The table below shows the compact tokens associated with each of the elements in this example.

Privacy tag	Compact token
<contact-and-other/>	CAO
<pseudo-analysis/>	PSA
<contact required="opt-in"/>	CONi
<other-recipient/>	OTR
<ours/>	OUR

Privacy tag	Compact token
<demographic/>	DEM
<online/>	ONL

We can form a compact policy for our example by aggregating these purpose, recipient, category, and access tokens. Compact policies are sent using a custom HTTP response header using the syntax shown in the following example.

```
P3P: CP="CAO PSA CONi OTR OUR DEM ONL"
```

This header can be added to an HTTP response using Active Server Pages (ASP) or through the computer management console on Microsoft® Windows® 2000 server and other popular Web servers. It is important to note that cookie compact policies are sent from the server along with the cookie data on HTTP responses, while decisions and settings regarding cookies are made on the client (Internet Explorer 6).

The cookie filtering of Internet Explorer 6 does not make use of full P3P policies. Compact policies are required for cookies. Cookies set through script or the meta element are governed by the compact policies on the associated HTTP response. Cookies without a compact policy are regarded by Internet Explorer 6 as not having a policy.

The purpose and recipient tags of a P3P policy have an optional attribute that can take the value of "opt-in," "opt-out," or "always." The use of "opt-in" denotes that users must approve the purpose of use or recipient of the data. The use of "opt-out" denotes that data is used for the purpose or recipient specified unless the user chooses not to allow it—that is, the user opts out. Using "always" indicates that the purpose or recipient is always required. "Always" is the default if this attribute is not specified. Within compact policies, this attribute is abbreviated by a single letter and appended to the token. In our example, the "i" appended to the CON token indicates that users have to "opt-in" to have their online information used for contact purposes ("always" is abbreviated as "a" and "opt-out" as "o"). Tokens which do not include a single letter abbreviation are handled in the same way as tokens with an "a." For example, CON and CONa are treated the same.

It is important to note that grouping of data categories, purposes, and recipients found in the P3P policy is lost in the aggregation process used to form a compact policy. This can lead to compact policies that have unintended consequences. In our example, the compact policy, "CAO PSA CONi OTR OUR DEM ONL", suggests that contact information can be shared with other recipients when this might not necessarily be the case. You can minimize this ambiguity by creating individual P3P policies for cookies in different data-collection scenarios.

In our example, the policies for cookies used for pseudonymous analysis and those used for collection of personal information could be separated into different P3P policies with different compact policy forms. The two compact policies would then be "CAO PSA OTR DEM" and "CAO CONi ONL OUR" and would clearly express the intention of each type of cookie.

Cookie Filtering

Internet Explorer 6 takes action on cookies based on the context in which the cookie was sent and on the content of its compact policy. Depending on the situation, Internet Explorer 6 will accept, deny, downgrade, or leash the cookie. A *downgraded cookie* is a persistent cookie that is deleted when the browsing session ends or the cookie expires, whichever comes first. A *leashed cookie* is one that is only sent on requests to download first-party content. When requests are made for third-party content, these cookies are suppressed—that is, they are not sent. For example, suppose *www.wingtiptoys.com* is in the first-party context and sets a cookie in Internet Explorer 6. Suppose also that this cookie is leashed. When *www.wingtiptoys.com* is later present in a third-party context, the cookie is suppressed.

A small icon on the status bar informs the user when Internet Explorer 6 has denied, downgraded, or suppressed cookies (see Figure C-2). Clicking the icon brings the user to a privacy report dialog box summarizing the actions made by Internet Explorer 6 on cookies. From the dialog box, users can elect to view full P3P policies in a user friendly format and grant "allow" or "block" cookie privileges to specific Web sites.

Figure C-2. An eye covered by a do-not-enter sign serves as the privacy icon on the IE6 status bar

The following table lists the potential cookie action values that might be found in the privacy report dialog box and their meanings.

Cookie Action	Meaning
Accepted	Cookie was accepted and might be leashed
Restricted	Cookie was accepted, but downgraded to a session cookie
Blocked	Cookie was either suppressed or rejected

Unsatisfactory Cookies

According to Internet Explorer 6, an unsatisfactory cookie contains or allows access to personally identifiable information that is used for unstated purposes or provided to unstated recipients without user consent. An unsatisfactory cookie's category and either purpose or recipient are contained in the following lists with neither opt-in nor opt-out specified. These categories, purposes, and recipients are only a subset of those in P3P used by Internet Explorer 6.

Note, this list includes short descriptions and the compact tokens for the data categories, purposes, and recipients of unsatisfactory cookies. Consult Chapter 6 or the

P3P 1.0 specification for detailed definitions. Chapter 7 includes a complete list of all P3P compact policy tokens.

Category	Compact token	Description
<physical/>	PHY	Contact or location information
<online/>	ONL	Contact or location information on the Internet (for example, e-mail address)
<government/>	GOV	Identification issued by the government (for example, Social Security number)
<financial/>	FIN	Information about an individual's finances

Purpose	Compact token	Description
<individual-analysis/>	IVA	Analysis that can be related to individual users
<individual-decision/>	IVD	Taking actions based on user history
<contact/>	CON	For contact by means other than telephone
<telemarketing/>	TEL	For contact by telephone
<other-purposes/>	OTP	Any other purpose not captured by other P3P purposes

Recipient	Compact token	Description
<same/>	SAM	Legal entities that use the data for their own purposes under equable practices
<other-recipient/>	OTR	Entities that are accountable to the provider but might use data in unknown ways
<unrelated/>	UNR	Entities that use data in ways unknown to the provider
<public/>	PUB	Public forums

In summary, unsatisfactory cookies are those where the policy contains a token from both columns in the following table and where the purpose/recipient token does not contain the optional attribute, "i" or "o." As an example, a cookie with a compact policy that contains the tokens PHY and OTR is an unsatisfactory cookie, while a cookie with the compact policy that contains PHY and OTRo is acceptable.

Category		Purpose/recipient	
PHY	Physical location	SAM	Same policies
ONL	Online location	OTR	Other recipients
GOV	Government ID	UNR	Unknown purposes
FIN	Financial information	PUB	Publicly available
		IVA	Individual Analysis
		IVD	Individual Decision
		CON	Contact Information
		TEL	Telephone Promotion
		OTP	Other Purposes

Internet Explorer 6 Privacy Preference Settings

Users can change their privacy preferences using a slider on the Privacy tab in Internet Options. The slider has six levels: Block All Cookies, High, Medium High, Medium (default level), Low, and Accept All Cookies. In the intermediate settings, compact policies are required of third-party cookies but not first-party cookies. However, first-party cookies without compact policies are *leashed*. This prohibits Web sites from setting a cookie without a compact policy in the first-party context for later use in a third-party context. First-party cookies are most effective when accompanied by a compact policy so they are reachable in the third-party context.

A change in privacy settings does not affect non-legacy cookies set prior to this change except when set to Block All Cookies and Accept All Cookies. To ensure all cookies follow the new settings, the user can delete all cookies before changing the privacy settings.

The user also has the option to define cookie management practices on a per-site basis. These per-site settings override all the default privacy preferences set with the slider except for Block All Cookies or Accept All Cookies.

The following sections describe the actions taken for first- and third-party cookies for each of the default privacy settings of the Internet zone.

Block All Cookies

This privacy setting is defined by the following:

- Deny all cookies.
- Do not send any cookies.
- Cookies already present are not deleted when this option is selected.
- This setting overrules any per-site cookie settings defined by the user.

High

Cookie type and policy	First-party context	Third-party context
Persistent cookie with no compact policy	Deny	Deny
Persistent cookie with unsatisfactory compact policy	Deny; also deny if the opt-out attribute is present.	Deny; also deny if the opt-out attribute is present
Persistent cookie with acceptable compact policy	Accept	Accept
Session cookie	Treat like a persistent cookie with regard to presence or content of the compact policy	Treat like a persistent cookie with regard to presence or content of the compact policy

The High setting uses a more stringent definition of unsatisfactory compact policies. First- and third-party cookies with compact policies that use the "opt-out" attribute with any of the purposes or recipients listed in the table of unsatisfactory tags are denied.

Medium High

Cookie type and policy	First-party context	Third-party context
Persistent cookie with no compact policy	Leash	Deny
Persistent cookie with unsatisfactory compact policy	Deny	Deny; also deny if the opt-out attribute is present
Persistent cookie with acceptable compact policy	Accept	Accept
Session cookie	Accept	Treat like a persistent cookie with regard to presence or content of the compact policy

The Medium High setting uses a more stringent definition of unsatisfactory compact policies. Third-party cookies with policies that use the "opt-out" attribute with any of the purposes or recipients listed in the table of unsatisfactory tags are denied.

Medium (Default)

Cookie type and policy	First-party context	Third-party context
Persistent cookie with no compact policy	Leash	Deny
Persistent cookie with unsatisfactory compact policy	Downgrade	Deny
Persistent cookie with acceptable compact policy	Accept	Accept
Session cookie	Accept	Treat like a persistent cookie with regard to presence or content of the compact policy

Low

Cookie type and policy	First-party context	Third-party context
Persistent cookie with no compact policy	Leash	Downgrade
Persistent cookie with unsatisfactory compact policy	Accept	Downgrade
Persistent cookie with acceptable compact policy	Accept	Accept
Session cookie	Accept	Treat like a persistent cookie with regard to presence or content of the compact policy

Accept All Cookies

This privacy setting is defined by the following:

- Accept all cookies regardless of the presence of a compact policy.

- Send all cookies.
- This setting overrides any per-site cookie settings defined by the user.

Legacy Cookies

Internet Explorer 6 defines a legacy cookie as a cookie that exists on the user's computer at the time Internet Explorer 6 is installed or that is imported from another browser using the Import/Export Wizard under the File menu of Internet Explorer. Legacy cookies are not deleted during installation.

Legacy cookies are leashed when the default privacy setting is set to High, Medium High, Medium, or Low. Under the Block All Cookies or Accept All Cookies settings, legacy cookies are treated the same as other cookies and unconditionally blocked or accepted respectively.

Unless the user's privacy setting is set to Accept All Cookies, legacy cookies are accessible only in a first-party context.

Special Provision for Legacy Opt-Out Cookies

Internet Explorer 6 has made a special provision for opt-out legacy cookies. Often when a user opts out of some online service, an opt-out cookie is used by the Web service to facilitate this choice. The success of this transaction sometimes relies on the ability of the browser to send this cookie in both first- and third-party contexts. However, with Internet Explorer 6, legacy cookies are leashed and are not sent in the third-party context. In response to this problem, Internet Explorer 6 does not leash cookies where the name/value pair is "ID=OPT_OUT". (Please note that this name/value string is case- and space-sensitive.) Web sites should upgrade their opt-out cookies to use this syntax to ensure legacy opt-out cookies are effective in Internet Explorer 6. Once Internet Explorer 6 is installed, new opt-out cookies are handled just like any other non-legacy cookie.

Cookie Filtering and the Internet Explorer Security Zones

Up until now, we have been talking about the Internet zone. However, the new privacy features also affect cookie handling in the other security zones. The following table describes the cookie management practices for each of the security zones.

Security zone	Cookie filtering
Internet	Cookie management is set by the user using the Privacy Preferences slider or Advanced Settings dialog box on the Privacy tab of Internet Options and on a per-site basis.
Intranet	Accept and send all cookies including legacy cookies. There is no per-site cookie management. (Same as Accept All Cookies setting on the Privacy Preferences slider.)

Security zone	Cookie filtering
Trusted	Accept and send all cookies including legacy cookies. There is no per-site cookie management. (Same as Accept All Cookies setting on the Privacy Preferences slider.)
Restricted	Reject all cookies. Do not send any cookies. There is no per-site cookie management. (Same as Block All Cookies setting on the Privacy Preferences slider.)
Local	Accept all cookies including legacy cookies. There is no per-site cookie management. (Same as Accept All Cookies setting on the Privacy Preferences slider.)

Other Key Privacy Features in Internet Explorer 6

P3P Privacy Policy Display
> Internet Explorer 6 retrieves full P3P policies and displays them in a user-friendly format.

Per-Site Cookie Management
> Through the Privacy Tab in the Internet Options dialog box, users can accept or deny cookies from individual Web sites. All existing cookies for a site are deleted when that site is added to the per-site list with the instruction to Deny all cookies from that site.

Advanced Settings
> Users can accept, deny, or be prompted for cookies in both the first- and third-party contexts. The user can also choose to always allow session cookies. When a user chooses to be prompted, a dialog box appears so a user can accept or reject a cookie. The dialog box also offers the user a chance to examine the cookie's name/value pair, expiration, compact policy, and whether it is sent in a first- or third-party context.

Import
> Users can import an XML file that can customize cookie handling for compact policies in all security zones, except for the Restricted and Local zones, and on a per-site basis. For more information see Appendix E, How to create a Customized Privacy Import File.

What If the Privacy Features "Broke" My Site?

It is likely that the Web site's behavior is dependent upon cookies that are unexpectedly being rejected or suppressed. To avoid this, users can move the privacy preferences slider down to "Accept All Cookies" or explicitly choose to allow a Web site's cookies by clicking the Site button on the Privacy tab of Internet Options and adding the site to the per-site list.

What Web Services Need to Do
for Internet Explorer 6

To continue the successful deployment of cookies for use with Internet Explorer 6 or its public preview, the best thing to do is deploy P3P on your site. This involves first assessing your business practices and then forming a comprehensive policy. Visit *http://p3ptoolbox.org* and take advantage of the tools and resources. Many cookies without compact policies will be rejected by default, so deploying P3P with compact policies is critical for maintaining your Web services. Addressing Internet privacy is the responsibility of the entire industry, and now is the time to take steps toward these sensible, interoperable solutions.

How to Create a Customized Privacy Import File for IE6

This appendix is an edited version of an article written by the IE6 privacy development and SDK team for the MSDN Library titled "How to Create a Customized Privacy Import File."* It is reprinted here with permission from Microsoft.

Customized privacy settings can be imported into Microsoft® Internet Explorer 6 using the Extensible Markup Language (XML) syntax described in this overview.

Customizing the Internet Explorer Privacy Settings

Privacy settings specify how Internet Explorer 6 handles cookies. Internet Explorer 6 makes decisions on cookies based on a number of factors including user preferences and the existence and content of a Web service's privacy policy. For most users, Internet Explorer 6 default privacy settings provides enough privacy protection without disrupting the browsing process. However, privacy settings can be customized through a variety of dialog boxes reachable from the Privacy tab in Internet Options on the Tools menu. Additionally, if the user chooses, privacy settings can be specified by importing custom settings using the XML syntax described in this overview. This is the only way that a user or Web service can directly specify rules for interpreting and acting on a cookie's compact policy.

Here are the XML elements that can be included in custom settings file. They are explained in more detail below, and described fully in the MSDN library.

XML Element	Definition
alwaysReplayLegacy	Specifies to always replay legacy cookies.
if	Specifies a rule describing how to act on a cookie based on its compact policy.
firstparty	Specifies rules for first-party cookies.

---

* *http://msdn.microsoft.com/library/default.asp?url=/workshop/security/privacy/overview/privacyimportxml.asp.*

XML Element	Definition
flushCookies	Specifies that all cookies be deleted when custom settings are loaded.
flushSiteList	Specifies that the privacy per-site list be deleted when custom settings are loaded.
MSIEPrivacy	Specifies custom privacy settings.
MSIEPrivacySettings	Specifies custom privacy settings as a function of security zone, Web page context (first-party vs. third-party), type (session vs. persistent cookie) and the content of a cookie's Platform for Privacy Preferences (P3P) compact policy.
MSIESiteRules	Specifies privacy per-site rules for cookies.
p3pCookiePolicy	Specifies how to handle cookies based on the P3P compact policy.
site	Specifies the per-site rules for a Web site.
thirdparty	Specifies rules for third-party cookies.

Note, comments are not allowed in custom privacy import files.

MSIEPrivacy

The MSIEPrivacy element is the XML document root, the outermost element of a custom privacy policy. Underneath this element are two optional children, MSIEPrivacySettings and MSIESiteRules. MSIEPrivacySettings is used to specify default actions on cookies, and MSIESiteRules specifies actions on a per-site basis.

The following example shows the basic XML structure of a custom privacy settings file. The formatVersion attribute is required and specifies the version of Internet Explorer to which these rules apply. For Internet Explorer 6, the formatVersion must be set to 6 and not 6.0. Comments are also not allowed in the custom privacy settings file.

```
<MSIEPrivacy>
<MSIEPrivacySettings formatVersion="6">
 ... child elements ...
</MSIEPrivacySettings>
<MSIESiteRules formatVersion="6">
 ... child elements ...
</MSIESiteRules>
</MSIEPrivacy>
```

MSIEPrivacySettings

The content of the MSIEPrivacySettings specifies cookie actions as a function of security zone, Web page context (first-party vs. third-party), type (session vs. persistent cookie) and the content of a cookie's P3P compact policy.

The MSIEPrivacySettings element has four children, p3pCookiePolicy, alwaysReplayLegacy, flushCookies, and flushSiteList. These elements must be specified in this order.

Specifying the `alwaysReplayLegacy` element allows all legacy cookies (cookies that existed when Internet Explorer 6 was installed) to be sent. If nothing is specified, legacy cookies are sent only in first-party context (that is, they are leashed). Specifying the `flushCookies` element deletes all cookies when these customized privacy settings are imported. Specifying the `flushSiteList` element deletes all per-site decisions when these customized privacy settings are imported.

The `p3pCookiePolicy` element specifies rules for handling cookies by security zone. Given a security zone, cookie actions are further defined for first-party and third-party cookies using the `firstParty` and `thirdParty` elements. The `firstParty` and `thirdParty` elements both have three required attributes—`noPolicyDefault`, `noRuleDefault`, and `alwaysAllowSession`. The `noPolicyDefault` attribute specifies the cookie action for a cookie with no compact policy. The `noRuleDefault` attribute specifies the cookie action for a cookie when none of the custom rule expressions evaluate to true when applied to the cookie's compact policy. Set the `alwaysAllowSession` attribute to "yes" to always accept session cookies. If `alwaysAllowSession` is set to "no," session cookies are evaluated in the same way as persistent cookies.

The following table lists acceptable cookie actions.

Action	Description
accept	Accept cookies.
prompt	Prompt the user.
forceFirstParty	Leash cookies so that they are only sent in a first-party context.
forceSession	Convert persistent cookies (cookies that have an expiration time independent of when browser session cookie ends) to session cookies (cookies that expire when browser session cookie ends).
reject	Reject cookies.

What follows is an example `MSIEPrivacySettings` statement that specifies rules for handling first- and third-party cookies and states that legacy cookies should always be sent.

```
<MSIEPrivacySettings formatVersion="6">
<p3pCookiePolicy zone="internet">
<firstParty noPolicyDefault="reject" noRuleDefault="accept" alwaysAllowSession="yes">
      <if expr="TEL" action="reject"></if>
      <if expr="FIN,CON" action="forceSession"></if>
      <if expr="FIN,CONa" action="forceSession"></if>
      <if expr="GOV,PUB" action="forceSession"></if>
</firstParty>
<thirdParty noPolicyDefault="accept" noRuleDefault="accept" alwaysAllowSession="yes">
</thirdParty>
</p3pCookiePolicy>
<alwaysReplayLegacy/>
</MSIEPrivacySettings>
```

Some compact tokens such as CON can include an opt-in, opt-out, or always attribute and therefore, produce different forms of a compact token (CON, CONa, CONi, CONo).

You must explicitly specify all the forms you want to intercept in an expression. For example, `expr="FIN,CON"` does not intercept a compact policy with the tokens `FIN` and `CONa`.

The following expression evaluates to true if a compact policy contains the tokens `FIN` and `CONa`.

```
expr="FIN,CONa"
```

The exclamation point (!) acts as a NOT operator in expressions. The following expression evaluates to true if a compact policy contains the token `CON` and does not contain the token `OTR`.

```
expr="CON,!OTR"
```

Rules are evaluated in the order they are defined in the customized import policy. The first expression to evaluate to true defines the cookie action taken.

MSIESiteRules

The `MSIESiteRules` element specifies cookie actions on a per-site basis. For each site, the cookie action can be set to accept or reject.

What follows is an example of an `MSIESiteRules` statement that specifies to accept all cookies from *www.BlueYonderAirlines.com*.

```
<MSIESiteRules formatVersion="6">
<site domain="www.BlueYonderAirlines.com"
    action="accept">
</site>
</MSIESiteRules>
```

Putting It All Together

Putting these pieces together creates the following custom privacy policy.[*]

```
<MSIEPrivacy>
<MSIEPrivacySettings formatVersion="6">
<p3pCookiePolicy zone="internet">
<firstParty noPolicyDefault="reject" noRuleDefault="accept" alwaysAllowSession="yes">
    <if expr="TEL" action="reject"></if>
    <if expr="FIN,CON" action="forceSession"></if>
    <if expr="FIN,CONa" action="forceSession"></if>
    <if expr="GOV,PUB" action="forceSession"></if>
</firstParty>
<thirdParty noPolicyDefault="accept" noRuleDefault="accept" alwaysAllowSession="yes">
</thirdParty>
```

---

[*] The MSDN Library version of this article also includes the complete settings file behind the IE6 Medium setting.

```
</p3pCookiePolicy>
<alwaysReplayLegacy/>
</MSIEPrivacySettings>
<MSIESiteRules formatVersion="6">
<site domain="www.BlueYonderAirlines.com"
    action="accept">
</site>
</MSIESiteRules>
</MSIEPrivacy>
```

Important Notes on Cookie Rules

- Given a set of rules on how to handle cookies, the first rule expression to evaluate to true takes precedence and the following rules are skipped.

- The presence of an invalid compact privacy policy token in the custom privacy settings import file cancels the import process.

Important Notes on Importing Customized Settings

- Privacy settings cannot be imported for the Restricted and Local security zones.[*]

- Privacy settings not overridden by the imported custom privacy settings remain as they were at the time of import. For example, if the imported custom settings do not define privacy settings for the Internet security zone, then the existing privacy settings for this zone are retained.

- Importing privacy preferences for a given security zone overrides all privacy preferences for that zone.

- When the MSIESiteRules element is specified, any per-site rules that exist when the custom privacy settings are imported are deleted.

- The import mechanism can only unleash legacy cookies. Non-legacy cookies cannot be unleashed. Also, with the exception of legacy cookies, imported privacy settings will not apply to old cookies. For this reason, you many want to delete old cookies.

- Once custom settings are imported for the Internet security zone, selecting either the Advanced or Default buttons on the Privacy tab in Internet Options on the Tools menu removes these imported settings.

- For information on restoring default privacy settings in Internet Explorer 6 for zones other than the Internet zone, see Knowledge Base article *http://support. microsoft.com/support/kb/articles/q301/6/89.asp*.

---

[*] See also Microsoft's information on security zones at *http://msdn.microsoft.com/library/default.asp?url=/ workshop/security/szone/overview/overview.asp*.

APPENDIX E
P3P Guiding Principles

The following appears as Appendix 7 of the P3P 1.0 Specification.

This appendix describes the intent of P3P development and recommends guidelines regarding the responsible use of P3P technology. An earlier version was published in the W3C Note *P3P Guiding Principles*.

The Platform for Privacy Preferences Project (P3P) has been designed to be flexible and support a diverse set of user preferences, public policies, service provider polices, and applications. This flexibility will provide opportunities for using P3P in a wide variety of innovative ways that its designers had not imagined. The P3P Guiding Principles were created in order to: express the intentions of the members of the P3P working groups when designing this technology and suggest how P3P can be used most effectively in order to maximize privacy and user confidence and trust on the Web. In keeping with our goal of flexibility, this document does not place requirements upon any party. Rather, it makes recommendations about 1) what *should* be done to be consistent with the intentions of the P3P designers and 2) how to maximize user confidence in P3P implementations and Web services. P3P was intended to help protect privacy on the Web. We encourage the organizations, individuals, policy-makers and companies who use P3P to embrace the guiding principles in order to reach this goal.

Information Privacy

P3P has been designed to promote privacy and trust on the Web by enabling service providers to disclose their information practices, and enabling individuals to make informed decisions about the collection and use of their personal information. P3P user agents work on behalf of individuals to reach agreements with service providers about the collection and use of personal information. Trust is built upon the mutual understanding that each party will respect the agreement reached.

Service providers should preserve trust and protect privacy by applying relevant laws and principles of data protection and privacy to their information practices. The following is a list of privacy principles and guidelines that helped inform the development of P3P and may be useful to those who use P3P:

- CMA Code of Ethics & Standards of Practice: Protection of Personal Privacy
- 1981 Council of Europe Convention For the Protection of Individuals with Regard to Automatic Processing of Personal Data
- CSA Q830-96 Model Code for the Protection of Personal Information
- Directive 95/46/EC of the European Parliament and of the Council of 24 October 1995 on the protection of individuals with regard to the processing of personal data and on the free movement of such data
- The DMA's Marketing Online Privacy Principles and Guidance and The DMA Guidelines for Ethical Business Practice
- OECD Guidelines on the Protection of Privacy and Transborder Flows of Personal Data
- Online Privacy Alliance Guidelines for Online Privacy Policies

In addition, service providers and P3P implementers should recognize and address the special concerns surrounding children's privacy.

Notice and Communication

Service providers should provide timely and effective notices of their information practices, and user agents should provide effective tools for users to access these notices and make decisions based on them.

Service providers should:

- Communicate explicitly about data collection and use, expressing the purpose for which personal information is collected and the extent to which it may be shared.
- Use P3P privacy policies to communicate about all information they propose to collect through a Web interaction.
- Prominently post clear, human-readable privacy policies.

User agents should:

- Provide mechanisms for displaying a service's information practices to users.
- Provide users an option that allows them to easily preview and agree to or reject each transfer of personal information that the user agent facilitates.
- Not be configured by default to transfer personal information to a service provider without the user's consent.
- Inform users about the privacy-related options offered by the user agent.

Choice and Control

Users should be given the ability to make meaningful choices about the collection, use, and disclosure of personal information. Users should retain control over their personal information and decide the conditions under which they will share it.

Service providers should:

- Limit their requests to information necessary for fulfilling the level of service desired by the user. This will reduce user frustration, increase trust, and enable relationships with many users, including those who may wish to have an anonymous, pseudonymous, customized, or personalized relationship with the service.
- Obtain informed consent prior to the collection and use of personal information.
- Provide information about the ability to review and if appropriate correct personal information.

User agents should:

- Include configuration tools that allow users to customize their preferences.
- Allow users to import and customize P3P preferences from trusted parties.
- Present configuration options to users in a way that is neutral or biased towards privacy.
- Be usable without requiring the user to store user personal information as part of the installation or configuration process.

Fairness and Integrity

Service providers should treat users and their personal information with fairness and integrity. This is essential for protecting privacy and promoting trust.

Service providers should:

- Accurately represent their information practices in a clear and unambiguous manner, never with the intention of misleading users.
- Use information only for the stated purpose and retain it only as long as necessary.
- Ensure that information is accurate, complete, and up-to-date.
- Disclose accountability and means for recourse.
- For as long as information is retained, continue to treat information according to the policy in effect when the information was collected, unless users give their informed consent to a new policy.

User agents should:

- Act only on behalf of the user according to the preferences specified by the user.
- Accurately represent the practices of the service provider.

Security

While P3P itself does not include security mechanisms, it is intended to be used in conjunction with security tools. Users' personal information should always be protected with reasonable security safeguards in keeping with the sensitivity of the information.

Service providers should:

- Provide mechanisms for protecting any personal information they collect.
- Use appropriate trusted protocols for the secure transmission of data.

User agents should:

- Provide mechanisms for protecting the personal information that users store in any data repositories maintained by the agent.
- Use appropriate trusted protocols for the secure transmission of data.
- Warn users when an insecure transport mechanism is being used.

Index

Symbols

\# (pound sign), in base data schema
    elements, 101
* (wildcard character)
    COOKIE-INCLUDE and
        COOKIE-EXCLUDE
        elements, 140
    INCLUDE and EXCLUDE elements, 137

A

A P3P Preference Exchange Language (see
    APPEL)
about attribute (POLICY-REF element), 136,
    279
absolute policy expiration times, 135
access-details extension, 107
access disclosures, 85, 195
ACCESS element, 85–87, 195, 269
accessibility, user interface design issues, 262
accountability principle, OECD, 24
action URLs (HTML forms), 142
ad networks, sample policy, 180
algorithms, encryption, 31
alt attribute (IMG element), 276
and (APPEL connective), 222
and-exact (APPEL connective), 223
anonymity tools, 36
    email, 39
    mix networks, 37
Anonymizer, 37
anonymizing proxies, 36
anonymous cookies, 70

Apache Web Server, including P3P
    headers, 284
APPEL, 8
    APPEL engine, 225
    connectives, 223
    goals, 214
    overview, 214
    privacy preferences, importing, 215, 216
    rule sets
        appel:RULESET element, 218
        elements, 218
        writing, 216
    rules, 220
        appel:RULE element, 220
        evaluating, 226
        implementing, 225
        limiting application of, 224
        normalizing attributes, 228
        normalizing DATA-GROUP and
            DATA elements, 229
        order of, 225
        pattern matching, 221–224
        PCDATA strings and, 227
appel:connective attribute (APPEL), 220
applets, 142
architecture, user agents, 203
assertions
    data-specific, 89–104
        CONSEQUENCE element, 90
        DATA element, 99–104
        NON-IDENTIFIABLE element, 91
        PURPOSE element, 92–96
        RECIPIENT element, 96–98
        RETENTION element, 98

We'd like to hear your suggestions for improving our indexes. Send email to *index@oreilly.com*.

assertions (*continued*)
    general, 82–89
        POLICY element, 83
        TEST element, 84
        ENTITY element, 84
        ACCESS element, 85–87
        DISPUTES element, 87–89
        DISPUTES-GROUP element, 87–89
asterisk (*) wildcard character
    COOKIE-INCLUDE and
        COOKIE-EXCLUDE
            elements, 140
    INCLUDE and EXCLUDE elements, 137
AT&T/Microsoft P3P browser helper object
        (user interfaces), 240–243
AT&T Privacy Bird, 7, 205
    privacy preferences, 230
    rule sets, 230
    user interfaces, 247–254
AT&T sample policy, 182
AT&T usability testing prototype (user
        interfaces), 243–246
attacks, brute force, 31
attributes
    attribute matching, 228
    XML, 82
    (see also individual element names)
authority (URIs), 157
automatic action user agents, 206
automatic data transfer, 50

B

base attribute (DATA-GROUP element), 273
base data schema, 4, 99–101
    business data set, 162
    certificate structure, 155
    contact structure, 156
    date structure, 154
    dynamic data set, 163
    elements, referencing in P3P policies, 101
    httpinfo structure, 159
    ipaddr structure, 158
    login structure, 156
    loginfo structure, 158
    online structure, 157
    overview, 154
    personname structure, 155
    postal structure, 156
    telecom structure, 157
    telephonenum structure, 156
    thirdparty data set, 162

    uri structure, 157
    user data set, 159–162
BBBOnLine program, 27
behavior rule (APPEL), 220, 221
Berners-Lee, Tim, 45
Better Business Bureau online, 27
blocking cookies, 19
browsers, user agents, 7
brute force attacks, 31
bugs, web, 20
business data set, 162

C

caller ID information, 44
Candidate Recommendation, 53
case-sensitivity, INCLUDE and EXCLUDE
        elements, 138
categories (see data categories)
CATEGORIES element, 102–104, 166, 270
CDT (Center for Democracy and
        Technology), 44
certificate structure, 155
chat rooms, sample policy, 177
Chaum, David, 37
Chief Privacy Officers, 28
child-protection filter software, 40
    GetNetWise web site, 41
Children's Online Privacy Protection Act
        (COPPA), 26
Choice and Control principle, 47, 308
cleanup tools, 41
clear gifs, 20
clients, user agents, 7
collection limitation principle, OECD, 23
comments, XML, 82
compact policies, 5, 62, 77
    IE6, 291–294
Compact Policy Translator web site, 209
compliance requirements (user agents),
        fetching and processing, 210
configuration
    IE6 privacy preference settings, 296
        accept all cookies, 298
        block all cookies, 296
        high, 297
        low, 297
        medium, 297
        medium high, 297
    P3P deployment and, 64
conflicts (policy references), avoiding, 148
connectives, rules for, 222

CONSEQUENCE element, 90, 271
contact structure, 156
contained expressions, 222, 226
content
    associating policies with, 136–138
    third-party, associating policies with, 139
continuous user agents, 205
cookie anchors, 20
cookie cutters, 40
cookie filtering, IE6 and, 289, 294
    compact policies, 291–294
    first- and third-party cookies, 291
    security zones, 299
    unsatisfactory cookies, 294
COOKIE-EXCLUDE element, 140, 271
COOKIE-INCLUDE element, 140, 271
cookies, 4, 18
    analyzing use of, 68–71
    anonymous, 70
    associating policies with, 136
    blocking, 19
    expiration, 141
    HTTP requests, 15
    legacy (IE6), 298
    linking, 70
    P3P deployment and, 63
    persistent, 18
        compared to session, 290
    policy references, 133
    policy scope, 141
    rejecting, 19
    replaying, 71
    requirements for including, 177
    rules, 305
    session, 18
    simple web sites, 170
    third-party, 19
        associating policies with, 140
    unsatisfactory, 294
    using as database keys, 178
    web beacons, 20
    web bugs, 20
COPPA (Children's Online Privacy
        Protection Act), 26
credit card numbers, categorizing, 201
criticisms of P3P, 56
crtdby attribute (RULESET element), 219
crtdon attribute (RULESET element), 220
cryptography, public-key, 32
customized user agents, 207
CyberScrub cleanup tool, 41

D

data categories, 101–104, 113, 154, 199–201
    used in AT&T Privacy Bird policy
        summary, 249
    (see also data schemas)
DATA element, 101–104, 153, 272
data elements, 114, 153
data practices, 4
data quality principle, OECD, 23
data schemas
    creating, 164–169
    data categories, 154
    overview, 153
    (see also base data schema)
data structures, 154
data transfer, automatic, 50
data use, planning, 115
database key cookies, sample policy, 178
DATA-DEF element, 153, 166, 272
DATA-GROUP element, 101, 104, 272
DATA-SCHEMA element, 273
DATASCHEMA element, 165
data-specific assertions (see assertions)
DATA-STRUCT element, 154, 166, 273
data-transfer mechanisms, 50
date attribute (EXPIRY element), 275
date structure, 154
default configuration settings, user
        interfaces, 257–259
default policy expiration time, 136
deployment of P3P, 63
DES Cracker computer, 31
description attribute (RULESET
        element), 220
design issues
    user interfaces
        accessibility, 262
        active versus passive alerts, 261
        AT&T/Microsoft P3P browser helper
            object, 240–243
        AT&T Privacy Bird, 247–254
        AT&T usability testing
            prototype, 243–246
        default configuration
            settings, 257–259
        filtering, 260
        layered, 256
        mismatches between policies and
            preferences, handling, 262
        policy representation, 262
        privacy considerations, 264

design issues, user interfaces (*continued*)
    Privacy Minder, 239
    symbols, 261
    user agents, 259
    vocabulary issues, 255
    W3C P3 Prototype, 237–239
  vocabulary, rating systems, 191–195
Direct Marketing Association (DMA), 44
disclosure URL, 83
discuri attribute (POLICY element), 278
dispute remedies tags, 89
dispute resolution, 87–89
  gathering site information, 112
DISPUTES element, 87–89, 274
DISPUTES-GROUP element, 87–89, 274
DMA (Direct Marketing Association), 44
domain attribute (COOKIE-INCLUDE and
    COOKIE-EXCLUDE
    elements), 271
dynamic data set, 163
dynamic negotiation, 43
dynamic.clickstream element, 163
dynamic.clientevents element, 164

E

editors, 207
  APPEL rule sets, 218
  IBM P3P Policy Editor, 121–128
    compact policies, 128
elements
  APPEL rule sets, 218
  base data schema, referencing, 101
  data, 153
  policy reference files, 134
  user data set, 161
  variable data, 154
  XML, 81, 269–283
email
  anonymous, 39
  comment forms, sample policy, 175
  encryption, 33
    web-based, 33
enabling web sites with P3P, 9
encryption
  56-bit encryption keys, 31
  algorithms, 31
  email encryption, 33
    web-based, 33
  file encryption, 32

network connections, 34
  SSH and, 35
  SSL and, 34
  private keys, 32
  public keys, 32
  tools, 31
  VPNs and, 34
ENTITY element, 84, 274
errors, avoiding, 131
Eudora, encryption and, 33
European Commission feedback, history
    and, 52
European Community Joint Research Center
    (see JRC)
European Union privacy laws, 25
evaluation, APPEL rules, 226
example policies (see policies, sample)
EXCLUDE element, 137, 275
expiration, cookies, 141
expiration notification, policies, 109, 135
EXPIRY element, 109, 135, 275
  policies, changing, 150
  POLICY-REFERENCES element, 134
EXTENSION element, 104–107, 135, 275

F

fair information practice principles, 22
Fairness and Integrity principle, 47, 308
fetching (user agent compliance
    requirements), 210
file encryption, 32
filters, 40
  child-protection software, 40
  cookie cutters, 40
first-party cookies (IE6), 291
fixed data categories, 154
forms
  HTML, 142
  sample policy, 174–177
    posting to other sites, 180
fullip element (ipaddr data structure), 158

G

general assertions (see assertions)
generators (see editors)
generic user agents, 207
GetNetWise web site (child protection), 41
Goldman, Janlori, 44

Graham-Leach-Bliley Act, 26
Guiding Principles (see P3P Guiding
        Principles)

H

headers, 16
    adding to web server responses, 284–288
    HTTP, 145–147
        Referer (HTTP), 30
        Set-Cookie (HTTP), 69
        testing, 147
    P3P, 62, 146, 286
headings, privacy policy, 68
height attribute (IMG element), 276
HINT element, 139, 276
history of P3P
    criticisms, 56
    feedback from European Commission, 52
    IPWG (Internet Privacy Working
        Group), 45
    legal implications, 55
    negotiation, 49
    origins, 43
    patent issue, 51
    Privacy Protection Commissioner's press
        release, 54
    specification
        evolution of, 47
        finishing, 53
    W3C P3P project launch, 46
hostname element (ipaddr data
        structure), 158
HTML (HyperText Markup Language)
    forms, 142
    web pages, associating policies with, 147
HTTP (HyperText Transfer Protocol), 4, 15
    headers (see headers, HTTP)
    methods, 141
    requests, 15
        cookies, 15
httpinfo structure, 159
human-readable policy explanation, 116
human-readable privacy policies, 111

I

IBM P3P Policy Editor, 121–128
    compact policies, 128
IBM sample policy, 186
Idcide Privacy Companion software, 243

identity-management tools, 41
IE6 (see Internet Explorer 6)
IIS (Microsoft Internet Information Server),
        including P3P headers, 286
IMG element, 88, 276
importing privacy preference settings
    APPEL, 215, 216
    AT&T Privacy Bird, 230
    IE6, 229, 301–305
INCLUDE element, 137, 276
individual participation principle, OECD, 23
infomediaries, 41
Information Privacy principle, 47, 306
information-only user agents, 206
Intelytics Site Sentinel, 66
Intermind Corporation, 51
Internet basics, 17
Internet Explorer 6, 8
    compact policies, 129
    cookie filtering, 294
    legacy cookies, 298
    privacy features, 299
        compact policies, 291–294
        first- and third-party cookies, 291
        overview, 289
    privacy settings, 230, 296
        accept all cookies, 298
        block all cookies, 296
        customizing, 301
        high, 297
        importing, 229, 301–305
        low, 297
        medium, 297
        medium high, 297
        MSIEPrivacy element, 302
        MSIEPrivacySettings element, 302
        MSIESiteRules element, 304
    security zones, cookie filtering and, 299
Internet Information Server (IIS), including
        P3P headers, 286
Internet Privacy Working Group (IPWG), 45
Internet service providers (ISPs), 17
Interoperability Session, W3C, 53
IP (Internet Protocol) addresses, 17
    proxies and, 36
ipaddr structure, 158
iPlanet Web Server, including P3P
        headers, 287
IPWG (Internet Privacy Working Group), 45
ISPs (Internet service providers), 17

J

Jigsaw web server, including P3P headers, 287
JRC (European Community Joint Research Center)
  APPEL editor, 218
  prototype user agent, 204

L

languages, policy considerations, 143
laws, privacy (see privacy laws)
layered user interfaces, 256
legacy cookies (IE6), 298
legal issues, 24, 55
  European Union, 25
  United States, 25
Lessig, Lawrence, xi–xiii
lifetime of policy reference files, 135
LINK tag, associating policies with web pages, 76, 147
linking cookies, 70
log files, 17
logical relationships, APPEL connectives, 222
login structure, 156
loginfo structure, 158
logs (server), disclosing information about, 165
LONG-DESCRIPTION element, 88, 277

M

mailing lists
  policy implementation information, 132
  registration forms, sample policy, 176
marketing purposes, 197
max-age attribute (EXPIRY element), 275
McAfee Privacy Service suite, 41
META element, 134
META element (HTTP), 78, 277
METHOD element, 141, 277
methods, HTTP, 141
Microsoft Outlook, encryption and, 33
Mitchell, Ross, 43
mix networks, 37
MSIE (see Internet Explorer 6)
MSIEPrivacy element, 302
MSIEPrivacySettings element, 302
MSIESiteRules element, 304
Mulligan, Deirdre, 44, 45

N

name attribute
  COOKIE-INCLUDE and COOKIE-EXCLUDE elements, 271
  data schemas, creating, 166
  DATA-DEF element, 272
  DATA-STRUCT element, 273
  POLICY element, 278
  statement, 113
naming policies, 111
negotiation, 49
  dynamic, 43
Netscape Messenger, encryption and, 33
Netscape Navigator, 8
networks
  encrypted connections, 34
    SSH and, 35
    SSL and, 34
  mix networks, 37
Newton MessagePads, 43
non-and (APPEL connective), 223
non-identifiable data, 113, 196
NON-IDENTIFIABLE element, 91, 277
non-or (APPEL connective), 223
Notice and Communication principle, 47, 307

O

OECD (Organization for Economic Co-operation and Development) Guidelines, 23
offline privacy concerns, 21
  security, 21
on-demand user agents, 205
online privacy concerns, 12
  offline concerns comparison, 21
  survey data, 13–14, 15
Online Privacy Store, 42
online structure, 157
openness principle, OECD, 23
OpenSSH, 36
OPS (Online Profiling Specification), 50
opt-in/opt-out, 24
  policies, 62, 111
optional attribute
  DATA element, 272
  EXTENSION element, 276
opt-out URL, 83

opturi attribute (POLICY element), 278
or (APPEL connective), 222
order forms, sample policy, 175
or-exact (APPEL connective), 223
Organization for Economic Co-operation and
        Development (OECD)
        Guidelines, 23
organizations, privacy-related, 29
origins of P3P, 43
OTHERWISE element, 224

P

P3P
    defined, 3
    history (see history of P3P)
    overview, 4
    reasons for using, 9
P3P Guiding Principles, 47, 306–309
    user agents, 211–213
P3P headers, 62, 146, 286
P3P Interoperability Session, 53
P3P Policy Editor (IBM), 74
P3P Proxy Service (JRC prototype user
        agent), 204
P3P Specification Working Group, 47
    finishing specification, 53
P3P Test Suite web site, 210
p3p:POLICY element, 221
packets, 17
padlock icon in browser, SSL and, 34
papers on P3P, 57
parcel delivery service example, mix
        networks, 37
patent issue, history and, 51
path attribute
        COOKIE-INCLUDE and
                COOKIE-EXCLUDE
                elements, 271
        HINT element, 139, 276
PCDATA, 82, 277
persistent cookies, 18
    compared to session cookies, 290
    sample policy, 178
personal home pages, sample policy, 170
personname structure, 155
PGP (Pretty Good Privacy), 33
    email plug-ins, 33
philosophy (P3P specification), 306
PICS (Platform for Internet Content
        Selection), 44

Platform for Privacy Preferences (see P3P)
policies, 4, 61
    access information, 111
    attributes, 83
    changing, 150
    combination files, 76
    compact policies, 5, 62, 77
        IBM P3P Policy Editor, 128
    contact information, 111
        ENTITY element, 84
    creating
        example, 116–120
        IBM P3P Policy Editor, 121–128
    data categories, 113
    data elements, 114
    data practices, information gathering, 112
    data recipients, 115
    data retention, 116
    data use, 115
    dispute resolution, 87, 112
    expiration, 109, 135
    generating, 74
    human-readable, 62, 111
    human-readable explanation, 116
    information-gathering templates, 110
    naming, 111
    non-identifiable data, 113
    opt-in/opt-out policies, 62, 111
    pattern matching and, 221
    pitfalls, 131
    safe zone, 78
    sample
        ad networks, 180
        AT&T, 182
        chat rooms, 177
        collecting any type of data, 171
        database key cookies, 178
        email comment forms, 175
        full web logs, 173
        IBM, 186
        mailing list registration forms, 176
        order forms, 175
        persistent cookies, 178
        posting forms to other sites, 180
        Robroydog.org, 181
        sanitized web logs, 174
        search engines, 177
        session cookies, 178
        simple policy, 170
        third-party agents, 179
    statement name, 113

policies (*continued*)
    test, 80, 84
    web pages, associating with, 147
POLICIES element, 82, 108, 278
POLICY element, 83, 107, 278
    policy naming recommendations, 111
policy reference files, 5, 61, 133
    combination files, 76
    conflicting policies, avoiding, 148
    cookies, associating with, 140
    creating, 133
    deployment and, 64
    generating, 74
    lifetime, 135
    LINK tags and, 76, 147
    pitfalls, 151
    policies, including, 149
    policy references, 136
    referencing, 144
        HTTP headers, 145
        well-known location mechanism, 144
    sample with all elements, 134
    third-party content, associating with, 139
    user agents and, 75
    web site content, associating
        with, 136–138
    web sites, 9
POLICY-REF element, 136, 279
POLICY-REFERENCES element, 134, 279
postal structure, 156
pound sign (#), in base data schema
    elements, 101
preference settings
    privacy (see importing privacy preference
        settings)
    user interfaces and, 254
        vocabulary issues, 255
press release, Privacy Protection
    Commissioner, 54
primary data uses, 196
privacy, 3
    fair information practice principles, 22
    laws (see privacy laws)
    preference settings, importing (see
        importing privacy preference
        settings)
    versus security, 22
    (see also offline privacy concerns; online
        privacy concerns)
Privacy Bird (see AT&T Privacy Bird)
Privacy Foundation, web bugs, 20

privacy laws, 24
    COPPA, 26
    European Union, 25
    Graham-Leach-Bliley Act, 26
    United States, 25
Privacy Minder (user interfaces), 239
privacy philosophy (P3P specification), 306
privacy policies, 4
    creating, 65
    deployment and, 63
    headings included, 68
    human-readable, 62
    information included, 67, 69
    number of, 73
    online resources, 67
Privacy Protection Commissioner's press
    release, 54
privacy-related organizations, 29
privacy seals, 27
Privacy Statements, developing, 65
PrivacyWall products, 66
private keys, 32
processing (user agent compliance
    requirements), 210
profiles, user data, 94
profiling purposes, 198
prompt attribute (APPEL), 220
promptmsg attribute (APPEL), 221
proxies
    anonymizing, 36
    IP addresses and, 36
pseudonymity tools, 36
public-key cryptography, 32
PURPOSE element, 92–96, 279
purpose specification principle, OECD, 23

Q

querystring (URIs), 157

R

rating system, PICS, 44
rating systems, vocabulary design, 191–195
reachability management systems, 43
Reagle, Joseph, 56
RECIPIENT element, 96–98, 280
recipient types, 198
recipient-description element, 281
recipients, 115
Reed, Drummond, 51
ref attribute (DATA element), 272

referencing policy reference files, 144
    HTTP headers, 145
    well-known location mechanism, 144
Referer header (HTTP)
    anonymity tools and, 30
    cookie-blocking tools and, 30
referers, 15, 20
Reidenberg, Joel, 44
rejecting cookies, 19
relative policy expiration times, 135
REMEDIES element, 88, 281
required attribute
    RECIPIENT element, 281
    PURPOSE element, 280
Resnick, Paul, 44
resolution-type attribute (DISPUTES
        element), 274
retention, 116
    policy lifetimes, 135
    sanitizing web logs, 174
RETENTION element, 98, 282
retrievable information, 14
Robroydog.org (sample policy), 181
routers, mix networks, 37
rule sets
    APPEL (see APPEL, rule sets)
    AT&T Privacy Bird, 230
RULESET element, attributes, 219

S

Safe Harbor framework, 25
safe zone, policies, 78
sample policies (see policies, sample)
sanitized web logs, sample policy, 174
schemas
    data categories, 154
    overview, 153
scope attribute (HINT element), 139, 276
scope, cookie policies, 141
search engines, 210
    sample policy, 177
secondary data uses, 196
security
    offline, 21
    versus privacy, 22
    zones (IE6), cookie filtering and, 299
Security principle, 47
security safeguards principle, OECD, 23
server logs, disclosing information
        about, 165
service attribute (DISPUTES element), 274

session cookies, 18
    compared to persistent cookies, 290
    sample policy, 178
Set-Cookie header (HTTP), 69
short-description attribute
    DATA-DEF element, 272
    DATA-STRUCT element, 273
    DISPUTES element, 88, 274
software
    email, encryption capabilities, 33
    file encryption, 32
    monitoring, automating, 66
    selection tips, 31
specification (P3P), xv
    evolution of, 47
    finishing, 53
src attribute (IMG element), 276
SSH (Secure Shell)
    encryption and, 35
    OpenSSH, 36
    telnet and, 36
    Windows and, 36
SSL (Secure Sockets Layer), encryption
        and, 34
STATEMENT element, 90, 282
    DATA elements and, 101
statement name, 113
statements, AT&T Privacy Bird, 253
stem (URIs), 157
structref attribute
    DATA-DEF element, 272
    DATA-STRUCT element, 273
structures, base data, 154–159
survey data, 13–14
    references, 15

T

telecom structure, 157
telephonenum structure, 156
telnet
    encryption and, 34
    SSH and, 36
templates, IBM P3P Policy Editor, 121
TEST element, 80, 84, 283
testing, HTTP headers, 147
test policies, 84
third-party agents, sample policy, 179
third-party content, analysis of, 68, 71
third-party cookies, 19
    IE6, 291
thirdparty data set, 162

Tivoli products, 66
tools, 30
    anonymity tools, 36
        email, 39
        mix networks, 37
    cleanup tools, 41
    encryption tools, 31–36
    filters, 40
        child-protection software, 40
        cookie cutters, 40
    IBM P3P Policy Editor, 121–128
        compact policies, 128
    identity-management tools, 41
    pseudonymity tools, 36
    selection tips, 31
    W3C web site, 203
tracker gifs, 20
TRUSTe seal program, 27
TST token, compact policies, 80

U

unique identifiers category, 200
United States privacy laws, 25
unsatisfactory cookies (IE6), 294
uri structure, 157
URIs (Uniform Resource Identifiers)
    components of, 157
    versus URLs, 84
URLs (Uniform Resource Locators), 15
    action (HTML forms), 142
    APPEL rules, limiting to, 224
    disclosure, 83
    human-readable privacy policies, 111
    opt-out pages, 83
    policy references, 133
use limitation principle, OECD, 23
user agents, 7, 203
    architecture, 203
    AT&T Privacy Bird, 7
    automatic action, 206
    browsers, 7
    clients, 7
    compliance requirements, fetching and
        processing, 210
    conflicting policies, avoiding, 148
    continuous, 205
    data elements, generating
        descriptions, 160
    generic versus customized, 207
    Guiding Principles, 211–213
    IE6, 8

    information-only, 206
    Netscape Navigator, 8
    on-demand versus continuous, 205
    referencing policy reference files, 75, 144
        HTTP headers, 145
        well-known location mechanism, 144
    (see also user interfaces)
user data set, 159–162
user interfaces
    accessibility, 262
    default configuration settings, 257–259
    layered, 256
    preference settings, 254
        vocabulary issues, 255
    privacy considerations, 264
    prototypes
        AT&T/Microsoft P3P browser helper
            object, 240–243
        AT&T Privacy Bird, 247–254
        AT&T usability testing
            prototype, 243–246
        Privacy Minder, 239
        W3C P3 Prototype, 237–239
    user agents, 259
        active versus passive alerts, 261
        filtering function, 260
        mismatches between policies and
            preferences, 262
        policy representation, 262
        symbols, 261
    (see also user agents)
user profiles, 94

V

validators, 208
value attribute (COOKIE-INCLUDE and
        COOKIE-EXCLUDE
        elements), 271
variable data elements, 154
Varney, Christine, 44
verification attribute (DISPUTES
        element), 274
version information
    including in POLICIES element, 108
    META element, 134
virtual private networks (VPNs), encryption
        and, 34
vocabulary
    access, 195
    credit card numbers, categorizing, 201
    data categories, 199

design issues, rating systems, 191–195
marketing purposes, 197
non-identifiable data, 196
omissions, 201
primary and secondary data uses, 196
profiling purposes, 198
recipient types, 198
unique identifiers category, 200
user interface design, 255
vocabulary subcommittee, IPWG, 45
VPNs (virtual private networks), encryption
and, 34

W

W3C (World Wide Web Consortium), 3, 48
Interoperability Session, 53
P3P-enabled sites, listing of, 108
P3P project launch, 46
P3P Prototype (user interfaces), 237–239
P3P Test Suite, 210
P3P tools, 203
P3P Validator, 64, 208
Wagner, Judith Decew, 43
web beacons, 20
web bugs, 20
web logs, disclosure requirements, 173
web pages, associating policies with, 147
web servers, adding headers to
responses, 284–288
web sites
monitoring tools, 210
P3P-enabling, 9
P3P policies, testing, 79
privacy policies, drafting, 67
reasons for using P3P, 9
sample policies (see policies, sample)
third-party content, 71
W3C (see W3C)
web-based encrypted email, 33
web browsing, user behavior data
elements, 163

WebCPO, 66
Weitzner, Daniel, 44
well-known location mechanism (policy
reference files), 144
width attribute (IMG element), 276
wildcard character (*)
COOKIE-INCLUDE and
COOKIE-EXCLUDE
elements, 140
INCLUDE and EXCLUDE elements, 137
Window Washer cleanup tool, 41
Windows, SSH and, 36
World Wide Web Consortium (see W3C)

X

X connections, SSH and, 35
XML (Extensible Markup Language), 6
APPEL rule sets, 216
attributes, 82
comments, 82
documents, P3P policies and, 61
elements, 81, 269–283
overview, 81
PCDATA, 82, 227
tags, 81
xml:lang attribute, 108
DATA-SCHEMA element, 273
META element, 134, 277
POLICIES element, 278
POLICY element, 279
xmlns attribute
DATA-SCHEMA element, 273
META element, 134, 277
POLICIES element, 278

Z

Zero-Knowledge P3P Analyzer, 66
Zero-Knowledge Systems privacy/security
tools, 42

About the Author

Dr. Lorrie Faith Cranor is a Principal Technical Staff Member in the Secure Systems Research Department at AT&T Labs-Research Shannon Laboratory in Florham Park, New Jersey. She is chair of the Platform for Privacy Preferences Project (P3P) Specification Working Group at the World Wide Web Consortium. Her research has focused on a variety of areas where technology and policy issues interact, including online privacy, electronic voting, and spam.

Dr. Cranor received her doctorate degree in Engineering & Policy from Washington University in St. Louis in 1996. While in graduate school, she helped found *Crossroads*, the ACM Student Magazine, and served as the publication's Editor-in-Chief for two years.

Dr. Cranor was chair of the Tenth Conference on Computers Freedom and Privacy (CFP2000) and program committee chair for the 29th Research Conference on Communication, Information and Internet Policy (TPRC 2001). She is frequently invited to speak about online privacy, and in 1998 *Internet Magazine* named her an unsung hero of the Internet for her work on P3P. In the spring of 2000 she served on the Federal Trade Commission Advisory Committee on Online Access and Security. She also serves on the editorial boards of the journals *ACM Transactions on Internet Technology* and *The Information Society*.

Dr. Cranor has been studying electronic voting systems since 1994. She maintains the e-lection electronic voting mailing list, and in 2000 she served on the executive committee of a National Science Foundation–sponsored Internet voting task force.

Dr. Cranor was also a member of the project team that developed the Publius censorship-resistant publishing system. In February 2001, the Publius team was honored by *Index on Censorship* magazine for the "Best Circumvention of Censorship."

Dr. Cranor plays the tenor saxophone in the Chatham Community Band. She spends most of her free time with her husband, Chuck, and her son, Shane, but sometimes she finds time to design and create quilts.

Colophon

Our look is the result of reader comments, our own experimentation, and feedback from distribution channels. Distinctive covers complement our distinctive approach to technical topics, breathing personality and life into potentially dry subjects.

The animal on the cover of *Web Privacy with P3P* is a lioness.

Leanne Soylemez and Rachel Wheeler were the production editors for *Web Privacy with P3P*. Rachel also copyedited the text; Leanne was the proofreader. Jane Ellin and Sheryl Avruch provided quality control. Tom Dinse wrote the index.

Ellie Volckhausen designed the cover of this book, based on a series design by Edie Freedman. The cover image is a 19th-century engraving from the Dover Pictorial Archive. Emma Colby produced the cover layout with QuarkXPress 4.1 using Adobe's ITC Garamond font.

David Futato and Melanie Wang designed the interior layout. This book was converted to FrameMaker 5.5.6 with a format conversion tool created by Erik Ray, Jason McIntosh, Neil Walls, and Mike Sierra that uses Perl and XML technologies. The text font is Linotype Birka; the heading font is Adobe Myriad Condensed; and the code font is LucasFont's TheSans Mono Condensed. The illustrations that appear in the book were produced by Robert Romano and Jessamyn Read using Macromedia FreeHand 9 and Adobe Photoshop 6. The tip icon were drawn by Christopher Bing. This colophon was written by XXX.

Other Titles Available from O'Reilly

Web Authoring and Design

HTML & XHTML: The Definitive Guide, 5th Edition

By Chuck Musciano & Bill Kennedy
5th Edition August 2002
672 pages, ISBN 0-596-00382-X

Our new edition offers web developers a better way to become HTML-fluent, by covering the language syntax, semantics, and variations in detail and demonstrating the difference between good and bad usage. Packed with examples, *HTML & XHTML: The Definitive Guide*, 5th Edition covers Netscape Navigator 6, Internet Explorer 6, HTML 4.01, XHTML 1.0, JavaScript 1.5, CSS2, Layers, and all of the features supported by the popular web browsers.

Cascading Style Sheets: The Definitive Guide

By Eric A. Meyer
1st Edition May 2000
470 pages, ISBN 1-56592-622-6

CSS is the HTML 4.0–approved method for controlling visual presentation on web pages. *Cascading Style Sheets: The Definitive Guide* offers a complete, detailed review of CSS1 properties and other aspects of CSS1. Each property is explored individually in detail with discussion of how each interacts with other properties. There is also information on how to avoid common mistakes in interpretation. This book is the first major title to cover CSS in a way that acknowledges and describes current browser support, instead of simply describing the way things work in theory. It offers both advanced and novice web authors a comprehensive guide to implementation of CSS.

Learning Web Design

By Jennifer Niederst
1st Edition March 2001
418 pages, ISBN 0-596-00036-7

In *Learning Web Design*, Jennifer Niederst shares the knowledge she's gained from years of experience as both web designer and teacher. She starts from the very beginning—defining the Internet, the Web, browsers, and URLs—assuming no previous knowledge of how the Web works. Jennifer helps you build the solid foundation in HTML, graphics, and design principles that you need for crafting effective web pages.

Web Design in a Nutshell, 2nd Edition

By Jennifer Niederst
2nd Edition September 2001
640 pages, ISBN 0-596-00196-7

Web Design in a Nutshell contains the nitty-gritty on everything you need to know to design web pages. Written by veteran web designer Jennifer Niederst, this book provides quick access to the wide range of technologies and techniques from which web designers and authors must draw. Topics include understanding the web environment, HTML, graphics, multimedia and interactivity, and emerging technologies.

The Web Design CD Bookshelf

By O'Reilly & Associates, Inc.
1st Edition, November 2001
(Includes CD-ROM)
640 pages, ISBN 0-596-00271-8

Six best selling O'Reilly Animal Guides are now available on CD-ROM, easily accessible and searchable with your favorite web browser: *HTML & XHTML: The Definitive Guide*, 4th Edition; *ActionScript: The Definitive Guide*; *Information Architecture for the World Wide Web*; *Designing Web Audio: RealAudio, MP3, Flash, and Beatnik*; *Web Design In a Nutshell*, 2nd Edition; and *Cascading Style Sheets: The Definitive Guide*. As a bonus, you also get the new paperback version of *Web Design in a Nutshell*, 2nd Edition.

Designing with JavaScript, 2nd Edition

By Nick Heinle & Bill Pena
2nd Edition November 2001
240 pages, ISBN 1-56592-360-X

This major revision to Nick Heinle's best-selling book, is written for the beginning web designers who are the focus of our Web Studio series, teaching core JavaScript with many useful examples and powerful libraries. The second half of the book goes beyond core JavaScript, explaining objects and more powerful event models, and showing how JavaScript can manipulate not only HTML but also XML, CSS (Cascading Style Sheets), and more.

O'REILLY®

To order: *800-998-9938* • *order@oreilly.com* • *www.oreilly.com*
Online editions of most O'Reilly titles are available by subscription at *safari.oreilly.com*
Also available at most retail and online bookstores.

How to stay in touch with O'Reilly

1. Visit our award-winning web site

http://www.oreilly.com/

★ "Top 100 Sites on the Web"—PC Magazine
★ CIO Magazine's Web Business 50 Awards

Our web site contains a library of comprehensive product information (including book excerpts and tables of contents), downloadable software, background articles, interviews with technology leaders, links to relevant sites, book cover art, and more. File us in your bookmarks or favorites!

2. Join our email mailing lists

Sign up to get email announcements of new books and conferences, special offers, and O'Reilly Network technology newsletters at:

http://www.elists.oreilly.com

It's easy to customize your free elists subscription so you'll get exactly the O'Reilly news you want.

3. Get examples from our books

To find example files for a book, go to:

http://www.oreilly.com/catalog

select the book, and follow the "Examples" link.

4. Work with us

Check out our web site for current employment opportunities:

http://jobs.oreilly.com/

5. Register your book

Register your book at:

http://register.oreilly.com

6. Contact us

O'Reilly & Associates, Inc.
1005 Gravenstein Hwy North
Sebastopol, CA 95472 USA
TEL: 707-827-7000 or 800-998-9938
       (6am to 5pm PST)
FAX: 707-829-0104

order@oreilly.com
For answers to problems regarding your order or our products. To place a book order online visit:

http://www.oreilly.com/order_new/

catalog@oreilly.com
To request a copy of our latest catalog.

booktech@oreilly.com
For book content technical questions or corrections.

corporate@oreilly.com
For educational, library, and corporate sales.

proposals@oreilly.com
To submit new book proposals to our editors and product managers.

international@oreilly.com
For information about our international distributors or translation queries. For a list of our distributors outside of North America check out:

http://international.oreilly.com/distributors.html

O'REILLY®